DEKKER'S

DRAMATIC WORKS

Printing Statement:

Due to the very old age and scarcity of this book, many of the pages may be hard to read due to the blurring of the original text, possible missing pages, missing text and other issues beyond our control.

Because this is such an important and rare work, we believe it is best to reproduce this book regardless of its original condition.

Thank you for your understanding.

THE DRAMATIC WORKS OF THOMAS DEKKER NOW FIRST COLLECTED WITH ILLUSTRATIVE NOTES AND A MEMOIR OF THE AUTHOR IN FOUR VOLUMES

VOLUME THE FIRST

LONDON
JOHN PEARSON YORK STREET COVENT GARDEN
1873

CONTENTS

VOLUME THE FIRST

MEMOIR OF THOMAS DEKKER

A PLEASANT COMEDIE OF THE GENTLE CRAFT

THE COMEDIE OF OLD FORTUNATUS

SATIRO-MASTIX, OR THE UNTRUSSING OF THE HUMOROUS POET

THE MAGNIFICENT ENTERTAINMENT GIVEN TO KING JAMES

NOTES AND ILLUSTRATIONS

VOLUME THE SECOND

THE HONEST WHORE

THE WHORE OF BABYLON

WESTWARD-HOE

NOTES AND ILLUSTRATIONS

VOLUME THE THIRD

NORTHWARD-HOE

THE FAMOUS HISTORY OF SIR THOMAS WYAT

THE ROARING GIRLE

LONDON TRIUMPHING

IF THIS BE NOT A GOOD PLAY THE DIVELL IS IN IT

NOTES AND ILLUSTRATIONS

VOLUME THE FOURTH

THE VIRGIN MARTIR

BRITTANNIA'S HONOR

LONDONS TEMPE

A TRAGI-COMEDY: CALLED MATCH MEE IN LONDON

THE WONDER OF A KINGDOME

THE SUN'S DARLING

THE WITCH OF EDMONTON

NOTES ATD ILLUSTRATIONS.

Memoir of

THOMAS DEKKER

THOMAS DEKKER was one of thoſe unfortunate poets to whom the Muſe is a cruel ſtepmother. The little that we know of his life ſuggeſts a painful and continual ſtruggle with poverty, in which he often ſuccumbed, and from which he never aroſe victorious. His ſtores of wiſdom and his wealth of imagination were for forty years laviſhed on the world, but with little or no reward to himſelf. He wrote continually under the bitter ſtreſs of want, and was often compelled to ſeek friendly aid to releaſe him from the walls of a debtor's priſon. A wretched hand-to-mouth exiſtence, a career made ſordid by the conſtant neceſſity of writing for daily bread, ſeems to have been his lot from firſt to laſt, relieved perhaps by occaſional glimpſes of happineſs and repoſe, ſuch as he muſt have enjoyed when compoſing ſome of the choiceſt of the long ſeries of dramas which conſtitute his chief title to fame.

That he was born in the metropolis we may infer from a proſe tract of his own, (1) where, apoſtrophiſing London, he ſays,—"O, thou beautifulleſt daughter of the two united Monarchies! from thy womb received I my being; from thy breſts my nouriſhment." The exact date of his birth is uncertain; in a tract dated February, 1637, he ſpeaks of "my three-ſcore years," (2) but the expreſſion is a vague one, and may mean any age from ſixty on towards ſeventy. Indeed, in the (unique) tract entitled "Warres, Warres, Warres," of date almoſt ten years earlier (1628), Dekker had already ſpoken of himſelf as an old man; (3) and in the Dedication to his Tragi-

---

1 *The Seuen deadly Sinnes of London* (1606). The paſſage cited will be found not far from the cloſe of "The Induction to the Booke."

2 *Engliſh Villanies Seven Severall Times Preſt to Death.* In his Dedication of this tract to the Middleſex juſtices of the Peace, he ſays:—"I preach without a Pulpit: this is no Sermon, but an Epiſtle Dedicatory, which dedicates theſe Diſcoveries, *and my threeſcore yeares* devotedly yours in my beſt ſervice."

3 "For my heart danceth ſprightly, when I ſee
(*Old as I am*) our Engliſh gallantry."

Comedy, called *Match mee in London* (1631), to Lodowick Carlell, he pathetically ſays: "I haue beene a Prieſt in APOLLO'S Temple, many yeares, my voyce is decaying with my Age, yet yours being cleare and aboue mine, ſhall much honour mee, if you but liſten to my old Tunes." (4) This is hardly the language of a man who has only juſt paſſed his fiftieth year; though Dekker, with ſuch a weight of ſorrow, if not of years, on his ſhoulders, might well feel old before his time. (5)

---

4 Vol. IV., p. 133.

5 It is curious to compare with the above lament the expreſſion of a ſimilar one written at the age of fifty-five (1864) by our greateſt living poet:—

"A Dedication.

Dear, near and true—no truer Time himſelf
Can prove you, though he make you evermore
Dearer and nearer, as the rapid of life
Shoots to the fall—take this and pray that he
Who wrote it, honouring your ſweet faith in him,
May truſt himſelf, and after praiſe and ſcorn,
As one who feels the immeaſurable world,
Attain the wiſe indifference of the wiſe;
And after Autumn paſt—if left to paſs
His autumn into ſeeming leafleſs days,
Draw toward the long froſt and longeſt night,
Wearing his wiſdom lightly, like the fruit
Which in our winter woodland looks a flower."

Another reaſon for fixing the date of his birth ſomewhat earlier than the "three-ſcore years" of 1637 would ſeem to imply, is that his earlieſt acknowledged publication (6) had already appeared in 1600, and that we hear of him in Henſlowe's Diary as a writer for the theatre as early as 1597. (7) We may ſafely aſſume him to have been born, therefore, ſomewhere in the ſecond decade of Elizabeth's reign; not earlier probably than 1570, and certainly not later than 1577.

We learn from the regiſters of St. Saviour's, Southwark, that the perſon who probably was Dekker's father, was buried there in 1594; and from the regiſters of St. Giles, Cripplegate (where Henſlowe's and Alleyn's theatre, the Fortune, for which Dekker wrote, was ſituated), that Thomas Dycker, gent., had a daughter Dorcas chriſtened there on 27th Oct., 1594, and that Thomas Decker, yeoman, had a daughter

---

6 *The Comedie of Old Fortunatus.*

7 "Lent unto Thomas Dowton, the 8 of Jeneway 1597, twenty ſhillinges, to by a booke of Mr. Dickers. xxs." *Diary of Philip Henſlowe*, From 1591 to 1609. *from the Original Manuſcript preſerved at Dulwich College*, London: Printed for the Shakeſpeare Society, 1845.

Anne chriſtened there on 14th Oct., 1602. Neither of theſe might be our poet, and it was not uſual to deſignate an author "yeoman." Thomas Dekker had a daughter Elizabeth buried there in 1598, and a ſon of Thomas Dekker was buried at St. Botolph's, Biſhopsgate, on 19th April in the ſame year. The widow of old Thomas Dekker, who died in 1594, was living in Maid Lane, Southwark, near the Globe Theatre, in 1596. (7)

We have ſaid that Dekker began to write for the ſtage as early as 1597. His firſt attempts, however, in moſt of which he ſeems to have been aſſociated with others, have not been preſerved. (8)

---

7 COLLIER'S *Bibliographical Account of Early Engliſh Literature* (Lond. 1865), I., 195.

8 Henſlowe records payments to Dekker and Chettle "in earneſte of their boocke called Troyelles and creſſida," on the 7th and 16th April, 1599. On the 2nd May, 1599, a payment of five ſhillings was made to Dekker "in earneſte of a Boocke called oreſtes fures," a play in which he does not appear to have had any coadjutor. In May, 1599, there are two payments to Dekker and Chettle for "the tragedie of Agamemnone." In July and August, 1599, he is mentioned in connexion with a play called the "ſtepmothers tragedy," and on 1ſt Auguſt, 1599, he receives forty ſhillings "for a booke called beare a braine."

His two earlieſt extant dramatic productions, *The Shomaker's Holiday* and *The Comedie of Old Fortunatus*—the firſt anonymous (9) and

---

In September, 1599, various payments are made to Dekker, Jonſon, and Chettle, and "another gentleman,' on account of a play called "Robert the ſecond, Kinge of Scottes tragedie."

In January, 1599—1600, Dekker receives a payment for a play called *Truth's Supplication to Candlelight*; in the following month payments are made to Dekker, Haughton, and Daye, for the *The Spaniſh Moor's Tragedy* [by ſome ſuppoſed to be identical with the play entitled *Luſt's Dominion*, firſt printed in 1657, and aſcribed to Marlowe]. In March, 1599—1600, Chettle, Dekker, Haughton, and Daye, received payment for a play called *The Seven Wiſe Maſters*. All theſe pieces appear to have remained in manuſcript, and to have periſhed.

9 The abſurdity of attributing this play to Barten Holiday (as in the Library Catalogue of the Britiſh Muſeum, in Lowndes, and elſewhere) muſt ſurely have ariſen from ſome blundering binder having lettered one of the later editions "The Shoemakers."—HOLIDAY. The date of the firſt edition alone ſhould have prevented the perpetuation of ſuch a piece of futility. Barten Holiday was born in 1593, and muſt have been, indeed, an infant prodigy to have produced ſuch a play as *The Shoemaker's Holiday* at the age of ſeven. Dekker's authorſhip of this play is corroborated by the following entry in Henſlowe's Diary:—"Lent unto Samewell Rowley and Thomas Dowton, the 15 of Julye, 1599, to bye a Boocke of Thomas Dickers, called the gentle Craft the ſome of iij^{l}."

the ſecond ſigned with his name at the end (10)—were publiſhed in 1600. With a ſingle exception, to be mentioned preſently, he probably never ſurpaſſed theſe earlier works, either in the lighter or the graver ſtrain. *The Shoemaker's Holiday,* both in the ſcenes of wild fun and buffoonery, and in the tender love-ſtory that runs through it like a ſilver thread, has all the charm of a Waverley novel, and poſſeſſes the very higheſt intereſt as an hiſtorical picture of manners. Simon Eyre is inimitable: there is no better type of jovial honeſt merriment in the whole range of Engliſh literature. He is as original and well-ſuſtained a character as Falſtaff himſelf. Of the *Comedie of Old Fortunatus,* Hazlitt might well ſay that it has "the idle garrulity of age, with the freſhneſs and gaiety of youth ſtill upon its cheek and in its heart." The ſongs in theſe two pieces are exquiſitely beautiful, and the Prologues to

10 *Tho. Dekker.*—The name is thus ſpelt in all the exiſting autograph ſignatures of the poet, and (we believe without exception) in all the original editions of thoſe pieces of which he was the ſole author. To this form we have ourſelves uniformly adhered. By his contemporaries, by his publiſhers, and by his critics and annotators, the name of Dekker has been ſpelt with almoſt as many variations as that of his illuſtrious contemporary Shakeſpeare: —*e.g.*, Decker, Deckers, Dickers, Dekker, Deker, Dekkers, Deckar, Dekkar, &c.

both contain ſome pleaſant flattery of Queen Elizabeth, before whom they were performed.

The Comedie of Old Fortunatus received a German dreſs in the preſent century. The tranſlator, Dr. Schmidt, makes the following obſervations on its ſtyle and verſification :—

"In Beziehung auf die Sprache will ich nur an Eins erinnern. Es iſt dies der Gebrauch des Reims, des reimloſen Iambus und der Proſa. Wie in den edleren Naturen Einſicht und höheres Gefühl beſtändig die Oberhand haben, ſo ſchläft in den gemeinem daſſelbe in fernſter Tiefe, und giebt kein Zeichen. Aber wenn von auſſen die Stimme des Höchſten donnert in plötzlich überraſchendem Segen oder Verderben, da entbrennt auch bei dieſen der göttliche Funken, und bricht hervor mit ungeahndeter Kraft, in treffendem Wort. So finden wir bei Shakſpeare und Decker den Reim als Organ jener höchſten Lebensblitze, die reimloſen Iamben für alle anderen unendlich mannigſachen Gemüthſzuſtände, bis zu dem gewöhnlichen gleichgültigen hinab, wo der Menſch ſich gehn läſſt, da tritt die Proſa ein, und iſt recht eigentlich zu Hauſe in den ſcherzhaften Maſſen. Denn die in demſelben abgeſpiegelte Kehrſeite des Lebens kann nur erfreulich und bedeutend ſein, wenn unbewuſst dahinter wie im Traume der Ernſt als Folie liegt, und nicht hervortritt mit ſeinem gewichtigen, gemeſſenen Wort. Dieſes ſo natürliche Verhältniſs zwiſchen der Sprache und dem Weſen des Dinges hat gewiſs auch ſeinen Theil an dem unergründlichen Wohlgefallen, mit welchem wir die Shakſpeareſchen Erzeugniſſe genieſſen. In unſerm Drama ſpricht der nichtige Schatte nur den einzigen Vers

'Doch Herr, daſs es nicht ende jämmerlich !'

In dem Augenblick ift er (ohne es zu wiffen) und daran zu glauben, wirklicher Profet, wie Lichtenberg verfichert, dafs der gewöhnlichfte Menfch wenigftens drei Mal im Jahr einen genialen Augenblick habe. Fortuna, Tugend, Lafter, Ampedo, Orleans, dagegen kommen in ihrer Feierlich keit niemals heraus aus den künftlich gemeffenen Worten."(11)

His next publifhed play was *Satiro-maftix, or The vntruffing of the Humorous Poet.* As a perfonal fatire of confiderable pungency directed againft the fuppofed arrogant pretenfions of Ben Jonfon, it feems to have enjoyed great popularity. In reading it now, more than two centuries after the grave has clofed over both the combatants, it is impoffible to fuppress a feeling of forrowful wonder that two men fo gifted fhould have proftituted their genius to the expreffion of fuch narrow jealoufies and hatreds.

---

11 *Fortunatus und feine Söhne, eine Zauber-Tragödie von Thomas Decker. Aufgeführt im Jahr* 1600 *vor der Königin Elifabeth. Aus dem Englifchen von* Dr. Fr. Wilh. Val. Schmidt, &c. *Mit einem Anhang ähnlicher Märchen diefes Kreifes, und einer Abhandlung über die Gefchichte von Fortunatus.* Berlin, 1819. A German edition (Englifh text) of *The Shoemaker's Holiday* appeared a few years ago, with fome interefting notes. The title is as follows:—"*The Shoemaker's Holiday, or The Gentle Craft. Nach einem Drucke aus dem Jahre* 1618 *neu heraufgegeben von Hermann Fritfche Lehrer am Gymnafium zu Thorn,* 1862." *Pp.* 67.

"Ah God! the petty fools of rhyme
That ſhriek and ſweat in pigmy wars
Before the ſtony face of Time,
And look'd at by the ſilent ſtars:
That ſtrain to make an inch of room
For their ſweet ſelves, and cannot hear
The ſullen Lethe rolling doom
On them and theirs and all things here."

That Dekker received provocation no one will deny. Unworthy perſonalities had been directed againſt him by his brother poet and former collaborator.(12) The *Poetaſter* had been flung like a fire-brand among the wits and witlings, among the poets and the ſmaller fry who only aſpired to that name. Dekker was choſen as the champion of all theſe, and acquitted himſelf of the

---

12 "On p. 155 of 'Henſlowe's Diary,' occurs the following entry:—

'Lent unto Wm Borne, alles birde, the 10 of auguſte 1529, to lend unto Bengemyne Johnſone, and thomas Dekkers, in earneſte of ther booke they are writtinge, called pagge of plimothe, the ſome xxxx^s.'

This tragedy was founded upon an event of comparatively recent occurrence. The play has been loſt, but the ſtory has come down to us. The event happened in February, 1591, and it appears that Ben Jonſon and Dekker had finiſhed their tragedy in September, 1599, when the laſt payment of £6 was made to them."—*Shakeſpeare Society's Papers*, vol. II. (1845), p. 79.

office in a moſt effective manner. The elder Diſraeli in his *Quarrels of Authors* has given the following account of the buſineſs, which we quote as containing ſome juſt and careful criticiſm :

"This quarrel is a ſplendid inſtance how genius of the firſt order, laviſhing its ſatirical powers on a number of contemporaries, may diſcover among the crowd, ſome individual who may return with a right aim the weapon he has himſelf uſed, and who will not want for encouragement to attack the common aſſailant : the greater genius is thus mortified by a victory conceded to the inferior, which he himſelf had taught the meaner one to obtain over him. . . . . . .

One of the 'ſcreaming graſſhoppers held by the wings,' boldly turned on the holder with a ſcorpion's bite ; and Dekker, who had been laſhed in *The Poetaſter*, produced his *Satiromaſtix, or the vntruſſing of the humorous Poet.* Dekker was a ſubordinate author, indeed ; but, what muſt have been very galling to Jonſon, who was the aggreſſor, indignation proved ſuch an inſpirer, that Dekker ſeemed to have caught ſome portion of Jonſon's own genius, who had the art of making even Dekker popular ; while he diſcovered that his own laurel-wreath had been dextrouſly changed by the *Satiromaſtix* into a garland of 'ſtinging nettles.'

In *The Poetaſter* Criſpinus is the picture of one of thoſe impertinent fellows who reſolve to become Poets, having an equal aptitude to become anything that is in faſhionable requeſt. When Hermogenes, the fineſt ſinger in Rome, refuſed to ſing, *Criſpinus* gladly ſeizes the occaſion, and whiſpers the lady near him—'Entreat the ladies to entreat me to ſing, I beſeech you.' This character is marked by a ludicrous peculiarity which turning on an individual characteriſtic, muſt have aſſiſted the audience in the true application. It is probable that Dekker had some remarkable head of hair, and that his locks hung not like 'the curls of Hyperion;'(13) for the jeweller's wife admiring among the company, the perſons of Ovid, Tibullus, &c., *Criſpinus* acquaints her that they were poets, and ſince ſhe admires them, promiſes to become a poet himſelf. The ſimple lady further inquires, 'if when he is a poet his looks will change? and particularly if his hair will change, and be like thoſe gentlemen's?' 'A man,' obſerves *Criſpinus*, 'may be a poet, and yet not change his hair.' 'Well!' exclaims the ſimple jeweller's wife, 'we ſhall ſee your cunning; yet if you can change your hair, I pray do it.'

The *Satiromaſtix* may be conſidered as a parody on *The Poetaſter*. Jonſon, with claſſical taſte, had raiſed his ſcene in the court of Auguſtus: Dekker, with great unhappineſs, places his in that of William Rufus. The intereſt of the piece ariſes from the dexterity with which Dekker has accommodated thoſe very characters which Jonſon has ſatiriſed in his *Poetaſter*. This gratified thoſe who came every day to the theatre, delighted to take this mimetic revenge on the Arch Bard. . . . . Some cenſured Dekker for barrenneſs of invention, in bringing on thoſe characters in his own play whom Jonſon had ſtigmatiſed; but 'it was not improper,' he ſays, 'to ſet the ſame dog

---

(13) If the rude woodcut on the title-page of *Dekker's Dream* be meant, as ſeems likely, for the *vera effigies* of our poet, it corroborates the above obſervation; for he is there repreſented with very ſhaggy locks indeed.

upon Horace, whom Horace had ſet to worry others. Dekker warmly concludes his ſpirited prefatory addreſs 'To the World' with defying the Jonſonians.

In Dekker's *Satiromaſtix* Horace junior is firſt exhibited in his ſtudy, rehearſing to himſelf an Ode: ſuddenly the Pindaric rapture is interrupted by the want of a rhyme; this is ſatirically applied to an unlucky line of Ben Jonſon's own. One of his *ſons,* Aſinius Bubo, who is blindly worſhipping his great idol, or his *Ningle,* as he calls him, amid his admiration of Horace, perpetually breaks out into digreſſive accounts of what ſort of a man his friends take him to be. For one Horace in wrath prepares an epigram; and for *Criſpinus* and *Fannius,* brother bards, who threaten 'they'll bring your life and death on the ſtage, as a bricklayer in a play,' he ſays, 'I can bring a prepared troop of gallants, who, for my ſake, ſhall diſtaſte every unſalted line in their fly-blown comedies.' 'Ay,' replies Aſinius, 'and all men of my rank!' *Criſpinus* Horace calls 'a light voluptuous reveller,' and *Fannius* 'the ſlighteſt cobweb-lawn piece of a poet.' Both enter, and Horace receives them with all friendſhip. The ſcene is here conducted not without ſkill. To the complaints of the querulous ſatiriſt, *Criſpinus* replies with dignified gravity, at which the galled Horace winces. *Fannius* too joins, and ſhows Ben the abſurd oaths he takes, when he ſwears to all parties that he does not mean them. Horace is awkwardly placed between theſe two friendly remonſtrants, to whom he promiſes perpetual love.

Captain Tucca, a dramatic perſonage in Jonſon's *Poetaſter,* and a copy of his own Bobadil, is here continued with the ſame ſpirit; and as that character permitted from the extravagance of its ribaldry, it is now made the vehicle for thoſe more perſonal retorts, exhibiting the ſecret hiſtory of Ben, which perhaps twitted the great bard more than the keeneſt wit, or the moſt ſolemn admonition which Dekker could ever attain. Jonſon had cruelly touched on Dekker being out at elbows, and made himſelf too merry with the hiſtrionic tribe: he who was himſelf a poet, and had been a Theſpian!

The greatneſs of Ben's genius is by no means denied by his rivals; and Dekker makes *Fannius* reply with noble feelings, and in an elevated ſtrain of poetry."

In the following year (1603) a play was publiſhed anonymouſly, of which Dekker is ſuppoſed to have written the principal portion, his aſſiſtants being Haughton and Chettle. This is entitled *The Comodie of Patient Griſſil* (14). From internal evidence there is little doubt that he had a ſhare in it; though, as the printed copy is entirely ſilent as to the authorſhip, which only reſts on ſome vague entries in Henſlowe's Diary, (15) this play has not been

---

14 *The Pleaſant Comodie of Patient Grisſill. As it hath beene ſundrie times lately plaid by the right honorable the Earle of Nottingham (Lord high Admirall) his ſeruants.* London. Imprinted for Henry Rocket, and are to be ſolde at the long Shop vnder S. Mildreds Church in the Poultry. 1603.

15 December 19th 1599, and again 26th Dec. payments were made to Dekker, Chettle and Haughton, and on 28th Dec. a ſeparate payment to Dekker.

included in the prefent collection. The following Song, however, has decidedly the ring of Dekker about it:—

Art thou poore yet haft thou golden Slumbers:
Oh fweet content!
Art thou rich yet is thy minde perplexed?
Oh punnifhment.
Doft thou laugh to fee how fooles are vexed?
To ad to golden numbers, golden numbers.
O fweet content, o fweet &c.
Worke apace, apace, apace, apace,
Honeft labour beares a louely face,
Then hey noney, noney: hey noney, noney.

Canft drinke the waters of the Crifped fpring,
O fweet content!
Swim'ft thou in wealth, yet finck'ft in thine owne teares,
O punnifhment.
Then hee that patiently want's burden beares,
No burden beares, but is a King, a King.
O fweet content, &c.
Worke apace, apace, &c.

The following pretty lullaby Song was probably alfo written by Dekker:—

Golden flumbers kiffe your eyes,
Smiles awake you when you rife:
Sleepe pretty wantons doe not cry,
And I will fing a lullabie,
Rocke them rocke them lullabie.

Care is heauy therefore fleepe you,
You are care and care muft keep you:

Sleepe pretty wantons doe not cry,
And I will ſing a lullabie,
Rocke them rocke them lullabie.

In 1604 appeared the firſt part of that beautiful play which moſt critics have agreed in conſidering as Dekker's maſterpiece. As Mr. Swinburne has ſaid in regard to one of the fineſt plays of Ford, "it is ſomewhat unfortunate that its very title ſhould ſound ſo ſtrangely in the ears of a generation whoſe ears are the chaſteſt part about them." (16) Although the name of Dekker ſtands alone on the title-page of all the editions of *The Honeſt Whore*, an entry in Henſlowe's Diary, corroborated by ſome internal evidence, would ſeem to imply that in the compoſition of at any rate the firſt part of the play he received ſome aid from Thomas Middleton, with whom he is known to have written conjointly on two other occaſions. Mr. Dyce has accordingly aſſumed a joint author-

---

16 *Fortnightly Review*, July, 1871, p.43. By the bye, it is curious and worthy of mention, as indicative of a contemplated change of title afterwards abandoned, that ſheet E of the ſingularly correct and intereſting edition of 1605, has the head-line of *The Conuerted Courtizan* throughout.

ſhip in both parts, and has included them in his edition of Middleton's works, though he admits that that writer's ſhare in the play was probably inſignificant. (17)

Conſidering, however, that the year before, when Middleton contributed a ſpeech of only ſixty lines to his *Magnificent Entertainment given to King James*, (1603) Dekker had gone out of his way to acknowledge the obligation, (18) I ſhould be inclined to think the aid given in the preſent caſe was of a very limited character, and was probably confined to a few ſuggeſtions on the general conduct and groundwork of the play; that at any rate it did not extend far enough to caſt a doubt on Dekker's creation and authorſhip of thoſe beautiful ſcenes and characters of which Hazlitt has ſpoken

---

17 "Of *The Roaring Girl*, I believe that Middleton wrote by far the greater portion; but of the two other plays which he produced in conjunction with Dekker—the Firſt and Second Parts of *The Honeſt Whore*—I have no doubt that his ſhare is comparatively ſmall."—Dyce's *Account of Middleton and his Works*, Lond. 1840 (Vol. I., lvi.).

18 "If there be any glorie to be won by writing theſe lynes, I doe freelie beſtow it (as his due) on *Tho. Middleton*, in whoſe braine they were begotten, though they were deliuered here: *Quæ nos non fecimus ipſi, vix ea noſtra voco.*"—p. 321.

with ſo much enthuſiaſm. I am moſt anxious to eſtabliſh this point in the reader's mind, more eſpecially becauſe in the plays which Dekker afterwards avowedly wrote in conjunction with Webſter, Middleton, Maſſinger, and Ford, it has been the faſhion from the time of Langbaine down to that of Gifford and Dyce, to attribute to him all the coarſe and careleſs ſcenes, and to aſſign all the tender and poetical paſſages to his collaborators, and thus to rob him of ſome of his chief claims to our conſideration as a dramatic writer.(19)

The Second part of *The Honeſt Whore* does

---

19 "Thomas Dekker," ſays old Gerard Langbaine, "was more famous for the contention he had with Ben Jonſon for the Bays, than for any great Reputation he had gained by his own Writings. Yet even in that age, he wanted not his Admirers nor his Friends amongſt the Poets: in which number I reckon the Ingenious Mr. Richard Brome; who always ſtyled him by the title of Father. He clubb'd with Webſter in writing Three Plays; and with Rowley and Ford in another: and I think I may venture to ſay, that theſe Plays as far exceed thoſe of his own Brain, as a platted Whipcord exceeds a ſingle Thread in ſtrength. Of thoſe which he writ alone I know none of much eſteem, except *The Untruſſing of the Humorous Poet*, and that chiefly on account of the Subject of it, which was the witty Ben Jonſon. Of *Fortunatus* I can give no other account than that I once barely ſaw it, and

not ſeem to have been printed until 1630; (20) at any rate no earlier edition is known to exiſt. As, however, the two plays ſucceed each other in proper and natural ſequence, we have departed in this inſtance from our otherwiſe uniform chronological order of arrangement.

Of *The Honeſt Whore* Hazlitt, in his *Lectures on the Dramatic Literature of the Age of Elizabeth*, writes in the following terms:—

"Old honeſt Dekker's Signior Orlando Friſcobaldo I ſhall never forget! I became only of late acquainted with

---

(that it) is printed in quarto."—GERARD LANGBAINE: *Account of the Engliſh Dramatick Poets*, Oxford, 1691, p. 121.

What are we to think of the *value* of a man's criticiſm who pronounces ſo ſweeping a judgment on works that he admits he has never read.

20 The text is very corrupt, as is alſo that of the later editions of the firſt part. Into the firſt edition of this (1604) ſome ſerious errors had crept, which were corrected in the excellent edition of 1605 (one of the moſt immaculate of Elizabethan plays in regard to accuracy of printing, and evidently ſuperintended by the author himſelf). The later editions, however, repeated all the errors of the firſt, and gathered a good many more by the way (eſpecially that of 1635). Mr. Dyce was the firſt to point out the exiſtence and peculiarities of the edition of 1605, which appears to be of extraordinary rarity. It has, of courſe, formed the baſis of our own text.

this laſt-mentioned worthy character; but the bargain between us is, I truſt, for life. We ſometimes regret that we had not ſooner met with characters like this, that ſeem to raiſe, revive, and give a new zeſt to our being. . . . . The execution is, throughout, as exact as the conception is new and maſterly. There is the leaſt colour poſſible uſed; the pencil drags; the canvas is almoſt ſeen through: but then, what preciſion of outline, what truth and purity of tone, what firmneſs of hand, what marking of character! The words and anſwers all along are ſo true and pertinent, that we ſeem to ſee the geſtures, and to hear the tone with which they are accompanied. So when Orlando, diſguiſed, ſays to his daughter, 'You'll forgive me,' and ſhe replies, 'I am not marble, I forgive you;' or again, when ſhe introduces him to her huſband, ſaying ſimply, 'It is my father,' there needs no ſtage-direction to ſupply the relenting tones of voice or cordial frankneſs of manner with which theſe words are ſpoken. It is as if there were ſome fine art to chiſel thought, and to embody the inmoſt movements of the mind in every-day actions and familiar ſpeech. Simplicity and extravagance of ſtyle, homelineſs and quaintneſs, tragedy and comedy, interchangeably ſet their hands and ſeals to this admirable production. We find the ſimplicity of proſe with the graces of poetry. The ſtalk grows out of the ground; but the flowers ſpread their flaunting leaves in the air. The mixture of levity in the chief character beſpeaks the bitterneſs from which it ſeeks relief; it is the idle echo of fixed deſpair, jealous of obſervation or pity. The ſarcaſm quivers on the lip, while the tear ſtands congealed on the eyelid. This 'tough ſenior,' this impracticable old gentleman, ſoftens into a little child; this choke-pear melts in the mouth like marmalade. In ſpite of his reſolute profeſſions of miſanthropy, he watches over his daughter with kindly ſolicitude; plays the careful houſewife; broods over her lifeleſs hopes; nurſes the decay of her huſband's fortune, as he had ſupported her tottering infancy; ſaves the high-flying Matheo from the gallows more than once, and is twice a father to them. The ſtory has all the romance of private life, all the pathos of bearing up againſt ſilent grief, all the tenderneſs of concealed affection: there is much ſorrow patiently borne, and then comes peace. Bellafront, in the two parts of this play taken together, is a moſt intereſting character. It is an extreme, and I am afraid almoſt an ideal caſe. She gives the play its title, turns out a true penitent, that is, a practical one, and is the model of an exemplary wife. The change of her relative poſition, with regard to Hippolito, who, in the firſt part, in the ſanguine enthuſiaſm of youthful generoſity, has reclaimed her from vice, and in the ſecond part, his own faith and love of virtue having been impaired with the progreſs of years, tries in vain to lure her back again to her former follies, has an effect the moſt ſtriking and beautiful. The pleadings on both ſides, for and againſt female faith and conſtancy are managed with great polemical ſkill, aſſiſted by the grace and vividneſs of poetical illuſtration. As an inſtance of the manner in which Bellafront ſpeaks of the miſeries of her former ſituation, I might give the lines in which ſhe contraſts the different regard ſhewn to the modeſt or the abandoned of her ſex. . . . Perhaps this ſort of appeal to matter of fact and popular opinion, is more convincing than the ſcholaſtic ſubtleties of the Lady in Comus. The manner too in which Infelice, the wife of Hippolito, is made acquainted with her huſband's infidelity, is finely dramatic; and in the cene where ſhe convicts him of his injuſtice, by taxing herſelf with incontinence firſt, and then turning his moſt galling reproaches to her into upbraidings againſt his own conduct, ſhe acquits herſelf with infinite ſpirit and addreſs. The contrivance by which, in the firſt part, after being ſuppoſed dead, ſhe is reſtored to life, and married to Hippolito, though perhaps a little far-fetched, is affecting and romantic. There is uncommon beauty in the Duke her father's deſcription of her ſudden illneſs. . . . . . . Candido, the good-natured man of this play, is a character of inconceivable quaintneſs and ſimplicity. His patience and good-humour cannot be diſturbed by anything. The idea (for it is nothing but an idea) is a droll one, and is well ſupported. . . . . The ſudden turn of the character of Candido, on his ſecond marriage, is, however, as amuſing as it is unexpected.

"Matheo, the 'high-flying' huſband of Bellafront, is a maſterly portrait, done with equal eaſe and effect. He is a perſon almoſt without virtue or vice, that is, he is in ſtrictneſs without any moral principle at all. He has no malice againſt others, and no concern for himſelf. He is gay, profligate, and unfeeling, governed entirely by the impulſe of the moment, and utterly reckleſs of conſequences. His exclamation, when he gets a new ſuit of velvet, or a lucky run on the dice, 'Do we not fly high,' is an anſwer to all arguments. Puniſhment or advice has no more effect upon him, than upon the moth that flies into the candle. He is only to be left to his fate. Orlando ſaves him from it, as we do the moth, by ſnatching it out of the flame, throwing it out of the window, and ſhutting down the caſement upon it."

In comparing the genius of Dekker and Webſter, he adds :—

"Dekker has, I think, more truth of character, more inſtinctive depth of ſentiment, more of the unconſcious ſimplicity of nature. He excels in giving expreſſion to certain habitual, deeply-rooted feelings, which remain pretty much the ſame in all circumſtances, the ſimple uncompounded elements of nature and paſſion."

The Whore of Babylon, which followed in 1607, is perhaps the worſt and leaſt intereſting of Dekker's dramatic pieces. The allegory is without fitneſs or beauty, the introduction of Queen Elizabeth, under the name of Titania, is clumſily managed; the perſonification of Time, Truth, and Plain-dealing is equally ſo. There is no dramatic unity or intereſt, no inſight into character, no beauty of dialogue. The ſpeeches are either bald and proſaic, or ſwell into turgid bombaſt. The introduction of the Spaniſh Armada is at once heavy and ridiculous. That this dull effuſion of loyalty may have given pleaſure at the time, is likely enough; but no one will read it now except for the ſake of its antiquarian intereſt. The only ſcenes in any way relieved from the general inſipidity are thoſe in which Plain-dealing deſcribes to Truth the faſhions of the city; and here and there throughout the play one comes on a line or two of poetry flaſhing out for a moment in the darkneſs.

In the ſame year (1607) appeared the three

plays written conjointly by Dekker and Webſter, viz., *Weſtward Hoe, Northward Hoe,* and *Sir Thomas Wyat.* The firſt two have little to diſtinguiſh them from the ordinary comedies of the time; and the latter, whatever merit it may have poſſeſſed in its original form, has been ſo mutilated by the tranſcriber or by the printer as to poſſeſs ſcarcely any value.

In his next dramatic production, *The Roaring Girle* (1611), Dekker was aſſociated with Middleton, who, as we have ſeen, in the opinion of Mr. Dyce, wrote the larger ſhare of this play. Middleton's name is printed firſt on the title-page, if that be any criterion, and the Preface is ſigned by him: it is certain, however, that there are many places where the hand of Dekker may clearly be recogniſed.

In 1612 Dekker was employed to write the Mayoralty Pageant, which he entitled *Troia Nova Triumphans: London Triumphing.* In the ſame year appeared his play entitled *If it be not good, the Diuell is in it;* to which much the ſame remarks apply as we have already made reſpecting *The Whore of Babylon.* The beginning of this play (obſerves Langbaine) ſeems to be written in imitation of Machiavel's novel, *Belphegor,* where Pluto ſummons the devils to council.

From 1613 to 1616 we learn, on the authority of Oldys, that Dekker was in King's Bench Prifon. In connexion with this circumftance, an interefting letter has been preferved in the archives of Dulwich College. Mr. Payne Collier, in his "Memoirs of Alleyn," writes as follows:—

"By the autumn of 1616, the conftruction of Dulwich College, which Alleyn named "The College of God's gift," muft have been confiderably advanced, and ready for the reception of fome of the objects of the founder's bounty. At this date Alleyn received a letter from one of Shakefpeare's moft popular and diftinguifhed contemporaries,—Thomas Dekker. He was a playwright of great celebrity fome years before the death of Queen Elizabeth, and had written moft of his pieces for companies with which Alleyn and Henflowe were connected. Like many of his class, he feems to have been a man of carelefs habits, as regarded his pecuniary affairs, living from hand to mouth, by turns affluent and needy, and fupplying his preffing wants by the produce of his prolific pen. At the date of the following communication he was a prifoner in the King's Bench; and it was, no doubt, intended to induce Alleyn to make him a prefent in return for fome enclofed verfes "in praife of charity," and in celebration of the benevolent work which was now approaching completion. The verfes themfelves have not furvived, but the letter containing them has:—

"To my worthy.and worll. freind Edw. Allin Efquier,
at his houfe at Dullidge.

"Sr

"Out of that refpect wch I ever caryed to yor Worth (now heightned by a Pillar of yor owne erecting) doe I ſend theis poore teſtimonies of a more rich Affection. I am glad (yf I bee the Firſt) that I am the firſt to Conſecrate to Memory (yf at leaſt you ſo embrace it) So noble and pious a Work, as This, yo[r] laſt and worthieſt is. A paſſionate deſire of expreſſing gladnes to See Goodnes ſo well delivered having bin long in labour in the world made mee thus far to venture. And it beſt becomes mee to Sing any thing in praiſe of Charity, becauſe, albeit I have felt few handes warme thorough that complexion, yett impriſonment may make me long for them. Yf any thing in my Eulogium (or Praiſe) of you and yo[r] noble Act bee offenſive, lett it be excuſed becauſe I live amongſt the Gothes and Vandalls, where Barbarouſnes is predominant. Accept my will howſoever And mee

"Ready to doe you any ſervice

"Tho. Dekker.

"King's Bench Sept. 12. 1616."

It is to be regretted that Dekker's tribute to Alleyn has ſhared the fate of many things he and his contemporaries compoſed. Few things in the long and honourable annals of Dulwich College would poſſeſs greater intereſt. We need entertain little doubt that Alleyn took ſteps to relieve his old friend's neceſſities; and as it is ſtated that Dekker was releaſed from priſon in the very year his letter bears date, it may not be too much to ſuppoſe that Alleyn had a hand in his liberation. (21)

21 *Memoirs of Edward Alleyn, Founder of Dulwich*

A ſubſequent undated letter from Dekker to Alleyn, exiſting among the papers at Dulwich, may here be added :—

"Sr.

"I give you thanks for the laſt remembrance of your love. I write nowe, not poetically, but as an orrator, not by waye of declamation, but by petition, that you would be pleaſed, upon my lovinge lynes, to receave a yong man (ſonn to a worthie yeoman of Kent here priſoner) able by his owne meanes to mayntayne himſelfe, whoſe fortunes will anſwere itt. Hee is a yonge man lovinge you, beinge of your name, and deſires no greater happines than to depend upon [you]. You ſhall doe mee much honor if you thinke him fitt to ſerve you as a ſervant, and him much love, becauſe of your name, to receave. The yonge man is of good parts, both of bodie and mynd. I knowe you reſpect ſuch a one, and I would not (upon that reputation I hold with you) offer a ſervant to bee unworthie of your attendance. If you pleaſe to receave him upon my commendation and your owne tryall, I ſhall thinck my ſelfe beholden to you, and you, as I hope, no waye repent the receavinge of ſuch a ſervant of your owne name. Soe I reſt

"Your lovinge freind

"THO. DEKKER."

When Dekker before made an appeal to

College, including ſome new Particulars reſpecting Shakeſpeare, Ben Jonſon, Maſſinger, Marſton, Dekker, &c. By J. Payne Collier, F.S.A. Lond. Printed for the Shakeſpeare Society, 1841, pp. 130—132.

Alleyn's known liberality, and ſent him ſome laudatory verſes, he was in confinement in the King's Bench, and we ſee that he was again a priſoner when he introduced a young man to Alleyn's notice as a ſervant. The expreſſion, "I give you thanks for the laſt remembrance of your love," warrants the concluſion that Alleyn had ſent pecuniary aſſiſtance to Dekker on more than one previous occaſſion. Reſpecting the date of the letter, we can give no information, and the back of the ſheet having been torn off, the addreſs has been loſt; but, conſidering its contents and the place where it was found, there can be no doubt at all on the latter point. (22).

After his releaſe from priſon, Dekker appears to have been occupied with ſome of his innumerable proſe pamphlets. His name is not connected with any new play until 1622, when *The Virgin-Martyr*, written conjointly with Maſſinger, appeared. Gifford has endeavoured to claim for Maſſinger nearly all the ſerious paſſages of this play, and to faſten on Dekker the ſtigma of having contributed all the coarſer ſcenes. Other critics have judged very differently. The reader ſhall hear both ſides of the queſtion, and form his own opinion.

---

(22) *Memoirs of Alleyn*, pp. 185, 186.

"It ſhould be obſerved," ſays Gifford, "in juſtice to our old plays, that few or rather none of them, are contaminated with ſuch deteſtable ribaldry as the preſent one. To "low wit," or indeed to wit of any kind, it has not the ſlighteſt pretenſion; being, in fact, nothing more than a loathſome ſooterkin engendered of filth and dulneſs. It was evidently the author's deſign to perſonify *Luſt* and *Drunkenneſs* in the characters of Hircius and Spungius, and this may account for the ribaldry in which they indulge. That Maſſinger is not free from dialogues of low wit and buffoonery (though certainly he is much more ſo than his contemporaries) may readily be granted; but the perſon who, after peruſing this execrable traſh, can imagine it to bear any reſemblance to his ſtyle and manner, muſt have read him to very little purpoſe. It was aſſuredly written by Dekker, as was the reſt of this act, in which there is much to approve.

On the paſſage beginning—

DOR. *My booke and taper* (vol. iv. p. 26),

he obſerves :—

"What follows, to the end of the ſcene, is exquiſitely beautiful. What pity that a man ſo capable of intereſting our beſt paſſions (for I am perſuaded that this alſo was written by Dekker) ſhould proſtitute his genius and his judgment to the production of what could only diſgrace himſelf, and diſguſt his reader.

And he concludes :—

"With a neglect of preciſion which pervades all the arguments of Mr. Monck Maſon, he declares it is eaſy to diſtinguiſh the hand of Dekker from that of Maſſinger, yet finds a difficulty in appropriating their moſt characteriſtic language. . . . . With reſpect to the ſcenes between the two buffoons, it would be an injury to the name of Maſſinger to waſte a ſingle argument in proving them not to be his. In ſaying this I am actuated by no hoſtility to Dekker, who in this Play has many paſſages which evince that he wanted not talents to rival, if he had pleaſed, his friend and aſſociate."

To this Mr. Kingſley rejoins :—

"Every pains has been taken to prove that the indecent ſcenes in the play were not written by Maſſinger, but by Dekker : on what grounds we know not. We are aware of no canons of internal criticiſm which will enable us to decide, as boldly as Mr. Gifford does, that all the indecency is Dekker's, and all the poetry Maſſinger's."(23)

A recent writer on the "Minor Elizabethan Dramatiſts," obſerves :—

"To prove how much finer, in its eſſence, his genius was than the genius of ſo eminent a dramatiſt as Maſſinger, we only need to compare Maſſinger's portions of the play of *The Virgin Martyr* with Dekker's. The ſcene between Dorothea and Angelo, in which ſhe recounts her firſt meeting with him as a "ſweet-faced beggar-boy," and the ſcene in which Angelo brings to Theophilus the basket of fruit and flowers which Dorothea has plucked in Paradiſe, are inexpreſſibly beautiful in their exquiſite

---

23 CHARLES KINGSLEY : *Plays and Puritans.* (Miſcellanies, 1859, vol. ii. p. 114.)

ſubtlety of imagination and artleſs elevation of ſentiment." (24)

But a ſtill better and earlier authority has ſettled the queſtion. In his Specimens of the Elizabethan Dramatiſts, Charles Lamb extracts the ſcene between Angelo and Dorothea, and ſays:

"This ſcene has beauties of ſo very high an order that, with all my reſpect for Maſſinger, I do not think he had poetical enthuſiaſm capable of furniſhing them. His aſſociate Dekker, who wrote *Old Fortunatus*, had poetry enough for anything. The very impurities which obtrude themſelves among the ſweet pieties of this play have a ſtrength of contraſt, a racineſs, and a glow in them, which are above Maſſinger. They ſet off the religion of the reſt."

In 1628 and 1629 Dekker was, for two ſucceſſive years employed to write the Mayoralty Pageants. *Britannia's Honor* and *London's Tempe* are the rareſt, though certainly far from the beſt of his pieces. In 1631 appeared the *Tragi-Comedy called, Match mee in London*, the plot of which is thus sketched in Geneſte's *Hiſtory of the Stage*:—

"Tormiella is the daughter of Malevento—her father had promiſed her to Gazetto—ſhe elopes from Cordova with Cordolente—they are married—he is a citizen and

---

24 *Atlantic Monthly*, December, 1867, p. 697.

ſhopkeeper of Seville—Malevento and Gazetto follow them to Seville—the King's Procureſs tells him of Tormiella—he viſits her in diſguiſe, and falls in love with her—he ſends for her to court, and makes her one of the Queen's attendants—the Queen is offended and jealous of Tormiella—the King endeavours to debauch Tormiella—ſhe continues firm in her attachment to her husband—at the concluſion, the King reſtores her to Cordolente, and is reconciled to the Queen. There is an underplot—Don John, the King's brother, wants to obtain the crown—in the laſt ſcene he renounces his ambitious views, and gains the King's pardon. The title ſeems to be a challenge to match Tormiella in London, if one can—the King concludes the play with ſaying that Tormiella has no parallel."

In 1632 Dekker prefixed ſome commendatory verſes to Richard Brome's comedy of *The Northern Laſſe.*

TO MY SONNE BROME AND HIS LASSE.

Which, then of Both ſhall I commend ?
Or Thee (that art my Sonne and Friend)
Or Her, by Thee begot ? A Girle
Twice worth the Cleopatrian Pearle.
No : 'tis not fit for Me to Grace
Thee, who art Mine ; and to thy Face.
Yet I could ſay, the merrieſt Mayd
Among the Nine, for Thee has layd
A Ghyrlond by ; and Iieres to ſee
Pied Ideots teare the Daphnean Tree ;
Putting their Eyes out with thoſe Boughes
With which Shee bids me deck thy Browes.

But what I bring ſhall crowne thy Daughter
(My grand child) who (though full of laughter)
Is Chaſt and Witty to the Time;
Not Lumpiſh Cold, as is her Clime
By Phœbus Lyre, Thy Northern Laſſe
Our Southern proudeſt Beauties paſſe:
  Be Iouiall with thy Braynes (her mother)
And helpe her (Dick) to ſuch Another.

THO. DEKKER.

Of *The Wonder of a Kingdom*, publiſhed in 1636, the German critic(25) already quoted ſpeaks as follows:

"Das gewaltige Jugendfeuer, welches den Fortunatus durch-dringt, iſt in dieſem Drama erloſchen. Beſtändiger Mangel an den erſten Bedürfniſſen des Lebens, Neid ſeiner Feinde, vielleicht eigene Schwäche und Sünde verbunden mit dem Alter, ſcheinen die Kraft des ſo viel verſprechenden Mannes gebrochen zu haben. Mit Wehmuth erinnern wir uns bei dieſer Gelegenheit der Worte ienes Dichters:

"Nicht bloſs erbleichen junge Roſenwangen,
Dem Geiſt auch droht's, daſs er ſich überlebe!"

Hazlitt, however, ſpeaks of the character of Iacomo Gentili in this play as "that truly ideal character of a magnificent patron."

The two remaining plays of Dekker, written in conjunction with Ford—*The Sun's Darling*

---

25 Dr. Schmidt, *ubi ſupra.*

and *The Witch of Edmonton*—were not publiſhed until ſome years after his death—the former in 1656, and the latter in 1658.

Of *The Sun's Darling* Gifford writes as follows :—

"I know not on what authority Langbaine ſpeaks [we have ſeen in another caſe on what a ſlender one] ; but he expreſſly attributes the greater part of this moral maſque to Ford. As far as concerns the laſt two acts, I agree with him ; and a long and clear examination of this poet's manner enables me to ſpeak with ſome degree of confidence. But I trace Dekker perpetually in the other three acts, and through the whole of the comic part. I think well of this poet, and ſhould pauſe before I admitted the inferiority of his genius—as far, at leaſt, as imagination is concerned—to that of Ford: but his rough vigour and his irregular metre generally enable us to mark the line between him and his more harmonious coadjutor."

He remarks thus on *The Witch of Edmonton* :—

"It is very eaſy to ſneer at the ſupernatural portions of this play—which I conſider creditable to the talents and feelings of both poets. I believe in witchcraft no more than the critics ; neither, perhaps, did Ford and Dekker, but they dealt with thoſe who did ; and we are leſs concerned with the viſionary creed of our forefathers than with the skill and dexterity of thoſe who wrote in conformity to it, and the moral or ethical maxims which they enable us to draw from it.

"The ferious part of this drama is fweetly written. The character of Sufan is delineated in Ford's [?] happieft manner; pure, affectionate, confiding, faithful, and forgiving; anxious as a wife to prove her love, but fearful to offend, there is a mixture of warmth and pudency in her language, particularly in the concluding fcene of the fecond act, which cannot fail to pleafe the moft faftidious reader. Winnifride is only fecond to her unfortunate rival; for, though highly culpable before marriage, fhe redeems her character as a wife, and infenfibly fteals upon our pity and regard. Even Katherine, with any other fifter, would not pafs unnoticed.

Carter is no unfair reprefentative of the refpectable yeoman (freeholder) of thofe days; and his frank and independent conduct is well contrafted with that of Banks, a fmall farmer, as credulous and ignorant as his labourers, pofitive, overbearing, and vindictive. The character of Sir Arthur Clarington is fuftained with care and ability. Terrified, but not reclaimed from his profligacy by the law, he is everywhere equally odious, and ends the fame mean, heartlefs, avaricious wretch he fhowed himfelf at firft.

"Of the two plays," fays Mr. Swinburne, "which bear conjointly the names of Ford and Dekker, *The Sun's Darling* is evidently, as Gifford calls it, a 'piece of patchwork' haftily ftitched up for fome momentary purpofe; I fufpect that the two poets did not work together on it, but that our prefent text is merely a recaft by Ford of an earlier mafque by Dekker: probably, as Mr. Collier has fuggefted, his loft play of *Phaeton*, for which we might be glad to exchange the 'loop'd and window'd nakedness' of this ragged verfion. In thofe parts which are plainly remnants of Dekker's handiwork there are ſome ſcattered lines of great ſweetneſs, ſuch as thoſe of lament for the dead ſpring. For the latter ſcenes, as Gifford obſerves, it is clear that Ford is in the main reſponſible; the intruſion in the fifth act of political ſatire and adulation is ſingularly perverſe and infelicitous. In the opening-ſcene, alſo, between Raybright and the Prieſt of the Sun, I recogniſe the moral tone and metrical regulation of Ford's verſe. Whatever the original may have been—and it was probably but a thin and haſty piece of work—it has doubtleſs ſuffered from the incongruous matter looſely ſewn on to it; and the maſque as it ſtands is too lax and incoherent in ſtructure to be worth much as a ſample of its ſlight kind, or to ſhew if there was anything of more ſignificance or value in the firſt conception.

The Witch of Edmonton is a play of rare beauty and importance both on poetical and ſocial grounds. It is perhaps the firſt proteſt of the ſtage againſt the horrors and brutalities of vulgar ſuperſtition; a proteſt all the more precious for the abſolute faith in witchcraft and devilry which goes hand in hand with compaſſion for the inſtruments as well as the victims of magic. . . . Victor Hugo could hardly ſhow a more tender and more bitter pity for the ſordid and grovelling agonies of outcaſt old age and reprobate miſery, than that which fills and fires the ſpeech of the wretched hag from the firſt ſcene where ſhe appears gathering ſticks to warm herſelf, ſtarved, beaten, lamed and bent double with blows, pitiable and terrible in her fierce abjection, to the laſt moment when ſhe is led to execution through the roar of the rabble. In all this part of the play I trace the hand of Dekker; his intimate and familiar ſcience of wretchedneſs, his great and gentle ſpirit of compaſſion for the poor and ſuffering, with whom his own lot in life was ſo often caſt, in priſon and out. The two chief ſoliloquies of Mother Sawyer, her firſt and laſt invocations of the familiar, are noble ſamples of his paſſionate dramatic power; their ſtyle has a fiery impulſe and rapidity quite unlike the uſual manner of his colleague. . . . The part of Suſan is one of Dekker's moſt beautiful and delicate ſtudies; in three ſhort ſcenes he has given an image ſo perfect in its ſimple ſweetneſs as hardly to be overmatched outſide the gallery of Shakeſpeare's women. The tender freſhneſs of his pathos, its plain frank qualities of grace and ſtrength, never ſhowed themſelves with purer or more powerful effect than here; the afterſcene where Frank's guilt is diſcovered has the ſame force and vivid beauty. The interview of Frank with the diſguiſed Winnifrede in this ſcene may be compared by the ſtudent of dramatic ſtyle with the parting of the ſame characters at the cloſe; the one has all the poignant ſimplicity of Dekker, the other all the majeſtic energy of Ford. The rough buffoonery and horſeplay of the clown and the familiar we may probably ſet down to Dekker's account; there is not much humour or meaning in it, but it is livelier and leſs offenſive than moſt of Ford's attempts in that line."(26)

The preciſe date of Dekker's death is as uncertain as that of his birth; but "we hear nothing of him," ſays Mr. Collier, "after 1638, and he is ſuppoſed to have died before the Civil Wars."

The only portrait of Dekker known to exiſt

---

26 *Fortnightly Review. Art.* on JOHN FORD by A. C. Swinburne, July 1871, pp. 55—57.

is in a rude woodcut on the title-page of *Dekker his Dreame*: Lond. 1620.

Mr. Halliwell, in the preface to his reprint (1860) of this pamphlet, ſays: "There can be but little doubt that the woodcut on the title-page contains a genuine portrait of Dekker; and, as ſuch, it is of great intereſt."

Some brief notices of a few of Dekker's proſe productions, extracted from Mr. Payne Collier's *Bibliographical Account of the Rareſt Books in the Engliſh Language*, may be not without intereſt here:—

The (unique) tract entitled *Warres, Warres, Warres*, 1628, 12mo, is dedicated to Hugh Hammerſley, Lord Mayor, and to the two Sheriffs of London and Middleſex for the year; and Dekker ſtates that, as City Poet, he had been employed to write the pageant for Hammerſley's Mayoralty, and he ſeems to have been not a little proud of it. He ſays, "What I offred up then was a Sacrifice *ex officio*. Cuſtome tooke my Bond for the Performance; and on the day of the Ceremony I hope the debt was fully diſcharged." If it were ever printed it has not ſurvived.

The Ravens Almanacke (1609) is ſubſcribed "T. Deckers," which was probably the printer's, certainly not the author's, mode of ſpelling his name. There is a good "ſong ſung by an olde Woman in a Medowe."

Of the Double PP, 1606, 4to, publiſhed anonymouſly, a preſentation copy, with Dekker's autograph, is in exiſtence. It has little but its rarity to recommend it; it is a violent, and, as far as we can underſtand the alluſions, not very witty attack upon the Catholics, provoked by the Gunpowder Plot of the year preceding its publication.

The Seven Deadly Sinnes of London. 1606. 4to.

This tract was one of thoſe which Dekker produced on the ſpur of his neceſſities, and he makes it a boaſt on his title-page that it only coſt him a week's work. . . . As if determined not to loſe any credit, or perhaps profit, by this production, Dekker not only placed his name prominently on the title-page, but he, ſomewhat unuſually, ſubſcribed it at the end, thus:—

"Dii me terrent, et Jupiter hoſtis."

Finis

Tho. Dekker.*

The *Jupiter* and *Dii* were, perhaps at this time a bailiff and his followers, in ſearch of the author for the non-payment of ſome debt.

The Guls Horne-booke, 1609, B. L. 4to.

This is unqueſtionably the moſt entertaining,

and, exclusive of his plays, perhaps the best of Dekker's numerous works in verse and prose. It is full of lively descriptions of the manners of the beginning of the reign of James I., including accounts of, or allusions to, most of the popular and fashionable amusements. The work is entirely prose, and is divided into eight chapters, which are introduced by a *Proemium.*

A writer, already quoted, has well summed up the character and career of Dekker in these words :—

"A man whose inborn sweetness and gleefulness of soul carried him through vexations and miseries which would have crushed a spirit less hopeful, cheerful, and humane. He was probably born about the year 1575 ; commenced his career as player and playwright before 1598 ; and for forty years was an author by profession, that is, was occupied in fighting famine with his pen. The first intelligence we have of him is characteristic of his whole life. It is from Henslowe's Diary, under date of February, 1598: 'Lent unto the company, to discharge Mr. Decker out of the counter in the powltry, the sum of 40 shillings.' Oldys tells us that 'he was in King's Bench Prison from 1613 to 1616;' and the antiquary adds ominously, 'how much longer I know not.' Indeed, Dr. Johnson's celebrated condensation of the scholar's life would stand for a biography of Dekker :—

'Toil, envy, want, the patron, and the jail.'

"This forced familiarity with poverty and distress does not seem to have imbittered his feelings or weakened the force and elaſticity of his mind. He turned his calamities into commodities. If indigence threw him into the ſociety of the ignorant, the wretched, and the depraved, he made the knowledge of low life he thus obtained ſerve his purpoſe as dramatiſt or pamphleteer. Whatever may have been the effect of his vagabond habits on his principles, they did not ſtain the ſweetneſs and purity of his ſentiments. There is an innocency in his very coarſeneſs, and a briſk, bright good-nature chirps in his very ſcurrility. In the midſt of diſtreſſes of all kinds, he ſeems, like his own Fortunatus, 'all felicity up to the brims;' but that his content with Fortune is not owing to an unthinking ignorance of her caprice and injuſtice is proved by the words he puts into her mouth." (27)

It is a ſad ſtory of genius allied to misfortune; of a man of the rareſt gifts and inſight, whom the iron tyranny of circumſtance prevented from being wiſe for himſelf. Even the guerdon of Fame—that fallacious conſolation and hope of the diſappointed—ſeemed as if it were to evade him. The renewed impulſe towards the ſtudy of our earlier poets has at laſt awakened a long-ſlumbering curioſity; but more than two centuries were to elapſe after Thomas Dekker was laid in his grave before his immortal contributions to the Engliſh drama were deſtined to be placed within the reach of general readers.

27 *Atlantic Monthly*, 1867. § *Minor Elizabethan Dramatiſts.*

The text has been reprinted *verbatim et literatim* from the original editions; the ſpelling and punctuation, and even the character of the type as far as poſſible, have been preſerved. A few Notes and Illuſtrations (elucidative of difficult paſſages, and embodying the reſearches of Malone, Steevens, Reed, Collier, Dilke, Gifford, Fairholt, Dyce, and others) have been added to each volume; but the bickerings of rival editors have been carefully eliminated. Only a few of the notes are entirely original, but thoſe borrowed from the ſources above indicated, have in many caſes been conſiderably altered, corrected, abridged, or amplified. This general acknowledgment will doubtleſs be deemed ſufficient.

THE SHOMAKERS Holiday.

OR

The Gentle Craft.

With the humorous life of Simon Eyre, ſhoomaker, and Lord Maior of London.

As it was acted before the Queenes moſt excellent Maieſtie on New-yeares day at night laſt, by the right honourable the Earle of Notingham, Lord high Admirall of England, his ſeruants.

Printed by Valentine Sims dwelling at the foote of Adling hill, neere Bainards Caſtle, at the ſigne of the White Swanne, and are there to be ſold.
1600.

[There are three later editions of *The Shoemakers' Holiday* publiſhed in Dekker's lifetime, bearing date 1610, 1618, and 1631 reſpectively. The preſent text has been formed by a careful collation of theſe with the firſt edition. Some of the verbal differences are indicated in footnotes.]

To all good Fellowes, Profeſſors of *the Gentle Craft; of what degree* ſoeuer.

KInde Gentlemen, and honeſt boone Companions, I preſent you here with a merrie conceited Comedie, called, *the Shoomakers Holyday*, acted by my Lorde Admiralls Players this preſent Chriſtmaſſe, before the Queenes moſt excellent Maieſtie. For the mirth and pleaſant matter, by her Highneſſe graciouſly accepted; being indeede no way offenſſiue. The Argument of the play I will ſet downe in this Epiſtle: Sir *Hugh Lacie* Earle of *Lincolne*, had a yong Gentleman of his owne name, his nere kinſman, that loued the Lorde Maiors daughter of London; to preuent and croſſe which loue, the Earle cauſed his kinſman to be ſent Coronell of a companie into France: who reſigned his place to another gentleman his friend, and came diſguiſed like a Dutch Shoomaker, to the houſe of *Symon Eyre* in Tower ſtreete, who ſerued the Maior and his houſhold with ſhooes. The merriments that paſſed in Eyres houſe, his comming to be Maior of *London*, *Lacies* getting his loue, and other accidents; with two merry Three-mens ſongs. Take all in good worth that is well intended, for nothing is purpoſed but mirth, mirth lengtheneth long life; which, with all other bleſſings I heartily wiſh you.

Farewell.

The firſt Three-mans

Song.

O the month of Maie, the merrie month of Maie,
So frolicke, ſo gay, and ſo greene, ſo greene, ſo greene:
O and then did I vnto my true loue ſay,
Sweete Peg, thou ſhalt be my Summers Queene.

NOw the Nightingale, the prettie Nightingale,
The ſweeteſt ſinger in all the Forreſt quier:
Intreates thee ſweete Peggie, to heare thy true loues tale,
Loe, yonder ſhe ſitteth, her breaſt againſt a brier.

But O I ſpie the Cuckoo, the Cuckoo, the Cuckoo,
See where ſhe ſitteth, come away my ioy:
Come away I prithee, I do not like the Cuckoo
Should ſing where my Peggie and I kiſſe and toy.

O the month of Maie, the merrie month of Maie,
So frolike, ſo gay, and ſo greene, ſo greene, ſo greene:
And then did I, vnto my true loue ſay,
Sweete Peg, thou ſhalt be my Summers Queene.

The ſecond Three-mans

Song.

This is to be ſung at the latter end.

COld's the wind, and wet's the raine,
Saint Hugh be our good ſpeede:
Ill is the weather that bringeth no gaine,
Nor helpes good hearts in neede.

Trowle the boll, the iolly Nut-browne boll,
And here kind mate to thee:
Let's ſing a dirge for Saint Hughes ſoule,
And downe it merrily.

Downe a downe, hey downe a downe,
Hey derie derie down a down, Cloſe with the tenor boy:
Ho well done, to me let come,
Ring compaſſe gentle ioy.

Trowle the boll, the Nut-browne boll,
And here kind, &c. *as often as there be men to drinke.*

At laſt when all haue drunke, this verſe.

Cold's the wind, and wet's the raine,
Saint Hugh be our good ſpeede:
Ill is the weather that bringeth no gaine,
Nor helpes good hearts in neede.

The Prologue as it was pronounced

before the Queenes Maieſtie.

AS wretches in a ſtorme (expecting day)
With trembling hands and eyes caſt vp to heauen,
Make Prayers the anchor of their conquerd hopes,
So we (deere Goddeſſe) wonder of all eyes,
Your meaneſt vaſſalls (through miſtruſt and feare,
To ſincke into the bottome of diſgrace,
By our imperfit paſtimes) proſtrate thus
On bended knees, our ſailes of hope do ſtrike,
Dreading the bitter ſtormes of your diſlike.
Since then (vnhappy men) our hap is ſuch,
That to our ſelues our ſelues no help can bring,
But needes muſt periſh, if your ſaint-like eares
(Locking the temple where all mercy ſits)
Refuſe the tribute of our begging tongues.
Oh graunt (bright mirror of true Chaſtitie)
From thoſe life-breathing ſtarres your ſun-like Eyes,
One gratious ſmile : for your celeſtiall breath
Muſt ſend vs life, or ſentence vs to death.

A pleaſant Comedie of

the Gentle Craft.

Enter Lord Maior, Lincolne.

Lincolne.

MY Lord Maior, you haue ſundrie times
Feaſted my ſelfe, and many Courtiers more,
Seldome, or neuer can we be ſo kind,
To make requitall of your curteſie:
But leauing this, I heare my coſen Lacie
Is much affected to your daughter Roſe.

L. Maior. True my good Lord, and ſhe loues him ſo wel,
That I miſlike her boldneſſe in the chace.

Lincol. Why my lord Maior, think you it then a ſhame,
To ioyne a Lacie with an Otleys name?

L. Maior. Too meane is my poore girle for his high birth,
Poore Cittizens muſt not with Courtiers wed,
Who will in ſilkes, and gay apparrell ſpend
More in one yeare, then I am worth by farre,
Therefore your honour neede not doubt my girle.

Lincolne. Take heede my Lord, aduiſe you what you do,
A verier vnthrift liues not in the world,
Then is my coſen, for Ile tel you what,

Tis now almoſt a yeare ſince he requeſted
To trauell countries for experience,
I furniſht him with coyne, billes of exchange,
Letters of credite, men to waite on him,
Solicited my friends in Italie
Well to reſpect him: but to ſee the end:
Scant had he iornied through halfe Germanie,
But all his coyne was ſpent, his men caſt off,
His billes imbezeld, and my iolly coze,
Aſham'd to ſhew his bankerupt preſence here,
Became a Shoomaker in Wittenberg,
A goodly ſcience for a gentleman
Of ſuch diſcent: now iudge the reſt by this.
Suppoſe your daughter haue a thouſand pound,
He did conſume me more in one halfe yeare,
And make him heyre to all the wealth you haue,
One twelue moneth's rioting wil waſte it all,
Then ſeeke (my Lord) ſome honeſt Cittizen
To wed your daughter to.

L. Maior. I thanke your Lordſhip,
Wel Foxe, I vnderſtand your ſubtiltie,
As for your nephew, let your lordſhips eie
But watch his actions, and you neede not feare,
For I haue my daughter farre enough,
And yet your coſen Rowland might do well
Now he hath learn'd an occupation,
And yet I ſcorne to call him ſonne in law.

Lincolne. I but I haue a better trade for him,
I thanke his grace he hath appointed him,
Chiefe colonell of all thoſe companies
Muſtred in London, and the ſhires about,
To ſerue his highneſſe in thoſe warres of France:
See where he comes: Louel what newes with you?

Enter Louell, Lacie, and Askew.

Louell. My Lord of Lincolne, tis his highneſſe will,
That preſently your coſen ſhip for France
With all his powers, he would not for a million,

But they ſhould land at Deepe within foure daies.

Linc. Goe certifie his grace it ſhall be done :

Exit Louell.

Now coſen Lacie, in what forwardneſſe
Are all your companies ?

Lacie. All wel prepar'd,
The men of Hartfordſhire lie at Mile end,
Suffolke, and Eſſex, traine in Tuttle fields,
The Londoners, and thoſe of Middleſex,
All gallantly prepar'd in Finſbury,
With frolike ſpirits, long for their parting houre.

L. Maior. They haue their impreſt, coates, and furniture,
And if it pleaſe your coſen Lacie come
To the Guild Hall, he ſhall receiue his pay,
And twentie pounds beſides my brethren
Will freely giue him, to approue our loues
We beare vnto my Lord your vncle here.

Lacie. I thanke your honour.

Lincoln. Thankes my good Lord Maior.

L. Ma. At the Guild Hal we wil expect your comming. *Exit.*

Lincolne. To approue your loues to me ? no. ſubtiltie
Nephew : that twentie pound he doth beſtow,
For ioy to rid you from his daughter Roſe :
But coſens both, now here are none but friends,
I would not haue you caſt an amorous eie
Upon ſo meane a proiect, as the loue
Of a gay wanton painted cittizen,
I know this churle, euen in the height of ſcorne,
Doth hate the mixture of his bloud with thine,
I pray thee do thou ſo, remember coze,
What honourable fortunes wayt on thee,
Increaſe the kings loue which ſo brightly ſhines,
And gilds thy hopes, I haue no heire but thee :
And yet not thee, if with a wayward ſpirit,
Thou ſtart from the true byas of my loue.

Lacie. My Lord, I will (for honor (not deſire

Of lands or liuings) or to be your heire)
So guide my actions in purſuit of France,
As ſhall adde glorie to the Lacies name.

Lincolne Coze, for thoſe words heres thirtie Portugues,
And Nephew Aſkew, there's a few for you,
Faire Honour in her loftieſt eminence
Staies in France for you till you fetch her thence,
Then Nephewes, clap ſwift wings on your diſſignes,
Be gone, be gone, make haſte to the Guild Hall,
There preſently Ile meete you, do not ſtay,
Where honour becomes, ſhame attends delay. *Exit.*

Askew. How gladly would your vncle haue you gone?

Lacie. True coze, but Ile ore-reach his policies,
I haue ſome ſerious buſineſſe for three dayes,
Which nothing but my preſence can diſpatch,
You therefore coſen with the companies
Shall haſte to Douer, there Ile meete with you,
Or if I ſtay paſt my prefixed time,
Away for France, weele meete in Normandie,
The twentie pounds my Lord Maior giues to me
You ſhall receiue, and theſe ten portugues,
Part of mine vncles thirtie, gentle coze,
Haue care to our great charge, I know your wiſedome
Hath tride it ſelfe in higher conſequence.

Askew. Coze, al my ſelfe am yours, yet haue this care,
To lodge in London with al ſecreſie,
Our vncle Lincolne hath (beſides his owne)
Many a iealous eie, that in your face
Stares onely to watch meanes for your diſgrace.

Lacie. Stay coſen, who be theſe?

Enter Symon Eyre, his wife, Hodge, Firk, Jane, & Rafe with a peece.

Eyre. Leaue whining, leaue whining, away with

this whimpering, this pewling, thefe blubbring teares, and thefe wet eies, Ile get thy hufband difcharg'd, I warrant thee fweete Jane: go to.

Hodge. Mafter, here be the captaines.

Eyre. Peace Hodge, hufht ye knaue, hufht.

Firke. Here be the caualiers, and the coronels, maifter.

Eyre. Peace Firke, peace my fine Firke, ftand by with your pifhery pafherie, away, I am a man of the beft prefence, Ile fpeake to them and they were Popes, gentlemen, captaines, colonels, commanders: braue men, braue leaders, may it pleafe you to giue me audience, I am Simon Eyre, the mad Shoomaker of Tower ftreete, this wench with the mealy mouth that wil neuer tire, is my wife I can tel you, heres Hodge my man, and my foreman, heres Firke my fine firking iourney-man, and this is blubbered Jane, al we come to be futers for this honeft Rafe keepe him at home, and as I am a true fhoomaker, and a gentleman of the Gentle Craft, buy fpurs your felf, and Ile find ye bootes thefe feuen yeeres.

Wife. Seuen yeares hufband?

Eyre. Peace Midriffe, peace, I know what I do, peace.

Firk. Truly mafter cormorant, you fhal do God good feruice to let Rafe and his wife ftay together, fhees a yong new married woman, if you take her hufband away from her a night, you undoo her, fhe may beg in the day time, for hees as good a workman at a pricke and awle, as any is in our trade.

Jane. O let him ftay, elfe I fhal be vndone.

Firke. I truly, fhe fhal be laid at one fide like a paire of old fhooes elfe, and be occupied for no vfe.

Lacie. Truly my friends, it lies not in my power,
The Londoners are preft, paide, and fet forth
By the Lord Maior, I cannot change a man.

Hodge. Why then you were as good be a corporall, as a colonel, if you cannot difcharge one good fellow, and I tell you true, I thinke you doe more then you can anſwere, to preſſe a man within a yeare and a day of his marriage.

Eyre. Wel ſaid melancholy Hodge, gramercy my fine foreman.

Wife. Truly gentlemen, it were il done, for ſuch as you, to ſtand ſo ſtiffely againſt a poore yong wife: conſidering her caſe, ſhe is newly married, but let that paſſe: I pray deale not roughly with her, her huſband is a yong man and but newly entred, but let that paſſe.

Eyre. Away with your piſherie paſherie, your pols and your edipolls, peace Midaffe, ſilence Ciſly Bumtrincket, let your head ſpeake.

Firke. Yea and the hornes too, maſter.

Eyre. Too ſoone, my fine Firk, too ſoone: peace ſcoundrels, ſee you this man? Captaines, you will not releaſe him, wel let him go, he is a proper ſhot, let him vaniſh, peace Jane, drie vp thy teares, theile make his powder dankiſh, take him braue men, Hector of Troy was a hackney to him, Hercules and Termagant ſcoundrelles, Prince Arthurs Round table, by the Lord of Ludgate, nere fed ſuch a tall, ſuch a dapper ſwordman: by the life of Pharo, a braue reſolute ſwordman, peace Jane, I ſay no more, mad knaues.

Firk. See, ſee Hodge, how my maiſter raues in commendation of Rafe.

Hodge. Raph, thou'rt a gull by this hand, an thou goeſt not.

Askew. I am glad (good maſter Eyre) it is my hap
To meete ſo reſolute a ſouldiour.
Truſt me, for your report, and loue to him,
A common ſlight regard ſhall not reſpect him.

Lacie. Is thy name Raph?

Raph. Yes ſir.

Lacie. Giue me thy hand,
Thou ſhalt not want, as I am a gentleman:
Woman, be patient, God (no doubt) wil ſend
Thy huſband ſafe againe, but he muſt go,

His countries quarrel ſayes, it ſhall be ſo.

Hodge. Thart a gull by my ſtirrop, if thou doſt not goe, I wil not haue thee ſtrike thy gimblet into theſe weake veſſels, pricke thine ememies Rafe.

Enter Dodger.

Dodger. My lord, your vncle on the Tower hill,
Stayes with the lord Mayor, and the Aldermen,
And doth requeſt you with al ſpeede you may
To haſten thither. *Exit Dodger.*

Askew. Coſin, come let vs go.

Lacy. *Dodger*, runne you before, tel them we come,
This *Dodger* is mine uncles paraſite,
The arrantſt varlet that e're breathd on earth,
He ſets more diſcord in a noble houſe,
By one daies broching of his pick-thanke tales,
Then can be ſalu'd againe in twentie yeares,
And he (I feare) ſhall go with vs to France,
To prie into our actions.

Askew. Therefore coze,
It ſhall behooue you to be circumſpect.

Lacy. Feare not good coſen: Raph, hie to your colours.

Raph. I muſt, becauſe there is no remedie,
But gentle maiſter and my louing dame,
As you haue alwaies beene a friend to me,
So in mine abſence thinke vpon my wife.

Jane. Alas my Raph.

Wife. She cannot ſpeake for weeping.

Eyre. Peace you crackt groates, you muſtard tokens, diſquiet not the brave souldier, goe thy waies Raph.

Jane. I I, you bid him go, what ſhal I do when he is gone?

Firk. Why be doing with me, or my fellow Hodge, be not idle.

Eyre. Let me ſee thy hand Jane, this fine hand, this white hand, theſe prettie fingers muſt ſpin, muſt card, muſt worke, worke you bombaſt cotten-candle-queane, worke for your liuing with a pox to you: hold thee Raph, heres fiue ſixpences for thee, fight for the honour of the *Gentle Craft*, for the gentlemen Shoomakers, the couragious Cordwainers, the flower of S. Martins, the mad knaues of Bedlem, Fleetſtreete, Towerſtreete, and white Chappell, cracke me the crownes of the French knaues, a poxe on them, cracke them, fight, by the lord of Ludgate, fight my fine boy.

Firke. Here Rafe, here's three two pences, two carry into France, the third ſhal waſh our ſoules at parting (for ſorrow is drie) for my ſake, Firke the *Baſa mon cues.*

Hodge. Raph, I am heauy at parting, but heres a ſhilling for thee, God ſend thee to cramme thy ſlops with French crownes, and thy enemies bellies with bullets.

Raph. I thanke you maiſter, and I thanke you all:
Now gentle wife, my louing louely Jane,
Rich men at parting, giue their wiues rich gifts,
Jewels and rings, to grace their lillie hands,
Thou know'ſt our trade makes rings for womens heeles:
Here take this paire of ſhooes cut out by Hodge,
Sticht by my fellow Firke, ſeam'd by my ſelfe,
Made vp and pinckt, with letters for thy name,
Weare them my deere Jane, for thy huſbands ſake,
And euerie morning when thou pull'ſt them on,
Remember me, and pray for my returne,
Make much of them, for I haue made them ſo,
That I can know them from a thouſand mo.

Sound drumme, enter Lord Maior, Lincolne, Lacy, Askew, Dodger, and ſouldiers, They paſſe ouer the ſtage, Rafe falles in amongeſt them, Firke and the reſt cry farewel, &c. and ſo Exeunt.

Enter Roſe alone making a Garland.

Roſe. Here ſit thou downe vpon this flowry banke,
And make a garland for thy *Lacies* head,

These pinkes, these roses, and these violets,
These blushing gilliflowers, these marigoldes,
The faire embrodery of his coronet,
Carry not halfe such beauty in their cheekes,
As the sweete countnaunce of my *Lacy* doth.
O my most vnkinde father! O my starres!
Why lowrde you so at my natiuity,
To make me loue, yet liue robd of my loue?
Here as a theefe am I imprisoned
(For my deere *Lacies* sake) within those walles,
Which by my fathers cost were builded vp
For better purposes: here must I languish
For him that doth as much lament (I know)
Mine absence, as for him I pine in woe.

Enter Sibil.

Sibil. Good morrow yong Mistris, I am sure you make that garland for me, against I shall be Lady of the Haruest.

Rose. *Sibil*, what news at London?

Sibil. None but good: my lord Mayor your father, and maister *Philpot* your vncle, and maister *Scot* your coosin, and mistris *Frigbottom* by Doctors Commons, doe all (by my troth) send you most hearty commendations.

Rose. Did *Lacy* send kind greetings to his loue?

Sibil. O yes, out of cry, by my troth, I scant knew him, here a wore a scarffe, and here a scarfe, here a bunch of fethers, and here pretious stones and iewells, and a paire of garters: O monstrous! like one of our yellow silke curtains, at home here in Old-ford house, here in maister *Bellymounts* chamber, I stoode at our doore in Cornehill, lookt at him, he at me indeed, spake to him, but he not to me, not a word, mary gup thought I with a wanion, he passt by me as prowde, mary foh, are you growne humorous thought I? and so shut the doore, and in I came.

Rose. O *Sibill*, how dost thou my *Lacy* wrong?
My Rowland is as gentle as a lambe,

No doue was euer halfe ſo milde as he.

Sibil. Milde? yea, as a buſhel of ſtampt crabs, he lookt vpon me as ſowre as veriuice: goe thy wayes thought I, thou maiſt be much in my gaſkins, but nothing in my neather ſtockes: this is your fault miſtris, to loue him that loues not you, he thinkes ſcorne to do as he's done to, but if I were as you, Ide cry, go by *Ieronimo,* go by, Ide ſet mine olde debts againſt my new driblets, and the hares foot againſt the gooſe giblets, for if euer I ſigh when ſleepe I ſhould take, pray God I may looſe my mayden-head when I wake.

Roſe. Will my loue leaue me then and go to France?

Sibill. I knowe not that, but I am ſure I ſee him ſtalke before the ſouldiers, by my troth he is a propper man, but he is proper that proper doth, let him goe ſnicke-vp yong miſtris.

Roſe. Get thee to London, and learne perfectly,
Whether my *Lacy* go to France, or no:
Do this, and I wil giue thee for thy paines,
My cambricke apron, and my romiſh gloues,
My purple ſtockings, and a ſtomacher,
Say, wilt thou do this *Sibil* for my ſake?

Sibil. Will I quoth a? at whoſe ſuite? by my troth yes, Ile go, a cambricke apron, gloues, and a paire of purple ſtockings, and a ſtomacher, Ile ſweat in purple miſtris for you, ile take any thing that comes a Gods name, O rich, a Cambricke apron; faith then haue at vp tailes all, Ile go, Jiggy, Joggy to London, and be here in a trice yong Miſtris. *Exit.*

Roſe. Do ſo good Sibill, meane time wretched I
Will ſit and ſigh for his loſt companie. *Exit.*

Enter Rowland Lacy like a Dutch Shooe-maker.

Lacy. How many ſhapes haue gods and kings deuiſde,
Thereby to compaſſe their deſired loues?
It is no ſhame for Rowland Lacy then,

To clothe his cunning with the Gentle Craft,
That thus difguifde, I may vnknowne poffeffe,
The onely happie prefence of my Rofe:
For her haue I forfooke my charge in France,
Incurd the kings difpleafure, and ftir'd vp
Rough hatred in mine vncle Lincolnes breft:
O loue, how powerfull art thou, that canft change
High birth to bafeneffe, and a noble mind,
To the meane femblance of a shooemaker:
But thus it muft be, for her cruell father,
Hating the fingle vnion of our foules,
Hath fecretly conueyd my Rofe from London,
To barre me of her prefence, but I truft
Fortune and this difguife will furder me
Once more to view her beautie, gaine her fight,
Here in Towerftreete with Eyre the fhooe-maker,
Meane I a while to worke, I know the trade,
I learn't it when I was at Wittenberge:
Then cheere thy hoping fprites, be not difmaide,
Thou canft not want, do fortune what fhe can,
The Gentle Craft is liuing for a man. *Exit.*

Enter Eyre making himfelfe readie.

Eyre. Where be thefe boyes, thefe girles, thefe drabbes, thefe fcoundrels, they wallow in the fat brewiffe of my boūtie, and licke vp the crums of my table, yet wil not rife to fee my walkes cleanfed: come out you powder-beefe-queanes, what Nan, what Madge-mumble-cruft, come out you fatte Midriffe-fwag-belly whores, and fweepe me thefe kennels, that the noyfome ftench offende not the nofe of my neighbours: (1) what Firke I fay, what Hodge? open my fhop windowes, what Firke I fay.

Enter Firke.

Firke. O Mafter, ift you that fpeake bandog and

(1) The later Editions read "that the noyfome filth offend not the nofes of neighbors."

Bedlam this morning, I was in a dreame, and muſed what mad-man was got into the ſtreet ſo earely, haue you drunk this morning that your throat is ſo cleere?

Eyre. Ah well ſaid *Firke*, well ſaid *Firke*, to worke my fine knaue, to worke, waſh thy face, and thou'lt be more bleſt.

Firke. Let them waſh my face that will eate it, good Maſter ſend for a Souſe-wife, if you will haue my face cleaner.

Enter Hodge.

Eyre. Away ſlouen, auant ſcoundrell, good morrow *Hodge*, good morrow my fine Fore-man.

Hodge. O Maſter, good morrow, y'are an earely ſtirrer, heere's a faire morning, good morrow *Firke*, I could haue ſlept this houre, heer's a braue day towards.

Eyre. O haſt to worke my fine Fore-man, haſt to worke.

Firke. Maſter, I am drie as duſt to heare my fellow *Roger* talke of faire weather, let vs pray for good leather, and let Clownes and Plow-boyes, and thoſe that worke in the fields pray for braue daies, wee worke in a drie ſhoppe, what care I if it raine?

Enter Eyres wife.

Eyre. How now dame *Margerie*, can you ſee to riſe? trip and go, call up the drabs your maides.

Wife. See to riſe? I hope tis time enough, tis early enough for any Woman to bee ſeene abroad, I maruell how many wiues in Tower ſtreet are vp ſo ſoone: Gods me tis not noone, heeres a yawling.

Eyre. Peace Margerie, peace, wher's *Ciſly Bumtrinket* your maid? ſhee hath a priuie fault, ſhee farts in her ſleepe, call the queane vp, if my men want ſhooe threed, Ile ſwinge her in a ſtirrop.

Firke. Yet that's but a drie beating, heere's ſtill a ſigne of drought.

Enter Lacy ſinging.

Lacy. **Der was een bore van Gelderland, Frolick ſi byen,**
He was als dronke he cold nyet ſtand, vp ſolce ſe byen,
Tap eens de canneken drinck ſchone mannekin.

Firke. Maiſter, for my life yonders a brother of the Gentle Craft, if hee beare not Saint *Hughes* bones Ile forfeit my bones, hee's ſome vplandiſh workeman, hire him good maſter, that I may learne ſome gibble gabble, 'twill make vs worke the faſter.

Eyre. Peace *Firke*, a hard world, let him paſſe, let him vaniſh, we haue iournymen enow, peace my fine *Firke.*

Wife. Nay nay y'are beſt follow your mans councell, you ſhall ſee what will come on't, we haue not men enow, but wee muſt entertaine euery butterboxe; but let that paſſe.

Hodge. Dame, fore God if my maſter follow your counſell hee'le conſume little beefe, he ſhall be glad of men, and he can catch them.

Firke. I that he ſhall.

Hodge. Afore God a proper man, and I warrant a fine workeman: Maſter farewell, dame adue, if ſuch a man as he cannot find worke, *Hodge* is not for you.

Offer to goe.

Eyre. Stay my fine *Hodge.*

Firke. Faith and your foreman goe, dame you muſt take a iourney to ſeeke a new iourneyman, if *Roger* remoue, *Firke* followes, if Saint *Hughes* bones ſhall not be ſet a worke, I may pricke mine awle in the wals, and goe play: fare ye wel maſter, God buy dame.

Eyre. Tarrie my fine *Hodge*, my briſke foreman, ſtay *Firke* peace pudding broth, by the Lord of Ludgate I loue my men as my life, peace you gallimafrey,

Hodge if hee want worke Ile hire him, one of you to him, ſtay he comes to vs.

Lacy. Goeden dach meeſter, ende v vro oak.

Firke. Nailes if I ſhould ſpeak after him without drinking, I ſhould choak, and you friend Oake, are you of the gentle craft?

Lacy. Yaw, yaw, ich beene den ſhoomaker.

Firke. Den ſhoomaker quoth a, and hearke you ſhoomaker, haue you all your tooles, a good rubbing pin, a good ſtopper, a good dreſſer, your foure ſorts of Aules, and your two balles of waxe, your paring knife, your hand and thum-leathers, and good Saint *Hughes* bones to ſmooth vp your worke.

Lacy. Yaw, yaw, bee niet vor veard, ik hab all de dingen, voour mack ſhooes groot and cleane.

Firke. Ha, ha, good maſter hire him, heele make me laugh ſo that I ſhall worke more in mirth than I can in earneſt.

Eyre. Heere you friend, haue you any ſkill in the myſtery of Cordwainers?

Lacy. Ick weet niet wat you ſeg ich verſtaw you niet.

Firk. Why thus man, Ich verſte v niet, quoth a.

Lacy Yaw, yaw, yaw, ick can dat well doen.

Firke. Yaw, yaw, he ſpeakes yawing like a Jack daw, that gapes to be fed with cheeſe curdes, O heele giue a villanous pull at a can of double beere, but *Hodge* and I haue the vantage, wee muſt drinke firſt, becauſe wee are the eldeſt Iourneymen.

Eyre. What is thy name?

Lacy. *Hans, Hans, Meulter.*

Eyre. Giue me thy hand, thou art welcome, *Hodge*, entertaine him, *Firke* bid, him welcome, come *Hans*, run wife, bid your maids, your trulli-bubs, make ready my fine mens breakfaſts: to him *Hodge.*

Hodge. Hans, th'art welcome, vſe thy ſelfe friendly, for we are good fellowes, if not, thou ſhalt be fought with, wert thou bigger than a Gyant.

Firk. Yea, and drunk with, wert thou *Gargantua*, my maſter keeps no Cowards, I tell thee: hoe, boy, bring him an heele-blocke, heers a new iourneyman.

Enter Boy.

Lacy. **O ich werſto you, ich moet een halbe doſſen Cans betalen: here boy nempt dis ſkilling, tap eens freelicke.**

Exit Boy.

Eyre. Quicke ſnipper ſnapper, away *Firk*, ſcowre thy throat, thou ſhalt waſh it with Caſtillian liquor.

Enter Boy.

Come my laſt of the fiues, give mee a Can, haue to thee *Hans*, here *Hodge*, here *Firke*, drinke you mad Greekes, and worke like true Troyans, and pray for *Simon Eyre* the Shoomaker, heere *Hans* and th'art welcome.

Firke. Lo dame, you would haue loſt a good fellow that will teach vs to laugh, this beere came hoping in well.

Wife. Simon, it is almoſt ſeuen.

Eyre. Iſt ſo dame clapper dudgeon, iſt ſeuen a clocke, and my mens breakfaſt not readie? trip and go you ſowſt cunger, away, come you madde Hiperboreans, follow me *Hodge*, follow me *Hans*, come after my fine *Firke*, to worke, to worke a while, and then to breakfaſt. *Exit.*

Firke. Soft, yaw, yaw, good *Hans*, though my maſter haue no more wit but to call you afore me, I am not ſo fooliſh to go behind you, I being the elder iourneymen. *Exeunt.*

Hollowing within. Enter Warner and Hammon, like hunters.

Hammon. Coſen beate euery brake, the game's not farre,
This way with winged feet he fled from death,
Whilſt the purſuing hounds ſenting his ſteps,
Find out his high way to deſtruction.
Beſides, the Millers boy told me euen now,
He ſaw him take ſoile and he hallowed him :
Affirming him ſo emboſt,
That long he could not hold.

Warner. If it be ſo,
Tis beſt we trace theſe meddowes by Old-Ford.

A noiſe of hunters within, enter a boy.

Hammon. How now boy, where's the Deere? ſpeak, ſawſt thou him?

Boy. O yea, I ſaw him leape through a hedge, and then ouer a ditch, then at my Lord Maiors pale ouer he ſkipt mee, and in he went me, and holla the hunters cride, and there boy, there boy, but there he is a mine honeſtie.

Ham. Boy God a mercie, Coſen lets away,
I hope we ſhall find better ſport to day. *Exeunt.*

Hunting within, enter Roſe and Sibill.

Roſe. Why *Sibill*, wilt thou proue a Forreſter?

Sibill. Upon ſome no. Forreſter go by : no faith miſtris, the Deere came running into the Barne, through the Orchard and ouer the pale, I wot well, I look't as pale as a new cheeſe to ſee him, but whip ſaies goodman Pincloſe, vp with his flaile, and our *Nicke* with a prong, and downe he fell, and they vpon him, and I vpon them, by my troth wee had ſuch ſport, and in the end we ended him, his throat wee cut, flead him, vnhorned him, and my Lord Maior ſhall eate of him anon when he comes.

Hornes ſound within.

Roſe. Heark, heark, the hunters come, y'are beſt take heed,
They'l haue a ſaying to you for this deed.

Enter Hammon, Warner, huntſmen, and boy.

Ham. God ſaue you faire Ladies.

Sibill. Ladies, O groſſe!

War. Came not a Bucke this way?

Roſe. No, but two Does.

Ham. And which way went they? faith wee'l hunt at thoſe.

Sibill. At thoſe? vpon ſome no: when, can you tell?

War. Vpon ſome, I.

Sibill. Good Lord!

War. Zounds then farewell.

Ham. Boy, which way went he?

Boy. This way ſir he ran.

Ham. This way he ran indeed, faire Miſtris *Roſe*,
Our game was lately in your orchard ſeene.

War. Can you aduiſe which way he tooke his flight?

Sibill. Follow your noſe, his hornes will guide you right.

War. Th'art a mad wench.

Sibill. O rich!

Roſe. Truſt me, not I,
It is not like that the wild forreſt deere,
Would come ſo neere to places of reſort,
You are deceiu'd, he fled ſome other way.

War. Which way my ſugar-candy, can you ſhew?

Sibill. Come vp good honniſops, vpon ſome, no.

Roſe. Why do you ſtay and not purſue your game?

Sibill. Ile hold my life their hunting nags be lame.

Ham. A deere, more deere is found within this place.

Roſe. But not the Deere (ſir) which you had in chace.

Ham. I chac'd the deere, but this deere chaſeth me.

Roſe. The ſtrangeſt hunting that euer I ſee,
But where's your parke?

She offers to go away.

Ham. Tis here: O ſtay.

Roſe. Impale me, and then I will not ſtray.

War. They wrangle wench, we are more kind than they.

Sibill. What kind of heart is that (deere heart) you ſeeke?

War. A Hart, deere heart.

Sibill. Who euer ſaw the like?

Roſe. To loſe your heart, is't poſſible you can?

Ham. My heart is loſt.

Roſe. Alacke good Gentleman.

Ham. This poore loſt heart would I wiſh you might find.

Roſe. You by ſuch luck might proue your heart a hind.

Ham. Why Lucke had hornes, ſo haue I heard ſome ſay?

Roſe. Now God and't be his will ſend luck into your way.

Enter L. Maior, and ſeruants.

L. Ma. What M. *Hammon,* welcome to Old Ford.

Sibill. Gods pittikins, hands off ſir, heeres my Lord.

L. Ma. I heare you had ill lucke, and loſt your game.

Ham. Tis true my Lord.

L. Ma. I am ſorrie for the ſame.
What gentleman is this?

Ham. My brother in law.

L. Ma. Y'are welcome both, ſith Fortune offers you
Into my hands, you ſhall not part from hence,
Untill you haue refreſht your wearied limbes.
Go Sibill couer the boord, you ſhall be gueſt
To no good cheere, but euen a hunters feaſt.

Ham. I thanke your Lordſhip : couſen, on my life,
For our loſt veniſon I ſhall find a wife. *Exeunt.*

L. Ma. In gentlemen, Ile not be abſent long.
This *Hammon* is a proper gentleman,
A citizen by birth, fairely allide,
How fit a huſband were he for my girle?
Well, I will in, and do the beſt I can,
To match my daughter with this gentleman. *Exit.*

Enter Lacy, Skipper, Hodge, and Firk.

Skip. **Ick ſal yow wat ſeggen Hans, dis ſkip dat comen from Candy is alwol, by gots ſacrament, van ſugar, ciuet, almonds, Cambrirke, end alle dingen towſand towſand ding, nempt it Hans, nempt it vor v meeſter, daer be bils van laden, your meeſter Symon Eyre ſal hae good copen, wat ſeggen yow Hans?**

Firke. What ſeggen de reggen de copen, ſlopen, laugh *Hodge* laugh.

Lacie. **Mine lieuer broder** *Firke*, **bringt meeſter** *Eyre* **lot det ſigne vn** ſwannekin, dare ſal you finde dis ſkip-per end me, wat seggen yow broder *Firke?* doot it *Hodge* come Skipper.

Exeunt.

Firke. Bring him qd. you, heeres no knauerie, to bring my maiſter to buy a ſhip, worth the lading of 2. or 3. hundred thouſand pounds, alas that's nothing, a trifle, a bable *Hodge.*

Hod. The truth is *Firke,* that the Marchant owner of the Ship dares not ſhew his head, and therfore this Skipper that deales for him, for the loue he beares to *Hans,* offers my maſter *Eyre* a bargaine in the commodities, he ſhal haue a reaſonable day of payment, he may ſell the wares by that time, and be an huge gainer himſelfe.

Firk. Yea, but can my fellow *Hans* lend my maſter twenty porpentines as an earneſt pennie.

Hod. Portegues thou wouldſt ſay, here they be *Firke,*
hark, they gingle in my pocket like S. *Mary Queries* bels.

Enter Eyre and his Wife.

Firk. Mum, here comes my Dame and my Maſter, ſheele ſcold on my life, for loytering this Monday, but al's one, let them all ſay what they can, Monday's our holyday.

Wife. You ſing ſir ſauce, but I beſhrew your heart, I feare for this your ſinging we ſhall ſmart.

Firk. Smart for me dame, why dame, why?

Hod. Maſter, I hope yowle not ſuffer my Dame to take downe your Journeymen.

Firk. If ſhe take me downe, Ile take her vp, yea and take her downe too, a button-hole lower.

Eyre. Peace *Firke,* not I *Hodge,* by the life of *Pharao,* by the Lord of *Ludgate,* by this beard, euery haire whereof I value at a Kings ranſome, ſhe ſhall not meddle with you, peace you bumbaſt-cotten-candle queane, away Queene of Clubs, quarrel not with me and my men, with me and my fine *Firke*, ile firke you if you do.

Wife. Yea yea man, you may vſe me as you pleaſe : but let that paſſe.

Eyre. Let it paſſe, let it vaniſh away : peace, am I not *Simon Eyre?* are not theſe my braue men? braue Shoomakers, all gentlemen of the Gentle Craft? Prince am I none, yet am I nobly borne, as being the ſole ſonne of a Shoomaker, away rubbiſh, vaniſh, melt, melt like kitchin ſtuffe.

Wife. Yea, yea, tis well, I muſt be cald rubbiſh, kitchin-ſtuffe, for a ſort of knaues.

Firke. Nay dame, you ſhall not weepe and waile in woe for me : maſter Ile ſtay no longer, heere's a vennentorie of my ſhop tooles : adue maſter, *Hodge* farewell.

Hodge. Nay ſtay *Firke*, thou ſhalt not go alone.

Wife. I pray let them go, there be more maids than Mawkin, more men than *Hodge*, and more fooles than *Firke.*

Firke. Fooles? nailes if I tarrie now, I would my guts might be turned to ſhoo-thread.

Hodge. And if I ſtay, I pray God I may be turnd to a Turk, and ſet in Finſburie for boyes to ſhoot at : come *Firke.*

Eyre. Stay my fine knaues, you armes of my trade, you pillars of my profeſſion, What, ſhall a tittle tattles words make you forſake *Simon Eyre?* auaunt Kitchin-ſtuffe, rippe you browne bread tannikin, out of my ſight, moue mee not, haue not I tane you from ſelling Tripes in Eaſtcheape, and ſet you in my ſhop, and made you haile fellow with *Simon Eyre* the Shoomaker? and now doe you deale thus with my Journey-men? Looke you powder-beefe queane on the face of *Hodge* : heeres a face for a Lord.

Firke. And heere's a face for any Lady in Chriſtendome.

Eyre. Rip you chitterling, auaunt boy, bid the Tapſter of the Bores head fill me a doozen Cannes of beere for my iourneymen.

Firke. A doozen Cans? O braue, *Hodge* now Ile ſtay.

Eyre. And the knaue fils any more than two, hee payes for them : a doozen Cans of beere for my Journemen, heere you mad *Meſopotamians*, waſh your liuers with this liquour, where bee the odde ten? no more Madge, no more, well ſaid, drink & to work : what work doſt thou *Hodge*? what work?

Hod. I am a making a paire of ſhooes for my Lord Maiors daughter, miſtreſſe *Roſe*.

Firk. And I a paire of ſhooes for *Sibill* my Lords maide, I deale with her.

Eyre. *Sibill*? fie, defile not thy fine workemanly fingers with the feet of Kitchin ſtuffe, and baſting ladles, Ladies of the Court, fine Ladies, my lads, commit their feet to our apparelling, put groſſe worke to *Hans* : yarke and ſeame : yarke and ſeame.

Firk. For yarking and ſeaming let me alone, & I I come toot.

Hod. Well maſter all this is from the bias, doe you remember the Shippe my fellow *Hans* told you of, the Skipper and he are both drinking at the Swan? here be the Portigues to giue earneſt, if you goe through with it, you cannot chooſe but be a Lord at leaſt.

Firk. Nay dame, if my maſter proue not a Lord, and you a Lady, hang me.

Wiſe. Yea like enough, if you may loyter and tipple thus.

Firke. Tipple Dame? no we haue beene bargaining with Skellum Scanderbag : can you Dutch ſpreaken, for a Shippe of Silke Cipreſſe, laden with Sugar Candy.

Enter the boy with a veluet coat, and an Aldermans gowne, Eyre puts it on.

Eyr. Peace *Firk*, ſilence tittle tattle : *Hodge*, ile go through with it, heers a ſeale ring, and I haue ſent for a garded gown and a damaſke caſocke, ſee where it comes, looke heere Maggy, helpe me *Firk*, apparrell me *Hodge*, ſilke and ſatten you mad Philiſtines, ſilke and ſatten.

Firk. Ha, ha, my maſter will be as proud as a dogge in a doublet, all in beaten damaſke and veluet.

Eyr. Softly *Firke*, for rearing of the nap, and wearing thread-beare my garments: how doſt thou like mee *Firke*? how do I looke my fine *Hodge*?

Hod. Why now you looke like your ſelfe maſter, I warrant you, ther's few in the citie, but will giue you the wall, and come vpon you with the right worſhipfull.

Firk. Nailes my maſter lookes like a thread-beare cloake new turn'd, and dreſt: Lord, Lord, to ſee what good raiment doth? dame, dame, are you not enamoured?

Eyr. How faiſt thou Maggy, am I not briſk? am I not fine?

Wife. Fine? by my troth ſweet heart very fine: by my troth I neuer likt thee ſo well in my life ſweet heart. But let that paſſe, I warrant there bee many women in the citie haue not ſuch handſome huſbands, but onely for their apparell, but let that paſſe too.

Enter Hans and Skipper.

Hans. Godden day meſter, dis be de ſkipper dat heb de ſkip van marchandize, de commodity ben good, nempt it meſter, nempt it.

Eyr. God a mercy *Hans*, welcome Skipper, where lies this ſhip of marchandize?

Skip. De ſkip beene in rouere: dor be van ſugar, ciuit, Almonds, Cambricke, and a towſand towſand tings, gots ſacrament, nempt it meſter, yo ſal heb good copen.

Firk. To him maiſter, O ſweet maiſter, O ſweet wares, Prunes, Almonds, Suger-candy, Carret roots,

Turnips, O braue fatting meat, let not a man buy a nutmeg but your ſelf.

Eyre. Peace *Firke*, come Skipper, Ile goe aboord with you, *Hans* haue you made him drinke?

Skip. Yaw, yaw, ic heb veale ge drunke.

Eyre. Come *Hans* follow me: Skipper thou ſhalt haue my countenance in the citie. *Exeunt.*

Firke. Yaw heb veale ge drunke, quoth a: they may well be called butter-boxes, when they drinke fat veale, and thicke beere too: but come Dame, I hope youle chide vs no more.

Wife. No faith *Firke*, no perdy *Hodge*, I do feele honour creepe vpon me, and which is more, a certaine riſing in my fleſh, but let that paſſe.

Firke. Riſing in your fleſh do you feele ſay you? I you may be with child, but why ſhould not my maſter feele a riſing in his fleſh, hauing a gowne and a gold ring on, but you are ſuch a ſhrew, youle ſoone pull him downe.

Wife. Ha, ha, prethee peace, thou makſt my worſhip laugh, but let that paſſe: come ile goe in *Hodge*, prethee goe before me, *Firke* follow me.

Firke. *Firke* doth follow, *Hodge* paſſe out in ſtate. *Exeunt.*

Enter Lincolne and Dodger.

Lincoln. How now good *Dodger*, whats the newes in France?

Dodg. My Lord, vpon the eighteenth day of May,
The French and Engliſh were prepared to fight,
Each ſide with eager furie gaue the ſigne
Of a moſt hot encounter, fiue long houres
Both armies fought together: at the length,
The lot of victorie fell on our ſides,
Twelue thouſand of the Frenchmen that day dide,
Four thouſand Engliſh, and no man of name,
But Captaine *Hyam*, and young *Ardington*,
Two gallant gentlemen, I knew them well.

Lin. But *Dodger*, prethee tell me in this fight,

How did my cozen *Lacy* beare himſelfe ?
Dod. My Lord, your cozen *Lacy* was not there.
Lin. Not there ?
Dod. No, my good Lord.
Lin. Sure thou miſtakeſt,
I ſaw him ſhipt, and a thouſand eyes beſide
Were witneſſe of the farewells which he gaue,
When I with weeping eyes bid him adew :
Dodger take heed.
Dodg. My Lord I am aduiſde
That what I ſpeake is true; to proue it ſo,
His cozen *Askew* that ſupplide his place,
Sent me for him from France, that ſecretly
He might conuey himſelfe hither.
Lin. Iſt euen ſo,
Dares he ſo careleſſely venture his life,
Upon the indignation of a King ?
Hath he deſpiſ'd my loue, and ſpurnd thoſe fauours
Which I with prodigall hand powr'd on his head ?
He ſhall repent his raſhneſſe with his ſoule,
Since of my loue he makes no eſtimate,
Ile make him wiſh he had not knowne my hate,
Thou haſt no other newes ?
Dodg. None elſe, my Lord.
Linc. None worſe I know thou haſt : procure the King
To crowne his giddie browes with ample honours,
Send him chiefe Colonell, and all my hope
Thus to be daſht ? but tis in vaine to grieue,
One euill cannot a worſe releeue :
Upon my life I haue found out this plot,
The old dog Loue that fawnd vpon him ſo,
Loue to that puling girle, his faire cheekt *Roſe*,
The Lord Maiors daughter hath diſtracted him.
And in the fire of that loues lunacie,
Hath he burnt vp himſelfe, conſum'd his credit,
Loſt the Kings loue, yea and I feare his life;
Onely to get a wanton to his wife :
Dodger, it is ſo.

D

Dodg. I feare ſo, my good Lord.
Linco. It is ſo, nay ſure it cannot be.
I am at my wits end *Dodger.*
Dodg. Yea my Lord.
Len. Thou art acquainted with my Nephewes haunts,
Spend this gold for thy paines, go ſeeke him out,
Watch at my Lord Maiors, there (if he liue)
Dodger, thou ſhalt be ſure to meet with him :
Prethee be diligent. *Lacy*, thy name
Liu'd once in honour, now dead in ſhame :
Be circumſpect. *Exit.*
Dod. I warrant you my Lord. *Exit.*

Enter Lord Maior, and Maſter Scot.

L. Ma. Good maſter *Scot*, I haue beene bold with you,
To be a witneſſe to a wedding knot,
Betwixt young maſter *Hammon* and my daughter.
O ſtand aſide, ſee where the louers come.

Enter Hammon and Roſe.

Roſe. Can it be poſſible you loue me ſo ?
No, no, within thoſe eye-balls I eſpie,
Apparant likelyhoods of flatterie,
Pray now let go my hand.
Ham. Sweet miſtres *Roſe*,
Miſconſtrue not my words, nor miſconceiue
Of my affection, whoſe deuoted ſoule
Sweares that I loue thee deerer than my heart.
Roſe. As deere as your owne heart ? I iudge it right.
Men loue their hearts beſt when th' are out of ſight.
Ham. I loue you by this hand.
Roſe. Yet hands off now :
If fleſh be fraile, how weak and frail's your vow ?
Ham. Then by my life I ſweare.

Rose. Then do not brawle,
One quarrell looseth wife and life and all,
Is not your meaning thus ?

Ham. In faith you iest.

Rose. Loue loues to sport, therefore leaue loue y'are best.

L. Ma. What ? square they master *Scot* ?

Scot. Sir, never doubt,
Louers are quickly in, and quickly out.

Ham. Sweet *Rose,* be not so strange in fansying me,
Nay neuer turne aside, shun not my sight,
I am not growne so fond, to fond my loue,
On any that shall quit it with disdaine,
If you will loue me, so : if not, farewell.

L. Ma. Why how now louers, are you both agreed ?

Ham. Yes faith my Lord.

L. Ma. Tis well, giue me your hand, give me yours daughter.
How now, both pull backe, what meanes this, Girle ?

Rose. I meane to liue a maide.

Ham. But not to die one, pawse ere that be said. *aside.*

L. Ma. Will you still crosse me ? still be obstinate ?

Ham. Nay chide her not my Lord for doing well,
If she can liue an happie virgins life,
Tis far more blessed than to be a wife.

Rose. Say sir I cannot, I haue made a vow,
Who euer be my husband, tis not you.

L. Ma. Your tongue is quicke, but M. *Hammon* know,
I bade you welcome to another end.

Ham. What, would you have me pule, and pine, and pray,
With louely Lady mistris of my heart,
Pardon your seruant, and the rimer play,
Rayling on *Cupid,* and his tyrants dart ?

Or ſhall I vndertake ſome martiall ſpoile,
Wearing your gloue at Turney, and at Tilt,
And tell how many gallants I vnhorſt,
Sweet, will this pleaſure you?

Roſe. Yes, when wilt begin;
What loue-rimes man? fie on that deadly ſinne.

L. Ma. If you will haue her, Ile make her agree.

Ham. Enforced loue is worſe than hate to me,
There is a wench keeps ſhop in the old change,
To her will I, it is not wealth I ſeeke,
I haue enough, and will prefer her loue
Before the world: my good Lord Maior adew,
Old loue for me, I haue no lucke with new. *Exit.*

L. Ma. Now mammet you haue well behau'd your ſelfe.
But you ſhall curſe your coyneſſe if I liue:
Who's within there? ſee you conuey your miſtris
Straight to th' old Ford, Ile keepe you ſtraite enough,
Fore God I would haue ſworne the puling girle
Would willingly accepted *Hammons* loue;
But baniſh him my thoughts, go minion in.
Exit Roſe.
Now tell me maſter *Scot,* would you haue thought
That maſter *Symon Eyre* the Shoomaker
Had beene of wealth to buy ſuch merchandize?

Scot. 'Twas well my Lord, your honour, and my ſelfe,
Grew partners with him, for your billes of lading
Shew that *Eyres* gaines in one commoditie
Riſe at the leaſt to full three thouſand pound,
Beſides like gaine in other merchandize.

L. Ma. Well, he ſhall ſpend ſome of his thouſands now.
For I haue ſent for him to the Guild Hall,

Enter Eyre.

See where he comes: good morrow maſter Eyre.

Eyre. Poore *Simon Eyre,* my Lord, your ſhoomaker.

L. Ma. Well well, it likes your ſelfe to terme you ſo,

Enter Dodger.

Now M. *Dodger*, whats the newes with you?

Dodg. Ide gladly ſpeake in priuate to your Honor.

L. Ma. You ſhall, you ſhall: maſter *Eyre*, and M. *Scot*,

I haue ſome buſineſſe with this gentleman,
I pray let me intreat you to walke before
To the Guild hall, Ile follow preſently,
Maiſter *Eyre*, I hope ere noone to call you Sherife.

Eyre. I would not care (my Lord) if you might call me king of Spaine, come maſter *Scot.*

L. Ma. Now maſter *Dodger*, what's the newes you bring?

Dod. The Earle of Lincolne by me greets your Lordſhip,

And earneſtly requeſts you (if you can)
Informe him where his nephew *Lacy* keepes.

L. Ma. Is not his nephew *Lacy* now in France?

Dod. No I aſſure your Lordſhip, but diſguiſ'd
Lurkes here in London.

L. Ma. London? iſt euen ſo?
It may be; but vpon my faith and ſoule,
I know not where he liues, or whether he liues,
So tell my Lord of Lincolne: lurke in London?
Well maſter *Dodger*, you perhaps may ſtart him,
Be but the meanes to rid him into France,
Ile giue you a dozen angells for your paines,
So much I loue his honor, hate his nephew,
And prethee ſo informe thy Lord from me.

Dodger. I take my leaue. *Exit Dodger.*

L. Ma. Farewell good maſter *Dodger.*
Lacie in London? I dare pawne my life,
My daughter knowes thereof, and for that cauſe,
Denied young Maſter *Hammon* in his loue,
Well, I am glad I ſent her to old Forde,
Gods Lord tis late, to Guild Hall I muſt hie,
I know my Brethren ſtay my companie. (2) *Exit.*

(2) lacke my companie. 1631.

Enter Firke, Eyres wife, Hans and Roger.

Wife. Thou goest too fast for me *Roger.* O *Firke.*

Firke. I forsooth.

Wife. I pray thee run (doe you heare) run to Guild Hall, and learne if my husband master *Eyre* will take that worshipfull vocation of M. Sherife vpon him, hie thee good *Firke.*

Firke. Take it? well I goe, and he should not take it, Firke sweares to forsweare him, yes forsooth I goe to Guild Hall.

Wife. Nay when? th'art two compendious and tedious.

Firk. O rare, your excellence if full of eloquence, how like a new Cart wheele my dame speakes, and she lookes like an old mustie Ale-bottle going to scalding.

Wife. Nay when? thou wilt make me melancholy.

Firke. God forbid your Worship should fall into that humour, I run. *Exit.*

Wife. Let me see now *Roger* and *Hans.*

Ro. I forsooth dame, (mistris I should say) but the old terme so stickes to the roofe of my mouth, I can hardly licke it off.

Wife. Euen what thou wilt good *Roger,* Dame is a faire name for any honest Christian, but let that passe, how dost thou *Hans*?

Hans. Me tanck you vro.

Wife. Well *Hans* and *Roger,* you see God hath blest your maister, and perdie if euer he come to be M. Sherife of London, (as we are all mortall) you shall see, I will haue some odde thing or other in a corner for you, I will not bee your backe friend, but let that passe, *Hans,* pray thee tye my shoe.

Hans. Yaw ic sal vro.

Wife. Roger, thou knowest the length of my foote, as it is none of the biggest, so I thanke God it is handsome enough, prethee let me haue a paire of shooes made, Corke good Roger, woodden heele too.

Hodge. You ſhall.

Wife. Art thou acquainted with neuer a Farding-ale-maker, nor a French-hood maker, I muſt enlarge my bumme, ha, ha, ha, how ſhall I looke in a hood I wonder ? perdie odly I thinke.

Roger. As a Cat out of a Pillory, very wel I warrant you Miſtreſſe.

Wife. Indeed all fleſh is graſſe, and *Roger*, canſt thou tell where I may buy a good haire ?

Roger. Yes forſooth, at the Poulterers in Gracious ſtreete.

Wife. Thou art an vngracious wag, perdye, I meane a falſe haire for my perewig.

Roger. Why Miſtris, the next time that I cut my beard, you ſhall have the ſhauings of it, but mine are all true haires.

Wife. It is very hot, I muſt get me a fan or elſe a maſke.

Roger. So you had need to hide your wicked face.

Wife. Fie vpon it, how coſtly this world's calling is, perdie, but that it is one of the wonderfull workes of God, I would not deal with it: is not *Firke* come yet ? *Hans*, be not ſo ſad, let it paſſe and vaniſh as my huſbands worſhip ſaies.

Hans. Ick bin vrolicke, lot ſee you ſoo.

Roger. Miſtris, will you drinke a pipe of Tobacco ?

Wife. O fie vpon it Roger, perdy, theſe filthy Tobacco pipes are the moſt idle ſlauering bables that euer I felt: out vpon it, God bleſſe vs, men looke not like men that vſe them.

Enter Raph being lame.

Roger. What fellow *Raph* ? Miſtreſſe looke heere, *Janes* huſband: why how now, lame ? *Hans* make much of him, hee's a brother of our Trade, a good workeman, and a tall Souldier.

Hans. You be welcome broder.

Wife. Pardie I knew him not, now doſt thou good *Raph* ?

I am glad to ſee thee well.

Raph. I would God you ſaw me dame as well
As when I went from London into France.

Wife. Truſt mee I am ſorrie *Raph* to ſee thee impotent, Lord how the warres haue made him Sunburnt: the left leg is not well, 'twas a faire giſt of God, the infirmitie took not hold a little higher, conſidering thou camſt from France, but let that paſſe.

Raph. I am glad to ſee you well, and I rejoyce
To heare that God hath bleſt my maſter ſo
Since my departure.

Wife. Yea truely *Raph*, I thanke my maker: but let that paſſe.

Roger. And ſirra *Raph*, what news, what news in France?

Raph. Tell me good *Roger* firſt what newes in England?
How does my *Jane*? when didſt thou ſee my wife?
Where liues my poore heart? ſheele be poore indeed,
Now I want limbs to get whereon to feed.

Rog. Limbes? haſt thou not hands man? thou ſhalt neuer ſee a ſhoomaker want bread, though he haue but three fingers on a hand.

Raph. Yet all this while I heare not of my *Jane.*

Wife. O *Raph* your wife, perdie wee know not what's become of her: ſhe was here a while, and becauſe ſhe was married, grew more ſtately than became her, I checkt her, and ſo forth, away ſhe flung, neuer returned, nor ſaid bih nor bah: and Raph you know, ka me, ka thee, And ſo as I tell ye, *Roger* is not *Firke* come yet?

Roger. No forſooth.

Wife. And ſo indeed we heard not of her, but I heare ſhee liues in London: but let that paſſe. If ſhee had wanted, ſhee might haue opened her caſe to me or my huſband, or to any of my men, I am ſure there is not any of them perdie, but would haue done her good to his power. *Hans*, looke if *Firke* bee come.

Hans. Yaw ic ſal vro. *Exit Hans*

Wife. And ſo as I ſaid : but *Raph*, why doſt thou weepe? thou knoweſt that naked we came out of our mothers womb, and naked we muſt returne, and therefore thanke God for all things.

Roger. No faith, *Jane* is a ſtranger heere, but *Raph* pull vp a good heart, I know thou haſt one, thy wiſe man is in London, one told me he ſaw her a while agoe very braue and neat, wee'le ferret her out, and London hold her.

Wife. Alas poore ſoule, hee's ouercome with ſorrow, he does but as I doe, weepe for the loſſe of any good thing : but *Raph*, get thee in, call for ſome meat and drink, thou ſhalt find me worſhipfull towards thee.

Raph. I thanke you dame, since I want limbs
and lands,
Ile truſt to God, my good friends, and to my hands. (3)
Exit.

Enter Hans and Firke running.

Firke. Runne good *Hans*, O *Hodge*, O Miſtris; *Hodge* heaue vp thine eares, miſtreſſe ſmugge vp your lookes, on with your beſt apparell, my maſter is choſen, my maſter is called, nay condemned by the cry of the Countrie to be ſherife of the Citie, for this famous yeare now to come : and time now being, a great many men in black gownes were aſkt for their voices, and their hands, and my maſter had all their fiſts about his eares preſently, and they cried I, I, I, I, and ſo I came away, wherefore without all other grieue, I doe ſalute you miſtris Shrieue.

Hans. Yaw, my meeſter is de groot man, de Shrieue.

Roger. Did not I tell you Miſtris, now I may boldly ſay, good morrow to your worſhip.

Wife. Good morrow good *Roger*, I thanke you my good people all, *Firke*, hold vp thy hand, heer's a three pennie peece for thy tydings.

(3) Ile to God, my good friends, and to theſe my hands.
1600—1610.

Firk. Tis but three halfe pence, I think : yes, tis three pence, I ſmell the Roſe.

Hodge. But Miſtris, be rul'd by me, and do not ſpeake ſo pulingly.

Firk. 'Tis her worſhip ſpeakes ſo and not ſhe, no faith miſtris ſpeake mee in the old key, to it *Firke*, there good *Firke*, ply your buſineſſe *Hodge*, *Hodge* with a full mouth : Ile fill your bellies with good cheare till they cry twang.

Enter Simon Eyre wearing a gold chaine.

Hans. See mine lieuer broder, heere compt my meeſter.

Wife. Welcome home maiſter Shrieue, I pray God continue you in health and wealth.

Eyre. See here my *Maggy*, a Chaine, a gold Chaine for *Simon Eyre*, I ſhall make thee a lady, heere's a French hood for thee, on with it, on with it, dreſſe thy browes with this flap of a ſhoulder of mutton, to make thee looke louely : where be my fine men ? *Roger*, Ile make ouer my ſhop and tooles to thee : *Firk*, thou ſhalt be the foreman : *Hans*, thou ſhalt haue an hundred for twenty, be as mad knaues as your maiſter *Sim Eyre* hath beene, and you ſhall liue to be Sherifes of London : how doſt thou like mee *Margerie*? Prince am I none, yet am I princely borne, *Firke*, *Hodge*, and *Hans*.

All 3. I forſooth, what ſayes your worſhip miſtris Sherife?

Eyre. Worſhip and honour ye Babilonian knaues, for the Gentle Craft : but I forgot my ſelfe, I am bidden by my Lord Maior to dinner to old Foord, hees gone before, I muſt after : come Madge, on with your trinkets : now my true Troians, my fine *Firke*, my dapper *Hodge*, my honeſt *Hans*, ſome deuice, ſome odde crochets, ſome morris, or ſuch like, for the honour of the gentle Shoo-makers, meet mee at old Foord, you know my mind : come Madge, away, ſhut vp the ſhop knaues, and make Holiday.

Exeunt.

Firke. O rare, O braue, come *Hodge*, follow me *Hans*,
Wee'le be with them for a Morris dance. *Exeunt.*

Enter Lord Maior, Eyre, his wife in a French hood, Sibill and other Seruants.

L. Maior. Truſt me you are as welcome to old Foord, as I myſelfe.

Wife. Truely, I thanke your Lordſhip.

L. Maior. Would our bad cheere were worth the thankes you giue.

Eyre. Good cheere my Lord Maior, fine cheere, a fine houſe, fine walles, all fine and neat.

L. Ma. Now by my troth, Ile tell thee maiſter *Eyre*,
It does me good and all my Brethren,
That ſuch a mad-cap fellow as thy ſelfe
Is entred into our ſocietie.

Wife. I but my Lord hee muſt learne now to put on grauitie.

Eyre. Peace *Maggy*, a fig for grauitie, when I goe to Guild Hall in my Scarlet gowne, i'le looke as demurely as a Saint, and ſpeake as grauely as a Juſtice of Peace, but now I am here at old Foord, at my good Lord Maiors houſe, let it goe by, vaniſh *Maggy*, i'le be merrie, away with flip flap, theſe fooleries, theſe gulleries: what hunny? Prince am I none, yet am I Princely borne: what ſayes my Lord Maior?

L. Ma. Ha, ha, ha, I had rather than a thouſand pound,
I had an heart but halfe ſo light as yours.

Eyre. Why what ſhould I doe my Lord? a pound of care payes not a dram of debt: hum, let's be merrie whiles wee are young, old Age, ſacke and ſugar will ſteale vpon vs ere we be aware.

L. Ma. Its well done, Miſtris *Eyre*, pray giue good counſell to my daughter.

Wife. I hope miſtris *Roſe* will haue the grace to take nothing that's bad.

L. Ma. Pray God ſhe doe, for ifaith miſtris *Eyre*,
I would beſtow vpon that peeuiſh girle
A thouſand markes more than I meane to giue her,
Upon condition ſheed be rul'd by me.
The Ape ſtill croſſeth me : there came of late
A proper gentleman of faire reuenewes,
Whom gladly I would call Sonne in law :
But my fine Cockney would haue none of him,
Youle proue a Cockſcombe for it ere you die,
A Courtier or no man muſt pleaſe your eye.

Eyre. Bee rul'd ſweet Roſe, th'art ripe for a man : marrie not with a boy that has no more haire on his face than thou haſt on thy cheekes : a Courtier, waſh, goe by, ſtand not vpon piſhery paſherie ; thoſe ſilken fellowes are but painted Images, outſides, outſides *Roſe*, their inner linings are torne : no my fine mouſe, marrie me with a Gentleman Grocer like my Lord Maior your father, a Grocer is a ſweet trade, plums, plums : had I a ſonne or daughter ſhould marrie out of the generation and blood of the ſhoomakers, he ſhould pack : what, the gentle trade is a liuing for a man through Europe, through the world.

A noyſe within of a Taber and a Pipe.

L. Ma. What noyſe is this ?

Eyre. O my Lord Maior, a crue of good fellowes that for loue to your honour, are come hither with a Morriſdance ; come in my Meſopotamians cheerily.

Enter Hodge, Hans, Raph, Firke, and other Shoomakers in a morris: after a little dancing the Lord Maior ſpeaks.

L. Ma. Maiſter *Eyre*, are all theſe Shoomakers ?

Eyre. All Cordwainers my good Lord Maior.

Roſe. How like my *Lacie* lookes yond Shoomaker.

Hans. O that I durſt but ſpeake vnto my loue !

L. Ma. *Sibill,* go fetch ſome wine to make theſe drinke,
You are all welcome.

All. We thanke your Lordſhip.

Roſe takes a cup of wine and goes to Hans.

Roſe. For his ſake whoſe faire ſhape thou repreſentſt,
Good friend I drinke to thee.

Hans. Ic be dancke good friſter.

Eyres Wife. I ſee miſtris *Roſe* you do not want iudgement, you haue drunke to the propereſt man I keepe..

Firke. Here be ſome haue done their parts to be as proper as he.

L. Ma. Well, vrgent buſineſſe cals me backe to London:
Good fellowes, firſt go in and taſt our cheare,
And to make merrie as you homeward goe,
Spend theſe two angels in beere at Stratford Boe.

Eyre. To theſe two (my mad lads) *Sim Eyre* addes another, then cheerily *Firke,* tickle it *Hans,* and all for the honour of Shoomakers.

All go dancing out.

L. Ma. Come maiſter *Eyre,* let's haue your company. *Exeunt.*

Roſe. *Sibill,* what ſhall I doe?

Sibil Why whats the matter?

Roſe. That *Hans* the ſhoo-maker is my loue *Lacy,*
Diſguiſd in that attire to find me out,
How ſhould I find the meanes to ſpeake with him?

Sib. What miſtris, neuer feare, I dare venter my maidenhead to nothing, and thats great oddes, that *Hans* the Dutchman when we come to London, ſhall not onely ſee and ſpeake with you, but in ſpight of all your Fathers pollicies, ſteale you away and marrie you, will not this pleaſe you?

Roſe. Do this, and euer be aſſured of my loue.

Sibil. Away then, and follow your father to London, leſt your abſence cauſe him to ſuſpect ſomething:

To morrow if my counſell be obaide,
Ile bind you prentiſe to the gentle trade.

Enter Iane in a Semſters ſhop working, and Hammon muffled at another doore, he ſtands aloofe.

Ham. Yonders the ſhop, and there my faire loue ſits,
Shee's faire and louely, but ſhe is not mine.
O would ſhe were, thrice haue I courted her,
Thrice hath my hand beene moiſtned with her hand,
Whilſt my poore famiſht eyes do feed on that
Which made them famiſh: I am infortunate,
I ſtill loue one, yet no bodie loues me,
I muſe in other men what women ſee,
That I ſo want? fine miſtris *Roſe* was coy,
And this too curious, oh no, ſhe is chaſt,
And for ſhe thinkes me wanton, ſhe denies
To cheare my cold heart with her ſunny eyes,
How prettily ſhe workes, oh prettie hand!
Oh happie worke, it doth me good to ſtand
Unſeene to ſee her, thus I oft haue ſtood,
In froſty euenings, a light burning by her,
Enduring biting cold, only to eye her,
One onely looke hath ſeem'd as rich to me
As a Kings crowne, ſuch is loues lunacie:
Muffeled Ile paſſe along, and by that try
Whether ſhe know me.

Jane. Sir, what iſt you buy?
What iſt you lacke ſir? callico, or lawne,
Fine cambricke ſhirts, or bands, what will you buy?

Ham. That which thou wilt not ſell, faith yet ile trie:
How do you ſell this handkercher?

Jane. Good cheape.

Ham. And how theſe ruffes?

Jane. Cheape too.

Ham. And how this band?

Jane. Cheape too.

Ham. All cheape, how ſell you then this hand?

Jane. My hands are not to be ſold.
Ham. To be giuen then, nay faith I come to buy.
Jane. But none knowes when.
Ham. Good ſweet, leaue worke a little while, lets play.
Jane. I cannot liue by keeping holliday.
Ham. Ile pay you for the time which ſhall be loſt.
Jane. With me you ſhall not be at ſo much coſt.
Ham. Looke how you wound this cloth, ſo you wound me.
Jane. It may be ſo.
Ham. Tis ſo.
Jane. What remedy?
Ham. Nay faith you are too coy.
Jane. Let go my hand.
Ham. I will do any taſke at your command,
I would let go this beautie, were I not
In mind to diſobey you by a power
That controules Kings: I loue you.
Jane. So, now part.
Ham. With hands I may, but neuer with my heart,
In faith I loue you.
Jane. I beleeue you doe.
Ham. Shall a true loue in mee breed hate in you?
Jane. I hate you not.
Ham. Then you muſt loue.
Jane. I doe, what are you better now? I loue not you.
Ham. All this I hope is but a womans fray,
That meanes come to me, when ſhe cries, away:
In earneſt miſtris I do not ieſt,
A true chaſt loue hath entred in my breſt,
I loue you dearely as I doe my life,
I loue you as a huſband loues a wife,
That, and no other loue my loue requires,
Thy wealth I know is little, my deſires
Thirſt not for gold, ſweet beautious *Jane* what's mine,
Shall (if thou make my ſelfe thine) all be thine,

Say, iudge, what is thy ſentence, life, or death ?
Mercy or crueltie lies in thy breath.

Jane. Good ſir I do beleeue you loue me well :
For tis a ſeely conqueſt, ſeely pride,
For one like you (I mean a gentleman)
To boaſt, that by his loue tricks he hath brought,
Such and ſuch women to his amorous lure :
I thinke you do not ſo, yet many doe,
And make it euen a very trade to wooe,
I could be coy, as many women be,
Feed you with ſun-ſhine ſmiles, and wanton lookes,
But I deteſt witch-craft ; ſay that I
Doe conſtantly beleeve you, conſtant haue.

Ham. Why doeſt thou not beleeue me ?

Jane. I beleeue you,
But yet good ſir, becauſe I will not greeue you,
With hopes to taſte fruit which will neuer fall,
In ſimple truth this is the ſumme of all,
My huſband liues, at leaſt I hope he liues,
Preſt was he to theſe bitter warres in France,
Bitter they are to me by wanting him,
I haue but one heart, and that heart's his due,
How can I then beſtow the ſame on you ?
Whileſt he liues, his I liue, be it neere ſo poore,
And rather be his wife, than a kings whore.

Ham. Chaſt and deare woman, I will not abuſe thee,
Although it coſt my life, if thou refuſe me,
Thy huſband preſt for France, what was his name ?

Jane. *Rafe Damport.*

Ham. *Damport,* heres a letter ſent
From France to me, from a deare friend of mine,
A gentleman of place, here he doth write,
Their names that haue beene ſlaine in euery fight.

Jane. I hope deaths ſcroll containes not my loues name.

Ham. Can you not read ?

Jane. I can.

Ham. Peruſe the ſame.

To my remembrance ſuch a name I read
Amongſt the reſt; ſee here.
Jane. Aye me, hee's dead,
Hee's dead, if this be true my deare hearts ſlaine.
Ham. Haue patience, deare loue.
Jane. Hence, hence.
Ham. Nay ſweet *Jane,*
Make not poore ſorrow prowd with theſe rich teares,
I mourne thy huſbands death becauſe thou mournſt.
Jane. That bill is forgde, tis ſignde by forgerie.
Ham. Ile bring thee letters ſent beſides to many
Carrying the like report: *Jane* tis too true,
Come, weep not: mourning though it riſe from loue,
Helpes not the mourned, yet hurts them that mourne.
Jane. For Gods ſake leaue me.
Ham. Whither doſt thou turne?
Forget the dead, loue them that are aliue.
His loue is faded, trie how mine will thriue.
Jane. Tis now no time for me to think on loue.
Ham. Tis now beſt time for you to thinke on loue, becauſe your loue liues not.
Jane. Though he be dead, my loue to him ſhal not be buried:
For Gods ſake leaue me to my ſelfe alone.
Ham. T'would kill my ſoule to leave thee drownd in mone:
Anſwere me to my ſute, and I am gone,
Say to me, yea, or no.
Jane. No.
Ham. Then farewell: one farewell will not ſerue.
I come againe, come drie theſe wet cheekes,
tell me faith ſweete Jane, yea, or no, once more.
Jane. Once more I ſay no, once more begone
I pray, elſe will I goe.
Ham. Nay then I will grow rude by this white hand,
Untill you change that cold no, here ile ſtand,
Till by your hard heart.
Jane. Nay for Gods loue peace,

My ſorrowes by your preſence more increaſe,
Not that you thus are preſent, but all griefe
Deſires to be alone, therefore in briefe
Thus much I ſay, and ſaying bid adew,
If euer I wed man it ſhall be you.

Ham. Oh bleſſed voice, deare *Jane*, ile urge no more,
Thy breath hath made me rich.

Jane. Death makes me poore. *Exit.*

Enter Hodge at his ſhop boord, Rafe, Firke, Hans, and a boy at worke.

All. Hey downe, a downe dery.

Hodge. Well ſaid my hearts, plie your worke to day, wee loytred yeſterday, to it pell mell, that we may liue to be Lord Maiors, or Aldermen at leaſt.

Firk. Hey downe a downe dery.

Hodge. Well ſaid ifaith, how ſaiſt thou *Hans*, doth not *Firk* tickle it ?

Hans. Yaw meſter.

Firke. Not ſo neither, my organe pipe ſqueaks this morning forwant of licoring : hey downe a downe dery.

Hans. Forward *Firk*, tow beſt vn iolly yongſter hort I meſter ic bid yo cut me vn paire vanpres vor meſter iffres boots.

Hodge. Thou ſhalt *Hans.*

Firke. Maiſter.

Hodge. How now, boy ?

Firke. Pray, now you are in the cutting vaine, cut me out a paire of counterfeits, or elſe my worke will not paſſe currant, hey downe a downe.

Hod. Tell me ſirs, are my cozen M. Priſcillaes ſhooes done ?

Firke. Your cozen ? no maſter, one of your aunts, hang her, let them alone.

Rafe. I am in hand with them, ſhe gaue charge that none but I ſhould do them for her.

Firke. Thou do for her ? then twill be but a lame

doing, and that ſhe loues not: *Rafe*, thou might'ſt haue ſent her to me, in faith I would haue yearkt and firkt your *Priſcilla*, hey downe a downe dery, this geere will not hold.

Hodge. How ſaiſt thou *Firk*? were we not merry at Old-Ford?

Firke. How merry? why our buttockes went Iiggy ioggy like a quagmire: well ſir Roger Oatemeale, if I thought all meate of that nature, I would eate nothing but Bag puddings.

Raph. Of all good fortunes, my fellow *Hans* had the beſt.

Firke. Tis true, becauſe miſtris *Roſe* dranke to him.

Hodge. Well, well, worke apace, they ſay ſeuen of the Aldermen be dead, or very ſick.

Firke. I care not, ile be none.

Rafe. No nor I, but then my M. *Eyre* will come quickly to be L. Maior.

Enter Sibill.

Firke. Whoope, yonder comes *Sibill.*

Hodge. *Sibill*, welcome ifaith, and how doſt thou madde wench?

Firke. *Sib* whoore, welcome to London.

Sibill. Godamercy ſweet *Firke*: good Lord, *Hodge*, what a delicious ſhop you haue got, you tickle it ifaith.

Rafe. God a mercy *Sibill* for our good cheere at old Ford.

Sibill. That you ſhall have *Rafe.*

Firke. Nay by the maſſe, we had tickling cheere *Sibill*, and how the plague doſt thou and miſtris *Roſe*, and my L. Maior? I put the women in firſt.

Sibill. Well Godamercy: but gods me, I forget my ſelfe, where's *Hans* the Flemming?

Firke. Hearke butter-boxe, now you muſt yelp out ſome ſpreken.

Hans. Vat begaie gon vat vod gon Friſter.

Sibill. Marry you muſt come to my young miſtris, to pull on her ſhooes you made laſt.

Hans. Var ben your egle fro, vare ben your miſtris ?

Sibil. Marrie here at our London houſe in Cornehill.

Firke. Will no bodie ſerue her turne but *Hans* ?

Sibil. No ſir, come, *Hans* I ſtand vpon needles.

Hod. Why then *Sibill*, take heed of pricking.

Sibill. For that let me alone, I haue a tricke in my budget, come *Hans.*

Hans. Yaw, yaw ic ſall meete yo gane.

Exit Hans and Sibill.

Hodge. Goe *Hans*, make haſt againe : come, who lackes worke ?

Firke. I maſter, for I lacke my breakefaſt, tis munching time, and paſt.

Hodge. Iſt ſo, why then leaue worke *Raph*, to breakefaſt, boy looke to the tooles, come *Rafe*, come *Firke.* *Exeunt.*

Enter a Seruingman.

Ser. Let me ſee now, the ſigne of the Laſt in Towerſtreet, mas yonders the houſe : what haw, whoes within ?

Enter Rafe.

Rafe. Who calls there, what want you ſir ?

Ser. Marrie I would haue a paire of ſhooes made for a Gentlewoman againſt to morrow morning, what, can you do them ?

Rafe. Yes ſir, you ſhall hane them, but what length's her foote?

Ser. Why, you muſt make them in all parts like this ſhooe, but at any hand faile not to do them, for the Gentlewoman is to be married very early in the morning.

Rafe. How? by this ſhooe muſt it be made? by this? are you ſure ſir by this?

Ser. How, by this am I ſure, by this? art thou in thy wits? I tell thee I muſt haue a paire of ſhooes, doſt thou marke me? a paire of ſhooes, two ſhooes, made by this very ſhooe, this ſame ſhooe, againſt to morrow morning by foure a clocke, doſt vnderſtand me, canſt thou do it?

Rafe. Yes ſir, yes, I, I, I can do't, by this ſhooe you ſay: I ſhould know this ſhooe? yes ſir, yes, by this ſhooe, I can do't, foure a clocke, well, whither ſhall I bring them?

Ser. To the ſigne of the golden ball in Watling-ſtreet, enquire for one maiſter *Hammon*, a Gentleman, my maſter.

Raph. Yea ſir, by this ſhooe you ſay.

Ser. I ſay maſter *Hammon* at the golden Ball, hee's the Bride-groome, and thoſe ſhooes are for his bride.

Raph. They ſhall be done by this ſhooe; well, well, maſter *Hammon* at the gold ſhooe, I would ſay the golden Ball, wel, very well, but I pray you ſir, where muſt maſter *Hammon* be married?

Ser. At Saint *Faith's* Church vnder Paules: but what's that to thee? prethee diſpatch thoſe ſhooes, and ſo farewell. *Exit.*

Raph. By this ſhooe ſaid he, how am I amazd
At this ſtrange accident? vpon my life,
This was the very ſhooe I gaue my wife
When I was preſt for France; ſince when, alas,
I neuer could heare of her. 'Tis the ſame,
And *Hammons* bride no other than my *Jane.*

Enter Firke.

Firke. Snailes *Raph* thou haſt loſt thy part of three pots, a countrieman of mine gaue me to breakefaſt.

Raph. I care not, I haue found a better thing.

Firke. A thing? away; is it a mans thing or a womans thing?

Raph. *Firke*, doſt thou know this ſhooe?

Firke. No by my troth, neither doth that know me: I haue no acquaintance with it, tis a meere ſtranger to me.

Raph. Why then I doe; this ſhooe I durſt be ſworne
Once couered the inſtep of my *Jane*:
This is her ſize, her breadth, thus trod my loue,
Theſe true-loue knots I prickt, I hold my life,
By this old ſhooe I ſhall find out my wife.

Firke. Ha, ha old ſhooe that wert new, how a murren came this ague fit of fooliſhneſſe vpon thee?

Raph. Thus *Firke* euen now here came a ſeruing-man,
By this ſhooe would he haue a new paire made,
Againſt to morrow morning for his miſtris,
That's to be married to a gentleman,
And why may not this be my ſweet *Jane*?

Firke. And why maieſt not thou be my ſweet Aſſe? ha, ha.

Raph. Well, laugh and ſpare not, but the truth is this,
Againſt to morrow morning Ile prouide
A luſty crew of honeſt ſhoomakers,
To watch the going of the bride to Church:
If ſhe proue *Jane*, Ile take her in diſpite
Of *Hammon* and the Deuill, were he by,
If it be not my *Jane*, what remedy?
Hereof I am ſure, I ſhall liue till I die,
Although I neuer with a woman lie.

Firke. Thou lie with a woman to build nothing but Cripplegates? Well God ſends fooles fortune, and it may be hee may light vpon his matrimony by ſuch a deuice, for wedding and hanging goes by deſtinie. *Exit.*

Enter Hans and Rose arme in arme.

Hans. How happie am I by embracing thee,
O I did feare ſuch croſſe miſhaps did raigne,
That I ſhould neuer ſee my *Roſe* againe.
Roſe. Sweet *Lacy*, ſince faire opportunitie,
Offers her ſelfe to further our eſcape,
Let not too ouer-fond eſteeme of me,
Hinder that happie houre, inuent the meanes,
And *Roſe* will follow thee through all the world.
Hans. Oh how I ſurfet with exceſſe of ioy,
Made happie by thy rich perfection:
But ſince thou payſt ſweet intereſt to my hopes,
Redoubling loue on loue, let me once more
Like to a bold-fac'd debtor craue of thee,
This night to ſteale abroad, and at *Eyres* houſe,
Who now by death of certaine Aldermen,
Is Maior of London, and my maiſter once,
Meete thou thy *Lacy*, where in ſpight of change,
Your fathers anger, and mine vncles hate,
Our happy nuptials will we conſummate.

Enter Sibil.

Sibill. Oh God, what will you do miſtris? ſhift for your ſelfe, your father is at hand, hee's comming, hee's comming, maſter *Lacy* hide your ſelfe in my miſtris, for Gods ſake ſhift for your ſelues.

Hans. Your father come, ſweet *Roſe*, what ſhall I doe?
Where ſhall I hide me? how ſhall I eſcape?
Roſe. A man, and want wit in extremitie,
Come come, be *Hans* ſtill, play the ſhoomaker,
Pull on my ſhooe.

Enter Lord Maior.

Hans. Mas and that's well remembred.

Sibill. Here comes your father.

Hans. For ware metreſſe, 'tis vn good ſkow, it ſall vel ſute, or ye ſal neit betallen.

Rose. O God it pincheth me, what will you do?

Hans. Your fathers presence pincheth, not the shooe.

L. Ma. Well done, fit my daughter well, and she shall please thee well.

Hans. Yaw, yaw, ick weit dat well, for ware tis vn good skoo, tis gi mait van neits leither, se euer mine here.

Enter a Prentise.

L. Maior. I do beleeue it, whats the newes with you?

Pren. Please you the Earle of Lincolne at the gate is newly lighted, and would speake with you.

L. Ma. The Earle of Lincolne come speake with me?
Well, well, I know his errand: daughter *Rose*
Send hence your shoomaker, dispatch, haue done:
Sib make things handsome, sir boy follow me. *Exit.*

Hans. Mine vncle come: O what may this portend?
Sweet *Rose*, this of our loue threatens an end.

Rose. Be not dismaid at this, what ere befall,
Rose is thine owne, to witnesse I speake truth,
Where thou appoints the place, Ile meet with thee;
I will not fixe a day to follow thee,
But presently steale hence: do not replie,
Loue which gaue strength to beare my fathers hate,
Shall now adde wings to further our escape. *Exeunt.*

Enter Lord Maior and Lincolne.

L. Maior. Beleeue me on my credit I speake truth,
Since first your nephew *Lacy* went to France,
I haue not seene him: It seem'd strange to me,
When *Dodger* told me that he staied behind,
Neglecting the high charge the king imposed.

Linc. Trust me (sir *Roger Otley*) I did thinke
Your counsell had giuen head to this attempt,
Drawne to it by the loue he beares your child,

Here I did hope to find him in your houſe,
But now I ſee mine error, and confeſſe
My iudgement wrong'd you by conceiuing ſo.

L. Ma. Lodge in my houſe, ſay you? truſt me my Lord,
I loue your nephew Lacy too too dearely,
So much to wrong his honour: and he hath done ſo,
That firſt gaue him aduice to ſtaie from France.
To witneſſe I ſpeake truth, I let you know
How carefull I haue beene to keepe my daughter
Free from all conference or ſpeech of him,
Not that I ſcorne your nephew, but in loue
I beare your honor, leſt your noble blood,
Should by my meane worth be diſhonoured.

Linc. How far the churles tongue wanders from his heart,
Well, well ſir *Roger Otley*, I beleeue you,
With more than many thankes for the kind loue,
So much you ſeeme to beare me: but my Lord,
Let me requeſt your helpe to ſeeke my nephew,
Whom if I find, i'le ſtraight imbarke for France;
So ſhall your Roſe be free, my thoughts at reſt,
And much care die which now lies in my breſt.

Enter Sibill.

Sibill. O Lord, helpe for Gods ſake my miſtris,
Oh my young miſtris.

L. Ma. Where is thy miſtris? what's become of her?

Sibill. Shee's gone, ſhee's fled.

L. Ma. Gone? whither is ſhe fled?

Sibill. I know not forſooth, ſhee's fled out of doores with *Hans* the Shoomaker, I ſaw them ſcud, ſcud, ſcud, apace, apace.

L. Ma. Which waie? what *John*? where be my men? which waie?

Sibill. I know not and it pleaſe your worſhip.

L. Ma. Fled with a ſhoomaker, can this be true?

Sibil. O Lord ſir, as true as you are L. Maior.(4)

Lin. Her loue turned ſhoomaker, I am glad of this.

L. Ma. A Flemming butter-boxe, a ſhoomaker.
Will ſhe forget her birth? requite my care
With ſuch ingratitude? ſcorn'd ſhe young *Hammon*,
To loue a honnikin, a needy knaue?
Well let her flie, ile not flie after her,
Let her ſtarue if ſhe will, ſhee's none of mine.

Lin. Be not ſo cruell ſir.

Enter Firke with ſhooes.

Sibill. I am glad ſhee's ſcapt.

L. Ma. Ile not account of her as of my child,
Was there no better obiect for her eyes,
But a foule drunken lubbery ſwill-bellie,
A ſhoomaker, that's braue.

Firke. Yea forſooth 'tis a verie braue ſhooe, and as fit as a pudding.

L. Ma. How now, what knaue is this, from whence commeſt thou?

Firke. No knaue ſir, I am *Firke* the ſhoomaker, luſtie *Rogers* chiefe luſty journey-man, and I come hither to take vp the prettie legge of ſweet miſtris *Roſe*, and thus hoping your worſhip is in as good health as I was at the making hereof, I bid you farewell, yours *Firke.*

L. Ma. Stay, ſtay, ſir knaue.

Lin. Come hither ſhoomaker.

Firke. Tis happie the knaue is put before the ſhoomaker, or elſe I would not haue vouchſafed to come backe to you, I am moued, for I ſtirre.

L. Ma. My Lord, this villaine calls vs knaues by craft.

Firke. Then 'tis by the Gentle Craft, and to call one knaue gently is no harme: ſit your worſhip merrie: *Sib* your young miſtris. I'le ſo bob them, now my maiſter M. *Eyre* is Lord Maior of London.

(4) as true as Gods in heauen. 1600.

L. Ma. Tell me ſirra, whoſe man are you?

Firke. I am glad to ſee your worſhip ſo merrie, I haue no maw to this geere, no ſtomacke as yet to a red petticoat. *Pointing to Sibil.*

Lin. He meanes not ſir to wooe you to his maid,
But onely doth demand whoſe man you are.

Firke. I ſing now to the tune of Rogero,
Roger my fellow is now my maiſter.

Linc. Sirra knowſt thou one *Hans* a ſhoomaker?

Fir. *Hans* Shoomaker, oh yes, ſtay, yes I haue him, I tell you what, I ſpeake it in ſecret, miſtris *Roſe* and he are by this time, no not ſo, but ſhortly are to come ouer one another, with Can you dance the ſhaking of the ſheets? it is that *Hans*, Ile ſo gull theſe diggers.

L. Ma. Knowſt thou then where he is?

Firke. Yes forſooth, yea marry.

Lin. Canſt thou in ſadneſſe?

Firke. No forſooth, no marry.

L. Ma. Tell me good honeſt fellow where he is,
And thou ſhalt ſee what Ile beſtow of thee.

Firke. Honeſt fellow, no ſir, not ſo ſir, my profeſſion is the Gentle Craft, I care not for ſeeing, I loue feeling, let me feel it heere, *aurium tenus*, ten peeces of gold, *genuum tenus*, ten peeces of ſiluer, and then Firke is your man in a new paire of ſtretchers.

L. Ma. Here is an angell, part of thy reward,
Which I will giue thee, tell me where he is.

Firke. No point, ſhall I betray my brother? no, ſhal I proue *Judas* to *Hans*? no; ſhal I crie treaſon to my corporation? no, I ſhall be firkt and yerkt then, but giue me your angell, your angell ſhall tell you.

Lin. Doe ſo good fellow, 'tis no hurt to thee.

Firke. Send ſimpring *Sib* away.

L. Ma. Huſwife get you in. *Exit Sib.*

Firke. Pitchers haue eares, and maids haue wide mouthes: but for *Hans* praunce, vpon my word to morrow morning hee and young miſtris *Roſe* goe to this geere, they ſhall be married together by this ruſh, or elſe turne *Firk* to a firkin of butter to tan leather withall.

L. Ma. But art thou ſure of this?

Firke. Am I ſure that Paules-ſteeple is a handfull higher than London ſtone? or that the piſſing Conduit leaks nothing but pure mother Bunch? am I ſure I am luſty *Firk*? Gods nailes do you thinke I am ſo baſe to gull you?

Lincolne. Where are they married? doſt thou know the Church?

Firke. I neuer goe to Church, but I know the name of it, it is a ſwearing Church, ſtay a while, 'tis, I by the mas: no, no, tis I by my troth, no nor that, tis I by my faith, that that, tis I by my Faiths Church vnder Paules Croſſe, there they ſhall bee knit like a paire of ſtockings in matrimony, there theyle be in cony.

Linc. Upon my life my Nephew *Lacy* walkes,
In the diſguiſe of this Dutch Shoomaker.

Firke. Yes forſooth.

Linc. Doth he not honeſt fellow?

Firke. No forſooth I thinke *Hans* is no body but *Hans*, no ſpirit.

L. Ma. My mind miſgiues me now tis ſo indeed.

Linc. My Coſen ſpeaks the language, knowes the trade.

L. Ma. Let me requeſt your company my Lord,
Your honorable preſence may, no doubt,
Refraine their head-ſtrong raſhneſſe, when my ſelfe
Going alone, perchance may be ore-borne:
Shall I requeſt this fauour?

Lin. This, or what elſe.

Firk. Then you muſt riſe betimes, for they meane to fall to their hey paſſe, and repaſſe, pindy pandy, which hand will you haue, very early.

L Ma. My care ſhall euery way equall their haſt,
This night accept your lodging in my houſe,
The earlier ſhal we ſtir, and at Saint Faiths
Preuent this giddy hare-braind Nuptiall,

This trafficke of hot loue ſhall yeeld cold gaines,
They ban our loues and weele forbid their baines.

Exit.

Lin. At Saint Faiths Church thou ſaiſt ?

Firk. Yes, by their troth.

Linc. Be ſecret on thy life. *Exit.*

Firk. Yes when I kiſſe your wife, ha, ha, heres no craft in the Gentle Craft, I came hither of purpoſe with ſhooes to Sir Rogers worſhip, whilſt Roſe his daughter be cony-catcht by *Hans* : ſoft now, theſe two gulles wil be at Saint Faithes Church to morrow morning to take maiſter Bridegroome, and miſtris Bride napping, and they in the meane time ſhall chop vp the matter at the Sauoy : but the beſt ſport is, Sir *Roger Otley* will find my fellow lame *Raphs* wife going to marrie a Genman : and then heele ſtop her in ſtead of his Daughter ; O braue, there will bee fine tickling ſport : ſoft now, what haue I to do ? O I know, now a meſſe of ſhoomakers meate at the Wooll-ſacke in Iuy lane, to cozen my Gentleman of lame *Raphs* wife, that's true, alacke alacke, girles hold out tacke, for now ſmockes for this iumbling ſhall go to wracke. *Exit.*

Enter Eyre, his wiſe, Hans and Roſe.

Eyre. This is the morning then, ſtay my bully, my honeſt *Hans*, is it not ?

Hans. This is the morning that muſt make vs two happie or miſerable, therefore if you——

Eyre. Away with theſe ifs and ands *Hans*, and theſe *et ceteraes*, by mine honor *Rowland Lacy*, none but the king ſhall wrong thee : come feare nothing, am not I *Sim Eyre* ? Is not *Sim Eyre* Lord Maior of London ? feare nothing *Roſe*, let them ſay all what they can, daintie come thou to mee, laugheſt thou ?

Wife. Good my Lord ſtand her friend in what thing you may.

Eyre. Why my ſweete Ladie Madgy, thinke you *Simon Eyre* can forget his fine Dutch iourneyman ? No vah. Fie I ſcorne it, it ſhall neuer be caſt in my teeth, that I was vnthankefull. Lady *Madgy*, thou hadſt neuer couered thy Saracens head with this French flappe, nor loaded thy bumme with this farthingale, tis traſh, trumperie, vanitie, *Simon Eyre* had neuer walkt in a red petticoate, nor wore a chaine of Gold but for my fine Journeymans Portigues, and ſhall I leaue him? No: Prince am I none, yet beare a Princely minde.

Hans. My Lord, 'tis time to part from hence.

Eyre. Lady *Madgy*, Lady *Madgy*, take two or three of my Pie-cruſt eaters, my Buffe-ierkin varlets, that doe walke in blacke gownes at *Simon Eyres* heeles, take them good Ladie *Madgy*, trip and go, my browne Queene of Perriwigs, with my delicate *Roſe*, and my iolly *Rowland* to the Sauoy, ſee them linkt, countenance the marriage, and when it is done, cling cling together, you Hamborow Turtle Doues, Ile beare you out, come to *Simon Eyre*, come dwell with me *Hans*, thou ſhalt eate minc'd pies, and marchpane. *Roſe*, away cricket, trip and goe, my Lady Madgy to the Sauoy. *Hans*, wed, and to bed, kiſſe and away, go vaniſh.

Wife. Farewell my Lord.

Roſe. Make haſt ſweet loue.

Wife. Sheede faine the deed were done.

Hans. Come my ſweet *Roſe*, faſter than Deere weele run. *They goe out.*

Eyre. Goe, vaniſh, vaniſh, auant I ſay: by the Lord of Ludgate, it's a mad life to be a Lord Maior, it's a ſtirring life, a fine life, a veluet life, a carefull life. Well *Simon Eyre*, yet ſet a good face on it, in the honour of Saint *Hugh*. Soft, the king this day comes to dine with me, to ſee my new buildings, his maieſtie is welcome, hee ſhall haue good cheere, delicate cheere, princely cheere. This day my fellow prentices of London come to dine with me too, they ſhal haue fine cheere, gentlemanlike cheere. I promiſed the mad Cappadoſians, when we all ſerued at the Conduit together, that if euer I came to bee

Maior of London, I would feaſt them all, and i'le doot, i'le doot by the life of *Pharaoh*, by this beard *Sim Eyre* will be no flincher. Beſides, I haue procured, that vpon euery Shrouetueſday at the ſound of the Pancake bell, my fine dapper Aſſirian lads ſhall clap vp their ſhop windowes, and away, this is the day, and this day they ſhall doot, they ſhall doot: boyes, that day are you free, let maiſters care, and prentiſes ſhall pray for *Simon Eyre.*

Enter Hodge, Firke, Raph, and fiue or ſix Shoomakers, all with cudgels, or ſuch weapons.

Hodge. Come *Rafe*, ſtand to it *Firke*: my maſters, as wee are the braue bloods of the Shoomakers, heires apparant to Saint *Hugh*, and perpetuall benefactors to all good fellowes: thou ſhalt haue no wrong: were *Hammon* a King of Spades, he ſhould not delue in thy cloſe without thy ſufferance; but tell me *Rafe*, art thou ſure tis thy wife?

Rafe. Am I ſure this is *Firke*? This morning when I ſtrokt on her ſhooes, I lookt vpon her, and ſhe vpon mee, and ſighed, aſkt me if euer I knew one *Rafe.* Yes ſaid I: for his ſake ſaid ſhe (teares ſtanding in her eyes) and for thou art ſomewhat like him, ſpend this peece of gold: I tooke it: my lame leg, and my trauell beyond ſea made me vnknowne, all is one for that, I know's ſhee's mine.

Firke. Did ſhee giue thee this gold? O glorious glittering gold: ſhees thine owne, tis thy wife, and ſhee loues thee, for Ile ſtand toot, there's no woman will giue gold to any man, but ſhe thinkes better of him than ſhee thinkes of them ſhee giues ſiluer to: and for *Hammon*, neither *Hammon* nor Hangman ſhall wrong thee in London: Is not our old Maſter *Eyre* Lord Maior? Speake my hearts.

All. Yes, and *Hammon* ſhall know it to his coſt.

Enter Hammon his man, Jane, and others.

Hodge. Peace my bullies, yonder they come.

Rafe. Stand toot my hearts, *Firk*, let me ſpeake firſt.

Hodge. No *Rafe*, let me : *Hammon*, whither away ſo earely ?

Ham. Unmannerly rude ſlaue, what's that to thee ?

Firk. To him ſir ? yes ſir, and to me, and others : good morrow *Jane*, how doſt thou ? good Lord, how the world is changed with you, God be thanked.

Ham. Villaines, hands off, how dare you touch my loue ?

All. Villaines : downe with them, cry clubs for prentiſes.

Hod. Hold, my hearts : touch her *Hammon* ? yea and more than that, weele carrie her away with vs. My maiſters and gentlemen, neuer draw your bird ſpits, ſhoomakers are ſteele to the backe, men euery inch of them, all ſpirit.

All of Hammons ſide. Well, and what of all this ?

Hod. Ile ſhew you : *Jane*, dooſt thou know this man ? tis *Rafe* I can tell thee : nay, tis he in faith, though he be lam'd by the warres, yet looke not ſtrange, but run to him, fold him about the necke and kiſſe him.

Jane. Liues then my huſband ? oh God let me go,
Let me embrace my *Rafe.*

Ham. What meanes my *Jane* ?

Jane. Nay, what meant you to tell me was he ſlaine ?

Ham. Pardon me deare loue for being miſled,
Twas rumord here in London thou wert dead.

Firke. Thou ſeeſt he liues : Laſſe, go packe home with him ? now M. *Hammon*, wheres your miſtris your wife ?

Seru. Swounds M. fight for her, will you thus loſe her ?

All. Downe with that creature, clubs, downe with him.

Hodge. Hold, hold.

Ham. Hold foole : ſirs he ſhall do no wrong,

Will my *Jane* leaue me thus, and breake her faith?

Firke. Yes ſir, ſhe muſt ſir, ſhe ſhall ſir, what then? mend it.

Hod. Hearke fellow *Rafe*, follow my counſell, ſet the wench in the midſt, and let her chuſe her man, and let her be his woman.

Jane. Whom ſhould I chuſe? whom ſhould my thoughts affect?
But him whom Heauen hath made to be my loue,
Thou art my huſband, and theſe humble weedes,
Makes thee more beautifull than all his wealth,
Therefore I will but put off his attire,
Returning it into the owners hand,
And euer after be thy conſtant wife.

Hodge. Not a ragge *Jane*, the law's on our ſide, hee that ſowes in another mans ground forfeits his harueſt, get thee home *Raph*, follow him *Jane*, hee ſhall not haue ſo much as a buſke point from thee.

Firke. Stand to that *Rafe*, the appurtenances are thine owne, *Hammon*, looke not at her.

Seru. O ſwounds no.

Firke. Blew coate be quiet, weele giue you a new liuerie elſe, weele make Shroue Tueſday Saint *Georges* day for you: looke not *Hammon*, leare not, Ile firke you, for thy head now, one glance, one ſheepes eye, any thing at her, touch not a ragge, leſt I and my brethren beate you to clowtes.

Ser. Come maiſter *Hammon*, theres no ſtriuing here.

Ham. Good fellowes, heare me ſpeake: and honeſt *Rafe*,
Whom I haue iniured moſt by louing *Jane*,
Marke what I offer thee: here in faire gold,
Is twentie pound, Ile giue it for thy *Jane*,
If this content thee not, thou ſhalt haue more.

Hodge. Sell not thy wife, *Rafe*, make her not a whore.

Ham. Say, wilt thou freely ceaſe thy claime in her,
And let her be my wife?

All. No do not *Raph.*

Raph. Sirra *Hammon Hammon*, doſt thou thinke a ſhooe-maker is ſo baſe, to be a bawd to his own wife for cõmodity ? take thy gold, choake with it: were I not lame, I would make thee eate thy words.

Firke. A ſhoomaker ſell his fleſh and blood, oh indignitie!

Hodg. Sirra, take vp your pelfe, and be packing.

Ham. I will not touch one pennie, but in liew,
Of that great wrong I offered thy *Jane*,
To *Jane* and thee I giue that twentie pound,
Since I haue faild of her, during my life,
I vow no woman elſe ſhall be my wife:
Farewell good fellowes of the Gentle trade,
Your morning mirth my mourning day hath made.

Exit.

Firke. Touch the gold creature if you dare, y'are beſt be trudging: here *Jane* take thou it, now lets home my hearts.

Hodge. Stay, who comes here? *Jane*, on againe with thy maſke.

Enter Lincolne, L. Maior, and ſeruants.

Lin. Yonders the lying varlet mockt vs ſo.

L. Ma. Come hither ſirra.

Firke. I ſir, I am ſirra, you meane me, do you not?

Linc. Where is my Nephew married?

Firke. Is he married? God giue him ioy, I am glad of it: they haue a faire day, and the ſigne is in a good Planet, *Mars* in *Venus.*

L. Ma. Villaine, thou toldſt me that my daughter *Roſe*,
This morning ſhould be married at Saint *Faiths*,
Wee haue watcht there theſe three houres at the leaſt,
Yet ſee we no ſuch thing.

Firke. Truely I am ſorry fort, a Bride's a prettie thing.

Hodge. Come to the purpoſe, yonder's the Bride

and Bridegroome you looke for I hope: though you be Lords, you are not to barre, by your authoritie, men from women, are you?

L. Ma. See ſee my daughter's maſkt.

Lin. True, and my nephew,
To hide his guilt, counterfeits him lame.

Firke. Yea truely, God helpe the poore couple, they are lame and blind.

L. Ma. Ile eaſe her blindneſſe.

Lin. Ile his lameneſſe cure.

Firke. Lye downe ſirs, and laugh, my fellow *Raph* is taken for *Rowland Lacy*, and *Jane* for miſtris damaſke Roſe, this is all my knauerie.

L. Ma. What haue I found you minion?

Lin. O baſe wretch,
Nay hide thy face, the horror of thy guilt
Can hardly be waſht off: where are thy powers?
What battells haue you made? O yes I ſee,
Thou foughtſt with ſhame, and ſhame hath conquer'd thee;
This lameneſſe with not ſerue.

L. Ma. Unmaſke your ſelfe.

Lin. Lead home your daughter.

L. Ma. Take your nephew hence.

Raph. Hence, ſwounds, what meane you? are you mad? I hope you cannot enforce my wife from me, wher's *Hammon*?

L. Ma. Your wife?

Lin. What *Hammon*?

Raph. Yea my wife, and therefore the proudeſt of you that laies hands on her firſt, Ile lay my Crutch croſſe his pate.

Firke. To him lame *Raph*, here's braue ſport.

Raph. *Roſe* call you her? why her name is *Jane*, looke here ſelfe, do you know her now?

Lin. Is this your daughter?

L. Ma. No nor this your nephew:
My Lord of Lincolne, we are both abuſ'd,
By this baſe craftie varlet.

Firke. Yea forſooth no varlet, forſooth no baſe, forſooth I am but meane, not craftie neither, but of the Gentle Craft.

L. Ma. Where is my daughter *Roſe*? where is my child?

Linc. Where is my Nephew *Lacy* married?

Firke. Why here is good lac'd mutton as I promiſt you.

Linc. Villaine Ile haue thee puniſht for this wrong.

Firke. Puniſh the Iourneyman villaine, but not the Iourneyman Shoomaker.

Enter Dodger.

Dodg. My Lord, I come to bring vnwelcome newes,
Your Nephew *Lacy* and your daughter *Roſe*,
Earely this morning wedded at the Sauoy,
None being preſent but the Lady Mayreſſe:
Beſides I learnt among the Officers,
The Lord Maior vowes to ſtand in their defence,
Gainſt any that ſhall ſeeke to croſſe the match.

Lin. Dares *Eyre* the Shoomaker vphold the deed?

Firk. Yes ſir, Shoomakers dare ſtand in a womans quarrel
I warrant you, as deepe as another, and deeper too.

Dod. Beſides his Grace to day dines with the Mayor,
Who on his knees humbly intends to fall,
And beg a pardon for your Nephews fault.

Lin But Ile preuent him, come Sir *Roger Otley*,
The King will do vs iuſtice in this cauſe,
How ere their hands haue made them man and wife,
I will diſioyne the match, or loſe my life. *Exeunt.*

Firk. Adue Monſieur *Dodger*, farewell fooles, ha, ha.
Oh if they had ſtaid I would haue ſo lamb'd them with flouts, O heart, my Codpeece-point is ready to flye in peeces euery time I thinke vpon miſtris *Roſe*, but let that paſſe, as my Ladie Mayreſſe ſaies.

Hodge. This matter is anſwerd : come *Raph*, home with thy wife, come my fine Shoomakers, lets to our maſters the new Lord Mayor, and there ſwagger this Shroue Tueſday, Ile promiſe you wine enough, for *Madge* keepes the Seller.

All. Oh rare ! *Madge* is a good wench.

Firk. And Ile promiſe you meat enough for ſimpring *Suſan* keeps the Larder, Ile lead you to victuals my braue ſouldiers, follow your Captaine, O braue, harke, harke. *Bell rings.*

All. The Pancake bell rings, the Pancake bell, tri-lill my hearts.

Firke. O braue, oh ſweet bell, O delicate Pancakes, open the doores my hearts, and ſhut vp the windowes, keepe in the houſe, let out the Pancakes, oh rare my hearts, let's march together for the honour of S. *Hugh*, to the great new hall in Gracious ſtreete corner, which our maſter the new Lord Maior hath built.

Rafe. O the crew of good fellowes that will dine at my Lord Maiors coſt to day !

Hodge. By the lord, my Lord Maior is a moſt braue man, how ſhall Prentiſes be bound to pray for him and the honor of the Gentlemen Shooemakers ? lets feed and bee fat with my Lordes bountie.

Firke. O muſicall Bell ſtill ; O *Hodge*, O my brethren ; there's cheere for the heauens, veniſon paſties walke vp and downe piping hot like Serieants : Beefe and brewes comes marching in drifattes, fritters and pancakes come trowling in in wheele-barrowes, hens and orenges hopping in Porters baſkets, collops and egges in ſcuttles, and tarts and cuſtards comes quauering in in malt ſhouels.

Enter more Prentiſes.

All. Whoop, looke here, looke here.

Hodge. How now mad lads whither away ſo faſt ?

1 *Pren.* Whither? why to the great new Hall, know

you not why? the Lord Maior hath bidden all the prentises in London to breakfast this morning.

All. Oh braue Shoomaker, oh braue Lord of incomprehensible good fellowship, whoo, hearke you, the Pancake-Bell rings. *Cast vp Caps.*

Firk. Nay more my hearts, euerie Shroue-tuesday is our yeare of Jubile : and when the Pancake-Bell rings, we are as as free as my Lord Maior, wee may shut up our shoppes and make holiday : I'le haue it cal'd Saint *Hughs* Holiday.

All. Agreed, agreed, Saint *Hughs* Holiday.

Hodge. And this shall continue for euer.

All. Oh braue; come come my hearts, away, away.

Firke. O eternall credit to vs of the Gentle Craft, march faire my hearts, O rare. *Exeunt.*

Enter the King and his traine ouer the stage.

King. Is our Lord Maior of London such a gallant?

Nobleman. One of the merriest madcaps in your Land,
Your Grace will thinke when you behold the man,
Hees rather a wild Ruffian than a Maior :
Yet thus much Ile ensure your Majestie,
In all his actions that concerne his state,
He is as serious, prouident, and wise,
As full of grauitie amongst the graue,
As any Maior hath been these many yeares.

King. I am with child till I behold this huffecap,
But all my doubt is when we come in presence,
His madnesse will be dasht cleane out of countenance.

Noblem. It may be so, my Liege.

King. Which to preuent,
Let some one giue him notice 'tis our pleasure,
That he put on his wonted merriment :
Set forward. *All.* On afore. *Exeunt.*

Enter Eyre, Hodge, Firke, Raph, and other Shoomakers, all with napkins on their ſhoulders.

Eyre. Come my fine *Hodge*, my iolly Gentlemen Shoomakers, ſoft, where be theſe Caniballes, theſe varlets my officers, let them all walke and wait vpon my brethren, for my meaning is, that none but Shoomakers, none but the liuerie of my Companie ſhall in their ſattin hoods wait vpon the trencher of my Soueraigne.

Firke. O my Lord, it will be rare.

Eyre. No more *Firke*, come liuely, let your fellow prentiſes want no cheere, let wine be plentifull as beere, and beere as water, hang theſe penny pinching fathers, that cram wealth in innocent Lambes ſkinnes, up knaues, auant, looke to my gueſts.

Hodge. My Lord, we are at our wits end for roome, thoſe hundred Tables will not feaſt the fourth part of them.

Eyre. Then couer me thoſe hundred Tables againe and againe, till all my iolly prentiſes be feaſted : auoyd *Hodge*, runne *Raph*, friſke about my nimble *Firke*, carowſe mee fadome healths to the honour of the ſhooemakers, doe they drinke liuely *Hodge*? do they tickle it *Firke*?

Firke. Tickle it? ſome of them haue taken their liquor ſtanding ſo long, that they can ſtand no longer : but for meat they would eat it and they had it.

Eyre. Want they meat? where's this ſwag-belly, this greaſie kitchinſtuffe cooke, call the varlet to me : want meat? *Firke, Hodge*, lame *Rafe*, runne my tall men, beleaguer the Shambles, begger all Eaſt-cheape, ſerue me whole Oxen in Chargers, and let Sheepe whine vpon the tables like Pigs, for want of good fellowes to eat them. Want meat? vaniſh Firke, auant *Hodge*.

Hodge. Your Lordſhip miſtakes my man *Firke*, he meanes their bellies want meat, not the boords, for they haue drunke ſo much they can eat nothing.

Enter Hans, Rose, and Wife.

Wife. Where is my Lord?

Eyre. How now Lady *Maggy*?

Wife. The Kings moſt excellent Maieſtie is new come, he ſends me for thy honor, one of his moſt worſhipfull Peeres bad me tell thou muſt be merrie, and ſo forth: but let that paſſe.

Eyre. Is my Soueraigne come? vaniſh my tall Shoomakers, my nimble brethren, looke to my gueſts the prentizes: yet ſtay a little, how now *Hans*, how lookes my little *Roſe*?

Hans. Let me requeſt you to remember me,
I know your honour eaſily may obtaine,
Free pardon of the King for me and *Roſe*,
And reconcile me to my Uncles grace.

Eyre. Haue done my good *Hans*, my honeſt Journeyman, looke cheerily, I'le fall vpon both my knees until they be as hard as horne, but I'le get thy pardon.

Wife. Good my Lord haue a care what you ſpeake to his Grace.

Eyre. Away you Iſlington whitepot, hence you hopper-arſe, you Barly pudding full of maggots, you broild Carbonado, auant, auant, auoyd Mephiſtophiles: ſhall *Sim Eyre* learne to ſpeake of you Lady *Maggy*? vaniſh mother Mineuer-Cap, vaniſh, goe, trip and goe, meddle with your platters and your piſherie paſherie, your flewes and your whirligigs, goe, rub out mine ally: *Sim Eyre* knowes how to ſpeake to a Pope, to *Sultan Solyman*, to *Tamberlaine* and he were here: and I ſhall melt, ſhall I droope hefore my Soueraigne? no, come my Lady *Maggy*, follow me *Hans*, about your buſineſſe my frolike freebooters: *Firke*, friſke about, and about, and about, for the honour of mad *Simon Eyre*, Lord Mayor of *London*.

Firke. Hey for the honour of the Shooemakers.

Exeunt.

A long flouriſh or two, enter the King, Nobles, Eyre, his Wife, Lacy, Roſe; Lacy and Roſe kneele.

King. Well *Lacy*, though the fact was very foule,
Of your reuolting from our Kingly loue,
And your owne dutie, yet we pardon you,
Riſe both, and Miſtris *Lacy*, thanke my Lord Mayor
For your young bridegroom here.

Eyre. So my deare Liege, *Sim Eyre* and my brethren the Gentlemen Shoomakers ſhall ſet your ſweet Maieſties image cheeke by iole by Saint *Hugh*, for this honour you haue done poore *Simon Eyre*, I beſeech your Grace pardon my rude behauiour, I am a handicrafts man, yet my heart is without craft, I would be ſorrie at my ſoule that my boldneſſe ſhould offend my King.

King. Nay, I pray thee good Lord Mayor, be euen as merry
As if thou wert among thy Shoomakers,
It does me good to ſee thee in this humour.

Eyre. Saiſt thou me ſo my ſweet *Diocleſian*? then humpe, Prince am I none, yet am I Princely borne, by the Lord of Ludgate my Liege, I'le be as merrie as a Pie.

King. Tell me in faith mad *Eyre*, how old thou art?

Eyre. My Liege, a very boy, a ſtripling, a yonker, you ſee not a white haire on my head, nor a gray in this beard, euery haire I aſſure thy Maieſty that ſtickes in this beard, *Sim Eyre* valews at the King of *Babilons* ranſome, *Tamar Chams* beard was a rubbing bruſh too't, yet I'le ſhave it off, and ſtuffe tennis balls with it to pleaſe my bully King.

King. But all this while I do not know your age.

Eyre. My Liege, I am ſix and fifty yeare old, yet I can cry humpe, with a ſound heart, for the honour of Saint *Hugh*: marke this old wench my King, I danc't the ſhaking of the ſheets with her ſix and thirtie yeares agoe, and yet I hope to get two or three yong

Lord Mayors ere I die: I am luſty ſtill, *Sim Eyre* ſtill: care and cold lodging brings white haires. My ſweet Maieſty, let care vaniſh, caſt it vpon thy Nobles, it will make thee looke always young like *Apollo*, and cry humpe: Prince am I none, yet am I Princely borne.

King. Ha, ha, ſay *Cornewall*, didſt thou euer ſee his like?

Noblem. Not I my Lord.

Enter Lincolne and Lord Mayor.

King. *Lincolne* what newes with you?

Lin. My gracious Lord haue care vnto your ſelfe,
For there are Traitors here.

All. Traitors, where? who?

Eyre. Traitors in my houſe? God forbid, where be my Officers? I'le ſpend my ſoule ere my King feele harme.

King. Where is the Traitor, *Lincolne*?

Lin. Here he ſtands.

King. *Cornewall*, lay hold on *Lacy*: *Lincolne* ſpeake,
What canſt thou lay vnto thy Nephewes charge?

Lin. This my deare Liege, your Grace to do me honour,
Heapt on the head of this degenerous boy,
Deſertleſſe fauours, you made choyce of him,
To be Commander ouer powers in *France*,
But he:

King. Good *Lincolne*, prethee pauſe a while,
Euen in thine eyes I read what thou wouldſt ſpeake,
I know how *Lacy* did neglect our loue,
Ran himſelfe deepely (in the higheſt degree)
Into vile treaſon.

Lin. Is he not a Traitor?

King. *Lincolne*, he was, now haue we pardoned him,
'Twas not a baſe want of true valours fire
That held him out of *France*, but loues deſire.

Lin. I will not beare his ſhame vpon my backe.
King. Nor ſhalt thou *Lincolne*, I forgiue you both.
Lin. Then good my Liege forbid the boy to wed
One whoſe meane birth will much diſgrace his bed.
King. Are they not married?
Lin. No my Liege.
Both. We are.
King. Shall I diuorce them then? O be it farre,
That any hand on earth ſhould dare vntie
The ſacred knot knit by Gods Maieſtie;
I would not for my Crowne diſioyne their hands,
That are conioyn'd in holy nuptiall bands:
How ſaiſt thou *Lacy*, wouldſt thou looſe thy *Roſe*?
Hans. Not for all Indians wealth, my Soueraigne.
King. But *Roſe* I am ſure her *Lacy* would forgoe.
Roſe. If *Roſe* were aſkt that queſtion, ſhee'd ſay no.
King. You heare them *Lincolne.*
Lin. Yea my Liege I do.
King. And canſt thou finde ith heart to part theſe two?
Who ſeekes beſides you to diuorce theſe louers?
L. Ma. I do (my gratious Lord) I am her father.
King. *Sir Roger Oteley*, our laſt Mayor I thinke.
Nob. The ſame my Liege.
King. Would you offend Loues lawes?
Well you ſhall haue your wills: you ſued to me
To prohibit the match: Soft, let me ſee,
You both are married, *Lacy* art thou not?
Hans. I am dread Soueraigne.
King. Then vpon thy life,
I charge thee not to call this woman wife.
L. Ma. I thanke your Grace.
Roſe. O my moſt gracious Lord. *kneele.*
King. Nay *Roſe* neuer wooe me, I tell you true,
Although as yet I am a Batchelor,
Yet I beleeue I ſhall not marrie you.
Roſe. Can you diuide the body from the ſoule,
Yet make the body liue?
King. Yea, ſo profound?

I cannot *Roſe*, but you I muſt diuide,
Faire maid this Bridegroome cannot be your Bride,
Are you pleaſ'd *Lincolne*? *Otley*, are you pleaſ'd?

Both. Yes my Lord.

King. Then muſt my heart be eaſ'd,
For credit me, my conſcience liues in paine,
Till theſe whom I diuorc'd be ioyned againe:
Lacy giue me thy hand, Roſe lend me thine,
Be what you would be: kiſſe now: ſo, that's fine,
At night (Louers) to bed: now let me ſee,
Which of you all miſlikes this harmony?

L. Ma. Will you then take from me my childe perforce?

King. Why tell me *Otley* ſhines not *Lacys* name,
As bright in the worlds eye, as the gay beames
Of any Citizen?

Lin. Yea but my gracious Lord,
I doe miſlike the match farre more than he,
Her bloud is too too baſe.

King. *Lincolne* no more,
Doſt thou not know, that loue reſpects no bloud?
Cares not for difference of birth or ſtate,
The maid is young, well borne, faire, vertuous,
A worthy Bride for any Gentleman:
Beſides your Nephew for her ſake did ſtoope
To bare neceſſitie; and as I heare,
Forgetting honours and all Courtly pleaſures,
To gaine her loue became a ſhoomaker:
As for the honour which he loſt in *France*,
Thus I redeeme it: *Lacy* kneele thee downe,
Ariſe Sir *Rowland Lacy*: tell me now,
Tell me in earneſt *Otley*, canſt thou chide?
Seeing thy *Roſe* a Lady and a Bride.

L. Ma. I am content with what your Grace hath done.

Linc. And I my Liege ſince there's no remedy.

King. Come on then, all ſhake hands, I'le haue you friends
Where there is much loue all diſcord ends:

What faies my mad Lord Mayor to all this loue?

Eyre. O my Liege, the honour you haue done to my fine Journeyman here, *Rowland Lacy*, and all thefe fauours which you haue fhowne to me this day in my poore houfe, will make *Simon Eyre* liue longer by one dozen of warme Summers more than he fhould.

King. Nay my mad Lord Mayor, (that fhall be thy name)
If any grace of mine can length thy life,
One honour more I'le doe thee, that new building,
Which at thy coft in Cornehill is erected,
Shall take a name from vs, wee'le haue it call'd,
The Leaden Hall, becaufe in digging it,
You found the lead that couereth the fame.

Eyre. I thanke your Maiefty.

Wife. God bleffe your grace.

King. *Lincolne*, a word with you.

Enter Hodge, Firke, Rafe, and more Shoomakers.

Eyre. How now my mad knaues? Peace, fpeake foftly, yonder is the King.

King. With the old troope which there we keepe in pay,
We will incorporate a new fupply:
Before one Summer more paffe ore my head,
France fhall repent *England* was iniured,
What are all thofe?

Hans. All Shoomakers my Liege,
Sometimes my fellowes, in their companies
I liu'd as merry as an Emperor.

King. My mad Lord Mayor, are all thefe Shoomakers?

Eyre. All Shoomakers my Liege, all Gentlemen of the Gentle Craft, true Troyans, couragious Cordwainers, they all kneele to the Shrine of holy Saint *Hugh.*

All. God faue your Maiefty all fhoomakers.

King. Mad *Simon*, would they any thing with vs?

Eyre. Mum, mad knaues not a word, I'le doo't I

warrant you. They are all Beggers my Liege, all for themſelues and I for them all, on both my knees doe intreat, that for the honour of poore *Simon Eyre*, and the good of his Brethren theſe mad knaues your Grace would vouchſafe ſome priuilege to my new Leaden hall, that it may be lawfull for vs to buy and ſell Leather there two dayes in a weeke.

King. Mad *Sim*, I grant your ſute, you ſhall haue Patent
To hold two market dayes in Leaden-Hall,
Mondayes and Fridays, thoſe ſhall be the times:
Will this content you?

All. Jeſus bleſſe your Grace.

Eyre. In the name of theſe my poore brethren Shoomakers, I moſt humblie thanke your Grace. But before I riſe, ſeeing you are in the giuing veine, and we in the begging, grant *Sim Eyre* one boone more.

King. What is it my Lord Mayor?

Eyre. Vouchſafe to taſt of a poore Banquet, that's ſweetly waiting for your ſweet preſence.

King. I ſhall vndoe thee *Eyre* only with this, (5)
Alreadie haue I beene too troubleſome,
Say, haue I not?

Eyre. O my deare King, *Sim Eyre* cannot ſay ſo; vpon a day of ſhrouing which I promiſt to all the merrie Prentiſes of *London:* for an't pleaſe you when I was prentiſe (6)
I bare the water-tankard, and my coat
Sits not a whit the worſe vpon my backe:
And then vpon a morning, ſome mad boyes
(It was Shroue-tueſday, euen as 'tis now)
Gaue me my breakfaſt, and I ſwore then by the

---

(5) only with feaſts. 1600.

(6) O my deere King *Sim Eyre* was taken vnawares vpon a day of ſhrouing which I promiſt long ago to the prentiſes of London: for andt pleaſe your Highnes, in time paſt, &c. 1600.

ſtopple of my Tankard, if euer I came to be Lord Mayor of *London*, I would feaſt al the Prentiſes. This day my Liege I did it, and the ſlaues had an hundred Tables fiue times couered, they are gone home and vaniſht.

Yet adde more glorie to the Gentle Trade,
Taſte of *Eyres* Banquet, *Simon's* happie made.

King. I will taſte of thy Banquet, and will ſay,
I haue not met more pleaſure on a day;
Friends of the Gentle Craft, thankes to you all,
Thankes my kinde Lady Mayreſſe for our cheere:
Come Lords a while let's reuell it at home,
When all our ſports, and banquetings are done
Warres muſt right wrongs which Frenchmen haue begun. (7) *Exeunt.*

---

(7) The later Editions read:
When all our words and banquetings are done,
We muſt right wrongs which Frenchmen haue begun.

FINIS.

THE

Pleaſant Comedie of

Old Fortunatus.

As it was plaied before the Queenes *Maieſtie this Chriſtmas, by the Right* Honourable the Earle of Notting-ham, Lord high Admirall of Eng-land his Seruants,

Aut Nunc Aut Nunquam.

LONDON

Printed by *S. S.* for William Aſpley, dwelling in Paules Church-yard at the ſigne of the Tygers head. 1600.

The Prologue at Court: Enter two old men.

1. ARe you then trauelling to the temple of Eliza? 2. Euen to her temple are my feeble limmes trauelling. Some cal her Pandora: ſome Gloriana, ſome Cynthia: ſome Delphœbe, ſame Aſtræa: all by ſeuerall names to expreſſe ſeuerall loues: Yet all thoſe names make but one celeſtiall body, as all thoſe loues meete to create but one ſoule.

1. I am one of her owne countrie, and we adore her by the name of Eliza.

2. Bleſſed name, happie countrie: Your Eliza makes your land Elizium: but what doe you offer?

1. That which all true Subiects ſhould: when I was young, an Armed hand; now I am crooked, an vpright heart: But what offer you?

2. That which all ſtraungers doe: two eyes ſtrucke blinde with admiration: Two lips (proud to ſound her glorie:) Two hands held vp full of prayers and praiſes: What not, that may expreſſe loue? what not, that may make her beloued?

1. How long iſt ſince you laſt beheld her?

2. A iuſt yeere: yet that yeere hath ſeemd to me but one day, becauſe her glorie hath beene my howrely contemplation, and yet that yeere hath ſeemd to me more then twice ſeuen yeres, becauſe ſo long I haue beene abſent from her. Come therefore, good father, lets goe faſter, leaſt we come too late: for ſee, the Tapers of the night are already lighted, and ſtand brightly burning in their ſtarrie Candleſtickes: See howe gloriouſly the Moone ſhines vpon vs. *Both kneele.*

1. Peace foole: tremble, and kneele: The Moone ſaiſt thou?

Our eyes are dazled by Elizaes beames,

See (if at leaſt thou dare ſee) where ſhee ſits :
This is the great Panthæon of our Goddeſſe,
And all thoſe faces which thine eyes thought ſtarres,
Are Nymphes attending on her deitie.
Prithee begin, for I want power to ſpeake.

2. No, no, ſpeake thou, I want words to begin.
Weepes.

1. Alacke what ſhall I doe? com'ſt thou with me,
And weepſt now thou beholdſt this Maieſtie?

2. Great land-lady of hearts, pardon me.

1. Blame not mine eyes, good father, in theſe teares.

2. My pure loue ſhines, as thine doth in thy feares:
I weepe for ioy to ſee ſo many heads
Of prudent Ladies, clothed in the liuerie
Of ſiluer-handed age, for ſeruing you,
Whilſt in your eyes youthes glory doth renue :
I weepe for ioy to ſee the Sunne looke old,
To ſee the Moone mad at her often change,
To ſee the Starres onely by night to ſhine,
Whilſt you are ſtill bright, ſtill one, ſtill diuine :
I weepe for ioy to ſee the world decay,
Yet ſee Eliza flouriſhing like May :
O pardon me your Pilgrim, I haue meaſurd
Many a mile to find you : and haue brought,
Old Fortunatus and his family,
With other Cipnots (my poore countrie men)
To pay a whole yeeres tribute : O vouchſafe,
Dread Queene of Fayries, with your gracious eyes,
T'accept theirs and our humble ſacrifice.

1. Now ile beg for thee too : and yet I need not :
Her ſacred hand hath euermore beene knowne,
As ſoone held out to ſtraungers as her owne.

2. Thou doeſt incourage me : Ile fetch them in,
They haue no princely gifts, we are all poore,
Our offrings are true hearts, who can wiſh more?
Exeunt.

THE PROLOGUE.

OF *Loues* ſweete war, our timerous Muſe doth ſing,
And to the boſome of each gentle deare,
Offence her Artles tunes, borne on the wing
Of ſacred Poeſy. A benumming feare,
(That your nice ſoules, cloyd with dilicious ſounds,
Will loath her lowly notes) makes her pull in
Her fainting pineons, and her ſpirit confounds
Before the weake voice of her ſong begin.
Yet ſince within the circle of each eye,
(Being like ſo many Suns in his round Sphere)
No wrinckle yet is ſeene, ſheele dare to flie,
Borne vp with hopes, that as you oft do reare
With your faire hands, thoſe who would els ſinke down,
So ſome will deigne to ſmile, where all might frown:
And for this ſmal Circumference muſt ſtand,
For the imagind Sur-face of much land,
Of many kingdomes, and ſince many a mile,
Should here be meaſurd out: our muſe intreats,
Your thoughts to helpe poore Art, and to allow,
That I may ſerue as Chorus to her ſcences,
She begs your pardon, for ſheele ſend one foorth,
Not when the lawes of Poeſy doe call,
But as the ſtorie needes, your gracious eye
Giues life to Fortunatus hiſtorie. *Exit.*

THE COMEDIE OF

Olde Fortunatus.

Enter Fortunatus meanely attired, hee walkes ere he ſpeake once or twice about cracking Nuts.

Fortunatus.

SO, ho, ho, ho, ho.

Eccho within. Ho, ho, ho, ho.

Fortun. There boy.

Eccho. There boy.

Fort. And thou bee'ſt a goodfellow, tel me how cal'ſt this wood.

Eccho. This wood.

Fort. I this wood, & which is my beſt way out.

Eccho. Beſt way out.

Fort. Ha, ha, ha, thats true, my beſt way out, is my beſt way out, but how that out will come in, by this Maggot I know not, I ſee by this we are all wormes meate: well, I am very poore and verie patient, Patience is a vertue: would I were not vertuous, thats to ſay, not poore, but full of vice, (thats to ſay, ful of chinckes) Ha, ha, ſo I am, for I am ſo full of chinckes, that a Horſe with one eye may looke through and through me, I haue ſighed long, and that makes me windie: I haue faſted long, and that makes me chaſt, marie I have praied little, and that makes mee I ſtill daunce in this coniuring circle: I haue wandred long, and that makes me wearie; but for my wearineſſe, anon Ile lie down, in ſteade of faſting ile feede vpon Nuts, and in ſtead of ſighing will laugh and bee leane, Sirra, *Eccho.*

Eccho. Sirra *Eccho.*

Fort. Heres a Nut.

Eccho. Heres a Nut.

Fort. Cracke it

Eccho. Cracke it.

Fort. Hang thy ſelfe.

Eccho. Hang thy ſelfe.

Fort. Th'art a knaue, a knaue.

Eccho. A knaue, a knaue.

Fort. Ha, ha, ha, ha.

Eccho. Ha, ha, ha, ha.

Fortunat. Why ſo, two fooles laugh at one another, I at my tittle tattle gammer eccho, and ſhee at me. Shortly there will creepe out in print ſome filthie booke of the old hoarie wandring Knight, meaning me: would I were that booke, for then I ſhould be ſure to creepe out from hence: I ſhould bee a good ſouldiour, for I trauerſe my ground rarely, marrie I ſee neither enemie nor friends, but Popiniayes, and Squirrels, and Apes, and Owles, and Dawes, and Wagtailes, and the ſpite is that none of theſe graſſe-eaters can ſpeake my language, but this foole that mockes me, and ſweares to haue the laſt word (in ſpite of my teeth) I, and ſhee ſhall haue it becauſe ſhee is a woman, which kind of cattell are indeede all Eccho, nothing but tongue, and are like the great bell of S. Michaels in Cyprus, that keepes moſt rumbling when men would moſt ſleepe. *Eccho,* a poxe on thee for mocking me.

Eccho.. A poxe on thee for mocking me.

Fortunat. Why ſo, Snip ſnap, this warre is at an end, but this wilderneſſe is world without end, to ſee how trauell can tranſforme: my teeth are turn'd into Nutcrackers, a thouſand to one I breake out ſhortly, for I am full of nothing, but waxing kernels, my tongue ſpeakes no language but an Almond for Parrat, and cracke me this Nut: If I hop three daies more vp and downe this cage of Coockooes neſts, I ſhall turne wilde man ſure, and be hyred to throw Squibs among the Cōminaltie vpon ſome terrible day. In the meane time to tell truth here will I lie. Farwell foole.

Eccho. Farwell foole.

Fort. Are not theſe comfortable words to a wiſe man? All haile Signior tree, by your leaue ile ſleepe vnder your leaues, I pray bow to me, and ile bend to you, for your backe and my browes muſt, I doubt, haue a game or two at Noddie erre I wake againe: downe great heart, downe. Hey, ho, well, well.

He lyes downe and ſleepes: Enter a Gardiner, a Smith, a Monke, a Shepheard all crown'd, a Nimph with a Globe, another with Fortunes wheele, then Fortune: After her fowre Kings with broken Crownes and Scepters, chained in ſiluer Giues and led by her. The foremoſt come out ſinging. Fortune takes her Chaire, the Kings lying at her feete, ſhee treading on them as ſhee goes vp.

The Song.

Fortune ſmiles, cry holyday,
Dimples on her cheekes doe dwell,
Fortune frownes, cry wellada,
Her loue is heauen, her hate is hell:
Since heauen and hell obey her power,
Tremble when her eyes doe lowre,
Since heauen and hell her power obey,
When ſhee ſmiles, crie holy day.
Holy-day with ioy we cry
And bend, and bend and merily,
Sing Hymnes to Fortunes deitie,
Sing Hymnes to Fortunes deitie.

All. Let vs ſing, merrily, merrily, merrily,
With our ſong let heauen reſound,
Fortunes hands our heads haue crown'd,
Let vs ſing merrily, merrily, merrily.

1. *King.* Accurſed Queene of chaunce, what had we done,
Who hauing ſometimes like young *Phaetons*,
Ryd in the burniſht Charriot of the Sun,
And ſometimes beene thy minions, when thy fingers
Weau'd wanton love-nets in our curled hayre,
And with ſweete iugling kiſſes warm'd our cheekes:
Oh how haue we offended thy proud eyes,
That thus we ſhould be ſpurnd and trod vpon,
Whilſt thoſe infected limmes of the ſicke world,
Are fixt by thee for ſtarres in that bright Sphere,
Wherein our Sunne like *Radiance* did appeare.

All the Kings.

Accurſed Queene of chaunce, damn'd ſorcereſſe.

The reſt.

Moſt powr'full Queene of chaunce dread ſoueraign-neſſe.

Fort. No more: curſe on: your cries to me are Muſicke,
And fill the ſacred roundure of mine eares,
With tunes more ſweete then mouing of the Spheres:
Curſe on: on our celeſtiall browes doe ſit
Un-numbred ſmiles, which then leaps from their throne,
When they ſee Peaſants daunce and Monarches groane.
Behold you not this Globe, this golden bowle,
This toy cal'd worlde at our Imperiall feete?
This world is Fortunes ball wherewith ſhe ſports.
Sometimes I ſtrike it vp into the ayre,
And then create I Emperours and kings:

Sometimes I ſpurne it: at which ſpurne crawles out
That wild beaſt multitude: curſe on you fooles,
Tis I that tumble Princes from their thrones,
And gild falſe browes with glittering diadems,
Tis I that tread on neckes of Conquerours,
And when like Semi-gods they haue beene drawne,
In Iuorie Charriots to the capitoll,
Circled about with wonder of all eyes,
The ſhouts of euery tongue, loue of all hearts,
Being ſwolne with their owne greatneſſe, I haue prickt
The bladder of their pride, and made them die,
As water bubbles (without memorie)
I thruſt baſe cowards into Honours chaire,
Whilſt the true ſpirited Souldiour ſtands by
Bare headed, and all bare, whilſt at his ſkarres
They ſkoffe, that nere durſt view the face of warres.
I ſet an Ideots cap on vertues head,
Turne learning out of doores, clothe wit in ragges,
And paint ten thouſand Images of Loame,
In gawdie ſilken colours: on the backes
Of Mules and Aſſes I make aſſes ride,
Onely for ſport, to ſee the Apiſh world
Worſhip ſuch beaſts with ſound idolatrie.
This Fortune does, and when this is done,
She ſits and ſmiles to heare ſome curſe her name,
And ſome with adoration crowne her fame.

Monck. True center of this wide circumference,
Sacred commaundreſſe of the deſtinies,
Our tongues ſhall onely ſownd thy excellence.

The reſt. Thy excellence our tongues ſhall onely ſound.

The ſecond King.

Thou painted ſtrumpet, that with honied ſmiles,
Openeſt the gates of heauen and crieſt, Come in,
Whoſe glories being ſeene, thou with one frowne,
(In pride) lower then hell tumbleſt vs downe.

All Kings. Euer for euer wil we banne thy name.

Fort. How ſweete your howlings relliſh in mine eares? *She comes downe.*
Stand by; now riſe, behold, here lies a wretch,
To vex your ſoules, this begger ile aduaunce
Beyond the ſway of thought, take inſtruments,
And let the raptures of choice Harmonie,
Through the hollow windings of his eare,

Muſicke a while, and he waketh.

Carrie their ſacred ſounds, & wake each ſence,
To ſtand amaz'd at our bright Eminence.
Fortunat. Oh, how am I tranſported? Is this earth?
Or bleſt Elizium?
Fortune. *Fortunatus*, riſe.
Fort. Dread Goddeſſe, how ſhould ſuch a wretch as I
Be knowne to ſuch a glorious deitie?
Oh pardon me: for to this place I come,
Lead by my fate, not folly; in this wood
With wearie ſorrow haue I wandered,
And three times ſeene the ſweating Sun take reſt,
And three times franticke Cynthia naked ride,
About the ruſtie high-waies of the ſkies
Stucke full of burning Starres, which lent her light
To court her Negro paramour grim night.
Fortune. This trauell now expires: yet from this circle,
Where I and theſe with fairie troopes abide,
Thou canſt not ſtir, unleſſe I be thy guide.
I the worlds Empreſſe am Fortune my name,
This hand hath written in thicke leaues of ſteele
An euerlaſting booke of changeleſſe Fate,
Shewing whoe's happie, who vnfortunate.
Fort. If euerie name (dread Queene) be there writ down,
I am ſure mine ſtands in Caracters of blacke,
Though happines her ſelfe lie in my name,
I am ſorrowes heire, and eldeſt ſonne to ſhame.

The Kings. No, we are ſons to ſhame, and ſorrowes heires.

Fortune. Thou ſhalt be one of Fortunes minions:
Behold theſe foure chain'd like Tartarian ſlaues,
Theſe I created Emperours and Kings,
And theſe are now my baſeſt vnderlings:
This ſometimes was a Germane Emperour,
Henry the fift, who being firſt depoſ'd,
Was after thruſt into a dungeon,
And thus in ſiluer chaines ſhall rot to death.
This Frederick Barbaroſſa Emperour
Of Almaine once: but by Pope Alexander
Now ſpurn'd and trod on when he takes his horſe,
And in theſe fetters ſhall he die his ſlaue.
This wretch once wore the diademe of Fraunce,
(Lewes the meeke,) but through his childrens pride,
Thus haue I cauſed him to be famiſhed.
Here ſtands the verie ſoule of miſerie
Poore Baiazet old Turkiſh Emperour,
And once the greateſt Monarch in the Eaſt;
Fortune her ſelfe is ſaid to view thy fall,
And grieues to ſee thee glad to licke vp crommes
At the proud feete of that great Scithian ſwaine,
Fortunes beſt minion, warlike Tamberlaine:
Yet muſt thou in a cage of Iron be drawne
In triumph at his heeles, and there in griefe
Daſh out thy braines.

The third King. Oh miſerable me.

Fortune. No teares can melt the heart of deſtinie:
Theſe haue I ruin'd and exalted thoſe:
Theſe hands haue conquerd Spaine, theſe browes fill vp
The golden circle of rich Portugall.
Viriat a Monarch now, but borne a ſhepherd.
This Primiſlaus (a Bohemian king)
Laſt day a Carter: this Monke Gregorie
Now lifted to the Papall dignitie,
Wretches, why gnaw you not your fingers off,
And teare your tongues out, ſeeing your ſelues trod downe,

And this Duch Botcher wearing Munſters crowne?
John Leyden borne in Holland poore and baſe,
Now rich in Emperie and Fortunes grace.
As theſe I haue aduanc'd, ſo will I thee.
Six giſts I ſpend vpon mortalitie,
Wiſedome, ſtrength, health, beautie, long life, and riches,
Out of my bountie: one of theſe is thine,
Chooſe then which likes thee beſt.

Fortunat. Oh moſt diuine:
Giue me but leaue to borrow wonders eye,
To looke (amaz'd) at thy bright maieſtie,
Wiſedome, ſtrength, health, beautie, long life and riches.

Fortune. Before thy ſoule (at this deepe Lotterie)
Draw foorth her prize, ordain'd by deſtinie,
Know that heres no recanting a firſt choice.
Chooſe then diſcreetly (for the lawes of Fate,
Being grauen in ſteele, muſt ſtand inuiolate.)

Fortunat. Daughters of Joue and the vnblemiſht night,
Moſt righteous Parce, guide my Genius right,
Wiſedome, ſtrength, health, beautie, long life, and riches.

Fortune. Staie, Fortunatus, once more heare me ſpeake,
If thou kiſſe wiſedomes cheeke and make her thine,
Sheele breath into thy lips diuinitie,
And thou (like Phebus) ſhalt ſpeake Oracle,
Thy heauen-inſpired ſoule, on wiſedomes wings,
Shall flie vp to the Parliament of Joue,
And read the Statutes of eternitie,
And ſee whats paſt, and learne what is to come.
If thou lay claime to ſtrength, Armies ſhall quake,
To ſee thee frowne: as Kings at mine doe lie,
So ſhall thy feete trample on Emperie;
Make Health thine obiect, thou ſhall be ſtrong proofe,
Gainſt the deepe ſearching darts of ſurfetting,
Be euer merrie, euer reuelling.

Wiſh but for beautie, and within thine eyes,
Two naked Cupids amorouſly ſhall ſwim,
And on thy cheekes ile mixe ſuch white and red,
That Joue ſhall turne away young Ganimede,
And with immortall armes ſhall circle thee.
Are thy deſires long life ? thy vitall thread
Shal be ſtretcht out, thou ſhalt behold the chaunge
Of Monarchies, and ſee thoſe children die,
Whoſe great great Graundſires now in cradles lie.
If through Golds ſacred hunger thou doſt pine,
Thoſe gilded wantons which in ſwarmes doe runne,
To warme their ſlender bodies in the ſunne,
Shall ſtand for number of thoſe golden piles,
Which in rich pride ſhall ſwell before thy feete,
As thoſe are ; ſo ſhall theſe be infinite.
Awaken then thy ſoules beſt faculties,
And gladly kiſſe this bounteous hand of Fate,
Which ſtriues to bleſſe thy name of Fortunate.

The Kings. Old man, take heede, her ſmiles wil murder thee.

Th' other. Old man, ſheele crowne thee with felicitie.

Fort. Oh, whither am I wrap't beyond my ſelfe ?
More violent conflicts fight in e'rie thought,
Than his whoſe fatall choice Troyes downfall wrought.
Shall I contract my ſelfe to wiſedomes loue ?
Then I loſe riches : And a wiſeman poore,
Is like a ſacred booke thats neuer read,
To himſelfe he liues, and to all els ſeemes dead.
This age thinks better of a gilded foole,
Then of a threedbare Saint in wiſedomes ſchoole.
I will be ſtrong : then I refuſe long life,
And though mine arme ſhould conquer twentie worlds,
Theres a leane fellow beates all conquerours :
The greateſt ſtrength expires with loſſe of breath.
The mightieſt (in one minute) ſtoope to death.
Then take long life, or Health : ſhould I doe ſo,
I might grow vgly, and that tedious Scrole
Of Months and yeeres, much miſerie may enrole :

Therefore ile beg for beautie ; yet I will not,
That faireſt cheeke hath oftentimes a ſoule
Leaprous as ſinne it ſelfe ; then hell more foule.
The wiſedome of this world is Idiotiſme,
Strength a weake reede : Health ſickneſſe enemie,
(And it at length will haue the victorie.)
Beautie is but a painting, and long life
Is a long iorney in December gon,
Tedious and full of tribulation.
Therefore dread ſacred Empreſſe make me rich,
Kneele downe.
My choice is ſtore of gold ; the rich are wiſe.
He that vpon his backe rich garments weares,
Is wiſe, though on his head grow Midas eares.
Gold is the ſtrength, the ſinnewes of the world,
The Health, the ſoule, the beautie moſt diuine,
A maſke of Gold hides all deformities ;
Gold is heauens phiſicke, lifes reſtoratiue,
Oh therefore make me rich : Not as the wretch,
That onely ſerues leane banquets to his eye,
Has Gold, yet ſtarues : is famiſht in his ſtore :
No, let me euer ſpend, be neuer poore.
Fortune. Thy lateſt words confine thy deſtinie,
Thou ſhalt ſpend euer, and be neuer poore :
For proofe receiue this purſe : with it this vertue,
Still when thou thruſts thy hand into the ſame,
Thou ſhalt draw foorth ten pieces of bright gold,
Currant in any Realme where then thou breatheſt ;
If thou can'ſt dribble out the Sea by drops,
Then ſhalt thou want : but that can nere be don,
Nor this grow emptie.
Fortanat. Thankes, great deitie.
Fortune. The vertue ends when thou and thy ſonnes end.
This path leades thee to Cyprus, get thee hence ;
Farewel, vaine couetous foole, thou wilt repent,
That for the loue of droſſe thou haſt deſpiſed
Wiſedomes diuine embrace, ſhe would haue borne thee
On the rich wings of immortalitie ;

But now goe dwell with cares and quickly die.

The Kings. We dwell with cares, yet cannot quickly die.

Exeunt all ſinging, manet Fortunatus.

Fortunat. But now goe dwell with cares and quickly die? How quickly? if I die to morrow, ile be merrie to day: if next day, ile be merrie to morrow: goe dwell with cares? Where dwels care? Hum ha, in what houſe dwels care, that I may chooſe an honeſter neighbor? In princes courts? No, among faire Ladies, neither, theres no care dwels with them: but care how to be moſt gallant. Among gallants then? Fie, fie, no: care is afraid ſure of a guilt Rapier, the ſent of Muſke is her priſon, Tobacco choakes her, rich attire preſſeth her to death. Princes, faire Ladies and gallants, haue amongſt you then, for this wet eide wench Care dwelles with wretches: they are wretches that feele want, I ſhall feele none if I be neuer poore, therefore care I caſheire you my companie. I wonder what blind Goſſip this minx is that is ſo prodigall, ſhe ſhould be a good one by her open dealing: her name's Fortune: Its no matter what ſhe is, ſo ſhe does as ſhe ſaies. *Thou ſhalt ſpend euer, and bee neuer poore*: Maſſe, yet I feele nothing here to make mee rich, heres no ſweete Muſicke with her ſiluer ſound. Trie deeper: ho God be here: Ha, ha, 1, 2, 3, 4, 5, 6, 7, 8, 9 and 10, good, iuſt ten. Its gold ſure, its ſo heauie, trie againe, 1, 2, &c. Good againe, iuſt ten, and iuſt ten. Ha, ha, ha, this is rare: a leather mint, admirable: an Indian mine in a Lambs ſkinne, miraculous: Ile fill three or fowre bagges full for my ſonnes, but keepe this for my ſelfe. If that leane tawnie face Tobacconiſt death, that turnes all into ſmoke, muſt turne me ſo quickly into aſhes, yet I will not mourne in aſhes, but in Muſicke, hey old lad be merrie. Heres riches, wiſdome, ſtrength, health, beautie, and long life. (If I die not quickly, ſweete purſe I kiſſe thee, Fortune, I adore thee, Care, I deſpiſe thee, death, I defie thee.

Enter Ampedo, Shaddow after him, both ſad: Andolocia after them.

Andelo. S'hart, why how now: two knights of the poſt?

Shad. I, maſter, and wee are both forſworne, as all ſuch woodden knights be, for we both tooke an oath (mary it was not corporall) you may ſee by our cheekes, that we would not faſt twentie fowre houres to amend, and we haue taſted no meate ſince the clocke told two dozen.

Andel. That lackes not much of twentie fowre, but I wonder when that halfe faced Moone of thine wil be at the ful.

Sha. The next quarter, not this, when the ſigne is in Taurus.

Andel. Ho thats to ſay, when thou eat'ſt bull biefe. But Shadow, what day is to day?

Shad. Faſting day.

Andel. What day was yeſter-day?

Shad. Faſting day too.

Andel. Will to morrow be ſo too?

Shad. I, and next day too.

Andel. That will be rare, you ſlaue:
For a leane dyet makes a fat wit.

Shad. I had rather be a foole & weare a fat paire of cheekes.

Andel. Now am I prowder of this pouertie, which I know is mine owne, then a wayting gentlewoman is, of a frizled groateſworth of haire, that neuer grewe on her head: Sirrha Shadow, now we can all three ſweare like puritans at one bare word: this want makes vs like good bowlers, we are able to rub out and ſhift in euery place.

Shad. Thats not ſo, we haue ſhifted our ſelues in no place this three moneths: marrie, we rub out in euery corner, but here followes no amendement either of life or of liuerie.

Andel. Why, brother Ampedo, art thou not yet

tir'd with riding poſt ? Come, come, light from this logger-headed Jade, and walke afoote, and talke with your poore friends.

Shad. Nay by my troth he is like me : if his belly be emptie, his heart is full.

Andelo. The famine of Gold gnawes his couetous ſtomacke, more then the want of good victuals : Thou haſt lookt very deuiliſhly euer ſince the good Angel left thee : come, come, leaue this broad brim faſhions, becauſe the world frownes vpon thee, wilt not thou ſmile vpon vs ?

Ampe. Did but the bitternes of mine owne fortunes
Infect my taſte, I could paint ore my cheekes
With ruddy-coloured ſmiles : tis not the want
Of coſtly dyet or deſire of gold,
Inforce this rupture in my wounded breſt.
Oh no, our Father (if he liue) doth lie
Under the Iron foote of miſerie,
And (as a Doue gript in a Faulcons claw)
There pant'th for life being moſt aſſur'd of death.
Brother, for him my ſoule thus languiſheth.

Shad. Tis not for my old Maſter that I languiſh.

Amped. I am not enamoured of this painted Idoll,
This ſtrumpet world ; for her moſt beautious lookes
Are poyſned baits, hung vpon golden hookes.
When fooles doe ſwim in wealth, her Cynthian beames
Will wantonly daunce on the ſiluer ſtreames :
But when this ſquinteide age ſees vertue poore,
And by a little ſparke ſits ſhiuering,
Begging at all, relieu'd at no mans doore,
She ſmiles on her (as the Sunne ſhines on fire)
To kill that little heate, and with her frowne
Is proud, that ſhe can treade poore vertue downe :
Therefore her wrinckled brow makes not mine ſowr e,
Her gifts are toyes, and I deride her power.

Shad. Tis not the crab-tree fac'd world neither that makes mine ſowre.

Andelo. Her gifts toyes : wel brother vertue, we

haue let ſlip the ripe plucking of thoſe toyes ſo long, that wee floriſh like Apple trees in September, (which hauing the falling ſicknes) beare neither fruit nor leaues.

Shad. Nay by my troth, maſter, none flouriſh in theſe withering times, but Auncient bearers and trumpettors.

Andelo. Shaddow, when thou proueſt a ſubſtance, then the tree of vertue and honeſtie, and ſuch fruit of heauen ſhall floriſh vpon earth.

Shad. True, or when the Sunne ſhines at midnight, or women flie, and yet they are light enough.

Andelo. Twas neuer merie world with vs, ſince purſes and bags were inuented, for now men ſet lime twigges to catch wealth : And gold, which ryſeth like the ſunne out of the Eaſt Indies, to ſhine vpon euery one, is like a Conie taken napping in a Purſenet, and ſuffers his gliſtring yellow face deitie to be lapt vp in Lambſkins, as if the innocencie of thoſe leather priſons, ſhould diſpence with the Cheuerill] conſciences of the Iron harted Jaylers.

Shad. Snudges may well be called Jaylers : for if a poore wretch ſteale but into a debt of tenne pound, they leade him ſtraight to execution.

Andel. Doth it not vex thee, Shaddow, to ſtalke vp and downe Cyprus, and to meete the out-ſide of a man, lapt all in Damaſke, his head and beard as white as milke, onely with coniuring in the ſnowie circles of the field Argent, and his noſe as red as Scarlet, onely with kiſſing the ruddie lippes of Angels, and ſuch an Image to weare on his thumbe, three mens liuings in the ſhape of a ſeale Ring, whilſt my brother vertue here,

Shad. And you his brother Vice.

Andel. Moſt true, my little leane Iniquitie, whilſt wee three, if we ſhould ſtarue, cannot borrow fiue ſhillings of him neither in word nor deede : does not this vexe thee, Shaddow?

Shad. Not me ; it vexes me no more to ſee ſuch

a picture, then to ſee an Aſſe laden with riches, becauſe I know when hee can beare no longer, he muſt leaue his burthen to ſome other beaſt.

Andel Art not thou mad, to ſee money on Goldſmithes ſtalles, and none in our purſes?

Shad. It mads not me, I thanke the deſtinies.

Andel. By my pouertie, and thats but a threedbare oath, I am more then mad, to ſee ſilkes and veluets, lie crowding together in Mercers ſhops, as in priſons, onely for feare of the ſmell of waxe (they cannot abide to ſee a man made out of waxe) for theſe Satten commodities haue ſuch ſmooth conſciences, that theile haue no man giue his word for them, or ſtand bownd for their comming foorth, but vow to lie till they rot in thoſe ſhop Counters, except Monſieur money baile them. Shaddow, I am out of my little wits to ſee this.

Shad. So is not Shaddow: I am out of my wits, to ſee fat gluttons feede all day long, whilſt I that am leane, faſt euery day: I am out of my wits, to ſee our Famagoſta fooles, turne halfe a ſhop of wares into a ſuite of gay apparrell, onely to make other Ideots laugh, and wiſe men to crie who's the foole now? I am mad, to ſee Souldiours beg, and cowards braue: I am mad, to ſee Schollers in the Brokers ſhop, and Dunces in the Mercers: I am mad, to ſee men that haue no more faſhion in them then poore Shaddow, yet muſt leape thrice a day into three orders of faſhions: I am mad, to ſee many things, but horne-mad, that my mouth feeles nothing.

Andel. Why, now ſhaddow, I ſee thou haſt a ſubſtance: I am glad to ſee thee thus mad.

Amped. The ſonnes of Fortunatus had not wont,
Thus to repine at others happines:
But fooles haue alwaies this looſe garment wore,
Being poore themſelues, they wiſh all others poore,
Fie, brother Andelocia, hate this madnes,
Turne your eyes inward, and behold your ſoule,
That wants more then your body: burniſh that

With glittering Vertue : and make Ideots grieue,
To fee your beautious mind in wifedome fhine,
As you at their rich pouertie repine.

Enter Fortunatus gallant.

And. Peace, good vertue, Shad. here comes another Shadow.

Shad. It fhould be a Camelion : for he is all in colours.

Amp. Oh, tis my Father. With thefe teares of ioye,
My loue and duetie greete your faire returne :
A double gladneffe hath refrefht my foule ;
One, that you liue, and one, to fee your fate
Lookes frefhly howfoeuer poore in ftate.

And. My father Fortunatus, & thus braue ?

Sha. Tis no wonder to fee a man braue, but a wonder how he comes braue.

Fortunat. Deere Andelocia and fonne Ampedo,
And my poore feruant Shaddow : plume your fpirits
With light-wingd mirth : for Fortunatus hand
Can now powre golden fhowers into their laps,
That fometimes fcorn'd him for his want of gold.
Boyes, I am rich, and you fhall ne're be poore ;
Weare gold, fpend gold, we all in gold will feede,
Now is your father Fortunate indeede.

Andel. Father, be not angrie, if I fet open the windowes of my mind : I doubt for all your bragging, you'le prooue like moft of our gallants in Famagofta, that haue a rich outfide, & a beggerly infide, and like Mules weare gay trappings, and good Veluet footeclothes on their backes, yet champe on the Iron bitte of penurie, I meane, want coyne : You gild our eares with a talke of Gold, but I pray dazell our eyes with the maieftie of it.

Fort. Firft will I wake your fences with the found
Of golds fweete muficke : tell me what you heare ?

Amp. Belieue me, Sir, I heare not any thing.

Andel. Ha, ha, ha. S'hart, I thought as much, if I heare any gingling, but of the purſe ſtrings that goe flip, flap, flip, flap, flip, flap, would I were turnd into a flip-flap, and ſolde to the Butchers.

Fort. Shaddow: Ile trie thine eares, harke, doſt rattle?

Shad. Yes, like three blew Beanes in a blew bladder, rattle bladder, rattle: your purſe is like my bellie, th'ones without money, th'other without meate.

Fort. Bid your eyes blame the error of your eares:
You miſbeleeuing Pagans, ſee, heres gold,
Ten golden pieces: take them, Ampedo.
Hold, Andelocia, here are ten for thee.

Ampe. Shaddow, theres one for thee, prouide thee foode.

Fort. Stay, boy: hold, Shad. here are ten for thee.

Shad. Ten maſter? then defiaunce to Fortune, & a Fig for famine.

Fort. Now tell me, wags, hath my purſe gold or no?

Andel. Wee the wags haue gold, Father; but I thinke theres not one Angell more wagging in this ſacred Temple; why this is rare: Shaddow, fiue will ſerue thy turne, giue me th' other fiue.

Shad. Nay, ſoft maſter, liberalitie dyed long agoe: I ſee ſome rich beggers are neuer well, but when they be crauing: My ten Duckets are like my ten fingers, they will not ieopard a ioynt for you: I am yours, and theſe are mine if I part from them, I ſhall neuer haue part of them.

Amp. Father, if heauen haue bleſt you once againe,
Let not an open hand diſperſe that ſtore;
Which gone, lifes gone; for all treade downe the poore.

Fort. Peace, Ampedo: talke not of pouertie,
Diſdaine, my boyes, to kiſſe the tawnie cheekes
Of leane neceſſitie: make not inquirie,
How I came rich: I am rich, let that ſuffice;

There are fowre leathern bags truſt full of gold:
Thoſe ſpent, ile fill you more : goe lads, be gallant:
Shine in the ſtreetes of Cyprus like two ſtarres,
And make them bow their knees that once did ſpurne
you;
For to effect ſuch wonders gold can turne you :
Braue it in Famagoſta, or els where,
Ile trauell to the Turkiſh Emperour :
And then ile reuell it with Preſter John,
Or banquet with great Cham of Tartarie,
And trie what frolicke Court the Souldan keepes;
Ile leaue you preſently : teare off theſe rags.
Glitter, my boyes, like Angels, that the world
May (whilſt our life in pleaſures circle romes)
Wonder at Fortunatus and his ſonnes.

Andel. Come, Shaddow : now wee'le feaſt it royally.

Shad. Doe, maſter, but take heede of beggerie.

Exeunt.

Muſick ſounds: Enter vice with a gilded face, and hornes on her head: her garments long, painted before with ſiluer halfe moones, increaſing by litle and litle, till they come to the full: in the midſt of them in Capitall letters this written: CRESCIT EVNDO : *her garment painted behind with fooles faces & diuels heads: and vnderneath it in the midſt this written, Ha, Ha, He: ſhe and others wearing gilded viſards, and attirde like deuils, bring out a faire tree of Gold with apples on it: after her comes Vertue, a coxecombe on her head, all in white before, and this written about the middle:* Sibi ſapit: *her attire behind painted with Crownes, and Laurell garlands, ſtuck full of ſtarres, held out by hands, thruſt out of bright cloudes, and among them this written:* Dominabitur aſtris : *Shee and other Nimphes all in white with coxecombs on their heads, bring a tree with greene and withered leaues mingled together, and litle fruit on it: after her Fortune, one bearing her Wheele, another her Globe; and laſt, the Prieſt.*

Fortune. You miniſters of Vertue, Vice, and Fortune,
Teare off this vpper garment of the earth,
And in her naked boſome ſticke theſe trees.

Vertue. How many kingdomes haue I meaſured,
Onely to find a Climat, apt to cheriſh
Theſe withering braunches? but no ground can prooue
So happie; (ay mee) none doe vertue loue;
Ile trie this ſoyle; if here I like wiſe fade,
To heauen ile flie, from whence I tooke my birth,
And tel the Gods, I am baniſht from the earth.

Vice. Vertue, I am ſworne thy foe: if there thou plant,
Here oppoſite to thine, my tree ſhall floriſh,
And (as the running wood-bind) ſpread her armes,
To choke thy withering boughes in their embrace,
Ile driue thee from this world: were Vertue fled,
Vice as an Angell ſhould be honoured.

Fort. Seruants of this bright diuell & and that poore Saint,
Applie your taſke whilſt you are labouring:
To make your paines ſeeme ſhort our prieſt ſhall ſing.

The ſong: whilſt he ſings, the reſt ſet the trees into the earth.

Prieſt, Vertues braunches wither, vertue pines,
O pittie, pittie, and alacke the time,
Vice doth flouriſh, Vice in glorie ſhines,
Her gilded boughs aboue the Cedar clime,
Vice hath golden cheekes, O pittie, pittie,
She in euery land doth monarchize.
Vertue is exilde from euery Cittie,
Vertue is a foole, Vice onely wiſe.
O pittie, pittie, Vertue weeping dies.
Vice laughs to ſee her faint (alacke the time)
This ſinckes: with painted wings the other flies,

Alacke that beſt ſhould fall, and bad ſhould clime,
O pittie, pittie, pittie, mourne, not ſing,
Vice is a Saint, Vertue an vnderling.
Vice doth floriſh, Vice in glorie ſhines,
Vertues braunches wither, Vertue pines.

Fort. Floriſh or wither, Fortune cares not which,
In eithers fall or height our Eminence
Shines equall to the Sunne: the Queene of chance
Both vertuous ſoules and vicious doth aduance.
Theſe ſhadowes of your ſelues ſhall (like your ſelues,)
Striue to make men enamoured of their beauties,
This groue ſhall be our temple; and henceforth
Be conſecrated to our deities.

Vert. How few will come and kneel at vertues ſhrine?

Vice. This contents vertue, that ſhe is cal'd diuine.

Fort. Poore Vertue, Fortune grieues to ſee thy lookes
Want cunning to intice: Why hang theſe leaues,
As looſe as Autumnes haire (which euery wind,
In mockerie blowes from his rotten browes?)
Why like a drunkard art thou pointed at?
Why is this Motley-ſcorne ſet on thy head?
Why ſtands thy Court wide open, but none in it?
Why are the Chriſtall pauements of thy temple,
Not worne, not trod vpon? All is for this,
Becauſe thy pride is to weare baſe attire,
Becauſe thine eyes flame not with amorous fire.

Vert. Vertue is faireſt in a poore aray.

Fort. Poore foole, tis not this badge of puritie,
Nor *Sibi ſapit*, (painted on thy breaſt,)
Allures mortalitie to ſeeke thy loue.
No: now the great wheele of thy Globe hath runne,
And met his firſt point of creation.
On Crutches went this world but yeſter-day,
Now it lies bed-rid, and is growne ſo old,
That its growne young; for tis a child againe,
A childiſh ſoule it hath, tis a meere foole:

And fooles and children are well pleaſde with toyes:
So muſt this world, with ſhewes it muſt be pleaſed,
Then Vertue, buy a golden face like Vice,
And hang thy boſome full of ſiluer Moones,
To tell the credulous world, As thoſe increaſe,
As the bright Moone ſwelles in her pearled Spheare,
So wealth and pleaſures them to heauen ſhall reare.

Vert. Vertue abhorres to weare a borrowed face.

Vice. Why haſt thou borrowed then that Idiots hood?

Vert. Fooles plac'd it on my head that knew me not,
And I am proud to weare the ſcorne of fooles.

Fort. Mourne in that pride & die, all the world hates thee.

Vert. Not all, ile wander once more through the world:
Wiſedome I know hath with her bleſſed wings
Fled to ſome boſome: if I meete that breſt,
There ile erect my temple, and there reſt.
Fortune nor Vice, ſhall then ere haue the power,
(By their looſe eyes) to intice my Paramour;
Then will I caſt off this deformitie,
And ſhine in glorie, and triumph to ſee
Your conquerd at my feete, that tread on me.

Fort. Vertue begins to quarrell: Vice, farewell.

Vice. Stay, Fortune, whilſt within this Groue we dwel,
If my Angelicall and Saint-like forme
Can win ſome amorous foole to wanton here,
And taſte the fruite of this alluring tree,
Thus ſhall his ſawcie browes adorned bee,
To make vs laugh. *Makes hornes.*

Fort. It will be rare: adiew,

Ver. Foule hel-bred fiend, Vertue ſhall ſtriue with you,
If any be enamoured of thine eyes,
Their loue muſt needes beget deformities.
Men are tranſformed to beaſtes, feaſting with ſinne;

But if (in ſpite of thee) their ſoules I winne,
To taſte this fruite, though thou diſguiſe their head,
Their ſhapes ſhall be re-metamorphoſed.

Vice. I dare thee doe thy worſt.

Ver. My beſt ile trie.

Fort. Fortune ſhall iudge who winnes the ſoueraigntie. *Exeunt.*

Enter Chorus.

Chorus. The world to the circumference of heauen,
Is as a ſmall point in Geometrie,
Whoſe greatnes is ſo little, that a leſſe
Cannot be made : into that narrow roome,
Your quicke imaginations we muſt charme,
To turne that world : and (turn'd) againe to part it
Into large kingdomes, and within one moment,
To carrie Fortunatus on the wings
Of actiue thought, many a thouſand miles.
Suppoſe then ſince you laſt beheld him here,
That you haue saild with him vpon the ſeas,
And leapt with him vpon the Aſian ſhores,
Beene feaſted with him in the Tartars palace,
And all the Courts of each Barbarian kings :
From whence (being cald by ſome vnluckie ſtarre,)
(For happines neuer continues long,)
Helpe me to bring him backe to Arragon :
Where for his pride (Riches make all men proude)
On ſlight quarrell, by a couetous Earle,
Fortunes deere minion is impriſoned ;
There thinke you ſee him ſit with folded armes,
Teares dropping downe his cheekes, his white haires torne,
His legges in ruſtie fetters, and his tongue
Bitterly curſing that his ſquint-eide ſoule
Did not make choice of wiſedomes ſacred loue,
Fortune (to triumph in vnconſtancie,)
From priſon bailes him, (libertie is wild)
For being ſet free, he like a luſtie Eagle,
Cuts with his ventrous feathers through the ſkie,

And lights not till he find the Turkiſh court.
Thither tranſport your eyes, and there behold him,
Reuelling with the Emperour of the Eaſt,
From whence (through feare) for ſafegard of his life,
(Flying into the armes of vgly night,)
Suppoſe you ſee him brought to Babylon ;
And that the Sunne (clothed all in fire) hath rid
One quarter of his hot celeſtiall way
With the bright morning, and that in this inſtant,
He and the Soldan meete, but what they ſay,
Liſten you, the talke of Kings none dare bewray.
Exit.

Enter the Souldan, his Noblemen, and Fortunatus.

Sould. Art thou that Fortunatus, whoſe great name,
Being carried in the Charriot of the winds,
Haſt fild the Courts of all our Aſian kings,
With loue and enuie, whoſe deere preſence tyes
The eyes of admiration to thine eyes?
Art thou that Joue that in a ſhower of gold
Appearedſt before the Turkiſh Emperour?
Fortunat. I am that Fortunatus, mightie Souldan.
Sould. Where is that purſe which threw abroad ſuch treaſure?
Fort. I gaue it to the Turkiſh Soliman,
A ſecond I beſtowed on Preſter Iohn,
A third the great Tartarian Cham receiued :
For with theſe Monarches haue I banquetted,
And rid with them in triumph through their courts,
In chriſtall Charriots drawne by Unicornes.
England, Fraunce, Spaine, and welthy Belgia,
And all the reſt of Europs bleſſed daughters,
Haue made my couetous eye rich in th' embrace
Of their celeſtiall beauties ; now I come,
To ſee the glorie of faire Babylon.
Is Fortunatus wel-come to the Soldan?
For I am like the Sunne, if Ioue once chide,
My gilded browes from amorous heauen I hide.

Sould. Moſt welcome, and moſt happie are mine armes
In circling ſuch an earthly deitie;
But will not Fortunatus make me bleſſed
By ſight of ſuch a purſe?
Fort. Ere I depart,
The Soldan ſhall receiue one at my hands:
For I muſt ſpend ſome time in framing it,
And then ſome time to breathe that vertuous ſpirit
Into the heart thereof, all which is don
By a moſt ſacred inſpiration.
Sould. Wel-come, moſt welcome to the Soldans court;
Stay here and be the king of Babylon,
Stay here, and I will more amaze thine eyes
With wondrous ſights, then can all Aſia:
Behold yon towre, there ſtands mine Armourie,
In which are Corſlets forg'd of beaten gold,
To arme ten hundred thouſand fighting men,
Whoſe glittering ſquadrons when the Sunne beholds,
They ſeeme like to ten hundred thouſand Ioues,
When Ioue on the proude backe of thunder rydes,
Trapt all in lightning flames: there can I ſhew thee
The ball of gold that ſet all Troy on fire;
There ſhalt thou ſee the ſkarfe of Cupids mother,
Snatcht from the ſoft moyſt Iuorie of her arme,
To wrap about Adonis wounded thigh,
There ſhalt thou ſee a wheele of Titans care,
Which dropt from heauen when Phaeton fir'd the world:
Ile giue thee (if thou wilt) two ſiluer Doues
Compoſ'd by Magicke to diuide the ayre,
Who (as they flie) ſhall clap their ſiluer wings,
And giue ſtraunge muſicke to the Elements;
Ile giue thee els the fanne of Proſerpine,
Which in reward (for a ſweete Thracian ſong,)
The black-browd Empreſſe threw to Orpheus,
Being come to fetch Euridice from hell.

Fort. Hath euer mortall eye beheld theſe wonders?

Sould. Thine ſhall behold them, and make choice of any,
So thou wilt giue the Souldan ſuch a purſe.

Fort. By Fortunes bleſſed hand (who chriſtned me)
The mightie Souldan ſhall haue ſuch a purſe,
Prouided I may ſee theſe prizeleſſe wonders.

Sould. Leaue vs alone: neuer was mortal eare
Exeunt Nobles.
Acquainted with the vertue of a Jewell,
Which now ile ſhew, (out-valuing all the reſt.)

Fort. It is impoſſible.

Sould. Behold this Caſket,—*Draw a Curtaine.*
Fettered in golden chaines, the Lock pure gold,
The key of ſollide gold, which my ſelfe keepe,
And heres the treaſure thats contained in it.
Takes out the Hat.

Fort. A courſe felt Hat? is this the precious Jewel?

Sould. Ile not exchange this, for ten Diadems.
On paine of death, none liſten to our talke.

Fort. What needes this ſolemne coniuration!

Sould. O, yes, for none ſhall vnderſtand the worth
Of this ineſtimâble ornament,
But you: and yet not you, but that you ſweare
By her white hand, that lent you ſuch a name,
To leaue a wondrous purſe in Babylon.

Fort. What I haue ſworne, I will not violate,
But now vncouer the vertues of this Hatte.

Sould. I thinke none liſten; if they doe, they die.

Fort. None liſten: tell: what needs this iealouſie?

Sould. You ſee tis poore in ſhew; did I want Jewels,
Gold could beget them, but the wide worlds wealth
Buyes not this Hat; this clapt vpon my head,
I (onely with a wiſh) am through the ayre,
Tranſported in a moment ouer Seas,

And ouer lands to any ſecrete place ;
By this I ſteale to euery Princes court,
And heare their priuate councels and preuent
All daungers which to Babylon are meant.
By helpe of this I oft ſee armies ioyne,
Though when the dreadfull Aluarado ſounds,
I am diſtant from the place a thouſand leagues,
Oh, had I ſuch a purſe and ſuch a Hat,
The Souldan were, of all, moſt fortunate.

Fort. Oh, had I ſuch a Hat, then were I braue.
Wheres he that made it ?

Sould. Dead, and the whole world
Yeelds not a workman that can frame the like.

Fort. No does ? by what trick ſhal I make this mine ? *Aſide.*
Me thinkes, me thinkes, when you are borne o're Seas,
And ouer lands, the heauineſſe thereof
Should waigh you downe, drowne you, or breake your necke.

Sould. No, tis more light then any Hat beſide :
Your hand ſhall peiſe it.

Fort. Oh, tis woudrous heauie.

Sould. Fie, ya're deceau'd : trie it vpon your head.

Fort. Would I were now in Cyprus with my ſons. *Exit.*

Sould. Stay, Fortunatus, ſtay, I am vndone.
Treaſon, Lords, treaſon, get me wings, ile flie
After this damn'd Traytor through the ayre.

Enter Nobles.

Nob. Who wrongs the mightie king of Babylon ?

Sould. This Fortunatus, this fiend wrongs your king.

Nobl. Locke the Court gates, where is the diuell hid ?

Sould. No gates no grates of Iron impriſon him,
Like a Magician breakes he through the clouds,
Bearing my ſoule with him, for that Iewell gon,

I am dead, and all is droſſe in Babylon.
Flie after him, tis vaine, on the winds wings,
Heele ride through all the Courts of earthly kings.

Nobl. What is the Iewell that your grace hath loſt?

Sould. He dies that troubles me: call me not king;
For ile conſume my life in ſorrowing. *Exeunt.*

Enter Andelocia very gallant, and Shaddow.

Andel. Shaddow? what haue I loſt to day at dice?

Shad. More then you will win againe in a month.

Andel. Why ſir, how much comes it to?

Shad. It comes to nothing, Sir, for you haue loſt your wits, and when a mans wittes are loſt, the man is like twentie poundes worth of Tobacco, which mounts into th' aire, and prooues nothing but one thing.

Andelo. And what thing is that, you Aſſe?

Shad. Marrie ſir, that he is an aſſe that melts ſo much money in ſmoke.

Andel. Twere a charitable deed to hang thee a ſmoking.

Shad. I ſhould neuer make good bacon, becauſe I am not fat.

Andel. Ile beſworne thy wit is leane.

Shad. Its happie I haue a leane wit: but maſter, you haue none; for when your money tript away, that went after it, and euer ſince you haue beene mad; here com's your brother; borrowe a dramme of him.

Enter Ampedo.

If his be not mouldie: for mens wits in theſe daies, Are like the Cuckoo, bald once a yeere, and that makes Motley ſo deere, and fooles ſo good cheape.

Andel. Brother, all haile.

Shad. There's a ratling ſalutation.

Andel. You muſt lend me ſome more money: Nay neuer looke ſo ſtraunge, and you will come off, ſo: if you will barre me from ſquare play, doe: come

come, when the old traueller my Father comes home, like a young Ape, full of fantasticke trickes, or a painted Parrat stucke full of outlandish feathers, heele leade the world in a string, and then (like a hot shot) Ile charge and discharge all.

Shad. I would be loth, master, to see that day: for he leades the world in a string that goes to hanging.

And. Take heede I turne not that head into the world, and leade you so?
Brother wilt be: Hay any ends of Gold or Siluer?

Amp. Thus wanton reuelling breedes beggerie.
Brother, twere better that you still liu'd poore.
Want would make wisedome rich: but when your Coffers
Swell to the brim, then royt sets vp sayles,
And like a desperate vnskild Mariner
Driues your vnsteddie fortunes on the point
Of wracke ineuitable; of all the wealth,
Left (by our Father, when he left vs last)
This little is vnspent, and this being wasted,
Your ryot ends; therefore consume it all,
Ile liue; or dying, find some buriall.
Thankes for my crownes.

Andel. Shaddow, I am villainous hungrie, to heare one of the seuen wise Masters talke thus emptily.

Shad. I am a villaine, master, if I am not hungrie.

Andel. Because ile saue this gold, sirra Shaddowe, weele feede our selues with Paradoxes.

Shad. Oh rare: what meat's that?

Andel. Meate, you gull: tis no meate: a dish of Paradoxes is a feast of straunge opinion, tis an ordinarie that our greatest gallants haunt nowadaies, because they would be held for Statesmen.

Shad. I shall neuer fil my belly with opinions.

And. In despite of sway-bellies, gluttons, & sweet mouth'd Epicures, Ile haue thee maintaine a Paradox in commendations of hunger.

Shad. I shall neuer haue the stomacke to doo't.

And. Seeſt thou this Cruſado? do it, & turne this into a feaſt.

Shad. Couetouſneſſe and lecherie are two diuels, they'lé tempt a man to wade through deepe matters: Ile doo't though good cheare cōſpire my death, for ſpeaking treaſon againſt her.

Andel. Fall to it then with a full mouth.

Shad. Oh famine, inſpire me with thy miſerable reaſons.
I begin, maſter.

Amp. O miſerable inuocation.

Andel. Silence.

Shad. Theres no mañ but loues one of theſe three beaſtes, a Horſe, a Hound, or a Whore; the Horſe by his goodwill, has his head euer in the maunger; the Whore with your ill will has her hand euer in your purſe; and a hungrie Dogge eates durtie puddings.

Andel. This is profound, forward: the concluſion of this now.

Shad. The concluſion is plaine: For ſince all men loue one of theſe three monſters, being ſuch terrible eaters, therefore all men loue hunger.

Amp. A very leane argument.

Shad. I can make it no fatter.

Andel. Proceede, good Shaddow; this fats me.

Shad. Hunger is made of Gun-powder.

Andel. Giue fire to that opinion.

Shad. Stand by, leſt it blow you vp: hunger is made of Gun-powder, or Gun-powder of hunger; for they both eate through ſtone walles; hunger is a grindſtone, it ſharpens wit, hunger is fuller of loue then Cupid, for it makes a man eate himſelfe; hunger was the firſt that euer open'd a Cookes ſhop; Cookes the firſt that euer made ſawce; ſawce being lickeriſh, lickes vp good meate; good meate preſerues life: Hunger therefore preſerues life.

Amp. By my conſent thou ſhouldeſt ſtill liue by hunger.

Shad. Not ſo, hunger makes no man mortall:

hunger is an excellent Phyſition : for hee dares kill any body : hunger is one of the ſeuen liberall ſciences.

Andel. O learned ? Which of the ſeuen ?

Shad. Muſicke, for ſheele make a man leapé at a cruſt : but as few care for her ſixe ſiſters, ſo none loue to daunce after her pipe : Hunger, maſter, is hungrie and couetous ; therefore the Cruſado.

Andel. But haſt thou no ſharper reaſons then this ?

Shad. Yes one : the dagger in Cyprus had neuer ſtabd out ſuch ſixe penie pipes, but for hunger.

And. Why, you dolt, theſe pies are but in their minority.

Shad. My belly and my purſe haue beene twentie times at daggers drawing, with parting the little vrchins.

Enter Fortunatus.

Ampe. Peace, Idiot, peace, my Father is return'd.

Fort. Touch mee not, boyes, I am nothing but ayre, let none ſpeake to me, till you haue markt me well.

Shad. Now ſpeake your mind.

Amp. Villaine, why haſt thou chalkt my Fathers backe ?

Shad. Onely to marke him, & to trie what colour aire is of.

Fort. Regard him not, Ampedo: Andelocia, Shaddowe : view me, am I as you are, or am I tranſform'd ?

And. I thought trauel would turne my father, mad man or foole.

Amp. How ſhould you be tranſform'd I ſee no chaunge.

Shad. If your wits be not planet ſtrucken, if your braines lie in their right place, you are well inough ; for your body is little mended by your fetching fegaries.

Andel. Mee thinkes, father, you looke as you did, onely your face is more withered.

Fort. Thats not my fault, age is like loue, it cannot be hid.

Shad. Or like Gun-powder a fire, or like a foole, or like a young nouice new come to his lands : for all these will ſhew of what houſe they come : now ſir, you may amplifie.

Fort. Shaddow, turne thy tongue to a ſhaddow, be ſilent : Boyes be proud, your Father hath the whole world in this compaſſe, I am all felicitie, vp to the brimmes. In a minute am I come from Babylon, I haue beene this half howre in Famagoſta.

And. How? in a minute, father? Ha, ha, I ſee trauellers muſt lie.

Shad. Tis their deſtinie : the Fates doe ſo conſpire.

Fort. I haue cut through the ayre like a Falcon ; I would haue it ſeeme ſtraunge to you.

Shad. So it does, Sir.

Fort. But tis true : I would not haue you belieue it neither.

Shad. No more we doe not, Sir.

Fort. But tis miraculous & true : deſire to ſee you, brought me to Cyprus ; ile leaue you more Gold, and goe viſite more Countries.

Sha. Leaue vs gold inough, and weele make all Countries come viſit vs.

Amp. The froſtie hand of age now nips your bloud,
And ſtrowes her ſnowie flowers vpon your head,
And giue you warning that within few yeeres,
Death needes muſt marrie you : thoſe ſhort liues minutes,
That dribble out your life, muſt needes be ſpent,
In peace not trauell : reſt in Cyprus then.
Could you ſuruaie ten worlds, yet you muſt die ;
And bitter is the ſweete thats reapt thereby.

And. Faith father, what pleaſure haue you met by walking your ſtations?

Fort. What pleaſure, boy? I haue reueld with kings, daunc'd with Queenes, dallied with Ladies, worne ſtraunge attires, ſeene fantaſticoes, conuerſt with humoriſts, beene rauiſht with diuine raptures of Dorick, Lidian and Phrigian harmonies, I haue ſpent the day in triumphes, and the night in banquetting.

Andel. Oh rare : this was heauenly.

Shad. Me thinkes t'was horrible.

Andel. He that would not be an Arabian Phenix to burne in theſe ſweete fires, let him liue like an Owle for the world to wonder at.

Amp. Why, brother, are not all theſe vanities?

Fort. Vanities? Ampedo, thy ſoule is made of lead, too dull, too ponderous to mount vp to the incomprehenſible glorie, that trauell liſts men to.

Shad. My olde maſters ſoule is Corke and feathers, and being ſo light doth eaſily mount vp.

Ande. Sweeten mine eares, good father, with ſome more.

Fort. When in the warmth of mine owne countries armes
We yawn'd like ſluggards, when this ſmall Horizon
Impriſon'd vp my body, then mine eyes
Worſhipt theſe clouds as brighteſt ; but, my boyes,
The gliſtring beames which doe abroad appeare,
(In other heauens) fire is not halfe ſo cleare.

Shad. Why, ſir, are there other heauens in other countries?

Andel. Peace, interrupt him not vpon thy life.

For. For ſtill in all the Regions I haue ſeene,
I ſcorn'd to crowd among the muddie throng
Of the rancke multitude, whoſe thickned breath,
Like to condenſed Fogs doe choake that beautie,
Which els would dwell in euery kingdomes cheeke.
No, I ſtill boldly ſtept into their Courts,
For there to liue tis rare, O tis diuine ;
There ſhall you ſee faces Angelicall,
There ſhall you ſee troopes of chaſt Goddeſſes,
Whoſe ſtar-like eyes haue power, (might they ſtill ſhine)
To make night day, and day more chriſtalline.
Neere theſe you ſhall behold great *Heroes*,

White headed Councellors and Jouiall ſpirites,
Standing like fierie Cherubins to gard
The Monarch, who in God-like glorie ſits.
In midſt of theſe, as if this deitie
Had with a looke created a new world;
The ſtanders by, being the faire workemanſhip.

Andel. Oh how my ſoule is rapt to a third heauen.
Ile trauell ſure, and liue with none but kings.

Shad. Then Shaddow muſt die among knaues; and yet why ſo? in a bunch of Cards, knaues waite vpon the kings.

And. When I turne king, then ſhalt thou waite on me.

Shad. Well, theres nothing impoſſible: a dog has his day, and ſo haue you.

Amp. But tell me, father, haue you in all courts
Beheld ſuch glorie, ſo maieſticall?
In all perfection? no way blemiſhed?

Fort. In ſome Courts ſhall you ſee ambition
Sit piecing Dedalus old waxen wings,
But being clapt on, and they about to flie,
Euen when their hopes are buſied in the clouds,
They melt againſt the Sunne of maieſtie,
And downe they tumble to deſtruction:
For ſince the heauens ſtrong armes teach kings to ſtand,
Angels are plac'd about their glorious throne,
To gard it from the ſtrokes of Traitrous hands.
By trauell, boyes, I haue ſeene all theſe things,
Fantaſticke complement ſtalkes vp and downe,
Trickt in out-landiſh Fethers, all his words,
His lookes, his oathes, are all ridiculous,
All apiſh, childiſh, and Italianate.

Enter Fortune: after her three deſtinies working.

Shad. I know a medicine for that maladie.

Fort. By trauell, beyes, I haue ſeene all theſe things.

Andel. And theſe are ſightes for none, but gods & kings.

Shad. Yes, and for Chriſten creatures, if they be not blind.

Fort. In theſe two hands doe I gripe all the world.
This leather purſe, and this bald woollen Hat
Make me a Monarch : heres my Crowne and Scepter.
In progreſſe will I now goe through the world,
Ile cracke your ſhoulders, boyes, with bags of gold
Ere I depart ; on Fortunes wings I ride,
And now ſit in the height of humane pride.

Fortune. Now, foole, thou lieſt ; where thy proud feete doe tread
Theſe ſhal throw downe thy cold & breathleſſe head.

Fort. O ſacred deitie, what sinne is don,
That deaths Iron fiſt ſhould wreſtle with thy ſonne ?

All kneele.

Fortune. Thou art no ſonne of Fortune, but her ſlaue :
Thy Cedar hath aſpir'd to his full height.
Thy Sunne like glorie hath aduaunc'd her ſelfe
Into the top of prides Meridian,
And downe amaine it comes. From beggerie
I plum'd thee like an Oſtrich, like that Oſtrich
Thou haſt eaten Metals, and abuſde my giftes,
Haſt plaid the Ruffian, waſted that in ryots,
Which as a bleſſing I beſtowed on thee.

Fort. Forgiue me, I will be more prouident.

Fortune. No, endleſſe follies follow endleſſe wealth.
Thou hadſt thy fancie, I muſt haue thy fate,
Which is, to die when th'art moſt fortunate.
This inckie thread thy vgly ſinnes haue ſpun,
Blacke life, blacke death ; faſter, that it were don.

Fort. Oh, let me liue, but till I can redeeme.

Fortune. The deſtinies denie thee longer life.

Fort. I am but now lifted to happines.

Fortune. And now I take moſt pride to caſt thee downe.
Hadſt thou choſen wiſedome, this blacke had beene white,
And deaths ſterne browe could not thy ſoule afright.

Fort. Take this againe: giue wiſedome to my ſonnes.

Fortune. No, foole, tis now too late: as death ſtrikes thee,
So ſhall their ends ſudden and wretched bee.
Ioues daughters (righteous deſtinies) make haſte,
His life hath waſtefull beene, and let it waſte.

Exeunt.

Andel. Why the pox doeſt thou ſweate ſo?

Shad. For anger to ſee any of Gods Creatures haue ſuch filthie faces as theſe Semſters had that went hence.

Andel. Semſters? why, you aſſe, they are deſtinies.

Shad. Indeede, if it bee ones deſtinie to haue a filthie face, I know no remedie but to goe Maſkt and crie, Woe worth the Fates.

Amp. Why droopes my father? theſe are onely ſhaddowes,
Raizd by the malice of ſome enemie,
To fright your life, o're which they haue no power.

Shad. Shaddowes? I defie their kinred.

Fort. O Ampedo, I faint; helpe me, my ſonnes.

Andel. Shaddow, I pray thee runne and call more helpe.

Shad. If that deſperate Don Dego death hath tane vp the Cudgels once, heres neuer a Fencer in Cyprus dare take my old maſters part.

Andel. Runne, villaine, call more helpe.

Shad. Bid him thanke the deſtinies for this. *Exit.*

Fort. Let me ſhrincke downe, & die betweene your armes,
Helpe comes in vaine. No hand can conquer Fate,
This inſtant is the laſt of my lifes date.
This Goddeſſe (if at leaſt ſhee be a goddeſſe)
Names her ſelfe Fortune; wandring in a wood,
Halfe famiſht, her I met. I haue, quoth ſhee,
Sixe gifts to ſpend vpon mortalitie,
Wiſedome, ſtrength, health, beautie, long life and riches.

Out of my bountie one of theſe is thine.

Amp. What benefit did from your choyce ariſe?

Fort. Liſten, my ſonnes: In this ſmall compaſſe lies,
Infinite treaſure: this ſhee gaue to mee,
And gaue to this, this vertue, Take (quoth ſhee)
So often as from hence thou drawſt thy hand,
Ten golden peeces of that kingdomes coyne,
Where er'e thou liu'ſt, which plenteous ſure ſhall laſt,
After thy death, till thy ſonnes liues doe waſte.

Andel. Father, your choice was rare, the gift diuine.

Fort. It had beene ſo, if riches had beene mine.

Amp. But hath this golden vertue neuer faild?

Fort. Neuer.

Andel. O admirable: heare's a fire
Hath power to thaw the very heart of death,
And giue ſtones life, by this moſt ſacred death,
See brother, heres all India in my hand.

Fort. Inherite you (my Sonnes) that golden land.
This Hat I brought away from Babylon,
I robd the Souldan of it, tis a prize
Worth twentie Empires. In this Jewell lies.

Andel. How, father? Jewell? call you this a Jewell? It's courſe Wooll, a bald faſhion, and greaſie to the brim; I haue bought a better Felt for a French crowne fortie times: Of what vertuous blocke is this Hat, I pray?

Fort. Set it vpon thy head, and wiſh a wiſh,
Thou in the moment on the winds ſwift wings,
Shalt be tranſported into any place.

Andel. A wiſhing Hat, and a golden mine?

For. O Andelocia, Ampedo, now death
Sounds his third ſommons: I muſt hence: theſe Jewels
To both I doe bequeath; diuide them not,
But vſe them equally: neuer bewray
What vertues are in them; for if you doe,

Much ſhame, much griefe, much daunger followes you.
Peruſe this booke : farwell : behold in me
The rotten ſtrength of proud mortalitie. *Dyes.*

Ampe. His ſoule is wandring to the Elizium ſhades.

Andel. The flowre thats freſh at noone, at Sun-ſet fades.
Brother, cloſe you downe his eyes, becauſe you were his eldeſt; and with them cloſe vp your teares, whilſt I (as all yonger brothers doe) ſhift for my ſelfe : let vs mourne, becauſe hee's dead, but mourne the leſſe, becauſe he cannot reuiue : the honour we can doe him, is to burie him royally, lets about it then, for ile not melt my ſelfe to death with ſcalding ſighes, nor drop my ſoule out at mine eyes, were my father an Emperour.

Amp. Hence, hence, thou ſtop'ſt the tide of my true teares.
True griefe is dumbe, though it hath open eares.

Andel. Yet God ſend my griefe a tongue, that I may haue good vtterance for it : Sob on, brother mine, whilſt you ſigh there, ile ſit & read what Storie my father has written here.

They both fall aſleepe : Fortune and a companie of Satyres enter with Muſicke, and playing about Fortunatus body, take them away ; They gone, Shaddow enters running.

Shad. I can get none, I can find none : where are you, maſter? Haue I tane you napping? and you too? I ſee ſorrowes eye-lids are made of a Dormouſe ſkin, they ſeldome open, or of a miſers purſe, that's alwaies ſhut : So ho, maſter.

Andel. Shaddow, why how now? whats the matter?

Shad. I can get none Sir, tis impoſſible.

Amp. What is impoſſible? what canſt not get.

Shad. No helpe for my old maſter.

Andel. Hast thou beene all this while calling for helpe?

Sha. Yes sir: he scornd all Famagosta when he was in his huffing, and now hee lies puffing for wind, they say they scorne him.

Amp. The poyson of their scorne infects not him;
He wants no helpe. See where he breathles lies:
Brother, to what place haue you borne his body?

Andel. I beare it? I toucht it not.

Amp. Nor I: a leaden slumber prest mine eyes.

Shad. Whether it were lead or lattin that haspt downe those winking casements, I knowe not, but I found you both snorting.

Amp. And in that sleepe (me thought) I heard the tunes
Of sullen passions apt for Funerals,
And saw my Fathers liuelesse body borne
By Satyres: O I feare that deitie
Hath stolne him hence, that Snudge his destinie.

And. I feare hees rysen againe, didst not thou meete him?

Shad. I sir? doe you thinke this white and red durst haue kist my sweete cheekes, if they had seene a ghost? But, master, if the destinies, or Fortune, or the Fates, or the Fayries haue stolne him, neuer indite them for the Felonie: for by this meanes the charges of a Tombe is sau'd, and you being his heyres, may doe as many rich Executors doe, put that money in your purses, and giue out that he dyed a begger.

Andel. Away, you Roague, my Father die a begger?
Ile build a Tombe for him of massie Gold.

Shad. Methinkes, master, it were better to let the memory of him shine in his owne vertues (if hee had any) than in Alablaster.

Andel. I shall mangle that Alablaster face, you whoreson vertuous vice.

Shad. He has a Marble heart, that can mangle a face of Alablaster.

Andel. Brother, come, come, mourne not, our Father is but ſtept to agree with Charon for his boate hyre to Elizium. See, heres a Storie of all his trauels; this booke ſhall come out with a new Addition: Ile treade after my Fathers ſteps; ile goe meaſure the world, therefore lets ſhare theſe Jewels, take this or this.

Amp. Will you then violate our Fathers Will?

Andel. A puritane? keepe a dead mans Will? Indeed in the old time, when men were buried in ſoft Church-yardes, that their Ghoſts might riſe, it was good: but, brother, now they are impriſond in ſtrong Brick and Marble, they are faſt: feare not: away, away, theſe are fooleries, gulleries, trumperies; heres this or this, or I am gon with both.

Amp. Doe you as you pleaſe, the ſinne ſhall not be mine.
Fooles call thoſe things prophane, that are diuine.

Andel. Are you content to weare the Jewels by turnes? Ile haue the purſe for a yeere, you the Hat, and as much gold, as youle aſke; & when my purſourſhip ends, ile reſigne, and cap you.

Amp. I am content to beare all diſcontents. *Exit.*

Andel. I ſhould ſerue this bearing Aſſe rarely now, if I ſhould load him, but I will not, though conſcience bee (like Phyſicke) ſeldome vſed, (for ſo it does leaſt hurt) yet ile take a dram of it: this for him, and ſome gold: this for me: for hauing this mint about me, I ſhall want no wiſhing Cap: gold is an Eagle, that can flie to any place, and like death, that dares enter all places.
Shaddow, wilt thou trauell withme?

Sha. I ſhal neuer fadge with the humor becauſe I cannot lie.

And. Thou dolt, weele viſit all the kings courts in the world.

Shad. So we may, and returne dolts home, but what ſhall we learne by trauaile?

Andel. Faſhions.

Shad. Thats a beaſtly diſeaſe: me thinkes its better ſtaying in your owne countrie.

Andel. How? In mine owne countrie? like a Cage-birde and ſee nothing?

Shad. Nothing? yes you may ſee things enough, for what can you ſee abroad that is not at home? The ſame Sunne cals you vp in the morning, and the ſame man in the Moone lights you to bed at night, our fields are as greene as theirs in ſummer, and their froſts will nip vs more in winter: Our birds ſing as ſweetly & our women are as faire: In other countries you ſhall haue one drinke to you, whilſt you kiſſe your hand, and ducke, heele poyſon you: I confeſſe you ſhall meete more fooles, and aſſes, and knaues abroad then at home (yet God be thanked we haue prettie ſtore of all) but for Punckes, wee put them downe.

And. Prepare thy ſpirits, for thou ſhalt goe with me,
To England ſhall our ſtarres direct our courſe,
Thither the prince of Cyprus (our kings ſonne)
Is gon to ſee the louely Agripyne,
Shaddow, weele gaze vpon that Engliſh dame,
And trie what vertue gold has to inflame.
Firſt to my brother, then away lets flie,
Shaddow muſt be a Courtier ere he die. *Exit.*

Shad. If I muſt, the Fates ſhall bee ſeru'd: I haue ſeene many clownes Courtiers, then why not Shaddow? Fortune, I am for thee. *Exit.*

Enter Orleans melancholike, Galloway with him, a boy after them with a Lute.

Orle. Be gone: leaue that with me, and leaue me to my ſelfe, if the King aſke for me, ſweare to him I am ſicke, and thou ſhalt not lie, pray thee leaue me.

Boy. I am gon, Sir. *Exit.*

Orle. This muſicke makes me but more out of tune.
O, Agripyna.
Gall. Gentle friend, no more.
Thou ſaieſt loue is a madnes, hate it then,
Euen for the names ſake.
Orle. O, I loue that madnes,
Euen for the names ſake.
Gall. Let me tame this frenzie,
By telling thee thou art a priſoner here,
By telling thee ſhees daughter to a king,
By telling thee the king of Cyprus ſonne
Shines like a Sunne, betweene her lookes and thine,
Whilſt thou ſeem'ſt but a ſtarre to Agripyne:
He loues her.
Orle. If he doe: why ſo doe I.
Gall. Loue is ambitious and loues maieſtie.
Orle. Deere friend, thou art deceiued, loues voice doth ſing
As ſweetely in a begger as a king.
Gall. Deere friend, thou art deceyu'd: O bid thy ſoule
Lift vp her intellectual eyes to heauen,
And (in this ample booke of wonders) read,
Of what celeſtiall mold, what ſacred eſſence,
Her ſelfe is formd, the ſearch whereof will driue
Sounds muſicall among the iarring ſpirits,
And in ſweete tune ſet that which none inherits.
Orle. Ile gaze on heauen if Agripyne be there:
If not: Fa, La, la, Sol, la, &c.
Gall. O, call this madnes in, ſee from the windowes
Of euery eye Deriſion thruſts out cheekes,
Wrinckled with Idiot laughter: euery finger
Is like a Dart ſhot from the hand of ſcorne,
By which thy name is hurt, thine honour torne.
Orle. Laugh they at me, ſweete Galloway?
Gall. Euen at thee.
Orle. Ha, ha, I laugh at them, are not they mad,

That let my true true ſorrow make them glad
I daunce and ſing onely to anger griefe,
That in that anger, he might ſmite life downe
With his Iron fiſt : good heart, it ſeemeth then,
They laugh to ſee griefe kill me : O, fond men,
You laugh at others teares, when others ſmile,
You teare your ſelues in peeces : vile, vile, vile,
Ha, ha, when I behold a ſwarme of fooles,
Crowding together to be counted wiſe,
I laugh becauſe ſweete Agripine's not there,
But weepe becauſe ſhee is not any where,
And weepe becauſe whether ſhee be or not,
My loue was euer and is ſtill forgot : forgot, forgot, forgot.

Gall. Draw backe this· ſtreame, why ſhould my Orleans mourne ?

Orle. Looke yonder, Galloway, doeſt thou ſee that Sunne ?
Nay good friend, ſtare vpon it, marke it well,
Ere he be two howres elder, all that glorie
Is baniſht heauen, and then (for griefe) this ſkie,
That's now ſo iocund, will mourne all in blacke,
And ſhall not Orleans mourne ? Alacke, alacke.
O what a Sauage tyrannie it were
T'inforce care, laugh and woe : not ſhed a teare ?
Dead is my loue, I am buried in her ſcorne,
That is my Sun-ſet, and ſhall I not mourne ?
Yes by my troth I will.

Gall. Deere friend forbeare,
Beautie (like ſorrow) dwelleth euery where.
Race out this ſtrong Idea of her face,
As faire as hers ſhineth in any place.

Orle. Thou art a Traytor to that white and red,
Which ſitting on her cheekes (being Cupids throne)
Is my hearts ſoueraigne : O when ſhee is dead,
This wonder (Beautie) ſhall be found in none.
Now Agripyne's not mine, I vow to be
In loue with nothing but deformitie.
O faire Deformitie, I muſe all eyes

Are not enamord of thee: thou didſt neuer
Murder mens hearts, or let them pine like wax,
Melting againſt the Sunne of thy deſtinie,
Thou art a faithfull nurſe to Chaſtitie,
Thy beautie is not like to Agripynes,
For cares, and age, and ſickneſſe hers deface,
But thine's eternall: O Deformitie,
Thy fairenes is not like to Agripynes,
For (dead) her beautie will no beautie haue,
But thy face lookes moſt louely in the graue.

Enter Prince of Cyprus and Agripyne.

Gall. See where they come together hand in hand.

Orle. O, watch ſweete Galloway, when their hands doe part,
Betweene them, ſhalt thou find my murdred heart.

Cypr. By this then it ſeemes a thing impoſſible, to know when an Engliſh Lady loues truely.

Agrip. Not ſo, for when her ſoule ſteales into her heart, and her heart leapes vp to her eyes, and her eyes drop into her hands, then if ſhee ſay, Heres my hand, ſhees your owne, elſe neuer.

Cyp. Heres a paire of your priſoners, lets try their opinion.

Agrip. My kind priſoners well encountred, the Prince of Cyprus here and my ſelfe haue beene wrangling about a queſtion of loue: my Lord of Orleans, you looke leane, and likeſt a louer; Whether is it more torment to loue a Lady and neuer enioy her, or alwaies to enioy a Lady, whome you cannot chooſe but hate?

Orle. To hold her euer in mine armes whome I loath in my heart, were ſome plague, yet the puniſhment were no more then to be enioyned to keepe poyſon in my hand, yet never to taſte it.

Agri. But ſay you ſhould be compeld to ſwallow the poyſon?

Orle. Then a ſpeedy death would end a ſpeeding miſerie: But to loue a Lady and neuer enioy her, oh it is not death, but worſe then damnation; Tis hell, tis.

Agrip. No more, no more, good Orleans, nay then I ſee my priſoner is in loue too.

Cypr. Me thinkes, ſouldiers cannot fal into the faſhion of loue.

Agrip. Me thinkes, a Souldier is the moſt faithfull louer of all men els: for his affection ſtands not vpon complement: his wooing is plaine home-ſpun ſtuffe; theres no outlandiſh thred in it, no Rethoricke: a Souldier caſts no figures to get his miſtris heart, his loue is like his valour in the field, when he payes downe-right blowes.

Gall. True, Madam, but would you receiue ſuch paiment?

Agrip. No, but I meane, I loue a Souldier beſt, for his plaine dealing.

Cypr. Thats as good as the firſt.

Agrip. Be it ſo, that goodneſſe I like: for what Lady can abide to loue a Spruce ſilken face Courtier, that ſtands euery morning two or three howres learning how to looke by his Glaſſe, how to ſpeake by his Glaſſe, how to ſigh by his glaſſe, how to court his Miſtris by his Glaſſe. I would wiſh him no other plague, but to haue a Miſtris as brittle as glaſſe.

Gall. And that were as bad as the horne plague.

Cypr. Are any louers poſſeſt with this madnes?

Agrip. What madman are not poſſeſt with this loue? yet by my troth, wee poore women doe but ſmile in our ſleeves to ſee all this fopperie: yet we all deſire to ſee our louers attirde gallantly, to heare them ſing ſweetely, to behold them daunce comely and ſuch like; but this apiſh monkie faſhion of effeminate niceneſſe, out vpon it: Oh, I hate it worſe then to be counted a ſcould.

Cypr. Indeede men are moſt regarded, when they leaſt regard themſelues.

Gall. And women moſt honored, when they ſhew moſt mercy to their louers.

Orle. But iſt not a miſerable tyrãnie, to ſee a Lady triumph in the paſſions of a ſoule languiſhing through her crueltie?

Cypr. Me thinkes it is.

Gall. Me thinkes tis more then tyrañie.

Agrip. So thinke not I; for as there is no reaſon to hate any that loue vs, ſo it were madnes to loue all that doe not hate vs; women are created beautifull, onely becauſe men ſhould wooe them; for twere miſerable tyrannie to inioyne poore women to wooe men: I would not heare of a woman in loue for my fathers kingdome.

Cyp. I neuer heard of any woman that hated loue.

Agrip. Nor I: but we had all rather die then confeſſe wee loue; our glorie is to heare men ſigh whilſt we ſmile, to kil them with a frowne, to ſtrike them dead with a ſharpe eye, to make you this day weare a Feather, and to morrow a ſicke nightcap: Oh, why this is rare, there's a certaine deitie in this, when a Lady by the Magicke of her lookes, can turne a man into twentie ſhapes.

Orle. Sweete friend, ſhee ſpeakes this but to torture mee.

Gall. Ile teach thee how to plague her: loue her not.

Agrip. Poore Orleans, how lamentably he lookes: if hee ſtay, heele make me ſurely loue him for pure pittie. I muſt ſend him hence, for of all ſortes of loue, I hate the French; I pray thee, ſweet priſoner, intreate Lord Longauile to come to me preſently.

Orle. I will: and eſteeme my ſelfe more then happie, that you will imploy me. *Exit.*

Agrip. Watch him, watch him for Gods ſake, if hee ſigh not or looke not backe.

Cyp. He does both: but what miſterie lyes in this?

Agrip. Nay, no miſterie, tis as plaine as Cupids forehead : why this is as it ſhould be : And eſteeme my ſelfe more then happie, that you will imploy me : my French priſoner is in loue ouer head and eares.

Cypr. Its wonder how he ſcapes drowning.

Gall. With whom thinke you?

Agrip. With his keeper, for a good wager : Ah, how glad is he to obey? And how proud am I to command in this Empire of affection? Ouer him and ſuch Spungy-liuerd youthes, (that lie ſoaking in loue) I triumph more with mine eye, then euer he did ouer a Souldier with his ſword. Iſt not a gallant victorie for me to ſubdue my Fathers enemy with a looke? Prince of Cyprus, you were beſt take heede, how you encounter an Engliſh Lady.

Cypr. God bleſſe me from louing any of you, if all bee ſo cruell.

Agryp. God bleſſe me from ſuffring you to loue me, if you be not ſo formable.

Cyp, Wil you commaund me any ſeruice, as you haue done Orleans?

Agrip. No other ſeruice but this, that (as Orleans) you loue me, for no other reaſon, but that I may torment you.

Cypr. I wil : conditionally, that in all companie I may call you my tormenter.

Agr. You ſhall : conditionally, that you neuer beg for mercy. Come, my Lord of Galloway.

Gall. Come, ſweete Madam. *Exeunt.*

Manet Cyprus.

Cypr. The Ruby-colourd portals of her ſpeech
Were cloſde by mercy : but vpon her eye,
(Attir'd in frownes) ſat murdring crueltie.

Enter Agrip. and liſtens.

Shees angrie, that I durſt ſo high aſpire.
O, ſhee diſdaines that any ſtraungers breſt

Should be a Temple for her deitie :
Shees full of beautie, full of bitternes.
Till uow, I did not dally with loues fire :
And when I thought to try his flames indeede,
I burnt me euen to cinders : O, my ſtarres,
Why from my natiue ſhore did your beames guide me,
To make me dote on her that doth deride me?

She kneeles : he walkes muſing.

Agri. Hold him in this mind, ſweete Cupid, I coniure thee. O, what muſick theſe hey-hoes make? I was about to caſt my litle litle ſelfe into a great loue trance for him, fearing his hart had been flint : but ſince I ſee tis pure virgin wax, he ſhal melt his belly full: for now I know how to temper him. *Exit.*

Cypr. Neuer beg mercy? yet be my tormenter. *He ſpies her.*
I hope ſhee heard me not : doubtleſſe ſhee did :
And now will ſhe inſult vpon my paſſions,
And vex my conſtant loue with mockeries.
Nay, then ile be mine owne Phyſician,
And out face loue, and make her thinke that I
Mournd thus, becauſe I ſaw her ſtanding by.
What newes, my Lord of Cornewall?

Enter Cornewall.

Cornew. This faire Prince,
One of your Countrie-men, is come to Court,
A luſtie gallant braue in Cyprus Ile,
With fiftie bard Horſes prawncing at his heeles,
Backt by as many ſtrong limbd Cypriots.
All whom he keepes in pay : whoſe offred ſeruice,
Our king with Armes of gladnes hath embrac'd.

Cypr. Borne in the Ile of Cyprus? whats his name?

Cornew. His ſeruants call him Fortunatus ſonne.

Cypr. Rich Fortunatus ſonne? Is he ariu'd?

Enter Longauile, Galloway, and Chester with Jewels.

Longa. This he beſtowed on me.

Cheſt. And this on me.

Gallow. And this his bounteous hand inforc'd mee take.

Longa. I prize this Jewell at a hundred Markes,
Yet would he needes beſtow this gift on me.

Cyp. My Lords, whoſe hand hath beene thus prodigal?

Gallow. Your countrieman my Lord, a Cypriot.

Longa. The gallant ſure is all compact of gold,
To euery Lady hath he giuen rich Jewels,
And ſent to euery ſeruant in the Court
Twentie faire Engliſh Angels.

Cypr. This is rare.

Enter Lincolne.

Lincol. My Lords, prepare your ſelues for reueling,
Tis the kings pleaſure that this day be ſpent
In royall paſtimes, that this golden Lord,
(For ſo all that behold him, chriſten him)
May taſt the pleaſures of our Engliſh court.
Here comes the gallant, ſhining like the Sunne.

Trumpets ſound: Enter Athelſtane, Andelocia, Agripyne, Orleans, Ladies, and other attendants, Inſultado a Spaniſh Lord: Muſicke ſounds within.

Andel. For theſe your royall fauours done to me,
(Being a poore ſtraunger) my beſt powres ſhall proue,
By Acts of worth, the ſoundnes of my loue.

Athelſt. Herein your loue ſhall beſt ſet out it ſelfe,
By ſtaying with vs: if our Engliſh Ile
Hold any obiect welcome to your eyes,

Doe but make choice, and claime it as your prize.

The King and Cyprus conferre aſide.

Ande. I thanke your grace: would he durſt keepe his word,
I know what I would claime: Tuſh, man, be bold,
Were ſhee a Saint, ſhee may be wonne with gold.

Cypr. Tis ſtraunge I muſt confeſſe, but in this pride,
His Father Fortunatus (if he liue)
Conſumes his life in Cyprus: ſtill he ſpends,
And ſtill his Coffers with abundance ſwell,
But how he gets theſe riches none can tell.

The King and Agripyne conferre aſide.

Athelſt. Hold him in talke: come hither, Agripyne.

Cypr. But what intic'de young Andelociaes ſoule
To wander hither?

Andel. That which did allure,
My ſoueraignes ſonne, the wonder of the place.

Agr. This curious heape of wonders, (which an Empreſſe
Gaue him) he gaue me, and by Venus hand,
The warlike Amorato needes would ſweare,
Hee left his countrie Cyprus for my loue.

Athelſt. If by the ſoueraigne Magicke of thine eye,
Thou canſt inchant his lookes to keepe the circles
Of thy faire cheekes, be bold to trie thy charmes,
Feede him with hopes, and find the royall veine,
That leades this Cypriot to his golden mine.
Here's Muſicke ſpent in vaine, Lords, fall to dauncing.

Cypr. My faire tormentor, will you lend a hand?

Agrip. Ile try this ſtrangers cunning in a daunce.

Andel. My cunning is but ſmall, yet whoo'le not proue
To ſhame himſele for ſuch a Ladies loue?

Orle. Theſe Cypriots are the diuels that torture me.
He courts her, and ſhee ſmiles, but I am borne,
To be her beauties ſlaue, and her loues ſcorne.

And. I ſhall neuer haue the face to aſke the queſtion twice.

Agrip. Whats the reaſon? Cowardlynes or pride?

Andel. Neither : but tis the faſhion of vs Cypriots, both men and women, to yeeld at firſt aſſault, and we expect others ſhould doe the like.

Agrip. Its a ſigne, that either your women are very black, & are glad to be ſped, or your men very fond, & wil take no denial.

Andel. Indeede our Ladies are not ſo faire as you.

Agrip. But your men more ventrous at a breach then you, or els they are all daſtardly ſouldiers.

Andel. Hee that fightes vnder theſe ſweete colours, & yet turnes coward, let him bee ſhot to death with the terrible arrowes of faire Ladies eyes.

Athelſt. Nay Inſultado, you muſt not denie vs.

Inſultad. *My Corocon es muy peſada, my Anima muy a-tormentada, No per los Cielos* :
La piede de Eſpagnoll, no haze muſica in Tierra Ingleſa.

Cypr. Sweete Inſultado let vs ſee you daunce.
I haue heard the Spaniſh daunce is full of ſtate.

Inſultad. *Verdad Signor* : *la danza ſpagnola, es muy alta,*
Maieſtica, y para Monarcas : *vueſtra Ingleſa,*
Baxa, Fantaſtica, y muy humilde.

Agrip. Doth my Spaniſh priſoner denie to daunce ? Hee has ſworne to me by the croſſe of his pure Toledo, to bee my ſeruant : by that oath (my Caſtilian priſoner) I coniure you to ſhew your cunning, though all your body bee not free, I am ſure your heeles are at libertie.

Inſultad. *Nolo quire contra dezir* : *vueſtra oio haze conqueſto a ſu priſionero* : *Oyres, la pauyne Hiſpanola, ſea vueſtra muſica y grauidad, y maieſtad* : *Paie, daaime Tabacca, Toma my capa, e my eſpada. Mas alta, Mas alta* : *Deſuiaios, Deſuiaios, Companieros, Mas alta, Mas alta.*

Hee daunces.

Athelſt. Thankes, Inſultado.

Cypr. Tis moſt excellent.

Agrip. The Spaniards daunce, is as his deedes bee, full of pride.

Athelst. The day growes old, & what remains vnſpent,
Shall be conſum'd in banquets, Agripyne,
Leaue vs a while, if Andelocia pleaſe,
Goe beare our beautious daughter companie.

And. Fortune I thanke thee : now thou ſmil'ſt on me. *Exeunt Agrip. and Andel. and Ladies.*

Athel. This Cipriot beares a gallant princely mind.
My Lord, of what birth is your country-man?
Thinke not, ſweete Prince, that I propound this queſtion,
To wrong you in your loue to Agripyne:
Our fauours grace him to an other end.
Nor let the wings of your affection droope,
Becauſe ſhee ſeemes to ſhun loues gentle lure.
Belieue it on our word, her beauties prize
Onely ſhall yeeld a conqueſt to your eyes.
But tell me whats this Fortunatus ſonne?

Cypr. Of honourable bloud, and more renownd
In forreine kingdomes (whither his proud ſpirit,
Plum'd with ambitious fethers, caries him)
Then in his natiue Countrie, but laſt day
The father and the ſonnes were through their riots,
Poore and diſdainde of all, but now they gliſter,
More bright than Midas : if ſome damned fiend
Fed not his bags, this golden pride would end.

Athelst. His pride weele ſomewhat tame, & curb the head
Of his rebellious prodigalitie :
He hath inuited vs, and all our Peeres,
To feaſt with him to morrow, his prouiſion,
I vnderſtand may entertaine three kings.
But Lincolne, let our Subiects ſecretly
Be chargde on paine of life that not a man
Sell any kind of Fewell to his ſeruants.

Cypr. This pollicy ſhall clip his golden wings,
And teach his pride what tis to ſtriue with kings.

Athelst. Withdraw awhile : *Exeunt.*
Manet Athelstane.

Athelst. None fild his hands with Gold, for we set spies,
To watch who fed his prodigalitie;
He hung the Marble bosome of our Court,
As thicke with glistring Spangles of pure gold,
As ere the spring hath stucke the earth with flowers.
Unlesse he melt himselfe to liquid gold,
Or be some God, some diuell, or can transport
A mint about him, (by inchanted power)
He cannot raine such showers: with his owne hands
He threw more wealth abroad in euery streete,
Then could be thurst into a Chariot:
Hees a Magician sure, and to some fiend,
His soule (by infernall couenants) has he sold,
Alwaies to swimme vp to the chin in gold.
Be what he can be, if those doting fires,
Wherein he burnes for Agripinaes loue,
Want power to melt from him this endlesse Myne,
Then (like a slaue) weele chaine him in our Tower,
Where tortures shall compell his sweating hands
To cast rich heapes into our treasorie.

Musicke sounding still: A curtaine being drawne, where Andelocia lies sleeping in Agripines lap, shee has his purse, and her selfe and another Lady tye another (like it) in the place, and then rise from him.

Agrip. I haue found the sacred spring that neuer ebs.
Leaue vs: *Exit Lady.* But ile not shew't your maiestie,
Till you haue sworne by Englands royall crowne,
To let me keepe it.
Athelst. By my Crowne I sweare,
None but faire Agripyne the Jem shall weare.
Agrip. Then is this mine: see Father, here's the fire,
Whose gilded beames still burne, this is the Sunne,
That euer shines, the tree that neuer dies,

Here growes the Garden of Hefperides,
The out-fide mockes you, makes you thinke tis poore,
But entring it, you find eternall ftore.

Athelft. Art fure of this? How didft thou driue it out?

Agrip. Feare not his waking yet, I made him drinke
That foporiferous Juice which was compofd,
To make the Queene (my Mother) rellifh fleepe,
When her laft ficknes fommond her to heauen.
He fleepes profoundly: when his amorous eyes
Had fingde their wings in Cupids wanton flames,
I fet him all on fire, and promift loue:
In pride whereof, he drew me forth this purfe,
And fwore, by this he multiplyed his gold.
I tride and found it true: and fecretly
Commaunded Muficke with her filuer tongue,
To chime foft lullabies into his foule,
And whilft my fingers wantond with his hayre,
(T'intice the fleepie Juice to charme his eyes)
In all points was there made a purfe, like his,
Which counterfet is hung in place of this.

Athelft. More then a fecond kingdome haft thou won.
Leaue him, that when he wakes he may fufpect,
Some els has robd him, come deere Agripyne,
If this ftrange purfe his facred vertues hold,
Weele circle England with a waft of Gold. *Exeunt.*

Muficke ftill: Enter Shaddow very gallant, reading a Bill, with emptie bags in his hand finging.

Shad. Thefe Englifh occupiers are mad Troians: let a man pay them neuer fo much, theile giue him nothing but the bag. Since my mafter created me fteward ouer his fiftie men, and his one and fiftie horfe, I haue rid ouer much bufineffe, yet neuer was gald, I thanke the deftinies: Muficke? O delicate warble: O thefe Courtiers are moft fweete triumphant creatures. Seignior, Sir, Monſieur : ſweete Seignior : this is the language of the accompliſhment : O delicious ſtrings : theſe heauenly wyre-drawers haue ſtretcht my maſter euen out at length : yet at length he muſt wake : maſter ?

Andel. Wake me not yet, my gentle Agripyne.

Shad. One word Sir, for the billets, and I vaniſh.

And. Theres heauen in theſe times : throw the muſicians
A bounteous largeſſe of three hundred Angels.

Andelocia ſtarts up.

Shad. Why, ſir, I haue but ten pound left.

And. Ha, . Shaddow ? where's the Princeſſe Agripyne ?

Shad. I am not Apollo, I cannot reueale.

Andel. Was not the princeſſe here, when thou cam'ſt in ?

Shad. Here was no Princeſſe but my princely ſelfe.

Andel. In faith ?

Shad. No in faith, Sir,

Andel. Where are you hid ? where ſtand you wantoning ? Not here ? gone ifaith ? haue you giuen me the ſlip ? well, tis but an amorous tricke and ſo I embrace it : my horſe, Shaddow, how fare my horſe ?

Shad. Upon the beſt Oates my vnderſteward can buy.

An. I meane, are they luſty, ſprightly, gallant, wanton, fiery ?

Shad. They are as all horſes are, Caterpillers to the Commonwealth, they are euer munching : but Sir, for theſe billets, and theſe fagots and bauins ?

Andel. S'hart what billets, what fagots ? doeſt make mee a Woodmonger ?

Shad. No ſweete Seignior, but you haue bid the King and his Peeres to dinner, and he has commaunded that no Woodmonger ſell you a ſticke of wood, and that no Collyer ſhall coſen you of your meaſure, but muſt tie vp the mouth of their Sackes, leaſt their Coales kindle your choler.

Andel. Iſt poſſible? iſt true, or haſt thou learnt of the Engliſh gallants to gull?

Shad. Hees a gul that would be taught by ſuch guls.

Andel. Not a ſticke of wood? Some child of enuie has buzd this ſtratagem into the kings eare, of purpoſe to diſgrace me: I haue inuited his maieſtie, and though it coſt me a Million, ile feaſt him. Shadow, thou ſhalt hyre a hundred or two of Carts, with them poſt to all the Grocers in London, buy vp all the Cynamon, Cloues, Nutmegs, Licoriſh and all other ſpices, that haue any ſtrong heart, and with them make fires to prepare our Cookerie:
Ere Fortunatus ſonne looke red with ſhame,
Heele dreſſe a Kings feaſt in a ſpiced flame.

Shad. This diuice, Sir, will bee ſomewhat a kin to Lady Pride, twill aſke coſt.

And. Fetch twentie Porters, ile laid all with gold.

Shad. Firſt, maſter, fil theſe bags.

And. Come then, hold vp, how now? trickes, new crochets, Madam Fortune? Drie as an Eele-ſkin? Shaddow, take thou my Gold out.

Shad. Why Sir, here's none in.

Andel. Ha, let me ſee: O heres a baſtard cheeke,
I ſee now tis not mine; tis counterfet,
Tis ſo: ſlaue thou haſt robd thy maſter.

Sha. Not of a peny, I haue beene as true a ſteward.

And. Vengeance on thee and on thy ſtewardſhip.
Yet wherefore curſe I thee? thy leaden ſoule
Had neuer power to mount vp to the knowledge
Of the rich miſterie cloſde in my purſe.
Oh no, ile curſe myſelfe, mine eyes ile curſe,
They haue betrayd me, I will curſe my tongue,
That hath betraid me: Ile curſe Agripyne,
Shee hath betraid me. Sirens ceaſe to ſing,
Your charmes haue tane effect, for now I ſee,
All your inchantments were, to coſen me.

Muſicke ceaſeth.

Shad. What ſhall I doe with this ten pound, Sir?

Andel. Goe buy with it a Chaine and hang thy ſelfe.
Now thinke I on my Fathers prophecie.
Tell none (quoth he) the vertue, if you doe,
Much ſhame, much griefe, much danger follows you.
With teares I credit his diuinitie.
O fingers, were you vpright Juſtices,
You would teare out mine eyes : had not they gazde
On the fraile colour of a painted cheeke,
None had betraid me : henceforth ile defie
All beautie, and will call a louely eye,
A Sun whoſe ſcorching beames burne vp our ioyes,
Or turne them blacke like Ethiopians.
O women, wherefore are you borne mens woe,
Why are your faces fram'd Angelicall ?
Your hearts of ſpunges, ſoft and ſmooth in ſhew,
But toucht, with poyſon they doe ouer-flow.
Had ſacred wiſedome beene my Fathers Fate,
He had died happie, I liu'd fortunate.
Shaddow, beare this to beautious Agripyne,
With it this meſſage, tell her, ile reprooue
Her couetous ſinne the leſſe, becauſe for gold,
I ſee that moſt mens ſoules too cheape are ſold.

Sha. Shal I buy theſe ſpices to day or to morrow ?

And, To morrow ? I, to morrow thou ſhalt buy them.
To morrow tell the Princeſſe I wil loue her,
To morrow tell the king, ile banquet him,
To morrow, Shaddow, will I giue thee gold,
To morrow pride goes bare and luſt acold.
To morrow will the rich man feede the poore.
And vice to morrow vertue will adore,
To morrow beggers ſhall be crowned kings,
This No-time, morrowes-time, no ſweetnes ſings :
I pray thee hence ; beare that to Agripyne.

Shad, Ile goe hence, becauſe you ſend me : but ile goe weeping hence, for griefe that I muſt turne villaine as many doe, and leaue you when you are vp to the eares in aduerſitie. *Exit.*

Andel. Shee hath robd me, and now ile play the thiefe,
I ſteale from hence to Cyprus, for blacke ſhame
Here (through my riots) brands my loftie name.
Ile fell this pride for helpe to beare me thither,
So pride and beggerie ſhall walke together:
This world is but a Schoole of villanie,
Therefore ile rob my brother, (not of gold,
Nor of his vertues, vertue none will ſteale :)
But (if I can,) ile ſteale his wiſhing Hat.
And with that, wandring round about the world,
Ile ſearch all corners to find miſerie,
And where ſhee dwels, ile dwell, languiſh and die.
Exit.

Chorus. Gentels, if ere you haue beheld the paſſions,
The combats of his ſoule who being a king,
By ſome vſurping hand hath beene depoſde
From all his royalties ; euen ſuch a ſoule,
Such eyes, ſuch heart ſwolne big with ſighes and teares,
The ſtar-croſt ſonne of Fortunatus weares.
The thoughts crownd him a Monarch in the morne,
Yet now hees bandyed by the Seas in ſcorne,
From waue to waue : his golden treaſures ſpoyle
Makes him in deſperate language to intreate,
The winds to ſpend their furie on his life :
But they (being milde in tyrannie) or ſcorning
To triumph in a wretches funerall,
Toſſe him to Cyprus. O what treacherie
Cannot this Serpent gold intice vs to?
He robs his brother of the Souldans prize,
And hauing got his wiſh (the wiſhing Hat)
He does not (as he voud) ſeeke miſerie,
But hopes by that to win his purſe againe,
And in that Hope from Cyprus is he fled.
If your ſwift thoughts clap on their wonted wings,
In Genoway may you take this fugitiue,
Where hauing cozened many Jewellers,
To England backe he comes, ſtep but to court,

And there (diſguizde) you find him bargoning
For Jewels with the beautious Agripyne,
Who wearing at her ſide the vertuous purſe,
He claſpes her in his armes, and as a Rauen,
Griping the tender-hearted Nightingale,
So flies he with her (wiſhing) in the ayre,
To be tranſported to ſome wilderneſſe:
Imagine this the place: ſee here they come.

Enter Andelocia and Agripyne.

Since they themſelues haue tongues, mine ſhall be dumbe. *Exit.*

Enter Andelocia with the wiſhing Hat on: Agripyna in his hand.

Agrip. What diuell art thou that affrightſt me thus,
Haling a Princeſſe from her fathers court,
To ſpoyle her in this ſauage wilderneſſe?

Andel. Indeed the diuel and the pick-purſe ſhould alwaies flie together, (for they are ſworne brothers:) but Madam Couetouſnes, I am neither a diuel as you cal me, nor a Jeweller as I call my ſelfe, no, nor a Jugler, yet ere you and I part, weele haue ſome leger-dimain together: do you know me?

Agrip. I am betrayd: this is the Cypriot.
Forgiue mee, twas not I that changde thy purſe,
But Athelſtane my father, ſend me home,
And heres thy purſe againe: here are thy Jewels,
And I in ſatiſſaction of all wrongs.

Andel. Talke not you of ſatiſſaction, this is ſome recompence that I haue you, tis not the purſe I regard: put it off, and ile mince it as ſmall as pie meate: the purſe? hang the purſe: were that gon, I can make another, and another, and another, I and another: tis not the purſe I care for, but the purſer: you, I you. Iſt not a ſhame that a kings daughter, a faire Lady, a Lady not for Lords, but for Monarches, ſhould for gold ſell her loue, and when ſhee has her owne aſking, and that there ſtands nothing betweene, then to cheate your ſweete heart? O fie, fie, a ſhee cony-catcher? You muſt be dealt ſoundly with.

Agrip. Inioyne what paines thou wilt, and ile endure them,
ſo thou wilt ſend me to my fathers court.

Ande. Nay gods lid, y' are not gon ſo: ſet your heart at reſt, for I haue ſet vp my reſt, that except you can runne ſwifter then a Hart, home you goe not: what paines ſhall I lay vpon you? Let me ſee: I could ſerue you now but a ſlipperie touch: I could get a young King or two, or three of you, and then ſend you home, and bid their grand-ſire king nurſe them: I could pepper you, but I will not.

Agrip. O, doe not violate my chaſtitie.

Andel. No, why I tell you I am not giuen to the fleſh, though I ſauor (in your noſe) a little of the diuell, I could run away elſe, and ſtarue you here.

Agrip. If I muſt die, doome me ſome eaſier death.

Andel. Or tranſforme you (becauſe you loue picking) into a Squirell, and make you picke out a poore liuing here among the Nut trees: but I will not neither.

Agrip. What will my gentle Andelocia doe?

Andel. Oh, now you come to your old byas of cogging.

Agrip. I pray thee Andelocia, let me goe:
Send me to England, and by heauen I ſweare,
Thou from all kings on earth my loue ſhalt beare.

And. Shall I in faith?

Agrip. In faith, in faith thou ſhalt.

Andel. Here, god a mercie: now thou ſhalt not goe.

Agrip. Oh God.

Andel. Nay doe you heare Lady? crie not y' are beſt: no nor curſe me not: if you thinke but a crabbed thought of me, the ſpirit that caried you in mine armes through the ayre, will tell me all: therefore ſet your Sunday face vpont. Since you'le loue me, ile loue you, ile marrie you, and lie with you, and beget little Juglers: marie home you get not: England you'le ſay is yours: but Agripyne, loue me, and I will make the whole world thine.

Agrip. I care not for the world, thou murdreſt me,
Betweene my ſorrow, and the ſcalding Sunne
I faint, and quickly will my life be done,
My mouth is like a Furnace, and drie heate
Drinks vp my bloud. Oh God, my heart will burſt,
I die, vnleſſe ſome moyſture quench my thirſt.

Andel. S' hart now I am worſe then ere I was before:
For halfe the world I would not haue her die.
Heres neither ſpring nor ditch, nor raine, nor dew,
Nor bread nor drinke: my louely Agripyne,
Be comforted, ſee here are Apple trees.

Agrip. Clime vp for Gods ſake, reach me ſome of them.

Andel. Looke vp, which of theſe Apples likes thee beſt?

Agrip. This hath a withered face, tis ſome ſweete fruit.
Not that, my ſorrowes are too ſowre already.

Andel. Come hither, here are Apples like gold.

Agrip. O, I for Gods ſake, gather ſome of theſe.
Ay me, would God I were at home againe.

Andel. Stand farder, leaſt I chance to fall on thee. *Climes vp.*
Oh here be rare Apples, rare red-cheekt Apples, that cry come kiſſe me: Apples, hold your peace, ile teach you to cry. *Eates one.*

Agrip. O England, ſhal I ne're behold thee more?

Andel. Agripyna, tis a moſt Sugred delicious taſt in ones mouth, but when tis downe, tis as bitter as gall.

Agrip. Yet gather ſome of them. Oh, that a Princeſſe
Should pine for foode: were I at home againe,
I ſhould diſdaine to ſtand thus and complaine.

And. Heres one Apple that growes higheſt, Agripyna, and I could reach that, ile come downe.

Hee ſtands fiſhing with his girdle for it.

Agrip. Make haſt, for the hot Sun doth ſcald my cheekes.

Andel. The ſunne kiſſe thee? hold, catch, put on my Hat, I will haue yonder higheſt Apple, though I die for 't.

Agrip. I had not wont be Sun-burnt, wretched mee.
O England, would I were againe in thee.

Exit. He leapes downe.

And. Swounds Agripyna, ſtay, O I am vndone,
Sweete Agripyna, if thou hearſt my voice,
Take pittie of me, and returne againe.
Shee flies like lightning: O ſhe heares me not,
I wiſh myſelfe into a wilderneſſe,
And now I ſhall turne wilde: here I ſhall famiſh,
Here die, here curſing dye, here rauing die,
And thus will wound my breſt, and rent mine hayre.
What hils of Flint are growne vpon my browes?
O me, two forked hornes, I am turn'd beaſt,
I haue abuzde two bleſſings, welth and knowledge,
Wealth in my purſe, and knowledge in my Hat,
By which being borne into the Courts of kings,
I might haue ſeene the wondrous workes of Joue,
Acquirde Experience, Learning, Wiſedome, Truth,
But I in wilderneſſe tottred out my youth,
And therefore muſt turne wild: muſt be a beaſt,
An vgly beaſt: my body hornes muſt beare,
Becauſe my ſoule deformitie doth weare.
Liues none within this wood? If none but I
Liue here (thankes heauen) for here none els ſhal die.

He lies downe and ſleepes under the tree: Enter Fortune, Vice, Vertue, the Prieſt: Satyres with Muſicke, playing as they come in before Fortune. They play awhile.

Fortune. See where my new-turnd diuel has built his hel.

Vice. Vertue, who conquers now? the foole is tane.

Vert. O ſleepie ſinne.

Vice. Sweete tunes wake him againe.

Muſicke awhile, and then ceaſe.

Fort. Vice ſets too heauie on his drowzy ſoule,
Muſicks ſweete concord cannot pierce his eare.
Sing and amongſt your Songs, mix bitter ſcorne.

Vert. Thoſe that teare Vertue, muſt by Vice be torne.

The Song.

1. *Verſe.* Vertue ſtand aſide: the foole is caught,
Laugh to ſee him, laugh alowd to wake him,
Follies nets are wide, and neately wrought,
Mocke his hornes, and laugh to ſee Vice take him.

Quire. Ha, ha, ha, ha, ha, laugh, laugh in ſcorne,
Who's the foole? the foole, he wears a horne.

Andel. wakens and ſtands vp.

2. *Verſe.* Vertue ſtand aſide, mock him, mock him, mock him
Laugh alowd to ſee him, call him foole.
Error gaue him ſucke, now ſorrowes rocke him,
Send the riotous beaſt to madnes ſchoole.

Quire. Ha, ha, ha, ha, ha, laugh, laugh in ſcorne,
Who's the foole? the foole, he weares a horne.

3. *Verſe.* Vertue ſtand aſide: your ſchoole he hates.
Laugh alowd to ſee him, mocke, mocke, mock him.
Vanitie and hell keepe open gates,
Hees in, and a newe nurſe (Deſpaire) muſt rocke him.

Quire. Ha, ha, ha, ha, ha, laugh, laugh in ſcorne,
Foole, foole, foole, foole, foole, weare ſtill the horne.

When they haue done ſinging, Vice and Vertue hold Apples out to him, Vice laughing, Vertue grieuing.

Andel. O me, what hell is this? fiends, tempt me not.
Thou glorious diuell hence. O now I ſee,
This fruit is thine, thou haſt deformed mee:
Ideot auoide, thy gifts I loath to taſt.
Away: ſince I am entred madnes Schoole,
As good to be a beaſt, as be a foole.
Away, why tempt you me? ſome powrefull grace
Come and redeeme me from this hideous place.

Fort. To her hath Andelocia (all his life)
Sworne fealtie, woudſt thou forſake her now?

Andel. Whose bleſſed tongue names Andelocia?

Fort. Hers, who (attended on by deſtinies)
Shortned thy Fathers life, and lengthens thine.

Andel. O ſacred Queene of chance, now ſhorten mine,
Elſe let thy deitie take off this ſhame.

Fort. Wooe her, t'was ſhee that ſet it on thy head.

Andel. She laughs to ſee me metamorphoſed. *Riſes.*

Vert. Wooe me, and ile take off this vgly ſcorne.

Vice. Wooe me, and ile clap on another horne,

Andel. I am beſet with anguiſh, ſhame and death.
O bid the Fates worke faſt, and ſtop my breath.

Fort. No Andelocia, thou muſt liue to ſee
Worſe torments (for thy follies) light on thee.
This golden tree, which did thine eyes intice,
Was planted here by Vice: loe, here ſtands Vice:
How often haſt thou ſued to win her grace?

Andel. Till now, I neuer did behold her face.

Fort. Thou didſt behold her at thy fathers death,
When thou in ſcorne didſt violate his will,
Thou didſt behold her, when thy ſtrecht-out arme
Catcht at the higheſt bough, the loftieſt vice,

The fairest Apple, but the fowlest price.
Thou didst behold her, when thy lickerish eye
Fed on the beautie of faire Agripyne,
Because th' adst gold, thou thoughtst al women thine.
When look'st thou off from her? for they whose soules
Still reuell in the nights of vanitie,
On the faire cheekes of Vice still fixe their eye.
Because her face doth shine, and all her bosome
Beares siluer Moones, thou wast enamord of her.
But hadst thou vpward lookt, and seene these shames,
Or viewd her round about, and in this glasse
Seene Idiots faces, heads of diuels and hell,
And read this ha, ha, he, this merrie storie,
Thou wouldst haue loathd her: where, by louing her,
Thou bearst this face, and wearst this vgly head,
And if shee once can bring thee to this place,
Lowd sounds these ha, ha, he, sheele laugh apace.

Andel. O, re-transforme me to a glorious shape,
And I will learne how I may loue to hate her.

Fort. I cannot re-transforme thee, wooe this woman.

Andel. This woman? wretched is my state, when I,
To find out wisedome, to a foole must flie.

Fort. Foole, cleere thine eyes, this is bright Arete,
This is poore Vertue, care not how the world
Doth crowne her head, the world laughes her to scorne,
Yet *Sibi sapit,* Vertue knowes her worth.
Runne after her, sheele give thee these and these
Crownes and Bay-garlands: (honours victories:)
Serue her, and shee will fetch thee pay from heauen,
Or giue thee some bright office in the starres.

Ande. Immortall Arete, Vertue diuine, *Kneeles.*
O smile on me, and I will still be thine.

Vert. Smile thou on me, and I will still be thine:
Though I am iealous of thy Apostasie,
Ile entertaine thee: here, come tast this tree,
Here's Physicke for thy sicke deformitie.

Andel. Tis bitter: this fruit I shall ne're disgest.

Vert. Trie once againe, the bitternes soone dies.

Vice. Mines ſweete, taſt mine.

Vert. But being downe tis ſowre,
And mine being downe has a delicious taſte.
The path that leades to Vertues court is narrow,
Thornie and vp a hill, a bitter iorney,
But being gon through, you find all heau'nly ſweetes,
The entrance is all flintie, but at th' end,
To towres of pearle and chriſtall you aſcend.

Ande. O delicate, O ſweete Ambroſian relliſh,
And ſee, my vglineſſe drops from my browes,
Thankes beautious Arete : O had I now
My Hat and purſe againe, how I would ſhine,
And gild my ſoule with none but thoughts diuine.

Fort. That ſhall be tride, take fruit from both theſe trees,
By helpe of them, winne both thy purſe and Hat,
I will inſtruct thee how, for on my wings
To England ſhalt thou ride; thy vertuous brother
Is (with that Shadow who attends on thee,)
In London, there ile ſet thee preſently.
But if thou loſe our fauours once againe,
To taſte her ſweetes, thoſe ſweetes muſt prooue thy bane.

Vert. Vice, who ſhall now be crownd with victorie?

Vice. Shee that triumphes at laſt, and that muſt I.

Exeunt.

Enter Athelſtane, Lincolne with Agripyne, Cyprus, Galloway, Cornewall, Cheſter, Longauile and Montroſſe.

Athelſt. Lincolne, how ſet'ſt thou her at libertie?

Lincol. No other priſon held her but your court,
There (in her chamber) hath ſhee hid her ſelfe
Theſe two daies, onely to ſhake off that feare,
Which her late violent rapture caſt vpon her.

Cypr. Where hath the beautious Agripyna been?

Agryp. In heauen or hel, in or without the world,
I know not which, for as I oft haue ſeene
(When angrie Thameſis hath curld her lockes,)

A whirle-wind come, and from her frizeld browes,
Snatch vp a handful of thoſe ſweatie pearles,
That ſtoode vpon her forhead, which awhile,
Being by the boyſtrous wind hung in the ayre,
At length hath flung them downe and raizd a ſtorme.
Euen with ſuch furie was I wherryed vp,
And by ſuch force held priſoner in the cloudes,
And throwne by ſuch a tempeſt downe againe.

Cornw. Some ſoule is dam'd in hell for this black deede.

Agrip. I haue the purſe ſafe, and anon your grace
Shall heare the wondrous hiſtorie at full.

Cypr. Tel me, tormenter, ſhall faire Agripyne,
Without more difference be now chriſtend mine ?

Agrip. My choice muſt be my Fathers faire conſent.

Athelſt. Then ſhall thy choyce end in this Cyprus prince.
Before the Sunne ſhall ſixe times more ariſe,
His royall marriage will we ſolemniſe.
Proclaime this honord match, come Agripyne,
I am glad th' art here, more glad the purſe is mine.

As they are all going in: Enter Andelocia and Shaddowe, like Iriſh Coſter-mongers, Agripyna, Longauyle, and Montroſſe ſtay liſtening to them, the reſt Exeunt.

Both. Buy any Apples, feene Apples of Tamaſco, feene Tamaſio peepins : peeps feene, buy Tamaſco peepins.

Agrip. Damaſco apples ? good my Lord Montroſſe,
Call yonder fellowes.

Montr. Sirra Coſter-monger.

Shad. Who cals : peeps of Tamaſco, feene peeps : I ſat tis de ſweeteſt apple in de world, tis better den de Pome water, or apple John.

Andel. By my trat Madam, tis reet Tamaſco peepins, looke here els.

Shad. I dare not ſay, as de Iriſhman my countrie-man ſay, taſt de goodneſſe of de fruit: No fayt tis farie teere miſtris, by Saint Patrickes hand tis teere Tamaſco apple.

Agrip. The faireſt fruit that euer I beheld,
Damaſco apples, wherefore are they good?

Longa. What is your price of halfe a ſcore of theſe?

Both. Halfe a ſcore, halfe a ſcore? dat is doos many meſter.

Longa. I, I, ten, half a ſcore, thats fiue and fiue.

Andel. Feeue and feeue? By my trat and as Creeze ſaue me la, I cannot tell, wat be de price of feeue and ſeeue, but tis tree crowne for one Peepin, dat is de preez if you take em.

Shad. I fat, tis no leſſe for Tamaſco.

Agrip. Three crownes for one? what wondrous vertues haue they?

Shad. O, tis feene Tamaſco apple, and ſhall make you a great teale wiſe, and make you no foole, and make feene memorie.

Andel. And make dis faſh be more faire and amiable, and make dis eyes looke alwaies louely, and make all de court & countrie burne in deſire to kiſſe di none ſweete countenance.

Montr. Apples to make a Lady beautifull?
Madam thats excellent.

Agrip. Theſe Iriſhmen,
Some ſay, are great diſſemblers, and I feare,
Theſe two the badge of their owne countrie weare.

Andel. By my trat, and by Saint Patrickes hand, and as Creez ſaue me la, tis no diſſembler: de Iriſh man now and den cut di countrie-mans throate, but yet in fayt hee loue di countrie-man, tis no diſſembler: dis feene Tamaſco apple can make di ſweete countenance, but I can take no leſſe but three crownes for one, I weare out my naked legs and my footes, and my tods, and run hidder and didder to Tamaſco for dem.

Shad. As Creez ſaue me la, hee ſpeakes true: Peeps ſeene.

Agrip. Ile trie what power lies in Damaſco fruit. Here are ten crownes for three. So fare you well.

Montr. Lord Longauyle, buy ſome.

Longa. I buy? not I:
Hang them, they are toyes, come Madam, let vs goe. *Exeunt.*

Both. Saint Patricke and Saint Peter, and all de holy Angels look vpon dat faſh and make it faire.

Enter Montroſſe ſoftly.

Shad. Ha, ha, ha, ſhees ſped, I warrant.

Andel. Peace, Shaddow, buy any peepins, buy.

Both. Peeps ſeene, ſeene Tamaſco apples.

Montr. Came not Lord Longauyle to buy ſome fruit?

Andel. No fat, maſter, here came no Lords nor Ladies, but di none ſweete ſelfe.

Montr. Tis well, ſay nothing, heres ſix crownes for two:
You ſay the vertues are to make one ſtrong.

Both. Yes fat and make ſweet countenance & ſtrong too.

Montr. Tis excellent, here: farwell, if theſe proue,
Ile conquer men by ſtrength, women by loue. *Exit.*

Enter Longauyle.

Both. Ha, ha, ha, why this is rare.

Shad. Peace, maſter, here comes another foole.

Both. Peepes ſeene, buy any peepes of Tamaſco?

Longa. Did not the Lord Montroſſe returne to you?

Both. No fat, ſweete maſter, no Lord did turne to vs: Peepes ſeene.

Longa. I am glad of it: here are nine crownes for thee:
What are the vertues beſides making faire?

Andel. O, twill make thee wondrous wiſe.

Shad. And dow ſhall bee no more a foole, but ſweete face and wiſe.

Longa. Tis rare, farwell, I neuer yet durſt wooe. None loues me : now ile trie what theſe can doe.

Exit.

Andel. Ha, ha, ha, So, this is admirable, Shaddow, here end my torments in Saint Patrickes Purgatorie, but thine ſhall continue longer.

Shad. Did I not clap on a good falſe Iriſh face ?

Andel. It became thee rarely.

Shad. Yet thats lamentable, that a falſe face ſhould become any man.

Andel. Thou art a gull, tis all the faſhion now, which faſhion becauſe weele keepe, ſtep thou abroad, let not the world want fooles : whilſt thou art commenſing thy knauerie there, ile proceede Doctor Dodipoll here : that done, thou Shaddow and I will ſat our ſelues to behold the tranſformation of theſe fooles : goe flie.

Shad. I feare nothing, but that whilſt wee ſtriue to make others fooles, we ſhall weare the Coxcombes our ſelues, Pips fine &c. *Exit Shaddow.*

Enter Ampedo.

Andel. S'hart, here's my brother whome I haue abuzde :
His preſence makes me bluſh, it ſtrikes me dead,
To thinke how I am metamorphoſed.
Feene peepins of Tamaſco &c.

Amp. For ſhame caſt off this Maſke.

Andel. Wilt thou buy any pips ?

Amp. Mocke me no longer
With idle apparitions : many a land
Haue I with wearie feete and a ſicke ſoule
Meaſurd to find thee ; and when thou art found,
My greateſt griefe is, that thou art not loſt :
Yet loſt thou art, thy fame, thy welth are loſt,
Thy wits are loſt, and thou haſt in their ſtead,
With ſhame and cares, and miſery crownd thy head.
That Shaddow that purſues thee, fild mine eares

With ſad relation of thy wretchedneſſe,
Where is the purſe, and where my wiſhing Hat?

Andel. Where? and where? are you created Conſtable, you ſtand ſo much vpon Intergatories? the purſe is gone, let that fret you, and the Hat is gone, let that mad you: I runne thus through all trades to ouer-take them, if youle bee quiet, follow me, and helpe, if not, flie from me, and hang your ſelfe: wilt thou buy any pippins? *Exit.*

Amp. O, how I grieue, to ſee him thus tranſformd?
Yet from the circles of my iealous eyes,
He ſhall not ſtart, till he haue re-poſſeſt
Thoſe vertuous Jewels, which found once againe,
More cauſe they ne're ſhall giue me to complaine,
Their worth ſhall be conſum'd in murdring flames,
And end my griefe, his ryot, and our ſhames. *Exit.*

Enter Athelſtane, Agripyne, Montroſſe and Longauyle with hornes, Lincolne and Cornwall.

Athelſt. In ſpite of ſorcerie trie once againe,
Trie once more in contempt of all dam'd ſpels.

Agrip. Your maieſtie fights with no mortall power.
Shame and not conqueſt, hangs vpon his ſtrife.
O, touch me not, you adde but paine to paine,
The more you cut, the more they grow againe.

Lincol. Is there no art to coniure downe this ſcorne?
I ne're knew Phiſicke yet againſt the horne.

Enter Cyprus.

Athelſt. See, prince of Cyprus, thy faire Agripyne
Hath turnd her beautie to deformitie.

Cypr. Then I defie thee, Loue, vaine hopes, adew,
You haue mockt me long; in ſcorne ile now mocke you.
I came to ſee how the Lord Longauyle
Was turnd into a monſter, and I find
An obiect, which both ſtrikes me dumbe and blind.
To morrow ſhould haue beene our marriage morne,

But now my bride is ſhame, thy bridegrome ſcorne.
O tell mee yet, is there no Art, no charmes,
No deſperate Phyſicke for this deſperate wound?

Athelſt. Al meanes are tride, but no meanes can be found.

Cypr. Then England, farwell: hapleſſe maide, thy ſtars,
Through ſpitefull influence ſet our hearts at warres.
I am infor'ſt to leaue thee, and reſigne
My loue to griefe.

Enter Orleans and Galloway.

Agrip. All griefe to Agripyne.

Cypr. Adew, I would ſay more, had I a tongue
Able to helpe his maſter: mightie king,
I humbly take my leaue, to Cyprus I,
My fathers Sonne, muſt all ſuch ſhame defie. *Exit.*

Orle. So doth not Orleans, I defie all thoſe,
That loue not Agripyne, and him defie,
That dares but loue her halfe ſo well as I.
O pardon me, I haue in ſorrowes Jayle,
Beene long tormented, long this mangled boſome
Hath bled, and neuer durſt expoſe her wounds,
Till now, till now, when at thy beautious feete,
I offer loue and life, O caſt an eye
Of mercy on me, this deformed face
Cannot affright my ſoule from louing thee.

Agri. Talk not of loue, good Orleans, but of hate.

Orle. What ſentence will my loue pronounce on me?

Gall. Will Orleans then be mad? O gentle friend.

Orle. O gentle, gentle friend, I am not mad:
Hees mad, whoſe eyes on painted cheekes doe doate,
O Galloway, ſuch read beauties booke by roate.
Hees mad, that pines for want of a gay flowre,
Which fades when grief doth blaſt, or ſicknes lowre,
Which heate doth wither, and white ages froſt
Nips dead: ſuch fairenes, when tis found, tis loſt.
I am not mad, for louing Agripyne,

My loue lookes on her eyes, with eyes diuine,
I doate on the rich brightnes of her mind,
That ſacred beautie ſtrikes all other blind,
O make me happie then, ſince my deſires
Are ſet a burning by loues pureſt fires.

Athelſt. So thou wilt beare her far from England ſight
Inioy thy wiſhes.

Agrip. Locke me in ſome caue,
Where ſtaring wonders eye ſhall not be guiltie
To my abhorred lookes, and I will die
To thee, as ful of loue as miſerie.

Athelſt. I am amazde and mad, ſome ſpeckled ſoule
Lies pawnd for this in Hell, without redemption,
Some fiend deludes vs all.

Cornw. O vniuſt Fates,
Why doe you hide from vs this miſterie?

Lincol. My Lord Montroſſe, how long haue your browes worne
This faſhion? theſe two feather-ſprings of horne?

Montr. An Iriſh kerne ſold me Damaſco apples,
Some two howres ſince, and (like a credulous foole)
Hee ſwearing to me that they had this power,
To make me ſtrong in body, rich in mind,
I did beleeue his words, taſted his fruit,
And ſince haue been attirde in this diſguize.

Longa. I feare that villaine hath beguild me too.

Cornw. Nay before God he has not cozend you,
You haue it ſoundly.

Longa. Me he made beleeue,
One apple of Damaſco would inſpire
My thoughts with wiſedome, and vpon my cheekes
Would caſt ſuch beautie, that each Ladies eye,
Which lookt on me, ſhould love me preſently.

Agrip. Deſire to looke more faire, makes me more fowle,
Thoſe apples did intice my wandring eye,
To be enamord of deformitie.

Athelst. This prooues that true, which oft I haue heard in schooles,
Those that would seeme most wise, doe turne most fooles.

Lincol. Here's your best hope, none needes to hide his face,
For horned foreheads swarme in euery place.

Enter Chester bringing Andelocia like a French Doctor.

Athelst. Now Chester, what Physitions hast thou found?

Chest. Many, my leige, but none that haue true skill
To tame such wilde diseases: yet here's one,
A Doctor and a Frenchman, whome report
Of Agripynes griefe hath drawne to court.

Athelst. Cure her, and Englands treasorie shall stand,
As free for thee to vse, as rayne from heauen.

Montr. Cure me, and to thy Coffers I will send,
More gold from Scotland then thy life can spend.

Logna. Cure Longauile, and all his wealth is thine.

Andel. He Monsieur Long-villaine gra tanck you: Gra tanck your mashestie a great teale artely by my trat: where be dis Madam Princeza dat be so mush tormenta? O Jeshu: one, 2: an tree, 4 & 5, seez horne: Ha, ha, ha, pardona moy prea wid al mine art, for by my trat, me can no point shose but laugh, Ha, ha, ha, to marke how like tree bul-beggera, dey stand. Oh, by my trat and fat, di diuela be whoreson, scuruie, paltry, ill fauore knaue to mocke de Madam, and gentill-home so: Ha, ha, ha, ha.

Lincol. This Doctor comes to mocke your maiestie.

Ande. No by my trat la, but me loua musha musha merymant: Come Madam, prea-artely stand still, and letta mee feele you: dis horne, O tis prettie horne, dis be facile, easie for pull de vey, but Madame dis O be grand, grand horne, difficill, and very deepe, tis perilous, a grand Laroone. But Madam, prea be patient, we shall take it off vell.

Athe. Thrice haue we parde them off, but with freſh paine,
In compaſſe of a thought they riſe againe.

Andel. Its true, tis no eaſie mattra, to pull horne off, tis eaſie for pull on, but hard for pull off, ſome horne bee ſo good fellow, hee will ſtill inhabit in de mans pate, but tis all one for tat, I ſhall ſnap away all dis: Madam truſt dis downe into your little belly.

Agrip. Father, I am in feare to taſte his phyſicke.
Firſt let him worke experiments on thoſe.

Andel. Ile ſawce you for your infidelitie. *Aſide.*
In no place can I ſpie my wiſhing Hat.

Longa. Thou learned Frenchman, trie thy ſkill on me,
More vgly then I am, I cannot be.

Montr. Cure me, and Montroſſe welth ſhall all be thine.

Andel. Tis all one for dat: ſhall doe preſently, Madam prea marke me: Monſieur, ſhamp dis in your two ſhaps, ſo, now Monſieur Long-villaine, dis ſo: nowe dis, feare noting, tis eſhelent medicyne: ſo, now cram dis into your guts, and belly: So, now ſnap away dis whoreſon fowre diuela; Ha, ha, Is no point good?

Puts Gallowayes hornes off.

Athelſt. This is moſt ſtrange.
Waſt painefull Longauyle?

Longa. Eaſe tooke them off, and there remaines no paine.

Agrip. O trie thy ſacred Phyſicke on me.

Andel. No by my trat, tis no poſſibla, tis no poſſibla, al de mattra, all de ting, all de ſubſtance, all de medicyne, be among his and his belly: tis no poſſibla, till me prepare more.

Athelſt. Prepare it then, and thou ſhalt haue more gold
From Englands Coffers, then thy life can waſt.

Andel. I muſh buy many coſtily tings dat grow in Arabia, in Aſia, and America, by my trat tis no poſſibla, till anoder time, no point.

Agrip. There's nothing in the world, but may for gold
Be bought in England, hold your lap ile rayne
A ſhower of Angels.

Andel. Fie, fie, fie, fie, you no credit le dockature? Ha, but vel, tis all one for tat: tis no mattera for gold: Vel, vel, vel, vel, vel, me haue ſome more, prea ſay noting, ſhall bee preſently prepara for your hornes.
Shee has my purſe, and yonder lies my Hat,
Worke braines, and once more make me fortunat.
Vel, vel, vel, vel, be patient Madam, preſently, preſently, be patient, mee haue two, tree, fowre and fiue medicines for de horne: preſently Madam, ſtand you der, prea wid all mine art, ſtand you all der: and ſay noting, ſo: nor looke noting dis vey: ſo, preſently, preſently Madam, ſnip dis horne off wid de ruſhes & anoder ting by and by, by and by, by and by, prea looke none dis vey, and ſay noting. *Gets his Hat vp.*

Athelſt. Let no man ſpeake, or looke, vpon his life.
Doctor, none here ſhall rob thee of thy ſkill.

Andel. So, taka dis hand: winck now prea artely wid your two nyes: why ſo.
Would I were with my brother Ampedo.

Exit with her.

Agrip. Helpe, Father, helpe, I am hurried hence perforce.

Athelſt. Draw weapons, wheres the princeſſe, follow him,
Stay the French Doctor, ſtay the Doctor there.

Cornwall and ſome other run out, and enter preſently.

Cornw. Stay him, ſh'art who dare ſtay him? tis the diuell
In likeneſſe of a Frenchman, of a Doctor.
Looke how a raſcall Kyte having ſwept vp
A Chicken in his clawes, ſo flies this hell-hound
In th' ayre with Agripyne in his armes.

Orle. Mount euery man vpon his ſwifteſt horſe.

Flie ſeuerall waies, he cannot beare her farre.

Gall. Theſe paths weele beate.

Exeunt Gall. and Orleans.

Lincol. And this way ſhall be mine.

Cornw. This way, my Leige, ile ride.

Athelſt. And this way I :
No matter which way, to ſeeke miſerie. *Exit Athelſt.*

Loga. I can ride no way, to out-runne my ſhame.

Montr. Yes, Longauile, lets gallop after too,
Doubtleſſe this Doctor was that Iriſh diuell,
That cozend vs, the medicine which he gaue vs,
Taſted like his Damaſco villanie.
To horſe, to horſe, if we can catch this fiend,
Our forked ſhame ſhall in his heart bloud end.

Longa. O how this mads me, that all tongues in ſcorne,
Which way ſo ere I ryde, cry, Ware the horne.

Exeunt.

Enter Andelocia, with Agripyne, Ampedo and Shaddow.

Agrip. O gentle Andelocia pittie me,
Take off this infamie, or take my life.

Andel. Your life ? you thinke then that I am a true Doctor indeede, that tie vp my liuing in the knots of winding ſheetes : your life ? no, keepe your life, but deliuer your purſe : you know the theifes ſalutation, Stand & deliuer. So, this is mine, and theſe yours : Ile teach you to liue by the ſweate of other mens browes.

Shad. And to ſtriue to be fairer then God made her.

Andel. Right, Shaddow : therefore vaniſh, you haue made me turne Iugler, and crie hey-paſſe, but your hornes ſhall nct repaſſe.

Agrip. O gentle Andelocia.

And. Andelocia is a Nettle : if you touch him gently, heele ſting you.

Shad. Or a roſe, if you pul his ſweete ſtalke heele prick you.

Andel. Therefore not a word, goe, trudge to your Father: ſigh not for your purſe, money may be got by you, as well as by the little Welſhwoman in Cyprus, that had but one horne in her head, you have two; and perhaps you ſhall caſt both: as you vſe me, marke thoſe words well, as you vſe me, nay, y'are beſt flie, ile not endure one word more. Yet ſtay too, becauſe you intreate me ſo gently, and that ile make ſome amends to your Father, although I care not for any King in Chriſtendome, yet hold you, take this Apple, eate it as you goe to court, and your hornes ſhall play the cowards and fall from you,

Agrip. O gentle Andelocia.

Andel. Nay away, not a word.

Shad. Ha, ha, ha, &c. Ware hornes.

Exit Agrip. weeping.

Andel. Why doeſt thou laugh, Shaddow?

Shad. To ſee what a horne plague followes coueteouſneſſe and pride.

Amp. Brother, what miſteries lie in all this?

Andel. Trickes, Ampedo, trickes, deuiſes, and mad Herogliphickes, mirth, mirth, and melody. O, there's more muſicke in this, then all the Gammoth ares, and Sol fa Res, in the world; here's the purſe, and here's the Hat: becauſe you ſhal be ſure ile not ſtart, weare you this you know his vertue; if danger beſet you, flie & away: A ſort of broken-ſhind limping legd Jades runne hobling to ſeeke vs: Shaddow, weele for all this haue one fit of mirth more, to make vs laugh and be fat.

Shad. And when we are fat, maſter, weele doe as all gluttons doe, laugh and lie downe.

Andel. Hiet hee to my chamber, make ready my richeſt attire, ile to Court preſently.

Shad. Ile goe to Court in this attire, for apparell is but the ſhaddow of a man, but ſhaddow is the ſubſtance of his apparell. *Exit Shaddow.*

Andel. Away, away, and meete me preſently.

Amp. I had more neede to crie, away to thee.

Away, away with this wilde lunacie,
Away with ryots.

Andel. Away with your puritie, brother, y'are an Aſſe, why doth this purſe ſpit out gold but to be ſpent? why liues a man in this world, to dwell in the Suburbs of it, as you doe? Away forren ſimplicitie, away: are not eyes made to ſee faire Ladies? hearts to loue them? tongues to court them, & hands to feele them? Out your Stocke, you ſtone, you logs end: Are not legs made to daunce, and ſhall mine limp vp and downe the world after your cloth-ſtockin-heeles? you haue the Hat, keepe it, anon ile viſit your vertuous countenance againe, adew, pleaſure is my ſweete miſtris, I weare her loue in my Hat, and her ſoule in my heart: I haue ſworne to bee merry, and in ſpite of Fortune and the blacke-browd deſtinies, ile neuer be ſad. *Exit.*

Amped. Goe, foole, in ſpite of mirth, thou ſhalt be ſad.
Ile burie halfe thy pleaſures in a graue
Of hungrie flames, this fire I did ordaine
To burne both purſe and Hat: as this doth periſh,
So ſhall the other; count what good and bad
They both haue wrought, the good is to the ill,
As a ſmall Pible to a mightie hill.
Thy glorie and thy miſchiefes here ſhall burne,
Good gifts abuzde to mans confuſion turne.

Enter Longauile, and Montroſſe with Souldiers.

Longa. This is his brother: Souldiers, bind his armes.

Montr. Bind armes and legs, and hale the fiend away.

Amp. Vnciuill: wherefore muſt I taſte your ſpite?

Longa. Art thou not one of Fortunatus ſonnes?

Amped. I am, but he did neuer doe you wrong.

Longa. The diuell thy brother has, villaine, looke here.

Montr. Where is the beautious purfe and wifhing Hat?

Amped. My brother Andelocia has the purfe,
This way heele come anon to paffe to court,
Alas, that finne fhould make mens hearts fo bold,
To kill their foules for the bafe thirft of gold.
The wifhing Hat is burnt.

Montr. Burnt? Souldiers bind him.
Tortures fhall wring both hat and purfe from you,
Villaine, ile be reueng'd for that bafe fcorne,
Thy hell-hound brother clapt vpon my head.

Longa. And fo will Longauyle.
Away with him.

Montr. Drag him to yonder towre, there fhackle him,
And in a paire of Stockes, locke vp his heeles,
And bid your wifhing Cap deliuer you.
Giue vs the purfe and Hat, weele fet thee free,
Els rot to death and ftarue.

Amp. Oh tyranny, you need not fcorne the badge which you did beare:
Beafts would you be, though hornes you did not weare.

Montr. Drag hence the cur: come noble Longauyle,
One's fure, and were the other fiend as faft,
Their pride fhould coft their liues: their purfe and Hat
Shall be both ours, weele fhare them equally.

Longa. That will be fome amends for arming me.

Enter Andelocia and Shaddow after him.

Montr. Peace, Longauyle, yonder the gallant comes.

Longa. Y'are well encountred.

Andel. Thankes, Lord Longauyle.

Longa. The king expects your prefence at the court.

Andel. And thither am I going.

Shad. Pips fine, fine apples of Tamafco, ha, ha, ha.

Montr. Wert thou that Irifhman that cozend vs?

Shad. Pips fine, ha, ha, ha, no not I: not Shaddow.

Andel. Were not your Apples delicate and rare?

Longa. The worft that ere you fold; Sirs, bind him faft.

Andel. What, wil you murder me? helpe, help, fome helpe.

Shad. Helpe, helpe, helpe. *Exit Shaddow.*

Montr. Follow that Dog, and ftop his balling throate.

Andel. Villaines, what meanes this barbarous trechery?

Louga. We meane to be reueng'd for our difgrace.

Montr. And ftop the golden current of thy waft.

Andel. Murder, they murder me, O call for helpe.

Long. Thy voice is fpent in vaine, come, come, this purfe,
This wel-fpring of your prodigalitie.

Andel. Are you appointed by the king to this?

Montr. No, no, rife, fpurne him vp: know you who's this?

Andel. My brother Ampedo? Alas, what fate
Hath made thy vertues fo infortunate?

Amp. They ryot and the wrong of thefe two Lords,
Who (caufeleffe) thus do ftarue me in this prifon.

Longa. Striue not y'are beft, villaines, lift in his legs.

Andel. Traitors to honor, what doe you intend?

Longa. That ryot fhall in wretchedneffe haue end.
Queftion thy brother with what coft hees fed,
And fo afsure thou fhalt be banquetted.

Exeunt they two.

Amp. In want, in miferie, in woe and care,
Poore Ampedo his fill hath furfeted:
My want is famine, bolts my miferie,
My care and woe fhould be thy portion.

Andel. Giue me that portion, for I haue a heart

Shall ſpend it freely, and make bankrowt
The proudeſt woe that euer wet mans eye.
Care with a miſchiefe ? wherefore ſhould I care ?
Haue I rid ſide by ſide by mightie kings,
Yet be thus bridled now ? Ile teare theſe fetters.
Murder, crie murder, Ampedo, alowd.
To beare this ſcorne our Fortunes are too proud.

Amp. O folly, thou haſt powre to make fleſh glad,
When the rich ſoule in wretchedneſſe is clad.

Ande. Peace, foole, am not I Fortunes minion ?
Theſe bands are but one wrincle of her frowne,
This is her Euening maſke, her next mornes eye
Shall ouer-ſhine the Sunne in maieſtie.

Amp. But this ſad night will make an end of me.
Brother, farwell, griefe, famine, ſorrow, want,
Haue made an end of wretched Ampedo.

Andel. Where is the wiſhing Hat ?

Amp. Conſum'd in fire.

Ande. Accurſed be thoſe hands that did deſtroy it,
That would redeeme vs, did we now enioy it.

Amp. Wanton, farwel, I faint, deaths frozen hand
Congeales lifes little Riuer in my breſt.
No man before his end is truely bleſt. *Dyes.*

Andel. O miſerable, miſerable foule.
Thus a foule life makes death to looke more foule.

Enter Longauyle and Montroſſe with a halter.

Longa. Thus ſhall this golden purſe diuided be,
One day for you, another day for me.

Montr. Of daies anon, ſay, what determine you,
Shall they haue libertie, or ſhall they die ?

Long. Die ſure : and ſee, I thinke the elder's dead.

And. I, murderers, he is dead, O ſacred wiſdom,
Had Fortunatus beene enamored
Of thy celeſtiall beautie, his two ſonnes
Had ſhind like two bright Sunnes.

Longa. Pul hard, Montroſſe.

Andel. Come you to ſtrangle me? are you the hangman?
Hell-hounds y' are dam'd for this impietie.
Fortune, forgiue me, I deſerue thy hate,
My ſelfe haue made myſelfe a reprobate:
Vertue, forgiue me, for I haue tranſgreſt
Againſt thy lawes, my vowes are quite forgot,
And therefore ſhame is falne to my ſinnes lot.
Riches and knowledge are two gifts diuine.
They that abuſe them both as I haue done,
To ſhame, to beggerie, to hell muſt runne.
O conſcience hold thy ſting, ceaſe to afflict me.
Be quicke, tormentors, I deſire to die.
No death is equall to my miſerie.
Cyprus, vaine world, and Vanitie farwell.
Who builds his heauen on earth, is ſure of hell.

Lon. He 's dead: in ſome deepe vault lets throw their bodies.

Montr. Firſt let us ſee the purſe, Lord Longauyle.

Longa. Here tis, by this weele fill this towre with gold.

Montr. Frenchman, this purſe is counterfeit.

Longa. Thou lyeſt.
Scot, thou haſt cozend me, giue me the right,
Els ſhall thy boſome be my weapons graue.

Montr. Villaine, thou ſhalt not rob me of my due.

They fight: Enter Athelſtane, Agripyna, Orleans, Galloway, Cornewall, Cheſter, Lincolne, and Shaddow with weapons at one dore: Fortune, Vice, and their attendants at another dore.

All. Lay hands vpon the murderers, ſtrike them downe.

Fortune. Surrender vp this purſe for this is mine.

All. Are theſe two diuels, or ſome powers diuine?

Shad. O ſee, ſee, O my two maſters, poore Shaddowes ſubſtances; what ſhall I doe? whoſe body ſhall Shaddow now follow?

Fort. Peace, Ideot, thou ſhalt find rich heapes of fooles,
That will be proud to entertaine a Shaddow.
I charme thy babbling lips from troubling me.
You need not hold them, ſee, I ſmite them downe
Lower then hell : baſe ſoules, ſincke to your heauen.

Vice. I doe arreſt you both my priſoners.

Fort. Stand not amazde, you gods of earth, at this,
Shee that arreſteth theſe two fooles is Vice,
They haue broke Vertues laws, Vice is her ſerieant,
Her Jayler and her executioner.
Looke on thoſe Cypriots, Fortunatus ſonnes,
They and their Father were my minions,
My name is Fortune.

All. O dread deitie.

Fort. Kneele not to me : if Fortune liſt to frowne,
You need not fal downe, for ſheele ſpurne you downe,
Arise, but fooles, on you ile triumph thus.
What haue you gaind by being couetous ?
This prodigall purſe did Fortunes bounteous hand
Beſtow on them, their ryots made them poore,
And ſet theſe markes of miſerable death,
On all their pride, the famine of baſe gold
Hath made your ſoules to murders hands be ſold,
Onely to be cald rich. But Ideots ſee
The vertues to be fled, Fortune hath cauſd it ſo,
Thoſe that will all deuowre, muſt all forgoe.

Athelſt. Moſt ſacred Goddeſſe.

Fortune. Peace, you flatterer.
Thy tongue but heapes more vengeance on thy head.
Fortune is angrie with thee, in thee burnes
A greedie couetous fire, in Agripyne
Pride like a Monarch reuels, and thoſe ſinnes
Haue lead you blind-fold to your former ſhames,
But Vertue pardond you, and ſo doth Fortune.

Athelſt. and Agrip. All thankes to both your ſacred deities.

Fort. As for theſe Mettall-eaters, theſe baſe thieues,
Who rather then they would be counted poore,

Will dig through hell for gold, you were forgiuen
By Vertues generall pardon ; her broade ſeale
Gaue you your liues, when ſhee tooke off your hornes.
Yet hauing ſcarce one foote out of the Jayle,
You tempt damnation by more deſperate meanes,
You both are mortall, and your paines ſhall ring
Through both your eares, to terrifie your ſoules,
As pleaſe the Judgement of this mortall king.

Athelſt. Faire Empreſſe of the world, ſince you reſigne
Your power to me, this ſentence ſhall be mine,
Thou ſhalt be torturd on a wheele to death,
Thou with wild horſes ſhalt be quartered.

Vice. Ha, ha, weake Judge, weake iudgement, I reuerſe
That ſentence, for they are my priſoners,
Embalme the bodies of thoſe Cypriots,
And honour them with princely buriall,
For thoſe doe as you pleaſe, but for theſe two,
I kiſſe you both, I loue you, y' are my minions.
Untie their bands, Vice doth repriue you both,
I ſet you free.

Both. Thankes, gracious deitie.

Vice. Be gon, but you in libertie ſhall find
More bondage then in chaines, fooles, get you hence,
Both wander with tormented conſcience.

Longa. O horrid Judgement, thats the hell indeede.

Mon. Come, come, our death ne're ends if conſcience bleede.

Both. O miſerable, miſerable men. *Exeunt.*

Fortune. Fortune triumphes at this, yet to appeare,
All like my ſelfe, that which from thoſe I tooke,
King Athelſtane I will beſtow on thee,
And in it the old vertue I infuſe :
But, king, take heede how thou my gifts doeſt vſe.
England ſhall ne're be poore, if England ſtriue,
Rather by vertue, then by wealth to thriue.

Enter Vertue, crownd: Nymphes and kings attending on her, crownd with Olive branches and lawrels, muſicke ſounding.

Vice. Vertue? alas good ſoule, ſhee hides her head.

Vert. What enuious tongue ſaid, Vertue hides her head?

Vice. Shee that will driue thee into baniſhment.

Fort. Shee that hath conquerd thee: how dar'ſt thou come,
Thus trickt in gawdy Feathers, and thus garded,
Which crowned kings and Muſes, when thy foe
Hath trod thus on thee, and now triumphes ſo?
Where 's vertuous Ampedo? See, hees her ſlaue,
For following thee this recompence they haue.

Vert. Is Ampedo her ſlaue? why thats my glorie.
The Idiots cap I once wore on my head,
Did figure him, thoſe that (like him) doe muffle
Vertue in clouds, and care not how ſhee ſhine,
Ile make their glorie like to his decline:
He made no vſe of me, but like a miſer,
Lockt up his wealth in ruſtie barres of ſloth:
His face was beautifull, but wore a maſke,
And in the worlds eyes ſeemd a Blackamore.
So periſh they that ſo keepe vertue poore.

Vice. Thou art a foole to ſtriue, I am more ſtrong,
And greater then thy ſelfe, then Vertue flie,
And hide thy face, yeeld me the victorie.

Vert. Is Vice higher then Vertue? thats my glorie,
The higher that thou art, thou art more horrid,
The world will loue me for my comlyneſſe.

Fortu. Thine owne ſelfe loues thy ſelfe: why on the heads
Of Agripyne, Montroſſe and Longauyle,
(Engliſh, Scot, French) did Vice clap vgly hornes,
But to approue that Engliſh, French and Scot,
And all the world els, kneele and honour Vice,

But in no Countrie, Vertue is of price ?

Vert. Yes, in all Countries Vertue is of price,
In euery kingdome ſome diuiner breſt
Is more enamord of me then the reſt.
Haue Engliſh, Scot, and French bowd knees to thee ?
Why that's my glorie too, for by their ſhame,
Men will abhor thee and adore my name.
Fortune, thou art too weake, Vice th' art a foole,
To fight with me, I ſuffred you awhile,
T' ecclips my brightnes, but I now will ſhine,
And make you ſweare your beautie's baſe to mine.

Fort. Thou art too inſolent, ſee here 's a court
Of mortall Judges, lets by them be tride,
Which of vs three ſhall moſt be deifide.

Vice. I am content.

Fort. And I.

Vert. So am not I.
My Judge ſhall be your ſacred deitie.

Vice. O miſerable me, I am vndon.

Exit Vice and her traine.

All. O ſtop the horrid monſter.

Vert. Let her runne.
Fortune, who conquers now ?

Fort. Vertue, I ſee,
Thou wilt triumph both ouer her and me.

All. Empreſſe of heauen and earth.

Fort. Why doe you mocke me ?
Kneele not to me, to her tranſfer your eyes,
There ſits the Queene of Chance, I bend my knees,
Lower then yours : dread goddeſſe, tis moſt meete,
That Fortune fall downe at thy conqu'ring feete.
Thou ſacred Empreſſe that commandſt the Fates,
Forgiue what I haue to thy handmaid don,
And at thy Chariot wheeles Fortune ſhall run,
And be thy captiue and to thee reſigne
All powers which heau'ns large Patent haue made mine.

Vert. Fortune th'art vanquisht: sacred deitie,
O now pronounce who winnes the victorie,
And yet that sentence needes not, since alone,
Your vertuous presence Vice hath ouer-throwne,
Yet to confirme the conquest on your side,
Looke but on Fortunatus and his sonnes
Of all the welth those gallants did possesse,
Onely poore Shaddow is left comfortlesse,
Their glorye's faded and their golden pride.

Sha. Onely poore Shaddow tels how poore they died.

Vert. All that they had, or mortall men can haue,
Sends onely but a Shaddow from the graue.
Vertue alone liues still, and liues in you,
I am a counterfeit, you are the true,
I am a Shaddow, at your feete I fall,
Begging for these, and these, my selfe and all.
All these that thus doe kneele before your eyes,
Are shaddowes like my selfe, dred Nymph it lyes
In you to make vs substances. O doe it,
Vertue I am sure you loue, shee woes you to it.
I read a verdict in your Sun-like eyes,
And this it is: Vertue the victorie.

All. All loudly cry, Vertue the victorie.

Vert. Vertue the victorie: for ioy of this,
Those selfe same himnes which you to Fortune sung
Let them be now in Vertues honour rung.

The Song.

Vertue smiles: crie hollyday,
Dimples on her cheekes doe dwell,
Vertue frownes, crie wellada,
Her loue is Heauen, her hate is Hell.
Since heau'n and hell obey her power,
Tremble when her eyes doe lowre.

Since heau'n and hell her power obey,
Where ſhee ſmiles, crie hollyday.
Hollyday with ioy we crie,
And bend, and bend, and merily,
Sing hymnes to vertues deitie :
Sing hymnes to Vertues deitie.

As they all offer to goe in, Enter the two old men.

THE EPILOGUE AT COURT.

1. NAy ſtay, poore pilgrims, when I entred firſt
The circle of this bright celeſtiall Sphære,
I wept for ioy, now I could weepe for feare.
2. I feare we all like mortall men ſhall proue
Weake (not in loue) but in expreſsing loue.
1. Let euery one beg once more on his knee,
One pardon for himſelfe, and one for mee,
For I intic'd you hither : O deere Goddeſſe,
Breathe life in our nombd ſpirits with one ſmile,
And from this cold earth, we with liuely ſoules
Shal riſe like men (new-borne) and make heau'n ſound
With Hymnes ſung to thy name, and praiers that we
May once a yeere ſo oft enioy this ſight,
Til theſe yong boyes change their curld locks to white,
And when gray-winged Age ſits on their heads,
That ſo their children may ſupply their Steads,
And that heau'ns great Arithmetician,
(Who in the Scales of Nomber weyes the world)
May ſtill to fortie two, and one yeere more,
And ſtil adde one to one, that went before,
And multiply fowre tennes by many a ten :
To this I crie Amen.
All. Amen, amen.
1. Good night (deere miſtris) thoſe that wiſh thee harme,
Thus let them ſtoope vnder deſtructions arme.
All. Amen, Amen, Amen. *Exeunt.*

FINIS.

Tho. Dekker.

Satiro-maſtix.

OR

The vntruſſing of the Humo-
rous Poet.

As it hath bin preſented publikely,
by the Right Honorable, the Lord Cham-
berlaine his Seruants; and priuately, by the
Children of Paules.

By *Thomas Dekker.*

Non recito cuiquam niſi Amicis *idq; coactus.*

LONDON,
Printed for *Edward VVhite*, and are to bee
ſolde at his ſhop, neere the little North doore of Paules
Church, at the ſigne of the Gun. 1602.

N

Dramatis personæ.

1. William Rufus.
2. Sir Walter Terill.
3. Sir Rees ap Vaughan.
4. S. Quintilian Shorthoſe.
5. Sir Adam Prickshaft.
6. Blunt.
7. Criſpinus.
8. Demetrius Fannius.
9. Tucca.
10. Horace.
11. Aſinius Bubo.
12. Peter Flash.
13. Cæleſtine.
14. Miſtris Miniuer.
15. Ladies.

Ad Detractorem.

Non potes in Nugas dicere plura meas,
Ipſe ego quam dixi.—Qui ſe mirantur, in illos
Virus habe : Nos hæc nouimus eſse nihil.

To the World.

WOrld, *J was once reſolu'd to bee round with thee, becauſe J know tis thy faſhion to bee round with euery bodie*: *but the winde ſhifting his point, the Veine turn'd*: *yet becauſe thou wilt ſit as Judge of all matters (though for thy labour thou wear'ſt* Midaſſes *eares, and art* Monſtrum horrendum, informe : Ingens cui lumen ademptum ; *whoſe great* Poliphemian *eye is put out) J care not much if I make deſcription (before thy* Vniuerſality) *of that terrible* Poetomachia, *lately commenc'd betweene* Horace the ſecond, *and a band of leane-witted* Poetaſters. *They haue bin at high wordes, and ſo high, that the ground could not ſerue them, but (for want of* Chopins) *haue ſtalk't vpon Stages.*

Horace *hal'd his* Poetaſters *to the Barre, the* Poetaſters *vntruſſ'd* Horace : *how worthily eyther, or how wrongfully,* (World) *leaue it to the Jurie*: Horace (*queſtionles*) *made himſelfe beleeue, that his* Burgonian wit *might deſperately challenge all commers, and that none durſt take vp the foyles againſt him*: *It's likely, if he had not ſo beleiu'd, he had not bin ſo deceiu'd, for hee was anſwer'd at his owne weapon*: *And if before* Apollo *himſelfe* (*who is* Coronator Poetarum) *an*

Inquiſition *ſhould be taken touching this lamentable merry murdering of Innocent Poetry : all mount* Helicon *to* Bun-hill, *it would be found on the* Poetaſters *ſide* Se defendendo. *Notwithſtanding the Doctors think otherwiſe. I meete one, and he runnes full Butt at me with his Satires hornes, for that in vntruſsing* Horace *J did onely whip his fortunes, and condition of life, where the more noble* Reprehenſion *had bin of his* mindes Deformitie, *whoſe greatnes if his* Criticall Lynx *had with as narrow eyes, obſeru'd in himſelfe, as it did little ſpots vpon others, without all diſputation :* Horace *would not haue left* Horace *out of* Euery man in's Hvmour. *His fortunes? why does not he taxe that onely in others? Read his* Arraignement *and ſee. A ſecond Cat-a-mountaine mewes, and calles me Barren, becauſe my braines could bring foorth no other* Stigmaticke *than* Tucca, *whome* Horace *had put to making, and begot to my hand : but I wonder what language* Tucca *would haue ſpoke, if honeſt Capten* Hannam *had bin borne without a tongue? Jſt not as lawfull then for mee to imitate* Horace, *as* Horace Hannam? *Beſides, If J had made an oppoſition of any other new-minted fellow, (of what Teſt ſo euer) hee had bin out-fac'd, and out-weyed by a ſettled former approbation : neyther was it much improper to ſet the ſame dog vpon* Horace, *whom* Horace *had ſet to worrie others.*

I could heere (eeuen with the feather of my pen) wipe off other ridiculous imputations : but my beſt way to anſwer them, is to laugh at them : onely thus much I proteſt (and ſweare by the diuineſt part of true Poeſie) that (howſoeuer the limmes of my naked lines may bee and I know haue bin, tortur'd on the racke) they are free from conſpiring the least disgrace to any man, but onely to our new Horace; *neyther should this ghost of* Tucca, *haue walkt vp and downe Poules Church-yard, but that hee was raiz'd vp (in print) by newe* Exorcismes. World, *if thy* Hugenes *will beleiue this*: *doe, if not, J care not*: *for J dedicate my booke not to thy* Greatnes, *but to the* Greatnes of thy scorne: *Defying which, let that mad Dog* Detraction *bite till his teeth bee worne to the stumps*: Enuy *feede thy Snakes so fat with poyson till they burst*: World, *let all thy Adders shoote out their* Hidra-headed-forked *Stinges,* Ha, ha, Nauci; *if none will take my part, (as I desire none) yet I thanke thee (thou true* Venusian Horace*) for these good wordes thou giu'st me*: Populus me sibylat at mihi plaudo. World *farewell.*

Malim Conuiuis quàm placuisse Cocis.

The Vntrussing of the Humo-
rous Poet.

Enter two Gentlewomen strewing of flowers.

1. COme bedfellow come, strew apace, strew, strew : in good troth tis pitty that these flowers must be trodden vnder feete as they are like to bee anon.

2. Pitty, alacke pretty heart, thou art sorry to see any good thing fall to the ground : pitty ? no more pitty, then to see an Innocent Mayden-head deliuered vp to the ruffling of her new-wedded husband. Beauty is made for vse, and hee that will not vse a sweete soule well, when she is vnder his fingers, I pray *Venus* he may neuer kisse a fair and a delicate, soft, red, plump-lip.

1. Amen, and that's torment enough.

2. Pitty ? come foole, fling them about lustily ; flowers neuer dye a sweeter death, than when they are smoother'd to death in a Louers bosome, or else paue the high wayes, ouer which these pretty, simpring, setting things, call'd brides, must trippe.

1. I pray thee tell mee, why doe they vse at weddings to furnish all places thus, with sweete hearbes and flowers ?

2. One reason is, because tis —— ô a most sweet thing to lye with a man.

1. I think tis a O more more more more sweet to lye with a woman.

2. I warrant all men are of thy minde: another reaſon is, becauſe they ſticke like the ſcutchions of madame chaſtity, on the ſable ground, weeping in their ſtalkes, and wincking with theyr yellow-ſunke eyes, as loathe to beholde the lamentable fall of a Maydenhead: what ſenceleſs thing in all the houſe, that is not nowe as melancholy, as a new ſet-vp Schoolemaſter ?

1. Troth I am.

2. Troth I thinke thou mournſt, becauſe th'aſt miſt thy turne, I doe by the quiuer of *Cupid*: you ſee the torches melt themſelues away in teares: the inſtruments weare theyr heart ſtringes out for ſorrow: and the Siluer Ewers weepe moſt pittifull Roſewater: fiue or ſixe payre of the white innocent wedding gloues, did in my ſight chooſe rather to be torne in peeces than to be drawne on; and looke this Roſemary, (a fatall hearbe) this dead-mans noſe-gay, has crept in amongſt theſe flowers to decke th' inuiſible coarſe of the Bride's Maydenhead, when (oh how much do we poore wenches ſuffer) about eleuen or twelue, or one a clock at midnight at furtheſt, it deſcends to purgatory, to giue notice that *Cæleſtine* (hey ho) will neuer come to lead Apes in hell.

1. I ſee by thy ſighing thou wilt not.

2. If I had as many Mayden-heads, as I have hayres on my head, Ide venture them all rather then to come into ſo hot a place; prethy ſtrew thou, for my little armes are weary.

1. I am ſure thy little tongue is not.

2. No faith that's like a woman bitten with fleas, it neuer lyes ſtil: fye vpont, what a miſerable thing tis to be a noble Bride, there's ſuch delayes in riſing, in fitting gownes, in tyring, in pinning Rebatoes, in poaking, in dinner, in ſupper, in Reuels, & laſt of all in curſing the poore nodding fidlers, for keeping Miſtris Bride ſo long vp from ſweeter Reuels; that, oh I could neuer endure to put it vp without much bickering.

1. Come th'art an odde wench, hark, harke, muſicke ? nay then the Bride's vp.

2. Is ſhe vp ? nay then I ſee ſhe has been downe : Lord ha mercy on vs, we women fall and fall ſtill, and when we haue husbands we play upon them like Virginall Jackes, they muſt ryſe and fall to our humours, or elſe they'l neuer get any good ſtraines of muſicke out of vs ; but come now, haue at it for a mayden-head. *ſtrew.*

As they ſtrew, enter Sir Quintilian Shorthoſe *with* Peeter Flaſh *and two or three ſeruingmen, with lights.*

Sir quin. Come knaues, night begins to be like my ſelfe, an olde man ; day playes the theefe and ſteales vpon vs ; O well done wenches, well done, well done, you haue couered all the ſtony way to church with flowers, tis well, tis well, ther's an Embleame too, to be made out of theſe flowers and ſtones, but you are honeſt wenches, in, in, in.

2. When we come to your yeares, we ſhal learne what honeſty is, come pew-fellow. *Exeunt.*

Sir quin. Is the muſicke come yet ? ſo much to do ! Iſt come ?

Omnes. Come ſir.

Sir quin. Haue the merry knaues pul'd their fiddle caſes ouer their inſtruments eares ?

Flaſh. As ſoone as they entred our gates, the noyſe went, before they came nere the great Hall, the faint hearted villiacoes ſounded at leaſt thrice.

Sir quin. Thou ſhouldſt haue reuiu'd them with a Cup of burnt wine and ſugar ; ſirra, you, horſe-keeper, goe, bid them curry theyr ſtrings : Is my daughter vp yet ?

Flaſh. Vp ſir ? ſhe was ſeene vp an houre agoe.

Sir quin. Shee's an early ſturrer, ah ſirra.

Flaſh. Shee'l be a late ſturrer ſoone at night ſir.

Sir Quint. Goe too *Peeter Flaſh*, you haue a good

ſodaine flaſh of braine, your wittes husky, and no maruaile, for tis like one of our Comedians beardes, ſtill ith ſtubble: about your buſines and looke you be nymble to flye from the wine, or the nymble wine will catch you by the noſe.

Flaſh. If youre wine play with my noſe Sir, Ile knocke's coxcombe.

Sir quin Doe *Peeter*, and weare it for thy labour; Is my Sonne in Law Sir *Walter Terell* ready yet?

Omnes. Ready Sir. *Exit another.*

Sir Quin. One of you attend him: Stay *Flaſh*, where's the note of the gueſtes you haue inuited?

Flaſh. Here Sir, Ile pull all your gueſtes out of my boſome; the men that will come, I haue croſt, but all the Gentlewomen haue at the tayle of the laſt letter a pricke, becauſe you may read them the better.

Sir Quin. My ſpectacles, lyght, lyght, knaues: Sir *Adam Prickſhaft*, thou haſt croſt him, heele come.

Flaſh. I had much a doe ſir, to draw Sir *Adam Prickeſhaft* home, becauſe I tolde him twas early, but heele come.

Sir quint. Juſtice *Crop*, what will he come?

Flaſh. He took phiſicke yeſterday ſir.

Sir quint. Oh then *Crop* cannot come.

Flaſh. O Lord yes, ſir yes, twas but to make more roome in his Crop for your good cheare, *Crop* will come.

Sir quint. Widdow *Mineuer.*

Flaſh. Shee's prickt you ſee ſir, and will come.

Sir quint. Sir *Vaughan ap Rees*, oh hee's croſt twiſe, ſo, ſo, ſo, then all theſe Ladyes, that fall downewardes heere, will come I ſee, and all theſe Gentlemen that ſtand right before them.

Flaſh. All wil come.

Sir quint. Well ſayd, heere, wryte them out agen, and put the men from the women; and *Peeter*, when we are at Church bring wine and cakes, be light & nimble good *Flaſh*, for your burden will be but light.

Enter ſir Adam *a light before him.*

Sir Adam Prickeſhaft. God morrow, god morrow: goe, in, in, in, to the Bridegroome, taſte a cup of burnt wine this morning, twill make you flye the better all the day after,

Sir Adam. You are au early ſtyrrer Sir *Quintilian Shorthoſe.*

Sir qui. I am ſo, it behoues me at my daughters wedding, in, in, in; fellow put out thy torch, and put thy ſelfe into my buttery, the torch burnes ill in thy hand, the wine will burne better in thy belly, in, in.

Flaſh. Ware there, roome for Sir *Adam Prickeſhaft*: your Worſhip— *Exit.*

Enter Sir Vaughan *and Miſtris* Mineuer.

Sir quin. Sir *Vaughan* and Widdow *Mineuer*, welcome, welcome, a thouſand times: my lips Miſtris Widdow ſhall bid you God morrow, in, in, one to the Bridegroome, the other to the Bride.

Sir Vaughan. Why then Sir *quintilian Shorthoſe*, I will ſtep into miſtris Bride, and Widdow *Mineuer*, ſhall goe vpon M. Bridegroome.

Mineu. No pardon, for by my truely Sir *Vaughan*, Ile ha no dealings with any M. Bridegroomes.

Sir quin. In widdow in, in honeſt knight in.

Sir Vaug. I will vſher you miſtris widdow.

Flaſh. Light there for Sir *Vaughan*; your good Worſhip—

Sir Vaug. Drinke that ſhilling Ma. *Peeter Flaſh*, in your guttes and belly.

Fla. Ile not drinke it downe ſir, but Ile turne it into that which ſhall run downe, oh merrily!

Exit Sir Vaughan.

Enter Blunt, Criſpinus, Demetrius, *and others with Ladies, lights before them.*

Sir quin. God morrow to theſe beauties, and Gentlemen, that haue Vshered this troope of Ladyes to my daughters wedding, welcome, welcome all; musick? nay then the bridegroome's comming, where are these knaues heere?

Flash. All here sir.

Enter Terill, Sir Adam, Sir Vaughan, Celestine, Mineuer, *and other Ladies and attendants with lights.*

Teri. Good morrow Ladies and fayre troopes of gallants, that haue depos'd the drowzy King of sleep, *to Crowne our* traine with your rich presences,
I salute you all;
Each one share thanks from thanks in generall.

Cris. God morrow M. Bride-groome, mistris Bride.

Omnes. God morrow M. Bride-groome.

Ter. Gallants I shal intreate you to prepare,
For Maskes and Reuels to defeate the night,
Our Soueraigne will in person grace our marriage.

Sir quin. What will the king be heer?

Ter. Father he will.

Sir quin. Where be these knaues? More Rosemary and gloues, gloues, gloues: choose Gentlemen; Ladyes put on soft skins vpon the skin of softer hands; so, so: come mistris Bride take you your place, the olde men first, and then the Batchelors; Maydes with the Bride, Widdows and wiues together, the priest's at Church, tis time that we march thether.

Ter. Deare *Blunt* at our returne from Church, take paines to step to *Horace*, for our nuptiall songs; now Father when you please.

Sir quin. Agreed, set on, come good Sir *Vaughan*, must we lead the way?

Sir Vau. *Peeter* you goe too fast for Mistris pride: so, gingerly, gingerly; I muse why Sir *Adam Pricke-shaft* sticks so short behinde?

Sir quin. He follows close, not too fast, holde vp knaues,

Thus we lead youth to church, they vs to graues.

Exeunt.

Horrace ſitting in a ſtudy behinde a Curtaine, a candle by him burning, bookes lying confuſedly: to himſelfe.

Hor. To thee whoſe fore-head ſwels with Roſes,
Whoſe moſt haunted bower
Giues life & ſent to euery flower,
Whoſe moſt adored name incloſes,
Things abſtruſe, deep and diuine,
Whoſe yellow treſſes ſhine,
Bright as *Eoan* fire.
O me thy Prieſt inſpire.
For I to thee and thine immortall name,
In—in—in golden tunes,
For I to thee and thine immortall name—
In—ſacred raptures flowing, flowing, ſwimming, ſwimming:
In ſacred raptures ſwimming,
Immortal name, game, dame, tame, lame, lame, lame,
Pux, hath, ſhame, proclaime, oh—
In ſacred raptures flowing, will proclaime, not—
O me thy Prieſt inſpyre!
For I to thee and thine immortall name,
In flowing numbers fild with ſpright and flame,
Good, good, in flowing numbers fild with ſpright & flame.

Enter Aſinius Bubo.

Aſini. *Horace*, *Horace*, my ſweet ningle, is alwayes in labour when I come, the nine Muſes be his midwiues I pray *Jupiter*: Ningle.

Ho. In flowing numbers fild with ſpright and flame,
To thee.

Aſini. To me? I pledge thee ſweet Ningle, by *Bacchus* quaffing boule, I thought th' adſt drunke to me.

Hor. It must haue been in the deuine lycour of *Pernassus*, then in which, I know you would scarce haue pledg'd me, but come sweet roague, sit, sit, sit.

Asini. Ouer head and eares ysaith? I haue a sacke-full of newes for thee, thou shalt plague some of them, if God send vs life and health together.

Hor. Its no matter, empty thy sacke anon, but come here first honest roague, come.

Asini. Ist good, Ist good, pure *Helicon* ha?

Hor. Dam me ist be not the best that euer came from me, if I have any iudgement, looke sir, tis an *Epithalamium* for Sir *Walter Terrels* wedding, my braines haue giuen assault to it but this morning.

Asin. Then I hope to see them flye out like gun powder ere night.

Hor. Nay good roague marke, for they are the best lynes that euer I drew.

Asin. Heer's the best leafe in England, but on, on, Ile but tune this Pipe.

Hor. Marke, *to thee whose fore-head swels with Roses.*

Asin. O sweet, but will there be no exceptions taken, because fore-head and swelling comes together?

Hor. Push away, away, its proper, besides tis an elegancy to say the fore head swels.

Asin. Nay an't be proper, let it stand for Gods loue.

Hor. Whose most haunted bower,
Giues life and sent to euery flower,
Whose most adored name incloses,
Things abstruse, deep and diuine.
Whose yellow tresses shine,
Bright as *Eoan* fire.

Asini. O pure, rich, ther's heate in this, on, on.

Hor. Bright as *Eoan* fire,
O me thy Priest inspire!
For I to thee and thine immortall name . . . *marke this.*
In flowing numbers fild with spryte and flame.

Asini. I mary, ther's spryte and flame in this.

Hor. A pox, a this Tobacco.

Asin. Wod this case were my last, if I did not marke, nay all's one, I haue always a consort of Pypes about mee, myne Ingle is all fire and water; I markt, by this Candle (which is none of Gods Angels) I remember, you started backe at sprite and flame.

Hor. For I to thee and thine immortall name,
In flowing numbers fild with sprite and flame,
To the Loues mightiest King,
Himen ô *Himen*, does our chase muse sing.

Asin. Ther's musicke in this;

Hor. Marke now deare *Asinius.*
Let these virgins quickly see thee,
Leading out the Bride,
Though theyr blushing cheekes they hide,
Yet with kisses will they see thee,
To vntye theyr Virgin zone,
They grieue to lye alone.

Asini. So doe I by *Venus.*

Hor. Yet with kisses wil they see thee, my Muse has marcht (deare roague) no farder yet: but how ist? how ist? nay prethee good *Asinius* deale plainly, doe not flatter me, come, how?—

Asin. If I haue any iudgement:

Hor. Nay look you Sir, and then follow a troope of other rich and labour'd conceipts, oh the end shall be admirable! but how ist sweet *Bubo,* how, how?

Asin. If I have any Iudgement, tis the best stuffe that euer dropt from thee.

Hor. You ha seene my Acrosticks?

Asi. Ile put vp my pypes and then Ile see any thing.

Hor. Th'ast a Coppy of mine Odes to, hast not Bubo?

Asi. Your odes? O that which you spoke by word a mouth at th' ordinary, when Musco the gull cryed Mew at it:

Hor. A pox on him poore braineles Rooke: and you remember, I tolde him his wit lay at pawne with

O

his new Sattin ſute, and both would be loſt, for not fetching home by a day.

Aſi. At which he would faine ha bluſht but that his painted cheekes would not let him.

Hor. Nay ſirra the Palinode, which I meane to ſtitch to my Reuels, ſhall be the beſt and ingenious piece that euer I ſwet for; ſtay roague, Ile fat thy ſpleane and make it plumpe with laughter.

Aſi. Shall I? fayth Ningle, ſhall I ſee thy ſecrets?

Hor. Puh my friends.

Aſi. But what fardle's that? what fardle's that?

Hor. Fardle, away, tis my packet; heere lyes intomb'd the loues of Knights and Earles, heere tis, heere tis, heere tis, Sir Walter Terils letter to me, and my anſwere to him: I no ſooner opened his letter, but there appeared to me three glorious Angels, whome I ador'd, as ſubiectes doe their Soueraignes: the honeſt knight Angles for my acquaintance, with ſuch golden baites—but why dooſt laugh my good roague? how is my anſwere, prethee, how, how?

Aſi. Anſwere, as God iudge me Ningle, for thy wit thou mayſt anſwer any Iuſtice of peace in England I warrant; thou writ'ſt in a moſt goodly big hand too, I like that, I readſt as leageably as ſome that haue bin ſau'd by their neck-verſe.

Hor. But how doſt like the Knights inditing?

Aſi. If I haue any iudgement; a pox ont, heer's worſhipfull lynes indeed, heer's ſtuffe: but ſirra Ningle, of what faſhion is this knights wit, of what blocke?

Hor. Why you ſee; wel, wel, an ordinary Ingenuity, a good wit for a knight, you know how, before God I am haunted with ſome the moſt pittyfull dry gallants.

Aſini. Troth ſo I think; good peeces of lantſkip, ſhew beſt a far off.

Hor. I, I, I, excellent ſumpter horſes, carry good cloaths; but honeſt roague, come, what news, what newes abroad? I haue heard a the horſes walking a' the top of Paules.

Asi. Ha ye? why thê Captain Tucca rayles vpon you moſt prepoſterouſly behinde your backe, did you not heare him?

Ho. A pox upon him.: by the white & ſoft hand of *Minerua*, Ile make him the moſt ridiculous: dam me if I bring not's humor ath ſtage: &—ſcuruy lymping tongu'd captaine, poore greaſie buffe Ierkin, hang him: tis out of his Element to traduce me: I am too well ranckt *Aſinius* to bee ſtab'd with his dudgion wit: ſirra, Ile compoſe an Epigram vpon him, ſhall goe thus—

Asi. Nay I ha more news, ther's Criſpinus & his Iorneyman Poet Demetrius Faninus too, they ſweare they'll bring your life & death vpon'th ſtage like a Bricklayer in a play.

Hor. Bubo they muſt preſſe more valiant wits than theyr own to do it: me ath ſtage? ha, ha. Ile ſtarue theire poore copper-lace work maſters, that dare play me: I can bring (& that they quake at) a prepar'd troope of gallants, who for my ſake ſhal diſtaſte euery vnſalted line, in their fly-blowne Comedies.

Asi. Nay that's certaine, ile bring 100 gallants of my ranke.

Hor. That ſame Criſpinus is the ſillieſt Dor, and Faninus the ſlighteſt cob-web-lawne peece of a Poet, oh God!
Why ſhould I care what euery Dor doth buz
In credulous eares, it is a crowne to me,
That the beſt iudgements can report me wrong'd.

Asi. I am one of them that can report it:

Hor. I thinke but what they are, and am not moou'd.
The one a light voluptuous Reueler,
The other, a ſtrange arrogating puffe,
Both impudent, and arrogant enough.

Asin. S'lid do not Criticus Reuel in theſe lynes, ha Ningle ha? *Knocking.*

Hor. Yes, they're mine owne.

Criſ. Horrace.

Dem. Flaccus.

Criſ. Horrace, not vp yet ;

Hor. Peace, tread ſoftly, hyde my Papers ; who's this ſo early ?
Some of my rookes, ſome of my guls ?

Criſ. Horrace, Flaccus.

Hor. Who's there ? ſtray, treade ſoftly : *Wat Terill* on my life : who's there ? my gowne ſweete roague, ſo, come vp, come in.

Enter Criſpinus and Demetrius.

Criſ. God morrow Horrace.

Hor. O, God ſaue you gallants.

Criſ. *Aſinius* Bubo well met.

Aſin. Nay, I hope ſo Criſpinus, yet I was ſicke a quarter of a yeare a goe of a vehement great tooth-atch : a pox ont, it bit me vilye, as God ſa me la I knew twas you by your knocking ſo ſoone as I ſaw you ; Demetrius Fannius, wil you take a whiffe this morning ? I haue tickling geare now, heer's that will play with your noſe, and a pype of mine owne ſcowring too.

Dem. I, and a Hodgſhead too of your owne, but that will neuer be ſcowred cleane I feare.

Aſin. I burnt my pype yeſternight, and twas neuer vſde ſince, if you will tis at your ſeruice gallants, and Tobacco too, tis right pudding I can tell you ; a Lady or two, tooke a pype full or two at my hands, and praizde it for the Heauens, ſhall I fill Flannius ?

Dem. I thanke you good Aſinius for your loue,
I ſildome take that Phiſicke, tis enough
Hauing ſo much foole to take him in ſnuffe.

Hor. Good Bubo read ſome booke, and giue vs leaue. . . .

Aſ. Leaue haue you deare Ningle, marry for reading any book Ile take my death vpont (as my Ningle ſayes) tis out of my Element : no faith, ever ſince I felt one hit me ith teeth that the greateſt Clarkes are not the wiſeſt men, could I abide to goe to Schoole, I was at *As in preſenti* and left there: yet becauſe Ile not be counted a worſe foole then I am, Ile turne ouer a new leafe.

Aſinius *reads and takes Tobacco.*

Hor. To ſee my fate, that when I dip my pen
In diſtilde Roſes, and doe ſtruie to dreine,
Out of myne Inke all gall; that when I wey
Each ſillable I write or ſpeake, becauſe
Mine enemies with ſharpe and ſearching eyes
Looke through & through me, caruing my poore labours
Like an Anotomy: Oh heauens to ſee,
That when my lines are meaſur'd out as ſtraight
As even Paralels, tis ſtrange that ſtill,
Still ſome imagine they are drawne awry.
The error is not mine, but in theyr eye,
That cannot take proportions.

Criſ. Horrace, Horrace,
To ſtand within the ſhot of galling tongues,
Proues not your gilt, for could we write on paper,
Made of theſe turning leaues of heauen, the cloudes,
Or ſpeake with Angels tongues: yet wiſe men know,
That ſome would ſhake the head, tho Saints ſhould ſing,
Some ſnakes muſt hiſſe, becauſe they 're borne with ſtings.

Hor. Tis true.

Criſ. Doe we not ſee fooles laugh at heauen? and mocke
The Makers workmanſhip; be not you grieu'd
If that which you molde faire, vpright and ſmooth,
Be ſkrwed awry, made crooked, lame and vile,
By racking coments, and calumnious tongues,
So to be bit it rankcles not: for innocence
May with a feather bruſh off the fouleſt wrongs.
But when your daſtard wit will ſtrike at men
In corners, and in riddles folde the vices
Of your beſt friends, you muſt not take to heart,

If they take off all gilding from their pilles,
And onely offer you the bitter Coare.

Hor. Crispinus.

Cri. Say that you haue not sworne vnto your Paper,
To blot her white cheekes with the dregs and bottome
Of your friends priuate vices : say you sweare
Your loue and your allegiance to bright vertue
Makes you descend so low, as to put on
The Office of an Executioner,
Onely to strike off the swolne head of sinne,
Where ere you finde it standing,
Say you sweare ;
And make damnation parcell of your oath,
That when your lashing iestes make all men bleed,
Yet you whip none. Court Citty, country, friends,
Foes, all must smart alike ; yet Court, nor Citty,
Nor foe, nor friend, dare winch at you ; great pitty.

Dem. If you sweare, dam me Faninus, or Crispinus,
Or to the law (*Our kingdomes golden chaine*)
To Poets dam me, or to Players dam me,
If I brand you, or you, tax you, scourge you :
I wonder then, that of fiue hundred, foure
Should all point with their fingers in one instant
At one and the same man ?

Hor. Deare Faninus.

Dem. Come, you cannot excuse it.

Hor. Heare me, I can—

Dem. You must daube on thicke collours then to hide it.

Cris. We come like your Phisitions, to purge
Your sicke and daungerous minde of her disease.

Dem. In troth we doe, out of our loues we come,
And not reuenge, but if you strike vs still,
We must defend our reputations :
Our pens shall like our swords be alwayes sheath'd,
Vnlesse too much prouockt, Horace if then
They draw bloud of you, blame vs not, we are men :

Come, let thy Muſe beare vp a ſmoother ſayle,
Tis the eaſieſt and the baſeſt Arte to raile.

Hor. Deliuer me your hands, I loue you both,
As deare as my owne ſoule, prooue me, and when
I ſhall traduce you, make me the ſcorne of men.

Both. Enough, we are friends.

Cri. What reads Aſinius?

Aſi. By my troth heer's an excellent comfortable booke, it's moſt ſweet reading in it.

Dem. Why, what does it ſmell of Bubo?

Aſi. Mas it ſmels of Roſe-leaues a little too.

Hor. Then it muſt be a ſweet booke, he would faine perfume his ignorance.

Aſi. I warrant he had wit in him that pen'd it.

Criſ. Tis good yet a foole will confeſſe truth.

Aſi. The whoorſon made me meete with a hard ſtile in two or three places as I went ouer him.

Dem. I beleeue thee, for they had need to be very lowe & eaſie Stiles of wit that thy braines goe ouer.

Enter Blunt *and* Tucca.

Blun. Wher's this gallant? Morrow Gentlemen: what's this deuiſe done yet Horace?

Hor. Gods ſo, what meane you to let this fellow dog you into my Chamber?

Blun. Oh, our honeſt Captayne, come, prethee let vs ſee.

Tuc. Why you baſtards of nine whoores, the Muſes, why do you walke heere in this gorgeous gallery of gallant inuentions, with that whooreſon poor lyme & hayre-raſcall? why—

Criſ. O peace good Tucca, we are all ſworne friends,

Tuc. Sworne, that Iudas yonder that walkes in Rug, will dub you Knights ath Poſte, if you ſerue vnder his band of oaths, the copper-fact raſcal wil for a good ſupper out ſweare twelue dozen of graund Iuryes.

Blun. A pox ont, not done yet, and bin about it three dayes?

Horr. By Ieſu within this houre, ſaue you Captayne Tucca.

Tuc. Dam thee, thou thin bearded Hermaphrodite, dam thee, Ile ſaue my ſelfe for one I warrant thee, is this thy Tub Diogines?

Hor. Yes Captaine this is my poore lodging.

Aſin. *Morrow Captaine Tucca*, will you whiffe this morning?

Tuc. Art thou there goates pizzel; no godamercy Caine I am for no whiffs I, come hether ſheep-skin-weauer, s'foote thou lookſt as though th' adſt beg'd out of a Iayle: drawe, I mean not thy face (for tis not worth drawing) but drawe neere: this way martch, follow your commaunder you ſcoundrell: So, thou muſt run of an errand for mee Mephoſtophiles.

Hor. To doe your pleaſure Captayne I will, but whether.

Tuc. To hell, thou knowſt the way, to hell my fire and brimſtone, to hell; doſt ſtare my Sarſens-head at Newgate? doſt gloate? Ile march through thy dunkirkes guts for ſhooting ieſtes at me.

Hor. Deare Captaine but one word.

Tuc. Out bench-whiſtler out, ile not take thy word for a dagger Pye: you browne-bread-mouth ſtinker, ile teach thee turne me into Bankes his horſe, and to tell gentlemen I am a Iugler, and can ſhew trickes.

Hor. Captaine Tucca, but halfe a word in your eare.

Tuc. No you ſtaru'd raſcal, thou't bite off mine eares then, you muſt haue three or foure ſuites of names, when like a lowſie Pediculous vermin th'aſt but one ſuite to thy backe: you muſt be call'd Aſper, and Criticus, and Horace, thy tytle's longer a reading then the Stile a the big Turkes: Aſper, Criticus, Quintus, Horatius, Flaccus.

Hor. Captaine I know vpon what euen baſes I ſtand, and therefore—

Tuc. Bafes? wud the roague were but ready for me.

Blun. Nay prethee deare Tucca, come you fhall fhake—

Tuc. Not hands with great Hunkes there, not hands, but Ile fhake the gull-groper out of his tan'd skinne.

Crifp. & Deme. For our fake Captaine, nay prethee holde.

Tuc. Thou wrongft heere a good honeft rafcall Crifpinus, and a poore varlet Demetrius Fanninus (bretheren in thine owne trade of Poetry) thou fayft Crifpinus Sattin dublet is Reauel'd out heere, and that this penurious fneaker is out of elboes, goe two my good full mouth'd ban-dog, Ile ha thee friends with both.

Hor. With all my heart captaine Tucca, and with you too, Ile laye my handes vnder your feete, to keepe them from aking.

Omnes. Can you have any more?

Tuc. Saift thou me fo, olde Coale come? doo't then; yet tis no matter neither, Ile haue thee in league firft with thefe two rowly powlies: they fhal be thy Damons and thou their Pithyaffe; Crifpinus fhall giue thee an olde caft Sattin fuite, and Demetrius fhall write thee a Scene or two, in one of thy ftrong garlicke Comedies; and thou fhalt take the guilt of confcience for't, and fweare tis thine owne olde lad, tis thine owne: thou neuer yet fels't into the hands of fattin, didft?

Hor. Neuer Captaine I thanke God.

Tuc. Goe too, thou fhalt now King Gorboduck, thou fhalt, becaufe Ile ha thee damn'd, Ile ha thee all in Sattin: Afper, Criticus, Quintus, Horatius, Flaccus, Crifpinus fhal doo't, thou fhalt doo't, heyre apparant of Helicon, thou fhalt doo't.

Afi. Mine Ingle weare an olde caft Sattin fuite?

Tuc. I wafer-face your Ningle.

Afi. If he carry the minde of a Gentleman, he'll fcorne it at's heeles.

Tuc. Mary muffe, my man a ginger-bread, wilt eate any fmall coale ?

Afi. No Captaine, wod you fhould well know it, great coale fhall not fill my bellie.

Tuc. Scorne it, doft fcorne to be arrefted at one of his olde Suites ?

Hor. No Captaine, Ile weare any thing.

Tuc. I know thou wilt, I know th'art an honeft low minded Pigmey, for I ha feene thy fhoulders lapt in a Plaiers old caft Cloake, like a Slie knaue as thou art: and when thou ranft mad for the death of Horatio: thou borrowedft a gowne of Rofcius the Stager, (that honeft Nicodemus) and fentest it home lowfie, didft not ? *Refponde*, didft not ?

Blun. So, fo, no more of this, within this houre—

Hor. If I can found retreate to my wits, with whome this leader is in skirmifh, Ile end within this houre.

Tuc. What wut end ? wut hang thy felfe now ? has he not writ Finis yet Jacke ? what will he bee fifteene weekes about this Cockatrices egge too ? has hee not cackeld yet ? not laide yet ?

Blunt. Not yet he fweares hee will within this houre.

Tuc. His wittes are fomewhat hard bound: the Puncke his Mufe has fore labour ere the whoore bee deliuered: the poore faffron-cheeke Sun-burnt Gipfie wantes Phificke; giue the hungrie-face pudding-pye-eater ten Pilles: ten fhillings my faire Angelica, they'l make his Mufe as yare as a tumbler.

Blu. He fhall not want for money if heele write.

Tuc. Goe by Ieronimo, goe by; and heere, drop the ten fhillings into this Bafon; doe, drop, when Iacke ? hee fhall call me his Mæcenas: befides, Ile dam vp's Ouen-mouth for rayling at's: So, ift right Iacke ? ift fterling ? fall off now to the vanward of yonder foure Stinkers, and aske alowde if wee fhal goe ? the Knight ſhall defray Iacke, the Knight when it comes to *Summa totalis*, the Knyght, the Knight.—

Blu. Well Gentlemen, we'll leaue you, ſhall we goe Captaine ? good Horrace make ſome haſt.

Hor. Ile put on wings.

Aſin. I never ſawe mine Ingle ſo daſht in my life before.

Criſ. Yes once Aſinius.

Aſi. Mas you ſay true, hee was daſht worſe once going (in a rainy day) with a ſpeech to 'th Tilt-yard, by Gods lyd has call'd him names, a dog would not put vp, that had any diſcreation.

Tuc. Holde, holde vp thy hand, I ha ſeene the day thou didſt not ſcorne to holde vp thy golles; ther's a Souldiers Spur-royall, twelue pence: Stay, becauſe I know thou canſt not write without quick-ſiluer: vp agen, this goll agen, I giue thee double preſſe-money: Stay, becauſe I know thou haſt a noble head, ile deuide my Crowne, ô royall Porrex, ther's a teſton more; goe, thou and thy Muſe munch, doe, munch; come my deare Mandrake, if Skeldring fall not to decay, thou ſhalt floriſh: farewell my ſweet *Amadis de Gaule*, farewell.

Hor. Deare Captaine.

Tuc. Come Iacke.

Dem. Nay Captaine ſtay, we are of your band.

Tuc. March faire then:

Cri. Horace farewell, adue Aſinius. *Exeunt.*

Aſi. Ningle lets goe to ſome Tauerne, and dine together, for my ſtomache riſes at this ſcuruy leather Captaine.

Hor. No, they haue choakt me with mine owne diſgrace,
Which (fooles) ile ſpit againe euen in your face. *Exeunt.*

Enter Sir Quintilian Shorthoſe, Sir Adam, Sir Vaugham, Mineuer *with ſeruingmen.*

Sir quinti. Knaues, Varlets, what Lungis, giue me a dozen of ſtooles there.

Sir Vau. Sefu pleffe vs all in our fiue fences a peece, what meane yee fir Kintilian Sorthofe to ftand fo much on a dozen ftooles, heere be not preeches inuffe to hyde a dozen ftooles, vnleffe you wiffe fome of vs preake his finnes.

Sir quin. I fay fir Vaughan no fhinne fhal be broken heer, what lungis, a chayre with a ftronge backe, and a foft bellie, great with childe, with a cufhion for this reuerend Lady.

Mineu. God neuer gaue me the grace to be a Lady, yet I ha beene worfhipt in my confcience to my face a thoufand times, I cannot denye fir Vaughan, but that I haue all implements, belonging to the vocation of a Lady.

Sir Vaughan. I truft miftris Mineuer you haue all a honeft oman fhud haue?

Min. Yes perdie, as my Coach, and my fan, and a man or two that ferue my turne, and other things which Ide bee loath euery one fhould fee, becaufe they fhal not be common, I am in manner of a Lady in one point.

Sir Vaug. I pray miftris Mineuers, let vs all fee that point for our better vnderftanding.

Mi. For I ha fome thinges that were fetcht (I am fure) as faire as fome of the Low Countries, and I payde fweetly for them too, and they tolde me they were good for Ladies.

Sir qui. And much good do't thy good heart faire widdow them.

Min. I am fayre enough to bee a Widdow, Sir Quintilian.

Sir Vaug. In my foule and confcience, and well fauoured enough to be a Lady: heere is fir Kintilian Sorthofe, and heere is fir Adam Prickfhaft, a fentleman of a very good braine, and well headed; you fee he fhootes his bolt fildome, but when Adam lets goe, he hits: and heere is fir Vaughan ap Rees, and I beleeue if God fud take vs all from his mercy, as I hope hee will not yet; we all three loue you, at the bottome of our bellyes, and our hearts: and therefore miſtris Mineuer, if you pleaſe, you ſhall be knighted by one of vs, whom you ſall deſire to put into your deuice and minde.

Min. One I muſt haue ſir Vaughan.

Sir quin. And one of vs thou ſhalt haue widdow.

Min. One I muſt haue, for now euery one ſeekes to crow ouer me.

Sir Vaug. By Seſu and if I finde any crowing ouer you, & he were a cocke (come out as farre as in Turkeys country) tis poſſible to cut his combe off.

Min. I muſe why ſir Adam Prickſhaft flyes ſo farre from vs.

Sir Adam. I am in a browne ſtudy, my deare, if loue ſhould bee turned into a beaſt, what beaſt hee were fit to bee turned into.

Sir quinti. I thinke Sir Adam an Aſſe, becauſe of his bearing.

Min. I thinke (ſauing your reuerence) Sir Adam a puppy, for a dog is the moſt louing creature to a chriſtian that is, vnles it be a childe.

Sir Ad. No, I thinke if loue ſhould bee turn'd away, and goe to ſerue any beaſt, it muſt bee an Ape, and my reaſon——

Sir Vaug. Sir Adam, an Ape? ther's no more reaſon in an Ape, than in a very plaine Monkey; for an Ape has no tayle, but we all know, or tis our duty to know, loue has two tailes; In my ſudſment, if loue be a beaſt, that beaſt is a bunce of Reddis; for a bunce of Reddis is wiſe meate without Mutton, and ſo is loue.

Mi. Ther's the yawning Captaine (ſauing your reuereuce that has ſuch a ſore mouth) would one day needes perſwade me, that loue was a Rebato; and his reaſon was (ſauing your reuerence) that a Rebato was worne out with pinning too often; and ſo he ſaid loue was.

Sir Vaug. And Maſter Captaine Tucca ſayd wiſely too, loue is a Rebato indeede: a Rebato muſt be poaked; now many women weare Rebatoes, and many that weare Rebatoes——

Sir Adam. Muſt be poakt.

Sir Vau. Sir Adam Prickſhaft has hit the cloute.

Muſicke.

Sir qui. The Muſicke ſpeakes to vs, we'll haue a daunce before dinner.

Enter Sir Walter Terrill, Cæleſtine, Blunt, Criſpinus, *and* Demetrius, *euery one with a Lady.*

All. The King's at hand.

Ter. Father the King's at hand.
Muſicke talke lowder, that thy ſiluer voice,
May reach my Soueraignes eares.

Sir Vaug. I pray doe ſo, Muſitions beſtir your fingers, that you may haue vs all by the eares.

Sir quin. His Grace comes, a Hall varlets, where be my men? blow, blow your colde Trumpets till they ſweate; tickle them till they ſound agen.

Blun. Beſt goe meete his Grace.

All. Agreed.

Sir Vaug. Pray all ſtand bare, as well men as women: Sir Adam is beſt you hide your head for feare your wiſe braines take key-colde: on afore Sir Kintilian; Sentlemen fall in before the Ladyes, in ſeemely order and faſhion; ſo this is comelye.

Enter Trumpets ſounding, they goe to the doore, and meete the King and his Traine, and whilſt the Trumpets ſound the King is welcom'd, kiſſes the Bride, and honors the Bridegroome in dumbe ſhew.

King. Nay if your pleaſures ſhrinke at ſight of vs,
We ſhall repent this labour, Miſtris Bride
You that for ſpeaking but one word to day,
Muſt looſe your head at night; you that doe ſtand
Taking your laſt leaue of virginity;
You that being well begun, muſt not be Maide:
Winne you the Ladies, I the men will wooe,
Our ſelfe will leade my bluſhing Bride with you.

Sir Vaughan. God bleſſe your Maieſty, and ſend you to be a long King William Rufus ouer vs, when he ſees his times & pleaſures.

King. Wee thanke you good Sir Vaughan, wee will take your meaning not your words..

Sir quint. Lowde Muſicke there.

Sir Vau. I am glad your Maieſty will take any thing at my hands; my words I truſt in Seſu, are ſpoken betweene my ſoule and body together, and haue neither Felonies nor treaſons about them, I hope.

King. Good words, Sir Vaughan, I prethee give vs leaue.

Vaug. Good words ſir Vaughan ? thats by interpretation in engliſh, you'r beſt giue good words ſir Vaughan : god and his Anſells bleſſe me, what ayles his maieſtye to be ſo tedious and difficult in his right mindes now, I holde my life that file raſcall-rymer Horace hath puzd and puzd aboue a hundred merie tales and lyce, into his great and princely eares : by god and he vſe it, his being Phœbus prieſt cannot ſaue him, if hee were his Sapline too ide preaſe vpon his coxcomb : good lord bleſſe me out of his maieſties celler : King Williams, I hope tis none offences to make a ſupplication to god a mightie for your long life : for by ſheſu I haue no meaning in't in all the world, vnles raſcalls be here that will haue your grace take ſhalke for ſhees, and vnleſſe Horace has ſent lyce to your maieſty.

King. Horace, what's he ſir Vaughan ?

Vaugh. As hard-fauourd a fellow as your maieſtie has ſeene in a ſommers day : he does pen, an't pleaſe your grace, toyes that will not pleaſe your grace : tis a Poet, we call them Bardes in our Countrie, ſinges ballads and rymes, and I was mightie ſealous, that his Inke which is blacke and full of gall, had brought my name to your maieſtie, and ſo lifted vp your hye and princely coller.

King. I neither know that Horace, nor mine anger,
If as thou ſaiſt our high and princely choller

Be vp, wee'l tread it downe with daunces ; Ladies
Looſe not your men ; faire meaſures muſt be tread,
When by ſo faire a dauncer you are lead.

Vaugh. Miſtris Miniuer :

Miu. Perdie ſir Vaughan I cannot daunce.

Vaugh. Perdie by this Miniuer cappe, and acording to his maſeſties leaue too, you ſall be put in among theiſe Ladies, & daunce ere long I treſt in god, the ſaking of the ſeetes.

They daunce a ſtraine, and whilſt the others keepe on, the King and Celeſtine ſtay.

Kin. That turne faire Bride ſhews you muſt turne at night,
In that ſweet daunce which ſteales away delight.

Cæl. Then pleaſure is a thiefe, a fit, a feauer :

Kin. True, he's the thiefe, but women the receiuer.

Another change ; they fall in, the reſt goe on.

Kin. This change ſweet Maide, ſaies you muſt change your life,
As Virgins doe.

Cæl. Virgins nere change their life,
She that is wiu'd a maide, is Maide and wife.

Kin. But ſhe that dyes a Maide ;—

Cæl. Thrice happy then.

Kin. Leades Apes in hell.

Cæl. Better leade Apes then men.

At this third change they end, and ſhe meetes the King.

Kin. Well met.

Cæl. Tis ouertaken.

Kin. Why faire ſweet ?

Cæl. Women are ouertaken when they meete ;

King. Your bloud ſpeakes like a coward.

Cæl. It were good,
If euery Maiden bluſh, had ſuch a bloud.

Kin. A coward bloud, why whom ſhould maidens feare ?

Cæ. Men, were Maides cowards, they'd not come ſo nere,
My Lord the Meaſure's done, I pleade my duetie.
Kin. Onelie my heart takes meaſure of thy beautie.
Sir quin. Now by my hoſe I ſweare, that's no deepe oath,
This was a fine ſweet earth-quake gentlie moou'd,
By the ſoft winde of whiſpring Silkes : come Ladies,
Whoſe ioynts are made out of the dauncing Orbes,
Come, follow me, walke a colde meaſure now ;
In the Brides Chamber ; your hot beautie's melt,
Take euerie one her fan, giue them their places,
And waue the Northerne winde vpon your faces.

Celeſtine and all the Ladyes doing obeyſance to the King, who onely kiſſes her, Exeunt, Short-hoſe manning them, the Gallants ſtand aloofe.

Kin. Sir Walter Terrill.
Ter. My confirmed Leige.
Ki. Beautie out of her bountie, thee hath lent
More then her owne with liberall extent.
Ter. What meanes my Lord ?
Kin. Thy Bride, thy choice, thy wife,
She that is now thy fadom, thy new world,
That brings thee people, and makes little ſubiects ;
Kneele at thy feete, obay in euerie thing,
So euerie Father is a priuate King.
Ter. My Lord, her beauty is the pooreſt part,
Chieflie her vertues did endowe my heart.
Kin. Doe not back-bite her beauties, they all ſhine,
Brighter on thee, becauſe the beames are thine,
To thee more faire, to others her two lips
Shew like a parted Moone in thine Eclipſe ;
That glaunce, which louers mongſt themſelues deuiſe,
Walkes as inuiſible to others eies :
Giue me thine eare.
Ter. What meanes the King ?
Dem. Tis a quaint ſtraine.

Ter. My Lord.

King. Thou darſt not Wat.

Ter. She is too courſe an obiect for the Court.

Kin. Thou darſt not Wat: let to night be to morrow,

Ter. For ſhee's not yet mine owne.

Rin. Thou darſt not Wat?

Ter. My Lord I dare, but——

King. But I ſee thou darſt not.

Ter. This night.

King. Yea, this night, tuſh thy minde repaires not,
The more thou talk'ſt of night, the more thou darſt not;
Thus farre I tend, I wod but turne this ſpheare,
Of Ladies eyes, and place it in the Court,
Where thy faire Bride ſhould for the Zodiacke ſhine,
And euery Lady elſe ſit for a ſigne.
But all thy thoughts are yellow, thy ſweet bloud
Rebels, th'art iealous Wat; thus with proude reuels
To emmulate the masking firmament,
Where Starres dance in the ſiluer Hall of heauen,
Thy pleaſure ſhould be ſeaſoned, and thy bed
Relish thy Bride, But, but thou darſt not Wat.

Ter. My Loord I dare.

Kin. Speake that agen.

Ter. I dare.

King. Agen kinde Wat, and then I know thou darſt.

Ter. I dare and will by that ioynt holy oath,
Which ſhe and I ſwore to the booke of heauen.
This very day when the ſurueying Sunne,
Riz like a witnes to her faith and mine,
By all the loyalty that ſubiects owe
To Maieſty, by that, by this, by both,
I ſweare to make a double guarded oath,
This night vntainted by the touch of man,
She ſhall a Virgin come.

Kin. To Court? *Ter*. To Court.
I know I tooke a woman to my wife,

And I know women to be earthly Moones,
That neuer ſhine till night, I know they change
Their Orbes (their husbands) and in ſickiſh hearts,
Steale to their ſweete Endimions, to be cur'd
With better Phiſicke, ſweeter dyet drinkes,
Then home can miniſter: all this I know
Yet know not all, but giue me leaue O King,
To boaſt of mine, and ſaie that I know none;
I haue a woman but not ſuch a one.

Kin. Why, ſhe's confirmed in thee; I now ap-
prooue her,
If conſtant in thy thoughts who then can mooue her?

Enter Sir Quintilian.

Sir qui. Wilt pleaſe your Highnes take your place
within,
The Ladies attend the Table.

Kin. I goe good Knight; Wat thy oath.

Ter. My Lord,
My oath's my honour, my honour is my life,
My oath is conſtant, ſo I hope my wife. *Exeunt.*

Enter Horace *in his true attyre,* Aſinius *bearing his Cloake.*

Aſi. If you flye out Ningle, heer's your Cloake; I thinke it raines too.

Ho. Hide my ſhoulders in't.

Aſi. Troth ſo th'adſt neede, for now thou art in thy Pee and Kue; thou haſt ſuch a villanous broad backe, that I warrant th'art able to beare away any mans ieſtes in England.

Hor. It's well Sir, I ha ſtrength to beare yours mee thinkes; fore God you are growne a piece of a Critiſt, ſince you fell into my hands: ah little roague, your wit has pickt vp her crums prettie and well.

Aſi. Yes faith, I finde my wit a the mending hand

Ningle; troth I doe not thinke but to proceede Poet-aſter next Commencement, if I haue my grace per-fectlie: euerie one that confer with me now, ſtop their noſe in merriment, and ſweare I ſmell ſomewhat of Horace; one calles me Horaces Ape, another Horaces Beagle, and ſuch Poeticall names it paſſes. I was but at Barbers laſt day, and when he was rencing my face, did but crie out, fellow thou makſt me *Conniue* too long, & ſayes he ſayes hyee, Maſter *Aſinius Bubo*, you haue eene Horaces wordes as right as if he had ſpit them into your mouth.

Hor. Well, away deare Aſinius, deliuer this letter to the young Gallant *Druſo*, he that fell ſo ſtrongly in loue with mee yeſternight.

Aſin. It's a ſweete Muske-cod, a pure ſpic'd-gull; by this feather I pittie his *Ingenuities*; but haſt writ all this ſince Ningle? I know thou haſt a good run-ning head and thou liſteſt.

Hor. Foh come, your great belly'd wit muſt long for euery thing too; why you *Rooke*, I haue a ſet of letters readie ſtarcht to my hands, which to any freſh ſuited gallant, that but newlie enters his name into my rowle, I ſend the next morning, ere his ten a clocke dreame has rize from him, onelie with clapping my hand to't, that my Nouice ſhall ſtart, ho and his haire ſtand an end, when hee ſees the ſodaine flaſh of my writing: what you prettie Diminitiue roague, we muſt haue falſe fiers to amaze theſe ſpangle babies, theſe true heires of Ma. Juſtice Shallow.

Aſi. I wod alwaies haue thee ſauce a foole thus.

Hor. Away, and, ſtay: 'here be Epigrams vpon Tucca, divulge theſe among the gallants; as for Criſpinus, that Criſpin-aſſe and Fannius his Play-dreſſer; who (to make the Muſes beleeue, their ſub-iects eares were ſtaru'd, and that there was a dearth of Poeſie) cut an Innocent Moore i'th middle, to ſerue him in twice; & when he had done, made Poules-worke of it, as for theſe Twynnes, theſe *Poet-apes*:
Their Mimicke trickes ſhall ſerue

With mirth to feaſt our Muſe, whilſt their owne ſtarue.

Aſin. Well Ningle Ile trudge, but where's the Randeuow?

Hor. Well thought off, marie at Sir Vaughans lodging the Welſh knight, I haue compoſ'd a loue-letter for the gallants worſhip, to his Roſamond: the ſecond, Miſtris Miniuer, becauſe ſhe does not thinke ſo ſoundly of his lame Engliſh as he could wiſh; I ha gull'd his Knight-ſhip heere to his face, yet haue given charge to his wincking vnderſtanding not to perceiue it: nay Gods ſo, away deare Bubo.

Aſi. I am gone. *Exit.*

Hor. The Muſes birdes the Bees were hiu'd and fled,
Vs in our cradle, thereby prophecying;
That we to learned eares ſhould ſweetly ſing,
But to the vulger and adulterate braine,
Should loath to proſtitute our Virgin ſtraine.
No, our ſharpe pen ſhall keep the world in awe,
Horace thy Poeſie, wormwood wreathes ſhall weare,
We hunt not for mens loues but for their feare. *Exit.*

Enter Sir Adam *and* Miniuer.

Min. O Sir Adam Prickſhaft, you are a the bow hand wide, a long yard I aſſure you: and as for Suitors, truelie they all goe downe with me, they haue all one flat anſwere.

Sir Adam. All Widdow? not all, let Sir Adam bee your firſt man ſtill.

Enter Sir Quintilian.

Sir quin. Widdow, art ſtolne from Table? I Sir Adam,
Are you my riuall? well, flye faire y' are beſt;
The King's exceeding merrie at the banquet,
He makes the Bride bluſh with his merrie words
That run into her eares; ah he's a wanton,
Yet I dare truſt her, had he twentie tongues,
And euerie tongue a Stile of Maieſtie.

Now Widdow, let me tell thee in thine eare,
I loue thee Widdow, by this ring; nay weare it.

Mineu. Ile come in no rings pardie, Ile take no golde.

Sir Ada. Harke in thine eare, take me, I am no golde.

Enter Sir Vaughan *and* Peter Flash.

Sir Vau. Master Peter Flash, I will grope about Sir Quintilian, for his terminations touching and considering you.

Flash. I thanke your Worship, for I haue as good a stomacke to your Worship as a man could wish.

Sir Vau. I hope in God a mightie, I shall fill your stomack Master Peter: What two vpon one Sentlemen; Mistris Miniuer, much good doo 't you Sir Adam.

Sir quin. Sir Vaughan, have you din'd well Sir Vaughan?

Sir Vau. As good seere as would make any hungrie man (and a were in the vilest prison in the world) eate and hee had anie stomacke: One word Sir Quintilian in hugger mugger; heere is a Sentleman of yours, Master Peter Flash, is tesirous to haue his blew coate pul'd ouer his eares; and . . . .

Flash. No, Sir, my petition runs thus, that your worshippe would thrust me out of doores, and that I may follow Sir Vaughan.

Sir Vau. I can tell you Master Flash, and you follow mee I goe verie fast, I thinke in my conscience, I am one of the lightest knights in England.

Flash. It's no matter Sir, the Flashes haue euer bin knowne to be quicke and light enough.

Sir quin. Sir Vaughan, he shal follow you, he shall dog you good Sir Vaughan.

Enter Horace *walking.*

Sir Vau. Why then Peter Flash I will set my foure markes a yeare, and a blew coate vpon you.

Fla. Godamercy to your worſhip, I hope you ſhall neuer repent for me.

Sir Vau. You beare the face of an honeſt man, for you bluſh paſſing well Peter, I will quench the flame out of your name, and you ſhall he chriſtned Peter Salamander.

Peter Flaſh. The name 's too good for me, I thanke your worſhip.

Sir Vau. Are you come Maſter Horace, you ſent mee the Coppie of your letters countenance, and I did write and read it; your wittes truelie haue done verie valliantlie: tis a good inditements, you haue put in enough for her ha you not ?

Hor. According to my inſtructions.

Sir Vau. Tis paſſing well, I pray Maſter Horace walke a little beſide your ſelfe, I will turne vpon you incontinent.

Sir quin. What Gentleman is this in the Mandilian, a ſoldyer ?

Sir Vau. No, tho he has a very bad face for a ſouldier, yet he has as deſperate a wit as euer any Scholler went to cuffes for; tis a Sentleman Poet, he has made rimes called Thalamimums, for M. Pridegroome, on vrd widdow.

Sir qui. Is this he ? welcome Sir, your name ? pray you walke not ſo ſtatelie, but be acquainted with me boldlie; your name Sir ?

Hor. Quintus, Horacius, Flaccus.

Sir Quint. Good Maſter Flappus welcome.

He walkes vp and downe.

Sir Vau. Miſtris Miniuer, one vrde in your corner heere; I deſire you to breake my armes heere, and read this Paper, you ſhall feele my mindes and affections in it, at full and at large.

Mini. Ile receiue no Loue libels perdy, but by word a mouth.

Sir Vaughan. By Sefu tis no libell, for heere is my hand to it.

Mini. Ile ha no hand in it Sir Vaughan, Ile not deale with you.

Sir Vau. Why then widdow, Ile tell you by word a mouth my deuices.

Mi. Your deuices come not neere my mouth Sir Vaughan perdy, I was vpon a time in the way to marriage, but now I am turn'd a tother ſide, I ha ſworne to leade a ſingle and ſimple life.

Sir Adam. She has anſwer'd you Sir Vaughan.

Sir Vau. Tis true, but at wrong weapons Sir Adam; will you be an Aſſe Miſtris Miniuers ?

Min. If I be you ſhall not ride me.

Sir Vaug. A ſimple life! by Seſu tis the life of a foole, a ſimple life!

Sir qui. How now Sir Vaughan ?

Sir Vaugh. My braines has a little fine quawme come vnder it, and therefore Sir Adam, and Sir Quintilian, and miſtris Miniuer caps God bo'y.

All. Good Sir Vaughan.

Sir Vaugh. Maſter Horace, your inuentions doe her no good in the Vniuerſalities; yet heere is two ſhillings for your wittes; nay by Seſu you ſhall take it if 't were more: yonder bald Adams, is put my noſe from his ioynt; but Adam I will be euen to you: this is my cogitations, I will indite the Ladies & Miniuer caps to a dinner of Plumbes, and I ſhall deſire you M. Horace, to ſpeake or raile; you can raile I hope in God a mighty.

Hor. You meane to ſpeake bitterlie:

Sir Vaughan. Right, to ſpitte bitterlie vpon baldnes, or the thinnes of haire; you ſall eate downe Plumbes to ſweeten your mouth, and heere is a good Anſell to defend you: Peter Salamander follow me.

Flaſh. With hue and crie and you will Sir.

Sir Vau. Come M. Horace, I will goe pull out the Ladies.

Ho. And Ile ſet out my wits, Baldnes the Theame ?
My words ſhall flow hye in a ſilver ſtreame. *Exeunt.*

Enter Tucca *bruſhing off the crumbes.*

Tuc. Wher 's my moſt coſtly and ſumptuous Short-hoſe ?

Sir Quint. Is the King riſen from table Captaine Tucca ?

Tuc. How ? riſen ? no my noble Quintilian, kings are greater men then we Knights and Caualliers, and therefore muſt eate more then leſſer perſons ; God-amercy good Diues for theſe crummes : how now ? has not Frier Tucke din'd yet ? he falles ſo hard to that Oyſter-pye yonder.

Sir quin. Oyſter-pye Captaine ? ha, ha, he loues her, and I loue her and feare both ſhall goe without her.

Tuc. Doſt loue her, my fineſt and firſt part of the Mirrour of Knighthood ? hange her ſhe lookes like a bottle of ale, when the corke flyes out and the Ale fomes at mouth, ſhee lookes my good button-breech like the ſigne of Capricorne, or like Tiborne when it is couer'd with ſnow.

Sir quin. All 's one for that, ſhe has a vizard in a bagge, will make her looke like an Angell ; I wod I had her, vpon condition, I gaue thee this chaine manlie Tucca.

Tuc. I ? ſaiſt thou ſo Friskin ? I haue her ath hip for ſome cauſes, I can ſound her, ſhe 'll come at my becke.

Sir quin. Wod I could ſound her too Noble commaunder.

Tuc. Thou ſhalt doo 't ; that Lady ath Lake is thine Sir Triſtram, lend mee thy chaine, doe, lend it, Ile make her take it as a token, Ile lincke her vnto thee ; and thou ſhalt weare hergloue in thy Worſhipfull hatte like to a leather brooch ; Nay and thou miſtruſts thy coller, be tyed in 't ſtill.

Sir quin. Miſtruſt Captaine ? no, heere tis, giue it her if ſhe 'll take it, or weare it thy ſelfe if ſhee 'll take mee, Ile watch him well enough too.

Tuc. No more, Ile ſhoote away yonder Prickſhaft,

and then belabour her, and flye you after yonder Cucko : doſt heere me my noble Gold-finch ? ——

Sir qui. No more.

Tuc. How doſt thou my ſmug Belimperia ? how doſt thou ? hands off my little bald Derricke, hands off : harke hether Suſanna, beware a theſe two wicked Elders, ſhall I ſpeake well or ill of thee ?

Min. Nay, eene as you pleaſe Captaine, it ſhal be at your choice.

Tuc. Why well ſaid, my nimble Short-hoſe.

Sir quin. I heare her, I heare her.

Tuc. Art angry father time ? art angrie becauſe I tooke mother-Winter aſide ? Ile holde my life thou art ſtrucke with Cupids Birde-bolt, my little prick-ſhaft, art ? doſt loue that mother Mumble-cruſt, doſt thou ? doſt long for that whim-wham ?

Sir Ada. Wod I were as ſure to lye with her, as to loue her.

Tuc. Haue I found thee my learned Dunce, haue I found thee ? If I might ha my wil, thou ſhouldſt not put thy ſpoone into that bumble-broth (for indeede Ide taſte her my ſelfe) no thou ſhouldſt not : yet if her beautie blinde thee, ſhe's thine, I can doo't, thou heardſt her ſay eene now, it ſhould bee at my choice.

Sir Ada. She did ſo, worke the match and Ile beſtow—

Tuc. Not a ſilke point vpon mee, little Adam ſhee ſhall be thy Eeue, for leſſe then an Apple ; but ſend, bee wiſe, ſend her ſome token, ſhee's greedie, ſhee ſhall take it, doe, ſend, thou ſhalt ſticke in her (Prickeſhaft) but ſend.

Sir Adam. Heer's a purſe of golde, thinke you that wil be accepted ?

Tuc. Goe to, it ſhall bee accepted, and twere but ſiluer, when that Flea-bitten Short-hoſe ſteppes hence : vaniſh too, and let mee alone with my Grannam in Gutter-Lane there, and this purſe of golde doe, let me alone.

Sir quin. The King, gods Lord, I doe forget the King;
Widdow, thinke on my wordes, I muſt be gone
To waite his riſing, Ile returne anone.

Sir Ad. Stay Sir Quintilian, Ile be a waiter too.

Sir quint. Widdow wee'll truſt that Captaine there with you. *Exeunt.*

Tuc. Now, now, mother Bunch how doſt thou? what doſt frowne Queene Gwyniuer? doſt wrinckle? what made theſe paire of Shittle-cockes heere? what doe they fumble for? Ile ha none of theſe Kites fluttering about thy carkas, for thou ſhalt bee my Weſt Indyes, and none but trim Tucca ſhall diſcouer thee.

Min. Diſcouer me? diſcouer what thou canſt of me.

Tuc. What I can? thou knowſt what I can diſcouer, but I will not lay thee open to the world.

Min. Lay me open to the world?

Tuc. No I will not my moldie decay'd Charing-croſſe, I will not.

Mi. Hang thee patch-pannell, I am none a thy Charing-croſſe: I ſcorne to be Croſſe to ſuch a ſcab as thou makſt thy ſelfe.

Tuc. No, tis thou makſt me ſo, my Long Meg a Weſtminſter, thou breedſt a ſcab, thou—

Min. I? dam thee filthie Captaine, dam thy ſelfe.

Tuc. My little deuill a Dow-gate, Ile dam thee, thou knowſt my meaning) Ile dam thee vp; my wide mouth at Biſhops-gate.

Min. Wod I might once come to that damming.

Tuc. Why thou ſhalt, my ſweet dame Annis a cleere thou ſhalt, for Ile drowne my ſelfe in thee; I, for thy loue, Ile ſinke, I, for thee.

Min. So thou wilt I warrant, in thy abhominable ſinnes; Lord, Lord, howe many filthy words haſt thou to anſwere for.

Tuc. Name one Madge-owlet, name one, Ile anſwer for none; my words ſhall be foorth comming at all times, & ſhall anſwer for them ſelues; my nimble Cat-a-mountaine: they ſhall Siſle Bum-trincket, for Ile giue thee none but Suger-candie words, I will not Puſſe: goody Tripe-wife, I will not.

Min. Why doſt call mee ſuch horrible vngodlie names then?

Tuc. Ile name thee no more Mother Red-cap vpon paine of death, if thou wilt Grimalkin, Maggot-a-pye I will not.

Min. Wod thou shouldſt wel know, I am no Maggot, but a meere Gentlewoman borne.

Tu. I know thou art a Gentle, and Ile nibble at thee, thou ſhalt be my Cap-a-maintenance, & Ile carrie my naked ſword before thee, my reuerend Ladie Lettice-cap.

Mi. Thou ſhalt carry no naked ſwords before me to fright me, thou—

Tuc. Go too, let not thy tongue play ſo hard at hot-cockles; for, Gammer Gurton, I meane to bee thy needle, I loue thee, I loue thee, becauſe thy teeth ſtand like the Arches vnder London Bridge, for thou't not turne Satyre & bite thy husband; No, come my Cub, doe not ſcorne mee becauſe I goe in Stag, in Buffe, heer's veluet too; thou ſeeſt I am worth thus much in bare veluet.

Min. I ſcorne thee not, not I.

Tuc. I know thou doſt not, thou ſhat ſee that I could march with two or three hundred linkes before me, looke here, what? I could ſhew golde too, if that would tempt thee, but I would not make my ſelfe a Gold-ſmithes ſtall I; I ſcorne to goe chain'd my Ladie ath Hoſpitall, I doe; yet I will and muſt bee chain'd to thee.

Min. To mee? why Maſter Captaine, you know that I haue my choiſe of three or foure payre of Knights, and therefore haue ſmall reaſon to flye out I know not how in a man of war.

Tuc. A man a warre? come thou knowſt not what a worſhipfull ſocation tis to be a Captaines wife:

three or foure payre of Knights? why doſt heare Ioane-a-bedlam, Ile enter into bond to be dub'd by what day thou wilt, when the next aćtion is layde vpon me, thou ſhalt be Ladified.

Min. You know I am offered that by halfe a dozen.

Tuc. Thou shalt little Miniuer, thou ſhalt, Ile ha this frocke turn'd into a foote-cloth : and thou ſhalt be carted drawne I meane, Coacht, Coacht, thou shalt ryde Iigga-Iogge ; a Hood shall flap vp and downe heere, and this shipskin-cap shall be put off.

Mini. Nay perdie, Ile put off my cap for no mans pleaſure.

Tuc. Wut thou be proude little Lucifer? well, thou shalt goe how then thou wilt Maide-marian; come buſſe thy little Anthony now, now, my cleane Cleopatria ; ſo, ſo, goe thy waies Alexis ſecrets, th'aſt a breath as ſweet as the Roſe, that growes by the Beare-garden, as ſweete as the proud'ſt head a Garlicke in England : come, wut march in, to the Gentle folkes?

Mini. Nay trulie Captaine you shall be my leader.

Tuc. I ſay Mary Ambree, thou shalt march formoſt,
Becauſe Ile marke how broad th'art in the heeles.

Mini. Perdie, I will be ſet ath laſt for this time.

Tuc. Why then come, we'll walke arme in arme,
As tho we were leading one another to Newgate.

Enter Blunt, Criſpinus, *and* Demetrius, *with papers, laughing.*

Cri. Mine's of a fashion, cut out quite from yours.

Dem. Mine has the sharpeſt tooth, yonder he is.

Blu. Captaine Tucca. *All hold vp papers.*

Tuc. How now? I cannot ſtand to read ſupplications now.

Criſ. They're bitter Epigrams compoſ'd on you
By Horace.

Dem. And difperft amongft the gallants
In feuerall coppies, by Afinius Bubo.

Tuc. By that liue Eele ? read, *Lege Legito*, read thou Iacke.

Blu. Tucca s growne monftrous, how ! rich ? that I feare,
He's to be feene for money euery where.

Tuc. Why true, shall not I get in my debts, nay and the roague write no better I care not, farewell blacke Iacke farewell.

Cri. But Captaine heer's a nettle.

Tuc. Sting me, doe.

Cri. Tucca's exceeding tall and yet not hye,
He fights with skill, but does moft vilye lye.

Tuc. Right, for heere I lye now, open, open, to make my aduerfarie come on; and then Sir, heere am I in's bofome : nay and this be the worft, I shal hug the poore honeft face-maker, Ile loue the little Atheift, when he writes after my commendation, another whip ? come yerke me.

Dem. Tucca will bite, how ? growne Satiricall,
No, he bites tables, for he feedes on all.

Tuc. The whorefon clouen-foote deuill in mans apparell lyes,
There ftood aboue forty dishes before me to day,
That I nere toucht, becaufe they were empty.

Min. I am witnes young Gentlemen to that.

Tuc. Farewell ftinckers, I fmel thy meaning Screech-owle, I doe, tho I ftop my nofe : and Sirra Poet, we'll haue thee vntruft for this; come, mother Mum-pudding, come. *Exeunt.*

Trumpets found a florifh, and then a fennate : Enter King *with* Cæleftine, Sir Walter Terrill, Sir Quintilian, Sir Adam, Blunt *and other Ladies and attendants : whilft the Trumpets found the King takes his leaue of the Bride-groome, and* Sir Quintilian, *and laft of the Bride.*

Kin. My fong in parting doth this burden beare

A kiſſe the Ditty, and I ſet it heere.
Your lips are well in tune, ſtrung with delight,
By this faire Bride remember ſoone at night;
Sir Walter.

Ter. My Leige Lord, we all attend,
The time and place.

Kin. Till then my leaue commend.

They bring him to the doore: Enter at another doore Sir Vaughan.

Sir Vau. Ladies, I am to put a verie eaſie ſuite vpon you all, and to deſire you to fill your little pellies at a dinner of plums behinde noone; there be Suckets, and Marmilads, and Marchants, and other long white plummes that faine would kiſſe your delicate and ſweet lippes; I indite you all together, and you eſpecially my Ladie Pride; what doe you ſaie for your ſelles? for I indite you all.

Cæl. I thanke you good Sir Vaughan, I will come.

Sir Vau. Say Sentlewomen will you ſtand to me too?

All. Wee'll ſit with you ſweet Sir Vaughan.

Sir Vau. God a mightie pleſſe your faces, and make your peauties laſt, when wee are all dead and rotten:—you all will come.

1 *Lady.* All will come.

Sir Vaug. Pray God that Horace bee in his right wittes to raile now. *Exit.*

Criſ. Come Ladie, you ſhall be my dauncing gueſt.
To treade the maze of muſicke with the reſt.

Dem. Ile lead you in.

Dicach. A maze is like a doubt:
Tis eaſie to goe in, hard to get out.

Blun. We follow cloſe behinde.

Philoca. That meaſure's beſt.
Now none markes vs, but we marke all the reſt.

Exeunt.

Exeunt all fauing Sir Quintilian, Cæleftine, *and* Sir Walter Terrill.

Ter. Father, and you my Bride ; that name to day
Wife comes not till to-morrow : but omitting
This enterchange of language ; let vs thinke
Vpon the King and night, and ca l our fpirits
To a true reckoning : firft to Arme our wittes
With compleat fteele of Iudgement, and our tongs
With found artillery of Phrafes : then
Our Bodies muft bee motions ; moouing firft
What we fpeake : afterwards, our very knees
Muft humbly feeme to talke, and fute out fpeech ;
For a true furnifht Cortyer hath fuch force,
Though his tongue faints, his very legs difcourfe.

Sir quin. Sonne Terrill, thou haft drawne his picture right,
For hee's noe full-made Courtier, nor well ftrung,
That hath not euery ioynt ftucke with a tongue.
Daughter, if Ladies fay, that is the Bride, that's fhe,
Gaze thou at none, for all will gaze at thee.

Cæl. Then, ô my father muft I goe? O my husband
Shall I then goe? O my felfe, will I goe?

Sir quin. You muft.

Ter. You fhall.

Cæl. I will, but giue me leaue,
To fay I may not, nor I ought not, fay not
Still, I muft goe, let me intreate I may not.

Ter. You muft and fhall, I made a deede of gift,
And gaue my oath vnto the King, I fwore
By thy true conftancy.

Cæl. Then keep that word
To fweare by, O let me be conftant ftill.

Ter. What fhall I cancell faith, and breake my oath?

Cæl. If breaking conftancie, thou breakft them both.

Ter. Thy conftancie no euill can purfue.

Cæl. I may be conſtant ſtill, and yet not true.

Ter. As how?

Cæ. As thus, by violence detain'd,
They may be conſtant ſtill, that are conſtrain'd.

Ter. Conſtrain'd? that word weighs heavy, yet my oath
Weighes downe that word; the kinges thoughts are at oddes,
They are not euen ballanſt in his breſt;
The King may play the man with me; nay more,
Kings may vſurpe; my wife's a woman; yet
Tis more then I know yet, that know not her,
If ſhe ſhould prooue mankinde, twere rare, fye, fye,
See how I looſe my ſelfe, amongſt my thoughts,
Thinking to finde my ſelfe; my oath, my oath.

Sir quin. I ſweare another, let me ſee, by what,
By my long ſtocking, and my narrow skirtes,
Not made to ſit vpon, ſhe ſhall to Court.
I haue a tricke, a charme, that ſhall lay downe
The ſpirit of luſt, and keep thee vndeflowred;
Thy husbands honor ſau'd, and the hot King,
Shall haue enough too. Come, a tricke, a charme.
Exit.

Cæl. God keep thy honour ſafe, my bloud from harme.

Ter. Come, my ſicke-minded Bride, Ile teach thee how,
To reliſh health a little: Taſte this thought,
That when mine eyes ſeru'd loues commiſſion,
Vpon thy beauties I did ſeiſe on them,
To a Kings vſe; cure all thy griefe with this,
That his great ſeale was grauen vpon this ring,
And that I was but Steward to a King. *Exeunt.*

A banquet ſet out: *Enter* Sir Vaughan, Horace, Aſinius Bubo, *Lady* Petula, Dicache, Philocalia, *Miſtris* Miniuer *and* Peter Flaſh.

Sir Vaugh. Ladies and Sentlemen, you are almoſt all welcome, to this ſweet nuncions of Plums.

Dicach. Almoſt all Sir Vaughan ? why to which of vs are you ſo niggardly, that you cut her out but a peice of welcome.

Sir Vaugh. My interpretations is that almoſt all are welcome, becauſe I indited a brace or two more that is not come, I am ſorrie my Lady Pride is not among you.

Aſi. Slid, he makes hounds of vs Ningle, a brace quoth a ?

Sir Vaug. Peter Salamanders draw out the pictures of all the ioynt ſtooles, & Ladies ſit downe vpon their wodden faces.

Flaſh. I warrant Sir, Ile giue euerie one of them a good ſtoole.

Sir Vau. Maſter Horace, Maſter Horace, when I pray to God, and deſire in hipocritnes that bald Sir Adams were heer, then, then, then begin to make your railes at the pouertie and beggerly want of haire.

Hor. Leaue it to my iudgment.

Sir Vau. M. Bubo ſit there, you and I wil thinke vpon our ends at the Tables : M. Horace, put your learned bodie into the midſt of theſe Ladies ; ſo tis no matter to ſpeake graces at nuncions, becauſe we are all paſt grace ſince dinner.

Aſini. Mas I thanke my deſtinie I am not paſt grace, for by this hand full of Carrawaies, I could neuer abide to ſay grace.

Dica. Miſtris Miniuer, is not that innocent Gentleman a kinde of foole ?

Min. Why doe you aske Madam ?

Dicach. Nay for no harme, I aske becauſe I thought you two had been of acquaintanc.

Min. I thinke he's within an Inch of a foole.

Dicach. Madam Philocalia, you ſit next that ſpare Gentleman, wod you heard what Miſtris Miniuer ſaies of you.

Philo. Why what ſaies ſhe Madam Dicache.

Dica. Nay nothing, but wiſhes you were married to that ſmall timber'd gallant.

Philo. Your wiſh and mine are twinnes, I wiſh ſo too, for then I ſhould be ſure to lead a merrie life.

Aſini. Yes faith Ladie, Ide make you laugh, my bolts now and then ſhould be ſoone ſhot; by theſe comfits, weed let'all ſlide.

Petu. He takes the ſweeteſt oathes that euer I heard a gallant of his pitch ſweare; by theſe Comfits, & theſe Carrawaies, I warrant it does him good to ſweare.

Aſin. .Yes faith tis meate and drinke to me. I am glad Ladie Petula (by this Apple) that they pleaſe you.

Sir Vau. Peter Salamanders wine, I beſeech you Maſter Aſinius Bubo, not to ſweare ſo deeplie, for there comes no fruite of your oathes; heere Ladies, I put you all into one corners together, you ſhall all drinke of one cup.

Aſi. Peter I prethee fill me out too.

Flaſh. Ide fling you out too and I might ha my will, a pox of all fooles.

Sir Vau. Miſtris Miniuers, pray bee luſtie, wod Sir Adams Prickshaft ſtucke by you.

Hor. Who, the balde Knight Sir Vaughan?

Sir Vau. The ſame M. Horace, he that has but a remnant or parcell of haire, his crowne is clipt and par'd away; me thinkes tis an excellent quallitie to bee balde; for and there ſtucke a noſe and two nyes in his pate, he might weare two faces vnder one hood.

Aſi. As God ſaue me la, if I might ha my will, Ide rather be a balde Gentleman then a hairy; for I am ſure the beſt and talleſt Yeomen in England haue balde heads: me thinkes haire is a ſcuruie lowſie commodity.

Hor. Bubo, herein you blaze your ignorance.

Sir Vau. Pray ſtop and fill your mouthes, and giue M. Horace all your eares.

Hor. *For, if of all the bodies parts, the head*
Be the moſt royall: if diſcourſe, wit, Iudgement,
And all our vnderſtanding faculties,
Sit there in their high Court of Parliament,
Enacting lawes to ſway this humorous world:

This little Ile of Man : needes muſt that crowne,
Which ſtands vpon this ſupreame head, be faire,
And helde inualuable, and that crowne's the Haire :
The head that wants this honour ſtands awry,
Is bare in name and in authority.

Sir Vau. He meanes balde-pates Miſtris Miniuers.

Hor. Haire, *tis the roabe which curious nature weaues,*
To hang vpon the head : and does adorne,
Our bodies in the firſt houre we are borne :
God does beſtow that garment : when we dye,
That (like a ſoft and ſilken Canopie)
Is ſtill ſpred ouer vs ; In ſpight of death
Our hayre growes in our graue, and that alone
Lookes freſh, when all our other beauty's gone.
The excellence of Haire, *in this ſhines cleere,*
That the foure Elements take pride to weare
The faſhion of it : when Fire *moſt bright does burne,*
The flames to golden lockes doe ſtriue to turne ;
When her laſciuious armes the Water *hurles,*
About the ſhoares waſt, her ſleeke head ſhe curles :
And rorid cloudes being ſuckt into the Ayre,
When downe they melt, hangs like fine ſiluer hayre.
You ſee the Earth (*whoſe head ſo oft is ſhorne*)
Frighted to feele her lockes ſo rudely torne,
Stands with her haire an end, and (*thus afraide*)
Turnes euery haire to a greene naked blade.
Beſides, (*when ſtrucke with griefe*) *we long to dye,*
We ſpoile that moſt, which moſt does beautifie,
We rend this Head-tyre *off. I thus conclude,*
Cullors ſet cullors out ; our eyes iudge right,
Of vice or vertue by their oppoſite :
So, if faire haire to beauty ad ſuch grace,
Baldnes muſt needes be vgly, vile and baſe.

Sir Vau. True M. Horace, for a bald reaſon, is a reaſon that has no haires vpon't, a ſcuruy ſcalded reaſon.

Mi. By my truely I neuer thought you could ha pickt ſuch ſtrange things out of haire before.

Asini. Nay my Ningle can tickle it, when hee comes too't.

Min. Troth I ſhall neuer be enameld of a bare-headed man for this, what ſhift ſo euer I make.

Sir Vaug. Then Miſtris Miniuer S. Adams Prick-ſhaft muſt not hit you; Peter take vp all the cloathes at the table and the Plums.

Enter Tucca *and his boy.*

Tuc. Saue thee my little worſhipfull Harper; how doe yee my little cracknels? how doe ye?

Sir Vau. Welcome M. Tucca, ſit and ſhoote into your belly ſome Suger pellets.

Tuc. No, Godamercy Cadwallader, how doe you Horace?

Ho. Thankes good Captaine.

Tu. Wher's the Sering thou carrieſt about thee? O haue I found thee my ſcowring-ſticke; what's my name Bubo?

Asini. Wod I were hang'd if I can call you any names but Captaine and Tucca.

Tuc. No Fye'ſt; my name's Hamlet reuenge; thou haſt been at Parris garden haſt not?

Hor. Yes Captaine, I ha plaide Zulziman there.

Sir Vau. Then M. Horace you plaide the part of an honeſt man.

Tuc. Death of Hercules, he could neuer play that part well in's life, no Fulkes you could not: thou call'ſt Demetrius Iorneyman Poet, but thou putſt vp a Supplication to be a poore Iorneyman Player, and hadſt beene ſtill ſo, but that thou couldſt not ſet a good face vpon't: thou haſt forgot how thou ambleſt (in leather pilch) by a play-wagon, in the high way, and took'ſt mad Ieronimoes part, to get ſeruice among the Mimickes: and when the Stagerites baniſht thee into the Ile of Dogs, thou turn'dſt Ban-dog (villanous Guy) & euer ſince biteſt therefore I aske if th'aſt been at Parris-garden, becauſe thou haſt ſuch a good mouth; thou baitſt well, read, *lege,* ſaue thy ſelfe and read.

Hor. Why Captaine these are *Epigrams* compos'd on you.

Tuc. Goe not out Farding Candle, goe not out, for trusty *Damboys* now the deed is done, Ile pledge this Epigram in wine, Ile swallow it, I, yes.

Sir Vau. God blesse vs, will he be drunke with nittigrams now.

Tuc. So, now arise sprite ath Buttry; no Herring-bone Ile not pull thee out, but arise deere Eccho rise, rise deuill or Ile coniure thee vp.

Min. Good Master Tucca lets ha no coniuring heere.

Sir Vau. Vddes bloud you scald gouty Captaine, why come you to set encombrances heere betweene the Ladies.

Tuc. Be not so tart my precious Metheglin, be not (my old whore a Babilon, sit fast.)

Min. O Iesu if I know where abouts in London Babilon stands.

Tuc. Feede and be fat my faire Calipolis, stir not my beauteous wriggle-tailes, Ile disease none of you, Ile take none of you vp, but onely this table-man, I must enter him into some filthy sincke point, I must.

Hor. Captaine, you doe me wrong thus to disgrace me.

Tuc. Thou thinkst thou maist be as sawcy with me as my Buffe Ierkin, to sit vpon me, dost?

Ho. Dam me, if euer I traduc'd your name,
What imputation can you charge me with?

Sir Vau. Sblud, I, what cōputations can you lay to. his sarge? answer, or by Sesu Ile canuas your cox-combe Tucky.

Min. If they draw sweet hearts, let vs shift for our selues.

Tuc. My noble swaggerer, I wil not fall out with thee, I cannot my mad Cumrade, finde in my heart to shed thy bloud.

Sir Vau. Cumrade? by Sesu call me Cumrade againe, and ile Cumrade ye about the sinnes and shoulders;

ownds, what come you to ſmell out heere ? did you not dine and feede horribly well to day at dinner, but you come to munch heere, and giue vs winter-plummes ? I pray depart, goe marſe, marſe, marſe out a doores.

Tuc. Adew Sir Eglamour, adew Lute-ſtringe, Curtin-rod, Gooſe-quill ; heere, giue that full-noſ'd Skinker, theſe rimes ; & harke Ile tagge my Codpeece point with thy legs, ſpout-pot Ile empty thee.

Aſin. Doſt threaten mee ? Gods lid Ile binde thee to the good forbearing.

Sir Vau. Will you amble Hobby-horſe, will you trot and amble ?

Tuc. Raw Artichocke I ſhall ſauce thee. *Exit.*

Min. I pray you Maſter Tucca, will you ſend me the fiue pound you borrowed on me ; O you cannot heare now, but Ile make you heare me and feele me too in another place, to your ſhame I warrant you, thou ſhalt not conny-catch mee for fiue pounds ; he tooke it vp Sir Vaughan in your name, hee ſwore you ſent for it to Mum withall, twas fiue pound in gold, as white as my kercher.

Sir Vaughan. Ownds, fiue pound in my name to Mum about withall.

Min. I, to Mum withall, but hee playes mum-budget with me.

Sir Vau. Peter Salamander, tye vp your great and your little ſword, by Seſu Ile goe ſing him while tis hot. Ile beate fiue pound out of his leather pilch : Maſter Horace, let your wittes inhabite in your right places ; if I fall ſanſomely vpon the Widdow, I haue ſome coſſens Garman at Court, ſhall beget you the reuerſion of the Maſter of the Kings Reuels, or elſe be his Lord of Miſ-rule nowe at Chriſtmas : Come Ladyes, whoreſon Stragling Captaine, Ile pound him. *Exeunt.*

Manet Horace *and* Aſinius.

Hor. How now, what ail'ſt thou, that thou look'ſt ſo pale ?

Aſin. Nay, nothing, but I am afraide the Welſh

Knight has giuen me nothing but purging Comfits: this Captaine ftickes pockily in my ftomack; read this fcroule, he faies they'r rimes, and bid me giue them you.

Hor. Rimes? tis a challenge fent to you.

Afin. To me?

Hor. He faies heere you divulg'd my Epigrams.

Afin. And for that dares he challenge me?

Hor. You fee he dares, but dare you anfwer him?

Afin. I dare anfwer his challenge, by word of mouth, or by writing, but I fcorne to meete him, I hope he and I are not Paralels.

Hor. Deere Bubo, thou fhalt anfwere him; our credites
Lye pawn'd vpon thy refolution,
Thy vallor muft redeeme them; charge thy fpirits,
To waite more clofe, and neere thee: if he kill thee
Ile not furuiue; into one Lottery
We'll caft our fates; together liue and dye.

Afi. Content, I owe God a death, and if he will make mee pay't againft my will, Ile fay tis hard dealing. *Exeunt.*

Enter Sir Adam, Tucca, *with two piftols by his fides, his boy laden with fwords and bucklers.*

Tuc. Did Apolloes Freeze gowne watchman (boy, doft heare Turkie-cockes tayle, haue an eye behinde, leaft the enemie affault our Rere-ward) on proceede Father Adam; did that fame tiranicall-tongu'd rag-a-muffin Horace, turne bald-pates out fo naked?

Sir Ad. He did, and whipt them fo with nettles, that
The Widdow fwore that a bare-headed man,
Should not man her: the Ladie Petula
Was there, heard all, and tolde me this.

Tuc. Goe too. Thy golde was accepted, it was, and fhe fhall bring thee into her Paradice, fhe fhall fmall Adam, fhe fhall.

Sir Ada. But how? but how Capten?

Tuc. Thus, goe, couer a table with ſweet meates, let all the Gentlewomen, and that ſame Paſquils-mad-cap (mother Bee there) nibble, bid them bite : they will come to gobble downe Plummes; then take vp that paire of Basket hiltes, with my commiſſion, I meane Criſpinus and Fannius; charge one of them to take vp the Bucklers, againſt that hayre-monger Horace, and haue a bout or two, in defence of baldepates : let them cracke euerie crowne that has haire on't : goe, let them lift vp baldenes to the skie, and thou ſhalt ſee, twill turne Miniuers heart quite againſt the haire.

Sir Ada. Excellent, why then M. Tucca——

Tuc. Nay, whir, nymble Prickſhaft; whir, away, I goe vpon life and death, away, flie Scanderbag flie.

Exit.

Enter Aſinius Bubo, *and* Horace *aloofe.*

Boy. Arme Captaine, arme, arme, arme, the foe is come downe.

Tucca *offers to ſhoote.*

Aſi. Hold Capten Tucca holde, I am Bubo, & come to anſwer any thing you can lay to my charge.

Tuc. What, doſt ſummon a parlie my little Drum-ſticke? tis too late; thou ſeeſt my red flag is hung out, Ile fill thy guts with thine owne carrion carcas, and then eate them vp in ſteed of Sawſages.

Aſin. Vſe me how you will; I am reſolute, for I ha made my Will.

Tuc. Wilt fight Turke-a-ten-pence? wilt fight then?

Aſini. Thou ſhalt finde Ile fight in a Godly quarrell, if I be once fir'd.

Tuc. Thou ſhalt not want fire, Ile ha thee burnt when thou wilt, my colde Cornelius : but come : *Reſpice funem*; looke, thou ſeeſt; open thy ſelfe my little Cutlers Shoppe, I challenge thee thou ſlender Gentleman, at foure ſundrie weapons.

Aſi. Thy challenge was but at one, and Ile anſwere but one.

Boy. Thou ſhalt anſwer two, for thou ſhalt anſwer me and my Capten.

Tuc. Well ſaid Cockrell out-crowe him: art hardy noble Huon? art Magnanimious? licke-trencher; looke, ſearch leaſt ſome lye in ambuſh; for this man at Armes has paper in's bellie, or ſome friend in a corner, or elſe hee durſt not bee ſo cranke.

Boy. Capten, Capten, Horace ſtands ſneaking heere.

Tuc. I ſmelt the foule-fiſted Morter-treader, come my moſt damnable faſtidious raſcall, I haue a ſuite to both of you.

Aſi. O holde, moſt pittifull Captaine holde.

Hor. Holde Capten, tis knowne that Horace is valliant, & a man of the ſword.

Tuc. A Gentleman or an honeſt Cittizen, ſhall not Sit in your pennie-bench Theaters, with his Squirrell by his ſide cracking nuttes; nor ſneake into a Tauerne with his Mermaid; but he ſhall be Satyr'd, and Epigram'd vpon, and his humour muſt run vpo'th Stage: you'll ha *Euery Gentleman in's humour*, and *Euery Gentleman out on's humour*: wee that are heades of Legions and Bandes, and feare none but theſe ſame ſhoulder-clappers, ſhall feare you, you Serpentine raſcall.

Hor. Honour'd Capten.

Tuc. Art not famous enough yet, my mad *Horaſtratus*, for killing a Player, but thou muſt eate men aliue? thy friends? Sirra wilde-man, thy Patrons? thou Anthropophagite, thy Mecænaſſes?

Hor. Captaine, I'm ſorry that you lay this wrong.
So cloſe vnto your heart: deare Captaine thinke
I writ out of hot bloud, which (now) being colde,
I could be pleaſ'd (to pleaſe you) to quaffe downe,
The poyſon'd Inke, in which I dipt your name.

Tuc. Saiſt thou ſo, my *Palinodicall* rimeſter?

Hor. Henceforth Ile rather breath out *Solœciſmes.*
(To doe which Ide as ſoone ſpeake blaſphemie)
Than with my tongue or pen to wound your worth,

Beleeue it noble Capten; it to me
Shall be a Crowne, to crowne your actes with praize,
Out of your hate, your loue Ile ſtronglie raize.

Tuc. I know now th'aſt a number of theſe *Quiddits* to binde men to'th peace: tis thy faſhion to flirt Inke in euerie mans face; and then to craule into his boſome, and damne thy ſelfe to wip't off agen: yet to giue out abroad, that he was glad to come to compoſition with me: I know *Monſieur Machiauell* tis one a thy rules; My long-heel'd *Troglodite*, I could make thine eares burne now, by dropping into them, all thoſe hot oathes, to which, thy ſelfe gau'ſt voluntarie fire, (when thou waſt the man in the Moone) that thou wouldſt neuer ſquib out any new Salt-peter Ieſtes againſt honeſt Tucca, nor thoſe Maligo-taſters, his *Poetaſters*; I could Cinocephalus, but I will not, yet thou knowſt thou haſt broke thoſe oathes in print, my excellent infernall.

Ho. Capten.

Tuc. Nay I ſmell what breath is to come from thee, thy anſwer is, that there's no faith to be helde with Heritickes & Infidels, and therfore thou ſwear'ſt anie thing: but come, lend mee thy hand, thou and I henceforth will bee *Alexander* and *Lodwicke*, the Gemini: ſworne brothers, thou ſhalt be *Perithous* and Tucca *Theſeus*; but Ile leaue thee 'i'th lurch, when thou mak'ſt thy voiage into hell: till then, *Thine-aſſuredly.*

Hor. With all my ſoule deare Capten.

Tuc. Thou'lt ſhoote thy quilles at mee, when my terrible backe's turn'd for all this, wilt not Porcupine? and bring me & my Heliconiſtes into thy Dialogues to make vs talke madlie, wut not Lucian?

Hor. Capten, if I doe——

Tuc. Nay and thou doſt, hornes of Lucifer, the *Parcell-Poets* ſhall Sue thy wrangling Muſe, in the Court of Pernaſſus, and neuer leaue hunting her, till ſhe pleade in *Forma Pauperis*: but I hope th'aſt more grace: come: friendes, clap handes tis a bargaine;

amiable Bubo, thy fiſt muſt walke too: ſo, I loue thee, now I ſee th'art a little Hercules, and wilt fight; Ile Sticke thee now in my companie like a ſprig of Roſemary.

Enter Sir Rees ap Vaughan *and* Peter Flaſh.

Fla. Draw Sir Rees he's yonder, ſhall I vpon him?

Sir Vau. Vpon him? goe too, goe too Peter Salamander; holde, in Gods name holde; I will kill him to his face, becauſe I meane he ſhall anſwer for it; being an eye-witnes; one vrde Capten Tucky.

Tuc. Ile giue thee ten thouſand words and thou wilt, my little Thomas Thomaſius.

Sir Vau. By Seſu, tis beſt you giue good vrdes too, leaſt I beate out your tongue, and make your vrde nere to bee taken more; doe you heare, fiue pounds, fiue pounds Tucky.

Tuc. Thou ſhalt ha fiue, and fiue, and fiue, and thou wantſt money my Iob.

Sir Vau. Leaue your fetches and your fegaries, you tough leather-Ierkins; leaue your quandaries, and trickes, and draw vpon me y' are beſt: you conny-catch Widdow *Miniuer-caps* for fiue pounds, and ſay tis for me to cry Mum, and make mee run vp and downe in diſhonors, and diſcredites; is 't not true, you winke-a-pipes raſcall? is not true?

Tuc. Right, true, guilty, I remember 't now; for when I ſpake a good word to the Widdow for thee my young Sampſon ——

Sir Vau. For fiue pounds you cheating ſcab, for 5. pounds, not for me.

Tuc. For thee ô Cæſar, for thee I tooke vp fiue pounds in golde, that lay in her lap, & ſaid Ide giue it thee as a token from her: I did it but to ſmell out how ſhe ſtood affected to thee, to feele her; I, and I know what ſhe ſaid, I know how I carried away the golde.

Sir Vau. By Seſu, I ha not the mercy to ſall vpon

him now: M. Tucky, did widdow Miniuers part quietly from her golde, becaufe you lyed, and faid it was for me?

Tuc. Quietly, in peace, without grumbling; made no noife. I know how I tempted her in thy behalfe, my little Trangdo.

Sir Vau. Capten Tucky, I will pay back her 5. £. (vnles you be damn'd in lyes) & hold you, I pray you pocket vp this; by the croffe a this fword & dagger, Capten you fhall take it.

Tuc. Doft fweare by daggers? nay then Ile put vp more at thy hands then this.

Flafh. Is the fray done fir?

Sir Vau. Done Peter, put vp your fmeeter.

Tuc. Come hether, my foure-fac'd Poet; fling away that beard-brufh Bubo, cafheere him and harke: Knight attend: So, that raw-head and bloudy-bones Sir Adam, has fee'd another brat (of thofe nine commcn wenches) to defend baldnes and to raile againft haire: he 'll haue a fling at thee, my noble Cock-Sparrow.

Sir Vau. At mee? will hee fling the cudgels of his witte at mee?

Tuc. And at thy button-cap too; but come, Ile be your leader, you fhall ftand, heare all, and not be feene; caft off that blew coate, away with that flawne, and follow, come: *Exit.*

Hor. *Bubo*, we follow Captaine.

Sir Vau. Peter, leaue comming behinde me, I pray any longer, for you and I muft part Peter.

Flafh. Sounds Sir, I hope you will not ferue me fo, to turne me away in this cafe.

Sir Vau. Turne you into a fooles coate; I meane I will go *folus*, or in folitaries alone; ounds y-are beft giue better words, or Ile turne you away indeed; where is Capten Tucky? come Horace; get you home Peter.

Flafh. Ile home to your coft, and I can get into the Wine-Seller. *Exit.*

Hor. Remember where to meete mee.

Aſin. Yes Ile meete; Tucca ſhould ha found I dare meete. *Exit.*

Ho. Dare defend baldnes, which our conquering Muſe
Has beaten downe ſo flat? Well, we will goe,
And ſee what weapons theyr weake wittes doe bring;
If ſharpe, we'll ſpred a large and nobler wing;
Tucca, heere lyes thy Peace: warre roares agen;
My Swoord ſhall neuer cutte thee, but my pen. *Exit.*

Enter Sir Adam, Criſpinus, Fannius, Blunt, Miniuer, Petula, Philocalia *and* Dicace.

Ladies. Thankes good Sir Adam.

Sir Ada. Welcome red-cheekt Ladies,
And welcome comely Widdow; Gentlemen,
Now that our ſorry banquet is put by,
From ſtealing more ſweete kiſſes from your lips
Walke in my garden: Ladyes let your eyes
Shed life into theſe flowers by their bright beames,
Sit, Sit, heere's a large bower, heere all may heare,
Now good Criſpinus let your praize begin.
There, where it left off Baldnes.

Criſ. I ſhall winne
No praiſe, by praiſing that, which to depraue,
All tongues are readie, and which none would haue.

Blu. To prooue that beſt, by ſtrong and armed reaſon,
Whoſe part reaſon feares to take, cannot but prooue,
Your wit's fine temper, and from theſe win loue.

Min. I promiſe you has almoſt conuerted me, I pray bring forward your bald reaſons M. Poet.

Cri. Miſtris you giue my Reaſons proper names,
For Arguments (like Children) ſhould be like,
The ſubiect that begets them; I muſt ſtriue,
To crowne *Bald heades*, therefore muſt baldlie thriue;
But be it as it can: To what before,
Went arm'd at table, this force bring I more,
If a *Bare head* (being like a dead-mans ſcull)

Should beare vp no praiſe els but this, it ſets
Our end before our eyes ; ſhould I diſpaire,
From giuing *Baldnes* higher place then haire ?

Mini. Nay perdie, haire has the higher place.

Cri. The goodlieſt & moſt glorious ſtrange-built wonder,
Which that great Architect hath made, is heauen ;
For there he keepes his Court, It is his Kingdome,
That 's his beſt Maſter-piece ; yet tis the roofe,
And Seeling of the world : that may be cal'd
The head or crowne of Earth, and yet that 's balde,
All creatures in it balde ; the louely *Sunne,*
Has a face ſleeke as golde ; the full-cheekt *Moone,*
As bright and ſmooth as ſiluer : nothing there
Weares dangling lockes, but ſometime blazing Starres,
Whoſe flaming curles, ſet realmes on fire with warres.
Deſcend more low ; looke through mans fiue-folde fence,
Of all, the *Eye,* beares greateſt eminence ;
And yet that 's balde, the haires that like a lace,
Are ſticht vnto the liddes, borrow thoſe formes,
Like Pent-houſes to ſaue the eyes from ſtormes.

Sir Adam. Right, well ſaid.

Criſ. A head and face ore-growne with Shaggie droſſe,
O, tis an Orient pearle hid all in Moſſe,
But when the head 's all naked and vncrown'd,
It is the worlds *Globe,* euen, ſmooth and round ;
Baldnes is natures *But,* at which our life,
Shootes her laſt Arrow : what man euer lead
His age out with a ſtaffe, but had a head
Bare and vncouer'd ? hee whoſe yeares doe riſe,
To their full height, yet not balde, is not wiſe.
The *Head* is Wiſedomes houſe, *Haire* but the thatch,
Haire ? It 's the baſeſt ſtubble ; in ſcorne of it,
This Prouerbe ſprung, *he has more haire then wit* :
Marke you not in deriſion how we call,
A head growne thicke with haire, *Buſh-naturall* ?

Min. By your leaue (Maſter Poet) but that Buſh-naturall, is one a the trimmeſt, and moſt intanglingſt beautie in a woman.

Criſ. Right, but beleeue this (*pardon me moſt faire*)
You would haue much more wit, had you leſſe haire:
I could more wearie you to tell the proofes,
(As they paſſe by) which fight on *Baldnes* ſide,
Then were you taskt to number on a head,
The haires: I know not how your thoughts are lead,
On this ſtrong Tower ſhall my opinion reſt,
Heades thicke of haire are goode, but balde the beſt.

Whilſt this Paradox is in ſpeaking, Tucca *Enters with* Sir Vaughan *at one doore, and ſecretly placeth him: then Exit and brings in* Horace *muffled, placing him:* Tucca *ſits among them.*

Tuc. Th' art within a haire of it, my ſweete *Wit whether wilt thou?* my delicate Poeticall Furie, th' aſt hit it to a haire.

Sir Vaughan *ſteps out.*

Sir Vau. By your fauour Maſter Tucky, his balde reaſons are wide aboue two hayres, I beſees you pardon mee Ladies, that I thruſt in ſo malepartly among you, for I did but mych heere, and ſee how this cruell Poet did handle bald heades.

Sir Ad. He gaue them but their due Sir Vaughan; Widdow did he not?

Mini. By my faith he made more of a balde head, than euer I ſhall be able: he gaue them their due truely.

Sir Vaugh. Nay vds bloud, their due is to bee a the right haire as I am, and that was not in his fingers to giue, but in God a Mighties: Well, I will hyre that humorous and fantaſticall Poet Maſter Horace, to breake your balde pate Sir Adam.

Sir Ada. Breake my balde pate?

Tuc. Doſt heare my worſhipfull block-head?

Sir Vaug. Patience Captaine Tucky, let me abſolue him; I meane he ſhal pricke, pricke your head or ſconce a little with his gooſe-quils, for he ſhal make another Thalimum, or croſſe-ſtickes, or ſome Polinoddyes, with a fewe Nappy-grams in them that ſhall lift vp haire, and ſet it an end, with his learned and harty commendations.

Hor. This is excellent, all will come out now.

Dica. That ſame Horace me thinkes has the moſt vngodly face, by my Fan; it lookes for all the world, like a rotten ruſſet Apple, when tis bruiz'd: Its better then a ſpoonefull of Sinamon water next my heart, for me to heare him ſpeake; hee ſoundes it ſo i' th noſe, and talkes and randes for all the world, like the poore fellow vnder Ludgate: oh fye vpon him.

Min. By my troth ſweet Ladies, it's Cake and pudding to me, to ſee his face make faces, when hee reades his Songs and Sonnets.

Hor. Ile face ſome of you for this, when you ſhall not budge.

Tuc. Its the ſtinckingſt dung-farmer—foh vpon him.

Sir Vau. Foh? oundes you make him vrſe than olde herring: foh? by Seſu I thinke he's as tidy, and as tall a Poet as euer drew out a long verſe.

Tuc. The beſt verſe that euer I knew him hacke out, was his white necke-verſe: noble Ap Rees thou wouldſt ſcorne to laye thy lippes to his commendations, and thou ſmeldſt him out as I doe, hee calles thee the burning Knight of the Salamander.

Sir Vaugh. Right, Peter is my Salamander; what of him? but Peter is neuer burnt: howe now? ſo, goe too now.

Tucca. And ſayes becauſe thou Clipſt the Kinges Engliſh.

Sir Vaughan. Oundes mee? that's treaſon: clip? horrible treaſons, Seſu holde my handes; clip? he baites mouſe-trappes for my life.

Tucca. Right little *Twinckler*, right: hee ſayes becauſe thou ſpeak'ſt no better, thou canſt not keepe a good tongue in thy head.

Sir Vaug. By God tis the beſt tongue, I can buy for loue or money.

Tuc. He ſhootes at thee too Adam Bell, and his arrowes ſtickes heere; he calles thee bald-pate.

Sir Vaugh. Oundes make him prooue theſe intollerabilities.

Tuc. And askes who ſhall carry the vineger-bottle? & then he rimes too't, and ſayes Prickſhaft: nay Miniuer hee cromples thy Cap too; and ——

Cri. Come Tucca, come, no more; the man's wel knowne, thou needſt not paint him, whom does he not wrong?

Tuc. Mary himſelfe, the vglie Pope Boniface, pardons himſelfe, and therefore my iudgement is, that preſently he bee had from hence to his place of execution, and there bee Stab'd, Stab'd, Stab'd.

He ſtabs at him.

Hor. Oh gentlemen, I am ſlaine, oh ſlaue art hyr'd to murder me, to murder me, to murder me?

Ladies. Oh God!

Sir Vaugh. Ounds Capten, you haue put all Poetrie to the dint of ſword, blow winde about him: Ladies for our Lordes ſake you that haue ſmocks, teare off peeces to ſhoote through his oundes: Is he dead and buried? is he? pull his noſe, pinch, rub, rub, rub, rub.

Tu. If he be not dead, looke heere; I ha the Stab and pippin for him: if I had kil'd him, I could ha pleaſ'd the great foole with an Apple.

Criſ. How now? be well good Horace, heer's no wound;
Y'are ſlaine by your owne feares; how doſt thou man?
Come, put thy heart into his place againe;
Thy out-ſide's neither peir'ſt, nor In-ſide ſlaine.

Sir Vau. I am glad M. Horace, to ſee you walking.

Ho. Gentlemen, I am blacke and blewe the breadth of a groate.

Tuc. Breadth of a groate? there's a teſton, hide thy infirmities, my ſcuruy Lazarus; doe, hide it, leaſt it prooue a ſcab in time : hang thee deſperation, hang thee, thou knowſt I cannot be ſharpe ſet againſt thee : looke, feele (my light-vptailes all) feele my weapon.

Mi. O moſt pittifull as blunt as my great thumbe.

Sir Vau. By Seſu, as blunt as a Welſh bag-pudding.

Tuc. As blunt as the top of Poules; tis not like thy Aloe, Cicatrine tongue, bitter: no, tis no ſtabber, but like thy goodly and glorious noſe, blunt, blunt, blunt: doſt roare bulchin? doſt roare? th' aſt a good rounciuall voice to cry Lanthorne & Candle-light.

Sir Va. Two vrds Horace about your eares: how chance it paſſes, that you bid God boygh to an honeſt trade of building Symneys, and laying downe Brickes, for a worſe handicraftnes, to make nothing but railes; your Muſe leanes vpon nothing but filthy rotten railes, ſuch as ſtand on Poules head, how chance?

Hor. Sir Vaughan.

Sir Va. You lye ſir varlet ſir villaine, I am ſir Salamanders, ounds, is my man Maſter Peter Salamanders face as vrſe as mine? Sentlemen, all and Ladies, and you ſay once or twice Amen, I will lap this little Silde, this Booby in his blankets agen.

Omnes. Agree'd, agree'd.

Tuc. A blanket, theſe crackt Venice glaſſes ſhall fill him out, they ſhall toſſe him, holde faſt wag-tailes: ſo, come, in, take this bandy with the racket of patience, why when? doſt ſtampe mad Tamberlaine, doſt ſtampe? thou thinkſt th' aſt Morter vnder thy feete, doſt?

Ladies. Come, a bandy ho.

Hor. O holde moſt ſacred beauties.

Sir Vau. Hold, ſilence; the puppet-teacher ſpeakes.

Ho. Sir Vaughan, noble Capten, Gentlemen,
Criſpinus, deare Demetrius ô redeeme me,
Out of this infamous —— by God by Ieſu ——

Cri. Nay, ſweare not ſo good Horace, now theſe Ladies,
Are made your executioners: prepare,

To ſuffer like a gallant, not a coward;
Ile trie t' vnlooſe, their hands, impoſſible.
Nay, womens vengeance are implacable.

Hor. Why, would you make me thus the ball of ſcorne?

Tuc. Ile tell thee why, becauſe th' aſt entred Actions of aſſault and battery, againſt a companie of honourable and worſhipfull Fathers of the law: you wrangling raſcall, law is one of the pillers ath land, and if thou beeſt bound too't (as I hope thou ſhalt bee) thou't prooue a skip-Jacke, thou't be whipt. Ile tell thee why, becauſe thy ſputtering chappes yelpe, that Arrogance, and Impudence, and Ignoraunce, are the eſſentiall parts of a Courtier.

Sir Vau. You remember Horace they will puncke, and pincke, and pumpe you, and they catch you by the coxcombe: on I pray, one laſh, a little more.

Tuc. Ile tell thee why, becauſe thou cryeſt ptrooh at worſhipfull Cittizens, and cal'ſt them Hat-caps, Cuckolds, and banckrupts, and modeſt and vertuous wiues punckes & cockatrices. Ile tell thee why, becauſe th' aſt arraigned two Poets againſt all lawe and conſcience; and not content with that, haſt turn'd them amongſt a company of horrible blacke Fryers.

Sir Vau. The ſame hand ſtill, it is your owne another day, M. Horace, admonitions is good meate.

Tuc. Thou art the true arraign'd Poet, and ſhouldſt haue been hang'd, but for one of theſe part-takers, theſe charitable Copper-lac'd Chriſtians, that fetcht thee out of Purgatory, (Players I meane) Theaterians pouch-mouth, Stage-walkers; for this Poet, for this, thou muſt lye with theſe foure wenches, in that blancket, for this ——

Hor. What could I doe, out of a iuſt reuenge,
But bring them to the Stage? they enuy me
becauſe I holde more worthy company.

Deme. Good Horace, no; my cheekes do bluſh for thine,
As often as thou ſpeakſt ſo, where one true

And nobly-vertuous ſpirit, for thy beſt part
Loues thee, I wiſh one ten, euen from my heart.]
I make account I put vp as deepe ſhare
In any good mans loue, which thy worth earne s,
As thou thy ſelfe; we enuy not to ſee,
Thy friends with Bayes to crowne thy Poeſie.
No, heere the gall lyes, we that know what ſtuffe
Thy verie heart is made of; know the ſtalke
On which thy learning growes, and can giue life
To thy (once dying) baſenes; yet muſt we
Dance Antickes on your Paper.

Hor. Fannius.

Cri. This makes vs angry, but not enuious,
No; were thy warpt ſoule, put in a new molde,
Ide weare thee as a Iewell ſet in golde.

Sir Vau. And Iewels Maſter Horace, muſt be hang'd you know.

Tuc. Good Pagans, well ſaid, they haue ſowed vp that broken ſeame-rent lye of thine, that Demetrius is out at Elbowes, and Criſpinus is falne out with Sattin heere, they haue; but bloate herring doſt heere?

Hor. Yes honour'd Captaine, I haue eares at will.

Tuc. Iſt not better be out at Elbowes, then to bee a bond-ſlaue, and to goe all in Parchment as thou doſt?

Horace. Parchment Captaine? tis Perpetuana I aſſure you.

Tuc. My Perpetuall pantaloone true, but tis waxt ouer; th'art made out of Wax; thou muſt anſwere for this one day; thy Muſe is a hagler, and weares cloathes vpon beſt-be-truſt: th'art great in ſome bodies books for this, thou knowſt where; thou wouldſt bee out at Elbowes, and out at heeles too, but that thou layeſt about thee with a Bill for this, a Bill—

Ho. I confeſſe Capten, I followed this ſuite hard.

Tuc. I know thou didſt, and therefore we haue Hiren heere, ſpeake my little diſh-waſhers, a verdit Piſſe-kitchins.

Omnes. Blancket.

Sir Vau. Holde I pray, holde, by Sesu I haue put vpon my heade, a fine deuice, to make you laugh, tis not your fooles Cap Mafter Horace, which you couer'd your Poetafters in, but a fine tricke, ha, ha, is iumbling in my braine.

Tuc. Ile beate out thy braines, my whorfon hanfome dwarfe, but ile haue it out of thee.

Omnes. What is it good Sir Vaughan?

Sir Vau. To conclude, tis after this manners, becaufe Ma. Horace is ambition, and does confpire to bee more hye and tall as God a mightie made him, wee'll carry his terrible perfon to Court, and there before his Mafeftie Dub, or what you call it, dip his Mufe in fome licour, and chriften him, or dye him, into collours of a Poet.

Omnes. Excellent.

Tuc. Super Super-excellent Reuellers goe, proceede you Mafters of Arte in kiffing thefe wenches, and in daunces, bring you the quiuering Bride to Court, in a Maske, come Grumboll, thou fhalt Mum with vs; come, dogge mee skneakes-bill.

Hor. O thou my Mufe!

Sir Vau. Call vpon God a mighty, and no Mufes, your Mufe I warrant is otherwife occupied, there is no dealing with your Mufe now, therefore I pray marfe, marfe, marfe, oundès your Moofe? *Exeunt.*

Cri. We fhal haue fport to fee them; come bright beauties,
The Sunne ftoops low, and whifpers in our eares,
To haften on our Maske, let's crowne this night,
With choife compofed wreathes of fweet delight.
Exeunt.

Enter Terrill *and* Cæleftine *fadly,* Sir Quintilian *ftirring and migling a cup of wine.*

Ter. O Night, that Dyes the Firmament in blacke,
And like a cloth of cloudes doft ftretch thy limbes;
Vpon the windy Tenters of the Ayre:

O thou that hang'ſt vpon the backe of Day,
Like a long mourning gowne : thou that art made
Without an eye, becauſe thou ſhouldſt not ſee
A Louers Reuels : nor participate
The Bride-groomes heauen ; ô heauen, to me a hell :
I haue a hell in heauen, a bleſſed curſſe ;
All other Bride-groomes long for Night, and taxe
The Day of lazie ſlouth ; call Time a Cripple,
And ſay the houres limpe after him : but I
Wiſh Night for euer baniſht from the skie,
Or that the Day would neuer ſleepe : or Time,
Were in a ſwound ; and all his little Houres,
Could neuer lift him vp with their poore powers.

Enter Cæleſtine.

But backward runnes the courſe of my delight ;
The day hath turn'd his backe, and it is night :
This night will make vs odde ; day made vs eeuen,
All elſe and damb'd in hel, but I in heauen.
Cæ. Let looſe thy oath, ſo ſhal we ſtill be euen.
Ter. Then am I damb'd in hell, and not in heauen.
Cæl. Muſt I then goe ? tis eaſie to ſay no,
Muſt is the King himſelfe, and I muſt goe ;
Shall I then goe ? that word is thine ; I ſhall,
Is thy commaund : I goe becauſe I ſhall ;
Will I then goe ? I aske my ſelfe ; ô ill,
King, ſaies I muſt : you, I ſhall ; I, I will.
Ter. Had I not ſworne.
Cæl. Why didſt thou ſweare ?
Ter. The King
Sat heauy on my reſolution,
Till (out of breath) it panted out an oath,
Cæl. An oath ? why, what's an oath ? tis but the ſmoake,
Of flame & bloud ; the bliſter of the ſpirit,
Which rizeth from the Steame of rage, the bubble

That fhootes vp to the tongue, and fcaldes the voice,
(For oathes are burning words, thou fwor'ft but one,
Tis frozen long agoe: if one be numbred,
What Countrimen are they? where doe they dwell,
That fpeake naught elfe but oathes?
Ter. They're men of hell.
An oath? why tis the trafficke of the foule,
Tis law within a man; the feale of faith,
The bond of euery confcience; vnto whom,
We fet our thoughts like hands: yea fuch a one
I fwore, and to the King: A King containes
A thoufand thoufand; when I fwore to him,
I fwore to them; the very haires that guard
His head, will rife vp like sharpe witneffes
Againft my faith and loyalty: his eye
Would ftraight condemne me: argue oathes no more,
My oath is high, for to the King I fwore.

Enter Sir Quintilian *with the cup.*

Cæ. Muft I betray my Chaftity? So long
Cleane from the treafon of rebelling luft;
O husband! O my Father! if poore I
Muft not liue chaft, then let me chaftly dye.
S. qui. I, heer's a charme fhall keep thee chafte, come, come,
Olde Time hath left vs but an houre to play
Our parts; begin the Sceane, who shall fpeake firft?
Oh, I, I play the King, and Kings fpeake firft;
Daughter ftand thou heere, thou Sonne Terrill there,
O thou ftandft well, thou lean'ft againft a poaft,
(For thou't be pofted off I warrant thee:)
The King will hang a horne about thy necke,
And make a poaft of thee; you ftand well both,
We neede no Prologue, the King entring firft,
He's a moft gracious Prologue: mary then
For the Cataftrophe, or Epilogue,
Ther's one in cloth of Siluer, which no doubt,

Will pleaſe the hearers well when he ſteps out;
His mouth is fil'd with words: ſee where he ſtands;
He'll make them clap their eyes beſides their hands.
But to my part; ſuppoſe who enters now,
A King, whoſe eyes are ſet in Siluer; one
That bluſheth golde, ſpeakes Muſicke, dancing walkes,
Now gathers neerer takes thee by the hand,
When ſtraight thou thinkſt, the very Orbe of heauen,
Mooues round about thy fingers, then he ſpeakes,
Thus—thus—I know not how.

Cæl. Nor I to anſwer him.

Sir Quint. No girle? knowſt thou not how to anſwer him?
Why then the field is loſt, and he rides home,
Like a great conquerour; not anſwer him?
Out of thy part already? foylde the Sceane?
Diſranckt the lynes? diſarm'd the action?

Ter. Yes, yes, true chaſtity is tongu'd ſo weake,
Tis ouer-come ere it know how to ſpeake.

Sir qui. Come come, thou happy cloſe of euery wrong,
Tis thou that canſt diſſolue the hardeſt doubt;
Tis time for thee to ſpeake, we are all out.
Daughter, and you the man whom I call Sonne,
I muſt confeſſe I made a deede of gift;
To heauen and you and gaue my childe to both:
When on my bleſſing I did charme her ſoule,
In the white circle of true Chaſtity,
Still to run true, till death: now Sir if not,
She forfeyts my rich bleſſing, and is Fin'd
With an eternall curſſe; then I tell you,
She shall dye now, now whilſt her ſoule is true.

Ter. Dye!

Cæl. I, I am deaths eccho.

Sir quin. O my Sonne,
I am her Father; euery teare I ſhed,
Is threeſcore ten yeere olde; I weepe and ſmile
Two kinde of teares: I weepe that ſhe muſt dye,

I ſmile that ſhe muſt dye a Virgin : thus
We ioyfull men mocke teares, and teares mocke vs.
Ter. What ſpeakes that cup ?
Sir quin. White wine and poiſon.
Ter. Oh :
That very name of poiſon, poiſons me ;
Thou Winter of a man, thou walking graue,
Whoſe life is like a dying Taper : how
Canſt thou define a Louers labouring thoughts ?
What Sent haſt thou but death ? what taſte but earth ?
The breath that purles from thee. is like the Steame
Of a new-open'd vault : I know thy drift,
Becauſe thou art trauelling to the land of Graues,
Thou coueſt company, and h ether bringſt,
A health of poiſon to pledge death : a poiſon
For this ſweete ſpring ; this Element is mine,
This is the Ayre I breath ; corrupt it not ;
This heauen is mine, I bought it with my ſoule,
Of him that ſelles a heauen, to buy a ſoule.
Sir quin. Well, let her goe ; ſhe's thine thou cal'ſt her thine,
Thy Element, the Ayre thou breath'ſt ; thou knowſt
The Ayre thou breath'ſt is common, make her ſo :
Perhaps thou't ſay ; none but the King ſhall weare
Thy night-gowne, ſhe that laps thee warme with loue ;
And that Kings are not common : Then to ſhew,
By conſequence he cannot make her ſo,
Indeede ſhe may promoote her ſhame and thine,
And with your ſhames, ſpeake a good word for mine :
The King ſhining ſo cleare, and we ſo dim,
Our darke diſgraces will be ſeene through him.
Imagine her the cup of thy moiſt life,
What man would pledge a King in his own wife ?
Ter. She dyes : that ſentence poiſons her : O life !
What ſlaue would pledge a King in his owne wife ?
Cæl. Welcome, ô poyſon, phiſicke againſt luſt,
Thou holeſome medicine to a conſtant bloud ;
Thou rare Apothecary that canſt keepe,
My chaſtity preſeru'd, within this boxe ;

Of tempting duſt, this painted earthen pot,
That ſtands vpon the ſtall of the white ſoule,
To ſet the ſhop out like a flatterer ;
To draw the cuſtomers of Sinne : come, come,
Thou art no poiſon, but a dyet-drinke,
To moderate my bloud : White-innocent Wine,
Art thou made guilty of my death ? oh no,
For thou thy ſelfe art poiſon'd, take me hence,
For Innocence, ſhall murder Innocence. *Drinkes.*

Ter. Holde, holde, thou ſhalt not dye, my Bride, my wife,
O ſtop that ſpeedy meſſenger of death ;
O let him not run downe that narrow path,
Which leades vnto thy heart ; nor carry newes
To thy remoouing ſoule, that thou muſt dye.

Cæl. Tis done already, the Spirituall Court,
Is breaking vp ; all Offices diſcharg'd,
My ſoule remooues from this weake ſtanding houſe,
Of fraile mortallity ; Deare Father, bleſſe
Me now and euer : Dearer Man, farewell,
I ioyntly take my leaue of thee and life,
Goe, tell the King thou haſt a conſtant wife.

Ter. I had a conſtant wife, Ile tell the King ;
Vntill the King—what doſt thou ſmile ? art thou
A Father ?

Sir quin. Yea, ſmiles on my cheekes ariſe,
To ſee how ſweetly a true virgin dyes.

Enter Blunt, Criſpinus, Fannius, Philocalia, Dicache, Petula, *lights before them.*

Creſ. Sir Walter Terrill gallants are all ready,

Ter. All ready.

Dem. Well ſaid, come, come, wher's the Bride ?

Ter. She's going to forbid the Banes agen.
She'll dye a maide ; and ſee ſhe keeps her oath.

All the men. Faire Cæleſtine !

Ladies. The Bride !

Ter. She that was faire,
Whom I cal'd faire and Cæleſtine.

Omnes. Dead!
Sir quin. Dead, ſhe's deathes Bride, he hath her maidenhead.
Cri. Sir Walter Terrill.
Onmes. Tell vs how.
Ter. All ceaſe,
The ſubiect that we treate of now is *Peace.*
If you demand how: I can tell: if why,
Aske the King that; he was the cauſe, not I.
Let it ſuffice, ſhe's dead, ſhe kept her vow,
Aske the King why, and then Ile tell you how:
Nay giue your Reuels life, tho ſhe be gone,
To Court with all your preparation;
Leade on, and leade her on; if any aske
The miſtery, ſay death preſents a maske,
Ring peales of Muſicke, you are Louers belles,
The loſſe of one heauen, brings a thouſand hels.
Exeunt.

Enter an arm'd Sewer, after him the ſeruice of a Banquet: the King at another doore meetes them, they Exeunt.

Kin. Why ſo, euen thus the Mercury of Heauen,
Vſhers th' ambroſiate banquet of the Gods,
When a long traine of Angels in a ranke,
Serue the firſt courſe, and bow their Chriſtall knees,
Before the Siluer table; where Ioues page
Sweet Ganimed filles Nectar: when the Gods
Drinke healthes to Kings, they pledge them; none but Kings
Dare pledge the Gods, none but Gods drinke to Kings.
Men of our houſe are we prepar'd?

Enter Seruants.

Ser. My Leige,
All waite the preſence of the Bride.
Kin. The Bride?
Yea, euery ſenceles thing, which ſhe beholdes,

Wil looke on her agen, her eyes reflection,
Will make the walles all eyes, with her perfection :
Obſerue me now, becauſe of Maskes and Reuels,
And many nuptiall ceremonies : Marke,
This I create the Preſence heere the State,
Our Kingdomes ſeate, ſhall ſit in honours Pride,
Like pleaſures Queene, there will I place the Bride :
Be gone, be ſpeedy, let me ſee it done. *Exeunt.*
A King in Loue, is Steward to himſelfe,
And neuer ſcornes the office, my ſelfe buy,
All glances from the Market of her eye.

Soft Muſicke, chaire is ſet vnder a Canopie.

Kin. Sound Muſicke, thou ſweet ſuiter to the ayre,
Now wooe the ayre agen, this is the houre,
Writ in the Calender of time, this houre,
Muſicke ſhall ſpend, the next and next the Bride ;
Her tongue will read the Muſicke-Lecture : Wat
I loue thee Wat, becauſe thou art not wiſe ;
Not deep-read in the volume of a man,
Thou neuer ſawſt a thought, poore ſoule thou thinkſt,
The heart and tongue is cut out of one peece,
But th'art deceau'd, the world hath a falſe light,
Fooles thinke tis day, when wiſe men know tis night.

Enter Sir Quintilian.

Sir quint. My Leige they're come a maske of gallants,

King. Now —— the ſpirit of Loue vſhers my bloud.

Sir quin. They come.
The Watch-word in a Maske is the bolde Drum.

Enter Blunt, Criſpinus, Demetrius, Philocalia, Petula, Dicache, *all maskt, two and two with lights like maskers* : Cæleſtine *in a chaire.*

Ter. All pleaſures guard my King, I heere preſent,
My oath vpon the knee of duety : knees
Are made for Kings, they are the ſubiects Fees.

King. Wat Terrill, th'art ill ſuited, ill made vp,

In Sable collours, like a night peece dyed,
Com'ſt thou the Prologue of a Maske in blacke;
Thy body is ill ſhapt; a Bride-groome too?
Looke how the day is dreſt in Siluer cloth,
Laide round about with golden Sunne-beames: ſo
(As white as heauen) ſhould a freſh Bride-groome goe.
What? Cæleſtine the Bride, in the ſame taske?
Nay then I ſee ther's miſtery in this maske,
Prethee reſolue me Wat?

Ter. My gracious Lord,
That part is hers, ſhe actes it; onely I
Preſent the Prologue, ſhe the miſterie.

Kin. Come Bride, the Sceane of bluſhing entred firſt,
Your cheekes are ſetled now, and paſt the worſt;
Vnmasks her.
A miſtery? oh none plaies heere but death,
This is deaths motion, motionles; ſpeake you,
Flatter no longer; thou her Bride-groome; thou
Her Father ſpeake,

Sir quint. Dead.

Ter. Dead.

Kin. How?

Sir quin. Poyſon'd.

King. And poyſon'd?
What villaine durſt blaſpheme her beauties, or
Prophane the cleare religion of her eyes.

Ter. Now King I enter, now the Sceane is mine,
My tongue is tipt with poiſon: know who ſpeakes,
And looke into my thoughts; I bluſh not King,
To call thee Tyrant: death hath ſet my face,
And made my bloud bolde: heare me ſpirits of men,
And place your eares vpon your hearts; the day
(The fellow to this night) ſaw her and me,
Shake hands together: for the booke of heauen,
Made vs eternall friends: thus, *Man and Wife*,
This man of men (the King) what are not kings?
Was my chiefe gueſt, my royall gueſt, his Grace
Grac'd all the Table, and did well become

The vpper end, where ſate my Bride : in briefe,
He tainted her chaſte eares ; ſhe yet vnknowne,
His breath was treaſon, tho his words were none.
Treaſon to her and me, he dar'd me then,
(Vnder the couert of a flattering ſmile,)
To bring her where ſhe is not as ſhe is,
Aliue for luſt, not dead for Chaſtity :
The reſolution of my ſoule, out-dar'd,
I ſwore and taxt my faith with a ſad oath ;
Which I maintaine ; heere take her, ſhe was mine,
When ſhe was liuing, but now dead, ſhe's thine.

Kin. Doe not confound me quite ; for mine owne guilt,
Speakes more within me then thy tongue containes ;
Thy ſorrow is my ſhame : yet heerein ſprings,
Ioy out of ſorrow, boldnes out of ſhame ;
For I by this haue found, once in my life,
A faithfull ſubiect, thou a conſtant wife.

Cœl. A conſtant wife.

Kin. Am I confounded twice ?
Blaſted with wonder.

Ter. O delude me not.
Thou art too true to liue agen, too faire
To be my Cæleſtine, too conſtant farre
To be a woman.

Cœl. Not to be thy wife,
But firſt I pleade my duetie, and ſalute
The world agen.

Sir quin. My King, my Sonne, know all,
I am an Actor in this miſterie,
And beare the chiefeſt part. The Father I,
Twas I that miniſtred to her chaſte bloud,
A true ſomniferous potion, which did ſteale
Her thoughts to ſleepe, and flattered her with death :
I cal'd it a quick poiſon'd drug, to trie
The Bride-groomes loue, and the Brides conſtancie.
He in the paſſion of his loue did fight,
A combat with affection ; ſo did both,
She for the poiſon ſtroue, he for his oath :

Thus like a happie Father, I haue won,
A conftant Daughter, and a louing Sonne.
Kin. Mirrour of Maidens, wonder of thy name,
I giue thee that art giuen, pure, chafte, the fame
Heere Wat: I would not part (for the worlds pride)
So true a Bride-groome, and fo chafte a Bride.
Cri. My Leige, to wed a Comicall euent,
To prefuppofed tragicke Argument:
Vouchfafe to exercife your eyes, and fee
A humorous dreadfull Poet take degree.
Kin. Dreadfull in his proportion or his pen?
Crif. In both, he calles himfelfe the whip of men.
Kin. If a cleare merrit ftand vpon his praife,
Reach him a Poets Crowne (the honour'd Bayes)
But if he claime it, wanting right thereto,
(As many baftard Sonnes of Poefie doe)
Race downe his vfurpation to the ground.
True Poets are with Arte and Nature Crown'd.
But in what molde fo ere this man bee caft,
We make him thine Crifpinus, wit and iudgement,
Shine in thy numbers, and thy foule I know,
Will not goe arm'd in paffion gainft thy foe:
Therefore be thou our felfe; whilft our felfe fit,
But as fpectator of this Sceane of wit.
Cri. Thankes royall Lord, for thefe high honors done,
To me vnworthie, my mindes brighteft fires
Shall all confume themfelues in pureft flame,
On the Alter of your deare eternall name.
Kin. Not vnder vs, but next vs take thy Seate,
"*Artes nourifhed by Kings make Kings more great,*
Vfe thy Authority.
Crif. Demetrius.
Call in that *felfe-creating Horace*, bring
Him and his *fhaddow* foorth.
Dem. Both fhall appeare,
"*No black-eyed ftar muft fticke in vertues Spheare.*

Enter Sir Vaughan.

Sir Va. Ounds did you fee him, I pray let all his Mafefties moft excellent dogs, be fet at liberties, and haue their freedoms to fmell him out.

Dem. Smell whom?

Sir Vaugh. Whom? the *Compofer*, the *Prince of Poets*, *Horace*, *Horace*, he's departed: in Gods name and the Kinges I farge you to ring it out from all our eares, for Horaces bodie is departed: Mafter hue and crie fhall——God bleffe King Williams, I crie you mercy and aske forgiuenes, for mine eyes did not finde in their hearts to looke vppon your Maieftie.

Kin. What news with thee Sir Vaughan?

Sir Vau. Newes? God tis as vrfe newes as I can defire to bring about mee: our vnhanfome-fac'd Poet does play at bo-peepes with your Grace, and cryes all-hidde as boyes doe.

Officers. Stand by, roome there, backe, roome for the Poet.

Sir Va. He's reprehended and taken, by Sefu, I reioyce very neere as much as if I had difcouer'd a New-found Land, or the North and Eaft Indies.

Enter Tucca, *his boy after him with two pictures vnder his cloake, and a wreath of nettles*: Horace *and* Bubo *pul'd in by th' hornes bound both like Satyres,* Sir Adam *following, Miftris* Miniuer *with him, wearing* Tuccaes *chaine.*

Tuc. So, tug, tug, pull the mad Bull in by' th hornes; So, baite one at that ftake my place-mouth yelpers, and one at that ftake Gurnets-head.

King. What bufie fellow 's this?

Tuc. Saue thee, my moft gracious King a Harts faue thee, all hats and caps are thine, and therefore I vaile: for but to thee great *Sultane Soliman*, I ſcorne to be thus put off or to deliuer vp this ſconce I wud.

Kin. Sir Vaughan, what's this iolly Captaines name?

Sir Va. Has a very ſufficient name, and is a man has done God and his Country as good and as hot Seruice (in conquering this vile Monſter-Poet) as euer did S. George his horſe-backe about the Dragon.

Tuc. I ſweate for 't, but Tawſoone, holde thy tongue Mon du, if thou't praiſe mee, doo't behinde my backe: I am my weighty Soueraigne one of thy graines, thy valliant vaſſaile; aske not what I am, but read, turne ouer, vnclaſpe thy Chronicles: there thou ſhalt finde Buffe-Ierkin; there read my points of war; I am one a thy Mandilian-Leaders; one that enters into thy royall bands for thee; *Pantilius Tucca*; one of thy Kingdomes chiefeſt quarrellers; one a thy moſt faithfull—fy—fy—fy——

Sir Vau. Drunkerds I holde my life.

Tuc. No *whirligig*, one of his faithfull fighters; thy drawer ô royall *Tamor Cham.*

Sir Vau. Goe too, I pray Captaine Tucca, giue vs all leaue to doe our buſines before the King.

Tuc. With all my heart, shi, shi, shi ſhake that *Beare-whelp* when thou wut.

Sir Vau. Horace and Bubo, pray ſend an anſwere into his Maſeſties eares, why you goe thus in Ouids Morter-Morpheſis and ſtrange faſhions of apparell.

Tuc. *Cur* why?

Aſini. My Lords, I was drawne into this beaſtly ſuite by head and ſhoulders onely for loue I bare to my Ningle.

Tuc. Speake Ningle, thy mouth's next, belch out, belch, why——

Hor. I did it to retyre me from the world;
And turne my *Muſe* into a *Timoniſt*,
Loathing the general Leprozie of Sinne,

Which like a plague runs through the ſoules of men:
I did it but to ——

Tu. But to bite euery Motley-head vice by'th noſe, you did it Ningle to play the Bug-beare Satyre, & make a Campe royall of faſhion-mongers quake at your paper Bullets; you Naſtie Tortois, you and your Itchy Poetry breake out like Chriſtmas, but once a yeare, and then you keepe a Reuelling, & Araigning & a Scratching of mens faces, as tho you were Tyber the long-tail'd Prince of Rattes, doe you?

Cri. Horace.

Sir Vaughan. Silence, pray let all vrdes be ſtrangled, or held faſt betweene your teeth

Cri. Vnder controule of my dreade Soueraigne,
We are thy Iudges; thou that didſt Arraigne,
Art now prepar'd for condemnation;
Should I but bid thy *Muſe ſtand to the Barre,*
Thy ſelfe againſt her wouldſt giue euidence:
For flat rebellion gainſt the Sacred lawes
Of diuine Poeſie: heerein moſt ſhe miſt,
Thy pride and ſcorne made her turne Saterijt,
And not her loue to vertue (as thou Preacheſt)
Or ſhould we miniſter ſtrong pilles to thee:
What lumpes of hard and indigeſted ſtuffe,
Of bitter *Satiriſme*, of *Arrogance*,
Of *Selfe-loue*, of *Detraction*, of a blacke
And ſtinking *Inſolence* ſhould we fetch vp?
But none of theſe, we giue thee what's more fit,
With ſtinging nettles Crowne his ſtinging wit.

Tuc. Wel ſaid my Poeticall huckſter, now he's in thy handling rate him, doe rate him well.

Hor. O I beſeech your Maieſty, rather then thus to be netled, Ile ha my Satyres coate pull'd ouer mine eares, and be turn'd out a the nine Muſes Seruice.

Aſin. And I too, let mee be put to my ſhiftes with myne Ningle.

Sir Vau. By Seſu ſo you ſhall M. Bubo; flea off this hairie skin M. Horace, ſo, ſo, ſo, vntruſſe, vntruſſe.

Tuc. His Poeticall wreath my dapper puncke-fetcher.

Hor. Ooh——

Sir Va. Nay, your oohs, nor your *Callin-oes* cannot ferue your turne; your tongue you know is full of bliſters with rayling, your face full of pockey-holes and pimples, with your fierie inuentions: and therefore to preferue your head from aking, this Biggin is yours, —— nay by Sefu you ſhall bee a Poet, though not Lawrefyed, yet Nettlefyed, fo:

Tuc. Sirra ſtincker, thou'rt but vntruſſ'd now, I owe thee a whipping ſtill, and Ile pay it: I haue layde roddes in Piſſe and Vineger for thee: It ſhall not bee the *Whipping a' th Satyre,* nor the Whipping of the blinde-Beare, but of a counterfeit Iugler, that ſteales the name of Horace.

Kin. How? counterfeit? does hee vſurpe that name?

Sir Vau. Yes indeede ant pleaſe your Grace, he does ſup vp that abhominable name.

Tuc. Hee does O King *Cambiſes*, hee does: thou haſt no part of Horace in thee but's name, and his damnable vices: thou haſt ſuch a terrible mouth, that thy beard's afraide to peepe out: but, looke heere you ſtaring Leuiathan, heere's the ſweete viſage of Horace; looke perboylde-face, looke; Horace had a trim long-beard, and a reaſonable good face for a Poet, (as faces goe now-a-dayes) Horace did not skrue and wriggle himſelfe into great Mens famyliarity, (impudentlie) as thou dooſt: nor weare the Badge of Gentlemens company, as thou dooſt thy Taffetie ſleeues tackt too onely with ſome pointes of profit: No, Horace had not his face puncht full of Oylet-holes, like the couer of a warming-pan: Horace lou'd Poets well, and gaue Coxcombes to none but fooles; but thou lou'ſt none, neither Wiſemen nor fooles, but thy ſelfe: Horace was a goodly Corpulent Gentleman, and not ſo leane a hollow-cheekt Scrag as thou art: No, heere's the Coppy of thy countenance, by this will I learne to make a number of villanous faces more, and to looke scuruily vpon'th world, as thou doſt.

Cri. Sir Vaughan will you miniſter their oath?

Sir Vau. Maſter Aſinius Bubo, you ſhall ſweare as little as you can, one oath ſhall damme vp your Innocent mouth.

Aſin. Any oath Sir, Ile ſweare any thing.

Sir Va. You ſhall ſweare by *Phœbus* (who is your Poets good Lord and Maſter,) that heere-after you will not hyre Horace, to giue you poeſies for rings. or hand-kerchers, or kniues which you vnderſtand not, nor to write your Loue-letters; which you (in turning of a hand) ſet your markes vpon, as your owne: nor you ſhall not carry Lattin Poets about you, till you can write and read Engliſh at moſt; and laſtlyc that you ſhall not call Horace your Ningle.

Aſin. By *Phœbus* I ſweare all this, and as many oathes as you will, ſo I may trudge.

Sir Vau. Trudge then, pay your legs for Fees, and bee diſſarg'd.

Tuc. Tprooth . . runne Red-cap, ware hornes there. *Exit Aſi.*

Sir Va. Now Maſter Horace, you muſt be a more horrible ſwearer, for your oath muſt be (like your wittes) of many collours; and like a Brokers booke of many parcels.

Tuc. Read, read; th'inuentory of his oath.

Hor. Ile ſweare till my haire ſtands vp an end, to bee rid of this ſting, oh this ſting.

Sir Vau. Tis not your ſting of conſcience, is it?

Tuc. Vpon him: *Inprimis.*

Sir Vaugh. *Inprimis*, you ſhall ſweare by *Phœbus* and the halfe a ſcore Muſes lacking one: not to ſweare to hang your ſelfe, if you thought any Man, Ooman or Silde, could write Playes and Rimes, as well-fauour'd ones as your ſelfe.

Tuc. Well ſayd, haſt brought him toth gallowes already?

Sir Vaugh. You ſhall ſweare not to bumbaſt out a

new Play, with the olde lynings of Ieſtes, ſtolen from the Temples Reuels.

Tuc. To him olde Tango.

Sir Va. Moreouer, you ſhall not ſit in a Gallery, when your Comedies and Enterludes haue entred their Actions, and there make vile and bad faces at euerie lyne, to make Sentlemen haue an eye to you, and to make Players afraide to take your part.

Tuc. Thou ſhalt be my Ningle for this.

Sir Vau. Beſides, you muſt forſweare to venter on the ſtage, when your Play is ended, and to exchange curtezies, and complements with Gallants in the Lordes roomes, to make all the houſe riſe vp in Armes, and to cry that's Horace, that's he, that's he, that's he, that pennes and purges Humours and diſeaſes.

Tuc. There boy, agen.

Sir Vau. Secondly, when you bid all your friends to the marriage of a poore couple, that is to ſay: your *Wits and neceſſities, alias dictus, to the rifling of your Muſe: alias, your Muſes vp-ſitting: alias a Poet Whitſon-Ale*; you ſhall ſweare that within three dayes after, you ſhall not abroad, in Booke-binders ſhops, brag that your *Vize-royes* or *Tributorie-Kings*, haue done homage to you, or paide quarterage.

Tuc. Ile buſſe thy head Holofernes.

Sir Vaugh. Moreouer and *Inprimis*, when a Knight or Sentlemen of vrſhip, does giue you his paſſe-port, to trauaile in and out to his Company, and giues you money for Gods ſake; I truſt in Seſu, you will ſweare (tooth and nayle) not to make ſcalde and wry-mouth Ieſtes vpon his Knight-hood, will you not?

Hor. I neuer did it by Parnaſſus.

Tuc. Wut ſweare by Parnaſſus and lye too, Doctor Doddipol?

Sir Va. Thirdly, and laſt of all ſauing one, when your Playes are miſſe-likt at Court, you ſhall not crye Mew like a Puſſe-cat, and ſay you are glad you write out of the Courtiers Element.

Tuc. Let the Element alone, tis out a thy reach.

Sir Vau. In brieflynes, when you Sup in Tauernes, amongſt your betters, you ſhall ſweare not to dippe your Manners in too much ſawce, nor at Table to fling Epigrams, Embleames, or Play-ſpeeches about you (lyke Hayle-ſtones) to keepe you out of the terrible daunger of the Shot, vpon payne to ſit at the vpper ende of the Table, a'th left hand of Carlo Buffon: ſweare all this, by Apollo and the eight or nine Muſes.

Hor. By Apollo, Helicon, the Muſes (who march three and three in a rancke) and by all that belongs to Pernaſſus, I ſweare all this.

Tuc. Beare witnes.

Criſ. That fearefull wreath, this honour is your due,
All Poets ſhall be Poet-Apes but you;
Thankes (*Learnings true Mecænas, Poeſies king*)
Thankes for that gracious eare, which you haue lent,
To this moſt tedious, moſt rude argument.

Kin. Our ſpirits haue well been feaſted; he whoſe pen
Draws both corrupt, and cleare bloud from all men:
(Careles what veine he prickes) let him not raue,
When his owne ſides are ſtrucke, blowes, blowes, doe craue.

Tuc. Kings-truce, my noble Hearbe-a-grace; my Princely ſweet-William, a boone—Stay firſt, Iſt a match or no match, Lady Furniuall Iſt?

Sir Ad. & Sir quint. A match?

Mini. I, a match, ſince he hath hit the Miſtris ſo often i'th fore-game, we'll eene play out a rubbers.

Sir Ada. Take her for me.

Sir quin. Take her for thy ſelfe, not for me.

Sir Vau. Play out your rubbers in Gods name, by Seſu Ile neuer boule more in your Alley, Iddow.

Sir Quin. My Chaine.

Sir Adam. My Purſe.

Tuc. Ile Chaine thee preſently, and giue thee ten pound and a purſe: a boone my Leige: . . . . daunce ô my delicate Rufus, at my wedding with this reuerend Antiquary; ist done? wut thou?

Kin. Ile giue thee Kingly honour: *Night* and *Sleepe*,
With silken Ribands would tye vp our eyes,
But Mistris Bride, one measure shall be led,
In scorne of Mid-nights hast, and then to bed.

Exeunt.

EPILOGUS.

Tucca. GEntlemen, Gallants, and you my little Swaggerers that fight lowe: my tough hearts of Oake that ſtand too't ſo valliantly, and are ſtill within a yard of your Capten: Now the Trumpets (that ſet men together by the eares) haue left their Tantara-ragboy, let's part friends. I recant, beare witnes all you Gentle-folkes (that walke i'th Galleries) I recant the opinions which I helde of Courtiers, Ladies, & Cittizens, when once (in an aſſembly of Friers) I railde vpon them: that Hereticall Libertine Horace, taught me ſo to mouth it. Beſides, twas when ſtiffe Tucca was a boy: twas not Tucca that railde and roar'd then, but the Deuill & his Angels: But now, Kings-truce, the Capten Summons a parlee, and deliuers himſelfe and his prating company into your hands, vpon what compoſition you wil. Are you pleaſ'd? and Ile dance Friskin for ioy, but if you be not, by'th Lord Ile ſee you all —— heere for your two pence a peice agen, before Ile looſe your company. I know now ſome be come hyther with cheekes ſwolne as big with hiſſes, as if they had the toot-ach: vds-foote, if I ſtood by them, Ide bee ſo bold as —— intreate them to hiſſe in another place. Are you aduiz'd what you doe when you hiſſe? you blowe away

Horace's reuenge: but if you ſet your hands and Seales to this, Horace will write againſt it, and you may haue more ſport: he ſhall not looſe his labour, he ſhall not turne his blanke verſes into waſt paper: No, my Poetaſters will not laugh at him, but will vntruſſe him agen, and agen, and agen. Ile tell you what you ſhall doe, caſt your little Tucca into a Bell: doe, make a Bell of me, and be al you my clappers, vpon condition, wee may haue a luſtie peale, this colde weather: I haue but two legs left me, and they are both yours: Good night my two penny Tenants Good night.

FINIS.

THE

MAGNIFICENT

Entertainment :

Giuen to King *Iames*, Queene *Anne* his wife, and *Henry Frederick* the Prince, vpon the day of his Maiesties Tryumphant Paſſage (from the Tower) through his Honourable Citie (and Chamber) of *London*, being the 15. of March. 1603.

*As well by the Engliſh as by the Strangers: With the ſpeeches and Songes, deliuered in the ſeue-*rall Pageants.

Mart. *Templa Deis, mores populis dedit, otia ferro,*
Aſtra ſuis, Cælo ſydera, ſerta Ioui.

Tho. Dekker.

Imprinted at London by T. C. for Tho. Man the yonger. 1604.

A DEVICE

(proiected downe, but till now not *publiſht,) that ſhould haue ſerued at his Maieſties firſt acceſſe to the Cittie.*

THe ſorrow and amazement, that like an earthquake began to ſhake the diſtempered body of this Ilād (by reaſon of our late Soueraigns departure,) being wiſely and miraculouſly preuented, and the feared wounds of a ciuill ſword, (as *Alexanders* fury was with Muſicke) being ſtopt from burſting forth, by the ſound of Trompets that proclaimed King *Iames*: All mens eyes were preſently turnd to the North, ſtanding euen ſtone ſtil in their Circles, like the poynts of ſo many Geometricall needles, through a fixed & Adamantine deſire to behold this 45. yeares wonder now brought forth by *Tyme*: their tongues neglecting all language elſe, ſaue that which ſpake zealous prayers, and vnceaſable wiſhes, for his moſt ſpeedy and longd-for arriuall. Inſomuch that the Night was thought vnworthy to be crownd with ſleepe, and the day not fit to be lookt vpon by the Sunne, which brought not ſome freſh tydings of his Maieſties more neare and neerer approach.

At the length *Expectation* (who is euer waking) and

that ſo long was great, grewe neare the time of her deliuery, *Rumor* comming all in a ſweate to play the Midwife, whoſe firſt comfortable words were, that this *Treaſure* of a Kingdome (a Man Ruler) hid ſo many yeares from vs, was now brought to light, and at hand.

Martiall. *Et populi vox erat vna, Venit.*

And that he was to be conducted through ſome vtter part of this his Citie, to his royall Caſtle the *Tower*, that in the age of a man (till this very minute) had not bene acquainted nor borne the name of a Kings Court. Which Entrance of his (in this maner) being fam'de abroad, ¡Becauſe his louing Subiects the Citizens would giue a taſte of their dutie and affection: The *Deuice* following was ſuddeinly made vp, as the firſt ſeruice, to a more royall and ſerious enſuing Entertainment; And this (as it was then purpoſed) ſhould haue bene performed about the Barres beyond Biſhops-gate.

The Deuice.

SAint *George*, Saint *Andrew*, (the Patrons of both Kingdomes) hauing along time lookt vpon each other, with countenances rather of meere ſtrangers, then of ſuch neare Neighbours, vpon the preſent aſpect of his *Maieſties* approach toward *London*, were (in his ſight) to iſſue from two ſeuerall places on horſe-backe, and in compleate Armour, their Breſtes and Capariſons ſuited with the Armes of *England* and *Scotland*, (as they are now quartered) to teſtifie their leagued Combination, and newe ſworne Brother-hood. Theſe two armed Knights, encountring one another on the way, were to ride hand in hand, till they met his *Maieſtie*. But the ſtrangeneſſe of this newly-begotten amitie, flying ouer the earth, It calles vp the *Genius* of the Cittie, who (not ſo much mazde, as wondring at the Noueltie) Interſepts their Paſſage.

And moſt aptly (in our Iudgement) might this *Domeſticum Numen* (the *Genius* of the place) lay iuſt clayme to this preheminence of firſt beſtowing Salutations and welcomes on his *Maieſtie*, *Genius* being held (*Inter fictos Deos*), to be God of Hoſpitalitie and Pleaſure: and none but ſuch a one was meet to receiue ſo excellent and princely a Gueſt.

Or if not worthy, for thoſe two former reſpects: Yet being *Deus Generationis*, and hauing a power aſ-well ouer Countries, hearbs and trees, as ouer men, and the Cittie hauing now put on a *Regeneration*, or new birth; the induction of ſuch a Perſon, might (without a Warrant from the court of *Critiſts*) paſſe very currant.

To made a falſe floriſh here with the borrowed weapons of all the old Maiſters of the noble Science of Poeſie, and to keepe a tyrannicall coyle, in Anatomizing *Genius*, from head to foote, (only to ſhew how nimbly we can carue vp the whole meſſe of the Poets) were to play the Executioner, and to lay our Cities houſhold God on the rack, to make him confeſſe, how many paire of Latin ſheets, we haue ſhaken & cut into ſhreds to make him a garment. Such feates of Actiuitie are ſtale, and common among Schollers, (before whome it is proteſted we come not now (in a Pageant) to Play a Maiſters prize) For *Nunc ego ventoſæ Plebis ſuffragia venor.*

The multitude is now to be our Audience, whoſe heads would miſerably runne a wooll-gathering, if we doo but offer to breake them with hard words. But ſuppoſe (by the way) contrary to the opinion of all the Doctors) that our *Genius* (in regarde the place is *Feminine*, and the perſon it ſelfe, drawne *Figura Humana, ſed Ambiguo ſexu*) ſhould at this time be thruſt into womans apparrell. It is no Schiſme: be it ſo: our *Genius* is then a female, Antique; and reuerend both in yeares and habit: a Chaplet of mingled flowres, Inter wouen with branches of the Plane Tree (crowning her Temples: her haire long and white: her Veſture a loose roabe, Changeable and powdred with Starres: And being (on horſebacke likewiſe) thus furniſhed, this was the tune of her voyce.

Genius Locj.

S*Tay : wee coniure you, by that Potent Name,*
Of which each Letter's (now) a triple charme :
Stay ; and deliuer vs, of whence you are,
And why you beare (alone) th'oſtent of Warre,
When all hands elſe reare Oliue-*boughs and* Palme :
And Halcyonean *dayes aſſure all's calme.*
When euery tongue ſpeakes Muſick : when each Pen
(Dul'd and dyde blacke in Galle) is white agen,
And dipt in Nectar, *which by* Delphick *fire*
Being heated, melts into an Orphean-*quire.*
When Troyes *proud buildings ſhew like* Fairie-*bowers,*
And Streets (like Gardens) are perfum'd with Flowers :
And Windowes glazde onely with wondring eyes ;
(In a Kings *looke ſuch admiration lyes !)*
And when ſoft handed Peace, *ſo ſweetly thriues,*
That Bees *in* Souldiers *Helmets build their Hiues :*
When Ioy a tip-toe ſtands on Fortunes *Wheele,*
In ſilken Robes : How dare you ſhine in Steele ?

Saint George.

Ladie, What are you that ſo queſtion vs?

Genius.

I *Am the places* Genius, *whence now ſprings*
A Vine, *whoſe yongeſt Braunch ſhall produce Kings*:
This little world of men; this precious Stone,
That ſets out Europe: *this (the glaſſe alone,)*
Where the neat Sunne each Morne himſelfe attires,
And gildes it with his repercuſsiue fires.
This Iewell of the Land; Englands *right Eye*:
Altar of Loue; *and Spheare of Maiestie*:
Greene Neptunes *Minion, bou't whoſe Virgin-wa'le,*
Iſis *is like a Criſtall girdle caſt.*
Of this are we the Genius; *here haue I,*
Slept (by the fauour of a Deity)
Fortie-foure Summers and as many Springs,
Not frighted with the threats of forraine Kings.
But held vp in that gowned State I haue,
By twice Twelue-Fathers politique and graue:
Who with a ſheathed Sword, and ſilken Law,
Do keepe (within weake Walles) Millions in awe.

I charge you therefore ſay, for what you come?
What are you?
Both. Knights at Armes.
S. George. *Saint George.*
Saint Andrew. *Saint Andrew.*
For *Scotlands* honour I.
S. George. For *Englands* I
Both ſworne into a League of Vnitie.

Genius.

I *Clap my hands for Ioy, and ſeate you both*
Next to my heart: *In leaues of pureſt golde,*
This moſt auſpicious loue ſhall be enrold.
Be ioynde to vs: *And as to earth we bowe,*

So, to thoſe royall feet, bende your ſteelde brow.
In name of all theſe Senators, (*on whom*
Vertue builds more, then theſe of Antique Rome)
Shouting a cheerefull welcome: Since no clyme,
Nor Age that has gon or'e the head of Time,
Did e're caſt vp ſuch Ioyes, nor the like Summe
(*But here*) *ſhall ſtand in the world, yeares to come,*
Dread King, *our hearts make good, what words do want,*
To bid thee boldly enter Troynouant.

Rerum certa ſalus, Terrarum gloria Cæſar ! Mart.
Sospite quo, magnos credimus eſse Deos :
Dilexere priùs pueri, Iuveneſque ſeneſque, Idem.
At Nunc Infantes te quoque Cæſar *amant.*

This ſhould haue beene the firſt Offring of the Citties Loue : But his *Maieſtie* not making his *Entrance* (according to expectation) It was (not vtterly throwne from the Alter) but layd by.

Mart. *Iam Crescunt media Pægmata celsa via.*

BY this time Imagine, that *Poets* (who drawe speaking Pictures) and *Painters* (who make dumbe Poesie) had their heads & hands full; the one for natiue and sweet Inuention; the other for liuely Illustration of what the former should deuise: Both of them emulously contending (but not striuing) with the proprest and brightest Colours of Wit and Art, to set out the beautie of the great *Triumphant day.*

For more exact and formall managing of which Businesse, a Select number both of Aldermen and Commoners (like so many Romane *Ædiles*) were (*Communi. Consilio*) chosen forth, to whose discretion, the *Charge*, *Contriuings*, *Proiects*, and all other *Dependences*, owing to so troublesome a worke, was intirely, and Iudicially committed.

Many dayes were thriftily consumed, to molde the bodies of these Tryumphes comely, and to the honour of the Place: & at last, the stuffe whereof to frame them, was beaten out. The Soule that should giue life, & a tongue to thls *Entertainment*, being to breathe out of Writers Pens. The Limmes of it to lye at the hard-handed mercy of Mychanitiens.

In a moment therefore of Time, are Carpenters, Ioyners, Caruers, and other Artificers sweating at their Chizzells.

Vir. *Accingunt Omnes operi.*

Not a finger but had an Office: He was held vn worthy euer after to *sucke the Hony dew of Peace*, that (*against his comming, by whom our Peace weares a triple Wreathe*) would offer to play the Droane. The Streets are surueyed; heigthes, breadths, and distances taken, as it were to make *Fortifications*, for the *Solemnities.* Seauen pieces of ground, (like so many fieldes for a battaile) are plotted foorth, vppon which these

Arches of Tryumph muſt ſhew themſelues in their glorie: aloft, in the ende doe they aduance their proude fore-heads.

Virg:—Circum pueri, Innuptæque Puellæ,
Sacra Canunt, funemq; manu contingere gaudent.

Euen childrẽ (might they haue bin ſuffred) would gladly haue ſpent their little ſtrength, about the *Engines*, that mounted vp the Frames: Such a fire of loue and ioy, was kindled in euery breſt.

The day (for whoſe ſake, theſe wonders of Wood, clymde thus into the clowdes) is now come; being ſo earely vp by reaſon of Artificiall Lights, which wakened it, that the Sunne ouer ſlept himſelfe, and roſe not in many houres after, yet bringing with it into the very boſome of the Cittie, a world of people. The Streets ſeemde to bee paued with men: Stalles in ſtead of rich wares were ſet out with children, open Caſements fild vp with women.

All Glaſſe windowes taken downe, but in their places, ſparkeled ſo many eyes, that had it not bene the day, the light which reflected from them, was ſufficient to haue made one: hee that ſhould haue compared the emptie and vntroden walkes of *London*, which were to be ſeen in that late mortally-deſtroying Deluge, with the thronged ſtreetes now, might haue belieued, that vpon this day, began a new *Creation*, & that the Citie was the onely Workhouſe wherein ſundry Nations were made.

A goodly and ciuil order was obſerued, in Martialling all the Companies according to their degrees: The firſt beginning at the vpper end of Saint *Marks* Lane, and the laſt reaching aboue the Conduit in *Fleetſtreete*: their Seats, being double-railde: vpon the vpper part wheron they leaned, the Streamers, Enſignes, and Bannerets, of each particular Company decently fixed: And directly againſt them, (euen quite through the body of the Citie, ſo hie as to

Temple-Barre) a ſingle Raile (in faire diſtance from the other) was likewiſe erected to put off the multitude. Amongſt whoſe tongues (which in ſuch Conſorts neuer lye ſtill,) tho there were no Muſicke, yet as the Poet ſayes:

Mart. *Vox diuerſa ſonat, populorum eſt vox tamen vna.*

NOthing that they ſpeake could bee made any thing, yet all that was ſpoken, ſounded to this purpoſe, that ſtill his Maieſtie was comming. They haue their longings: And behold, A farre off they ſpie him, richly mounted on a white Iennet, vnder a rich Canopy, ſuſtained by eight Barons of the *Cinqueports*; the Tower ſeruing that morning but for his with-drawing Chamber, wherein hee made him ready: and from thence ſtept preſently into his Citie of *London*, which for the time might worthily borrow the name of his *Court Royall*: His paſſage alongſt that Court, offering it ſelfe for more State) through ſeuen Gates, of which the firſt was erected at *Fanchurch.*

Thus preſenting it ſelfe.

IT was an vpright Flat-ſquare, (for it contained fiftie foote in the perpendiculer, *Fanchurch.* and fiftie foote in the Ground-lyne) the vpper roofe thereof (one diſtinct *Grices*) bore vp the true moddells of all the notable Houſes, Turrets, and Steeples, within the Citie. The Gate vnder which his Maieſtie did paſſe, was 12. foote wide, and 18. foote hie: A Poſterne likewiſe (at one ſide of it) being foure foote wide, and 8. foote in heigth: On either ſide of the Gate, ſtood a great French Terme, of ſtone, aduanced vpon wodden Pedeſtalls; two half Pilaſters of Ruſtick, ſtanding ouer their heads. I could ſhoote more Arrowes at this marke, and teach you without the Carpenters Rule how to meaſure all the proportions belonging to this *Fabrick.* But an excellent hand being at this inſtant curiouſly deſcribing all the ſeuen, and beſtowing on them their faire proſpectiue limmes, your eye ſhall hereafter rather be delighted in beholding thoſe Pictures, than now be wearied in looking vpon mine.

☞ The Perſonages (as well Mutes as Speakers) in this Pageant, were *theſe*: *viz.*

1 THe higheſt Perſon was *The Brittayne Monarchy.*

2 At her feet, ſate *Diuine Wiſdome.*

3 Beneath her, ſtood *The Genius of the City*, A man.

4 At his right hand was placed a Perſonage, figuring, *The Counſell of the City.*

5 Vnder all theſe lay a perſon repreſenting *Thameſis the Riuer.*

Sixe other perſons (being daughters to *Genius*) were aduaunced aboue him, on a ſpreading *Aſcent*, of which the firſt was,

1 *Gladneſſe.*

2 The ſecond, *Veneration.*

3 The third, *Promptitude.*

4 The fourth, *Vigilance.*

5 The fift, *Louing affection.*

6 The ſixth, *Vnanimity.*

Of all which perſonages, *Genius* and *Thameſis* were the only Speakers: *Thameſis* being preſented by one of the children of her Maieſties Reuels: *Genius* by M. *Allin* (ſeruant to the young Prince) his gratulatory ſpeach (which was deliuered with excellent Action, and a well tun'de audible voyce) being to this effect:

That London may be prowd to behold this day, and therefore in name of the Lord *Maior* and *Aldermen*, the *Councell*, *Commoners* and *Multitude*, the heartieſt Welcome is tendered to his Maieſty, that euer was beſtowed on any King, &c.

The Wayts & Hault-boyes of London. Which Banquet being taken away with ſound of Muſicke, there, ready for the purpoſe, his Maieſtie made his entrance into this his Court Royall: vnder this firſt Gate, vpon the Battlements of the worke, in great Capitalls was inſcribed, thus:

LONDINIVM.

And vnder that, in a ſmaller (but not different) *Caracter*, was written,

CAMERA REGIA:
The Kings Chamber.

Too ſhort a time (in their opinions that were glewed there together ſo many houres, to behold him) did his Maieſtie dwell vpon this firſt place: yet too long it ſeemed to other happy Spirits, that higher vp in theſe *Elizian* fields awaited for his preſence: he ſets on therefore (like the Sunne in his Zodiaque) bountifully diſperſing his beames amongſt particular Nations: the brightneſſe and warmth of which, was now ſpent firſt vpon the *Italians*, & next vpon the *Belgians*: The ſpace of ground, on which their *magnificent Arches* were builded, being not vnworthy to beare the name of the great Hall to this our Court Royal: wherein was to be heard & ſeene the ſundry languages & habits of Strangers, which vnder Princes Roofes tender excellent harmony.

In a paire of Scales doe I weigh theſe two Nations, and finde them (neither in hearty loue to his Maieſtie, in aduancement of the Cities honor, nor in forwardneſſe to glorifie theſe *Triumphes*) to differ one graine.

To diſpute which haue done beſt, were to doubt that one had done well. Call their inuentions therefore *Twynnes*: or if they themſelues doe not like that name, (for happily they are emulous of one glory) yet thus may we ſpeake of them.

——— Facies non omnibus vna,
Nec diuerſa tamen, Qualem decet eſſe ſororum. *Ouid.*

Becauſe, whoſoeuer (*fixis oculis*) beholds their proportions,

Virg. *Expleri mentem nequit, ardeſcitq; tuendo.*

The ſtreet, vpon whoſe breaſt, this *Italian* Iewell was worne, was neuer worthy of that name which it carries, till this houre: For here did the Kings eye meete a ſecond Obiect, that inticed him by tarrying to giue honor to the place. And thus did the queintneſſe of the *Engine* ſeeme to diſcouer it ſelfe before him. *Gracious ſtreet.*

The Italians Pageant.

THe building tooke vp the whole bredth of the Street, of which, the lower part was a Square, garniſhed with foure great Columnes: In the midſt of of which Square, was cut out a fayre and ſpacious high Gate, arched, being twenty ſeuen foot in the perpendicular lyne, and eyghteene at the ground lyne: ouer the Gate, in golden Caracters, theſe verſes (in a long ſquare) were inſcribed:

Tu Regere Imperio populos Iacobe memento,
Hæ tibi erunt Artes, Paciq; imponere morem,
Parcere Subiectis, & debellare ſuperbos.

And directly aboue this, was aduanc'd the Armes of the Kingdome, the Supporters fairely cut out to the life: ouer the Lyon (ſome prety diſtance from it) was written,

IACOBO REGI MAGN.

And aboue the head of the *Vnicorne*, at the like diſtance, this,

HENRICI VII. ABNEP.

In a large Sqnare erected aboue all theſe, King *Henry* the ſeuenth was royally ſeated in his Imperiall Robes, to whome King *Iames* (mounted on horſe-backe) approches, and receyues a Scepter, ouer both their heads theſe words being written,

HIC VIR, HIC EST.

Betweene two of the *Columnes*, (on the right hand) was fixed vp a Square table, wherein, in liuely and excellent colours, was lim'd a woman, figuring *Peace*, her head ſecurely leaning on her left hand, her body modeſtly beſtowed (to the length) vpon the earth: In her other hand, was held an *Oliue* branch, the *Enſigne* of Peace, her word was out of *Virgil*, being thus,

——— *Deus nobis hæc otia fecit.*

Beneath that peece, was another ſquare Table, reaching almoſt to the Baſes of the two *Columnes*: In which, 2. (ſeeming) Sea perſonages, were drawne to the life, both of them lying, or rather leaning on the boſome of the earth, naked; the one a woman, her backe onely ſeene; the other a man, his hand ſtretching and faſtning it ſelfe vpon her ſhoulder: the word that this dead body ſpake, was this,

I Decus, I Noſtrum.

Vpon the left-hand ſide of the Gate, betweene the other two *Columnes*, were alſo two ſquare Tables: In the one of which were two perſons portrayed to the life, naked, and wilde in lookes, the word,

Expectate ſolo Trinobanti.

And ouer that, in another ſquare, carying the ſame proportion, ſtoode a woman vpright, holding in her hand a Shield, beneath whom was inſcribed in golden *Caracters*,

——— *Spes ô fidiſsima rerum.*

And this was the ſhape and front of the firſt great *Square*, whoſe top being flat, was garniſhed with *Pelaſters*, and vpon the roofe was directed a great *Padeſtall*, on which ſtood a Perſon carued out to the life (a woman) her left hand leaning on a ſword, with the poynt downeward, and her right hand reaching foorth a Diadem, which ſhee ſeemde by bowing of her knee and head, to beſtow vpon his Maieſtie.

On the foure corners of this vpper part, ſtoode foure naked portraytures (in great) with artificiall Trumpets in their hands.

In the Arch of the Gate, was drawne (at one ſide) a companie of Palme trees, young, and as it were but newly ſpringing, ouer whoſe branches, two naked winged Angels, flying, held foorth a Scroll, which ſeem'd to ſpeake thus,

Spes altera.

On the contrarie ſide, was a Vine, ſpreading it ſelfe into many branches, and winding about *Oliue*, and

Palme trees : two naked winged Angels hanging likewiſe in the Ayre ouer them, and holding a Scrol betweene them, fild with this inſcription,

Vxor tua, ſicut vitis abundans,
Et filii tui, ſicut palmites Oliuarum.

If your imaginations (after the beholding of theſe obiects) will ſuppoſe, that his Maieſtie is now gone to the other ſide of this *Italian Trophee*; doe but caſt your eyes backe, and there you ſhall finde iuſt the ſame proportions, which the fore-part, or Breſt of our Arch carrieth, with equall number of *Columnes*, Pedeſtals, Pilaſters, Lim'd peeces, and Carued Statues. Ouer the Gate, this *Diſtichon* preſents it ſelfe.

Nonne tuo Imperio ſatis eſt Iacobe potiri ?
Imperium in Muſas, Aemule quæris ? Habes.

Vnder which verſes, a wreathe of *Lawrell* ſeem'd to be ready to be let fall on his Maieſties head, as hee went vnder it, being held betweene two naked Antique women, their bodies ſtretching (at the full length) to compaſſe ouer the Arch of the Gate. And aboue thoſe verſes, in a faire Azure table, this inſcription was aduanc'd in golden *Capitals*:

EXPECTATIONI ORBIS TERRARVM,
REGIB. GENITO NVMEROSISS.
REGVM GENITORI FÆLICISS.
REGI MARTIGENARVM AVGVSTISS.
REGI MVSARVM GLORIOSISS.

Itali ſtatuerunt lætitiæ & cultus Signum.

On the right hand of this backe-part, betweene two of the *Columnes* was a ſquare table, in which was drawne a Woman, crown'd with beautifull and freſh flowres, a *Caducæus* in her hand : All the notes of a plenteous and liuely Spring being caried about her, the ſoule that gaue life to this ſpeaking picture, was :

——— *Omnis feret omnia Tellus.*

Aboue this peece, in another ſquare, was portrayed a *Tryton*, his Trumpet at his mouth, ſeeming to vtter this much,

Dum Cœlum ſtellas.

Vpon the left hand of this back-part, in moſt excellent colours, Antikely attir'd, ſtood the 4. kingdoms, *England*, *Scotland*, *France* and *Ireland*, holding hands together; this being the language of them all,

Concordes ſtabili Fatorum Numine.

The middle great Square, that was aduaunced ouer the *Freeze* of the Gate, held *Apollo*, with all his Enſignes and properties belonging vnto him, as a *Sphere*, *Bookes*, a *Caducæus*, an *Octoedron*, with other *Geometricall* Bodies, and a Harpe in his left hand: his right hand with a golden Wand in it, poynting to the battel of *Lepanto* fought by the *Turks*, (of which his Maieſtie hath written a *Poem*) and to doe him Honour, *Apollo* himſelfe doth here ſeeme to take vpon him to deſcribe: his word,

Fortunate Puer.

Theſe were the Mutes, and properties that helpt to furniſh out this great *Italian Theater*: vpon whoſe Stage, the ſound of no voice was appointed to be heard, but of one, (and that, in the preſence of the *Italians* themſelues) who in two little oppoſite galleries vnder & within the Arch of the gate, very richly and neately hung, deliuered thus much Latine to his Maieſtie:

The Italians ſpeach.

S*Alue, Rex magne, ſalue. Salutem Maieſtati tuæ Itali, fœliciſsimum Aduentum læti, fœlices ſub Te futuri, precamur. Ecce hic Omnes, Exigui munere, pauculi Numero: Sed magni erga Maieſtatem tuam animi, multi obſequij. At nec Atlas, qui Cœlum ſuſtinet, nec ipſa Cœli conuexa, altitudinem attingant meritorum Regis optimi; Hoc eſt, eius, quem de Teipſo expreſsiſti doctiſsimo (Deus!) et admirabili penicillo: Beatiſsimos populos, vbi & Philoſophus regnat, & Rex Philoſophatur. Salue, Rex nobiliſsime, ſalue, viue, Rex potentiſsime, fœliciter. Regna, Rex ſapientiſsime, fœliciter, Itali optamus omnes, Itali clamamus omnes: Omnes, omnes.*

Hauing hoyſted vp our Sailes, and taken leaue of this *Italian* ſhore, let our next place of caſting anker, be vpon the Land of the 17. Prouinces; where the *Belgians*, (attired in the coſtly habits of their own natiue Countrey, without the fantaſticke mixtures of other Nations) but more richly furniſhed with loue, ſtand ready to receyue his Maieſtie: who (according to their expectation) does moſt gratiouſly make himſelfe & his Royall traine their Princely gheſts. The houſe which theſe *Strangers* haue builded to entertaine him in, is thus contriu'de.

The Pageant of the Dutch-men,
by the Royall Exchange.

THe Foundation of this, was (as it were by *Fate*) layd neere vnto a royall place ; for it was a royall and magnificent labour : It was bounded in with the houſes on both ſides the ſtreet, ſo prowdly (as all the reſt alſo did) did this extend her body in bredth. The paſſage of State, was a Gate, large, aſcending eighteene foot high, aptly proportion'd to the other lymmes, and twelue foot wyde, arched ; two leſſer Poſternes were for common feet, cut out and open'd on the ſides of the other.

Within a ſmall *Freeze*, (and kiſſing the very forhead of the Gate) the *Aedifice* ſpake thus,

Vnicus à Fato ſurgo non Degener Hæres.

Whil'ſt lifting vp your eye to an vpper larger *Freeze*, you may there be enriched with theſe golden Capitalls,

IACOBO, ANGL. SCOT. FRANC. HIBERN. REGI OPT. PRINC. MAX. BELGAE ded.

But beſtowing your ſight vpon a large Azure Table, lyned quite through with Caracters of gold, likewiſe you may for your paynes receiue this inſcription,

ORBIS RESTITVTOR. PACIS FVND. RELIG. PROPVG. D. IAC. P. F. REGI. P. P.
D. ANNAE REGIAE CONIVG. SOR. FIL. NEPTI, ET D. HENRICO I. FIL. PRINC. IVVENT.
IN PVBL. VRBIS ET ORBIS LAETITIA, SECVLIQVE FAELICITAT. XVII. BELGIAE PROV. MERCATORES BENIGNE REGIA HAC IN VRBE EXCEPTI, ET
S. M. VESTRAE OB ANTIQ. SOCIALE FOEDVS, ET D. ELIZ. BENEFICENT. DEVOTI.

FAVSTA OMNIA ET FOELICIA AD IMPERII ÆTERNITAT. PRECANTVR.

Aboue which (being the heart of the *Trophee*) was a ſpacious ſquare roome, left open, Silke Curtaines drawne before it, which (vpon the approch of his Maieſtie) being put by, 17. yong *Damſels*, (all of them ſumptuouſly adorned, after their countrey faſhion,) ſate as it were in ſo many Chaires of State, and figuring in their perſons, the 17. *Prouinces* of *Belgia*, of which euery one caried in a Scutchion (excellently pencilde) the Armes and Coate of one.

Aboue the vpper edge of this large Square Roome, and ouer the firſt Battlement, in another front, aduanc'd for the purpoſe, a ſquare Table was faſtened vpright, in which was drawne the liuely picture of the *King*, in his Imperial Robes; a Crowne on his head, the Sword and Scepter in his handes: vpon his left ſide ſtood a woman, her face fixed vpon his, a burning hart in her right hand, her left hanging by, a *Heron* ſtanding cloſe vnto her: vpon his other ſide ſtood vpright (with her countenance directed likewiſe vpon him) another woman, winged, and in a *Freeze* beneath them, which tooke vp the full length of this Square: this inſcription ſet out it ſelfe in golden wordes;

—— *Vtroque Satellite Tutus.*

Suffer your eyes to be wearied no longer with gazing vp ſo high at thoſe *Sun-beams*, but turne thê aſide to looke below through the little *Poſternes*: whoſe State ſweld quickly vp to a greatnes, by reaſon of 2. *Columnes*, that ſupported them on either ſide. In a Table, ouer the right-hand *Portall*, was in perfect colours, drawne a Serpêt, purſude by a Lion: betweene them, Adders and Snakes, chaſing one another, the Lion ſcornfully caſting his head backe, to behold the violence of a blacke ſtorme, that heauen powred downe, to ouertake them: the ſound that came from all this, was thus:

—— *Sequitur grauis Ira feroces.*

The oppoſite body to this (on the other ſide, and directly ouer the other *Portall*, whoſe pompe did in like maner leane vpon, and vphold it ſelfe by two mayne *Columnes*) was a ſquare peece, in which were to be ſeene, Sheepe browzing, Lambes nibbling, Byrds flying in the Ayre, with other arguments of a ſerene and vntroubled ſeaſon, whoſe happineſſe was proclaymed in this maner,

— *Venit alma Cicuribus Aura.*

Directly aboue this, in a ſquare Table, were portrayed two *Kings*, reuerently and antiquely attyrde, who ſeem'd to walke vpon theſe golden lines,

Naſcitur in noſtro Regum par Nobile Rege
Alter Ieſiades, Alter Amoniades.

From whome, leade but your eye, in a ſtraight line, to the other ſide, (ouer the contrary Poſterne) and there in a ſecond vpper Picture, you may meete with two other *Kings*, not fully ſo antique, but as rich in their Ornaments; both of them, out of golden letters, compoſing theſe wordes,

Lucius ante alios, Edwardus, & inde IACOBVS
Sextus, & hic ſanxit, ſextus & ille fidem.

And theſe were the *Nerues*, by which this great *Triumphall* Body was knit together, in the inferiour parts of it, vpon the ſhoulders whereof, (which were garniſhed with rowes of *Pilasters*, that ſupported Lions, rāpant, bearing vp Banners) there ſtood another leſſer Square, the head of which wore a Coronet of *Pilasters* alſo; and aboue thẽ, vpon a *Pedestal*, curiouſly cloſed in betweene the tayles of two Dolphins, was aduanced a Woman, holding in one hand, a golden Warder, and poynting with the fore-finger of the other hand vp to heauen. She figur'd *Diuine Prouidence*, for ſo at her feete was written.

Prouida Mens Cœli.

Somewhat beneath which, was to bee ſeene an Imperiall Crowne, two Scepters being faſtened (croſſewiſe) vnto it, and deliuering this ſpeach,

——*Sceptra hæc concredidit vni.*

At the elbowes of this vpper Square, ſtood vpon the foure corners of a great *Pedeſtall*, foure *Pyramides*, hollow, and ſo neately contriu'de, that in the night time (for anger that the Sunne would no longer looke vpon theſe earthly beauties) they gaue light to themſelues, and the whole place about them: the windowes, from whence theſe artificiall beames were throwne, being cut out in ſuch a faſhion, that (as *Ouid*, deſcribing the Palace of the Sunne, ſayes)

Clara micante Auro, Flammaſq; imitante Pyropo,

So did they ſhine afarre off, like Cryſolites, and ſparkled like Carbuncles: Betweene thoſe two *Pyramides* that were lifted vp on the right hand, ſtood *Fortitude*; her Piller reſting it ſelfe vpon this golden line,

Perfero curarum pondus, Diſcrimina temno.

Betweene the two *Pyramides* on the other ſide, Iuſtice challenged her place, being knowne both by her habit and by her voyce, that ſpake thus,

Auſpice me Dextra ſolium Regale perennat.

Wee haue held his Maieſtie too long from entring this third Gate of his *Court Royall*; It is now hie time, that thoſe eyes, which on the other ſide ake with rolling vp and downe for his gladſome preſence, ſhould inioy that happineſſe. Beholde, hee is in an inſtance paſſed thorough; The Obiects that there offer themſelues before him, being theſe:

Our *Belgick Statue* of Triumph, weares on her backe, as much riches, as ſhe caried vpon her breſt, being altogether as glorious in *Columnes*, ſtanding on Tiptoe, on as loftie and as proude *Pyramides*; her walkes encompa'ſt with as ſtrong and as neate *Pilaſters*: the colours of her garments are as bright, her adornements as many: For,

In the ſquare Field, next and loweſt, ouer one of the Portals, were the Dutch Countrey people, toyling at their Husbandrie; women carding of their Hemp, the men beating it, ſuch excellent Art being expreſt in their faces, their ſtoopings, bendings, ſweatings, &c. that nothing is wanting in them but life (which no colours can giue) to make them bee thought more than the works of Paynters.

Lift vp your eyes a little aboue them, and beholde their *Exchange*; the countenaunces of the Marchants there being ſo liuely, that bargaines ſeeme to come from their lippes.

But in ſtead of other ſpeach, this is onely to bee had,

PIO INVICTO,
R. IACOBO,

QVOD FEL. EIVS AVSPICIIS VNIVERSVM BRIT. IMPERIVM PACAT, MARE TVTVM PORTVS APERIT.

Ouer the other Portall, in a ſquare (proportion'd, to the bignes of thoſe other) men, women, & childrê (in Dutch habits) are buſie at other workes: the men

Weauing, the women Spinning, the children at their Hand-loomes, &c. Aboue whofe heads, you may with little labour, walke into the *Mart*, where as well as the *Froe*, as the *Burger*, are buying and felling, the praife of whofe induftrie (being worthy of it) ftands publifht in gold, thus,

QVOD MVTVIS COMMERCIIS, ET ARTIFICVM NAVTARVMQVE SOLERTIA CRESCAT, DESIDIA EXVLAT, MVTVAQVE AMICITIA CONSERVETVR.

Iuft in the midft of thefe foure Squares, and directly ouer the Gate, in a large Table, whofe feete are faftned to the *Freeze*, is their fifhing & fhipping liuely and fweetely fet downe: The *Skipper* (euen though he be had tugging at his Net) loudly finging this:

Quod Celeb: hoc Emporium prudenti induftria fuos,
Quouis Terrarum Negotiatores emittat, exteros
Humaniter admittat, foris famam, domi diuitias augeat.

Let vs now clime vp to the vpper battlementes; where, at the right hand *Time* ftandes: at the left (in a direct line) his daughter *Trueth*; vnder her foote is written, *Sincera.*
And vnder his,

Durant.

Sincera Durant.

In the midft of thefe two, three other perfons are rancked togeather, *Art*, *Sedulitie*, and *Labour*: beneath whom, in a Freeze rouing along the whole breadth of that Square, you may find thefe wordes in gold.

Artes, Perfecit, Sedulitate, Labor.

As on the forefide, fo on this, and equall in heigth

to that of *Diuine Prouidence*, is the figure of a Woman aduaunced : beneath whom, is an imperiall Crowne, with branches of Oliue, fixed (croſſe-wiſe) vnto it, and giues you this word.

Sine Cæde at Sanguine.

And thus haue we beſtowed vpon you, all the dead Cullours of this Picture, (wherein notwithſtanding, was left ſo much life) as can come from Art. The ſpeaking inſtrument, was a Boy, attyred all in white Silke, a wreath of Lawrell about his temples: from his voyce came this ſound.

Sermo ad Regem.

QVæ tot Sceptra tenes forti, Rex maxime, dextra,
Prouida Mens ſummi Numinis illa dedit.
Aſpice ridentem per gaudia Plebis Olympum,
Reddentem et plauſus ad ſua verba ſuos,
Tantus honos paucis, primi poſt ſecula mundi
Obtigit, et paucis tantum vnus incubuit,
Nam Regere imperijs populum fœlicibus vnum,
Arduares, magnis res tamen apta viris.
At non vnanimes nutu compeſcere gentes,
Non homines penſum, ſed labor ille Dei,
Ille ideò ingentes qui temperet orbis habenas,
Adiungit longas ad tua fræna manus.
Et menti de mente ſua prælucet, et Artem
Regnandi, regnum qui dedit illa, docet.
Creſcentes varijs Cumulat virtutibus annos,
Quas inter pietas, culmina ſumma tenet.
Hac proauos reddis patriæ, qui barbara Gentis
Flexêre inducto Numine, corda feræ.
Hac animos tractas rigidos, ſubigiſq ; rebelles,
Et leue perſuades quod trahis ipſe iugum,

Illi fida comes terram indignata profanum,
Aut nunc te tanto Rege reuersa Themis.
Afsidat et robusta soror, ingentibus ausis
Pro populo carum tradere prompta caput.
Quin et Regis amor, musæ et dilectus Apollo,
Regali gaudent subdere plectra manu.
Aurea et vbertas solerti nata labore,
Exhibet aggestas Ruris et vrbis opes.
Sunt hæc dona Poli, certa quæ prodita fama
Miratum vt veniat, venit vterq ; polus.
Venimus et Belgæ, patrijs Gens exul ab oris
Quos fouit tenero mater Eliza sinu.
Matri sacratum, Patri duplicamus amorem,
Poscimus et simili posse fauore frui.
Sic Deum Panthaeci tibi proferat alitis æuum,
Sceptra per Innumeros qui tibi tradit Auos.
Sic Regina tua pars altera, et altera proles,
Spes populi longum det, capiatq ; decus.

Whilst the tongnes of the *Strangers* were imployed in extolling the gracious Aspect of the King, and his Princely behauiour towardes them, his Maiestie (by the quicknes of *Time*, and the earnestnesse of expectation, whose eyes ran a thousand wayes to finde him) had won more ground, and was gotten so far as to *S. Mildreds* Church in the *Poulterie*: close to the side of which, a Scaffold was erected; where (at the Citties cost) to delight the Queene with her owne country Musicke, nine Trumpets, and a Kettle Drum, did very sprightly & actiuely sound the *Danish march*: Whose cunning and quicke stops, by that time they had toucht the last Ladyes eare in the traine, behold, the *King* was aduaunced vp so hie as to *Cheapeside*: into which place (if *Loue* himselfe had entered, and seene so many gallant Gentlemen, so many Ladyes, and beautifull creatures, in whose eyes glaunces (mixt with modest lookes) seemed to daunce courtly Measures in their motion) he could not haue chosen, to haue giuen the Roome any other name, then, *The Presence Chamber.*

Soper lane. The ſtately entraunce into which, was a faire Gate in height 18. foote. In breadth 12. The thickneſſe of the paſſage vnder it, being 24. Two Poſternes ſtoode wide open on the two ſides, either of them being 4. foote wide, and 8. foote high. The two Portals that ietted out before theſe Poſternes, had their ſides open foure ſeuerall wayes, and ſerued as Pedeſtalles (of Ruſticke) to ſupport two *Pyramides*, which ſtoode vpon foure great Balles, and foure great Lions: the Pedeſtalles, Balles, and *Pyramides*, deuowring in their full vpright heigth, from the ground line to the top, iuſt 60. foote. But burying this Mechanicke Body in ſcilence, let vs now take note in what faſhion it ſtood attyred. Thus then it went appareled.

The Deuice at

Soper-lane end.

VVIthin a large Compartiment, mounted aboue the forehead of the Gate, ouer the Freeze, in Capitalles was inſcribed this Title:

NOVA FÆLIX ARABIA.

Vnder that ſhape of *Arabia*, this Iland being figured: which two names of *New*, and *Happie*, the Countrey could by no merit in it ſelfe, challenge to be her due, but onely by meanes of that ſecret influence accompanying his Maieſtie whereſoeuer hee goes, and working ſuch effectes.

The moſt worthy perſonage aduaunced in this place, was *Arabia Britannica*, a Woman, attyred all in White, a rich Mantle of Greene caſt about her, an imperiall Crowne on her head, and a Scepter in one hand, a Mound in the other: vpon which ſhe ſadly leaned: a rich Veyle (vnder the Crowne) ſhadowing her eyes, by reaſon that her countenaunce (which till his Maieſties approach, could by no worldly obiect be drawne to looke vp) was penſiuely deiected: her ornamentes were markes of *Chaſtetie* and *Youth*: the Crowne, Mound, and Scepter, badges of Soueraigntie.

Directly vnder her in a Cant by her ſelfe, *Fame* ſtood vpright: A Woman in a Watchet Roabe, thickly ſet with open Eyes, and Tongues, a payre of large golden Winges at her backe, a Trumpet in her hand, a Mantle of ſundry cullours trauerſing her body: all these Ensignes desplaying but the propertie of her swiftnesse, and aptnesse to disperse Rumors.

In a Descent beneath her, being a spatious Concaue roome, were exalted fiue Mounts, swelling vp with different ascensions; vpon which sate the fiue *Sences*, drooping: *Viz.*

1	*Auditus,*	Hearing.
2	*Visus,*	Sight.
3	*Tactus,*	Feeling.
4	*Olfactus.*	Smelling.
5	*Gustus.*	Taste.

Appareled in Roabes of distinct cullours, proper to their natures; and holding Scutchions in their handes: vpon which were drawne Herogliphicall bodyes, to expresse their qualities.

Some prettie distaunce from them (and as it were in the midst before them) an artificiall Lauer or Fount was erected, called the *Fount of Arate* (*Vertue.*) Sundry Pipes (like veines) branching from the body of it: the water receiuing libertie but from one place, and that very slowly.

At the foote of this Fount, two personages (in greater shapes then the rest) lay sleeping: vpon their brestes stucke their names, *Detractio*, *Obliuio*: The one holdes an open Cuppe; about whose brim, a wreath of curled Snakes were winding, intimating that whatsoeuer his lippes toucht, was poysoned: the other helde a blacke Cuppe couerd, in token of an enuious desire to drowne the worth and memorie of Noble persons.

Vpon an Ascent, on the right hand of these, stood the three *Charites* or *Graces*, hand in hand, attyred like three Sisters.

Aglaia.		Brightneſſe, or Maieſtie.
Thalia,	*Figuring*	Youthfulnes, or floriſhing.
Euphroſine,		Chearfulnes, or gladnes.

They were all three Virgins : their countenaunces laboring to ſmother an innated ſweetnes and cheare-fulnes, that appareled their cheekes ; yet hardly to be hid : their Garmentes were long Roabes of ſundry coloures, hanging looſe : the one had a Chaplet of ſundry Flowers on her head, cluſtard heere and there with the Fruites of the earth. The ſeconde, a Garland of eares of Corne. The third, a wreath of Vine-branches, mixt with Grapes and Oliues.

Their haire hung downe ouer their ſhoulders looſe, and of a bright cullour, for that *Epithite* is properly beſtowed vpon them, by *Homer* in his Himne to *Apollo.*

PVLCHRICOMÆ CHARITES.

The Bright Hayrde Graces.

They helde in their handes penſild Shieldes : vpon the firſt, was drawne a Roſe : on the ſecond, 3. Dyce : on the third, a branch of Mirtle.

Figuring { *Pleaſantneſſe.* / *Accord.* / *Floriſhing.*

In a direct line againſt them, ſtoode the three *Howres,* to whom in this place we giue the names of *Loue, Iuſtice,* and *Peace* : they were attyred in looſe Roabes of light cullours, paynted with Flowers : for ſo *Ouid* apparrels them.

Conueniunt pictis incinctæ vestibus Horæ.

Winges at their feete, expresing their swiftnesse, because they are Lackies to the Sunne : *Iungere equos Tytan velocibus imperat Horis. Ouid.*

Each of them helde two Goblets ; the one full of Flowers (as Ensigne of the *Spring*,) the other full of rypened Figges, the Cognisance of *Summer*.

Vpon the approch of his Maiestie (sad and solemne Musicke hauing beaten the Ayre all the time of his absence, and now ceasing,) *Fame* speakes.

Fama.

Turne into Ice mine eye-balls, whilst the sound
Flying through this brazen trump, may back rebound
To stop *Fames* hundred tongues, leauing them mute,
As in an vntoucht Bell, or stringlesse Lute,
For *Vertues* Fount, which late ran deepe and cleare,
Drie, and melts all her body to a teare.
You *Graces* ! and you houres that each day runne
On the quicke errands of the golden Sunne,
O say ! to *Vertues* Fount what has befell,
That thus her veines shrinke vp.

Charites Horæ.

Wee cannot tell.

Euphrosine.

Behold the fiue-folde guard of *Sence* which keepes
The sacred streame, sit drooping : neere them sleepe
Two horred Monsters : *Fame* ! summon each *Sence*,
To tell the cause of this strange accidence.

Heereupon *Fame* sounding her Trumpet ; *Arabia Britannica*, lookes cheerefully vp, the sences are startled : *Detraction* and *Obliuion* throw off their iron ſlumber, buſily beſtowing all their powers to fill their cups at the Fount with their olde malitious intention to ſucke it drie ; But a ſtrange and heauenly muſicke ſuddainly ſtriking through their eares, which cauſing a wildnes and quicke motion in their lookes, drew them to light vpon the glorious preſence of the King, they were ſuddainly thereby daunted and ſunke downe ; The Fount in the ſame moment of *Tyme*, flowing freſh and aboundantly through ſeuerall pipes, with Milke, Wine, and Balme, whilſt a perſon (figuring *Circumſpection*) that had watcht day and night, to giue note to the world of this bleſſed *Tyme*, which hee foreſawe would happen, ſteps forth on a mounted Stage extended 30. foote in length from the maine building, to deliuer to his Maieſtie the interpretation of this dumbe Myſterie.

This Preſenter was a Boy, one of the Choriſters, belonging to Paules.

His Speech.

Great Monarch of the Weſt, whoſe glorious Stem,
Doth now ſupport a triple Diadem,
Weying more thā that of thy grand Grandſire *Brute*,
Thou that maiſt make a King thy ſubſtitute,
And doeſt beſides the Red-roſe and the white,
With the rich flower of *France* thy garland dight,
Wearing aboue Kings now, or thoſe of olde,
A double Crowne of Lawrell and of gold,
O let my voyce paſſe through thy royall eare,
And whiſper thus much, that we figure here,
A new *Arabia*, in whoſe ſpiced neſt
A *Phœnix* liu'd and died in the Sunnes breſt,
Her loſſe, made ſight, in teares to drowne her eyes,
The Eare grew deafe, Taſtelike a ſick-man lyes,
Finding no relliſh : euery other Sence,
Forgat his office, worth and excellence,
Whereby this Fount of Vertue gan to freeze,

Threatned to be drunke by two enemies,
Snakie *Detraction*, and *Obliuion*,
But at thy glorious preſence, both are gone,
Thou being that ſacred *Phœnix*, that doeſt riſe,
From th'aſhes of the firſt : Beames from thine eyes
So vertually ſhining, that they bring,
To *Englands* new *Arabia*, a new Spring :
For ioy whereof, Nimphes, Sences, Houres, & Fame,
Eccho loud Hymnes to his imperiall name.

At the ſhutting vp of this Speech, his Maieſtie (being readie to goe on,) did moſt graciouſlie feede the eyes of beholders with his preſence, till a Song was ſpent : which to a loude and excellent Muſicke (compoſed of Violins & an other rare Artificiall Inſtrumêt, wherein beſides ſundrie ſeuerall ſounds effus'd (all at one time) were alſo ſenſibly diſtinguiſht the chirpings of birds, was by two Boyes (Choriſters of Paules) deliuered in ſweete and rauiſhing voyces.

Cant.

Troynouant is now no more a Citie :
O great pittie ! is't not pittie ?
And yet her Towers on tiptoe ſtand,
Like Pageants built on Fairie land,
And her Marble armes,
Like to Magicke charmes,
binde thouſands faſt vnto her,
That for her wealth & beauty daily wooe her,
yet for all this, is't not pittie ?
Troynouant is now no more a Cittie.

2

Troynouant is now a Sommer Arbour,
or the neſt wherein doth harbour
The Eagle, of all birds that flie,
The Soueraigne, for his piercing eie

If you wiſely marke,
Tis beſides a Parke,
Where runnes (being newly borne)
With the fierce Lyon, the faire Vnicorne,
or elſe it is a wedding Hall,
Where foure great Kingdomes holde a Feſtiuall.

3

Troynouant is now a Bridall Chamber,
whoſe roofe is gold; floore is of Amber,
By vertue of that holy light,
That burnes in *Hymens* hand, more bright,
Than the ſiluer Moone,
or the Torch at Noone,
Harke what the Ecchoes ſay !
Brittaine till now nere kept a Holiday:
for *Ioue* dwels heere : And tis no pittie,
If *Troynouant* be now no more a Cittie.

Nor let the ſcrue of any wreſting comment vpon theſe words,

Troynouant is now no more a Citie.

Enforce the Authors inuention away frõ his owne cleare ſtraight and harmeleſſe meaning: all the ſcope of this fiction ſtretching onely to this point, that *London* (to doo honour to this day, wherein ſprings vp all her happines) beeing rauiſhed with vnutterable ioyes, makes no account (for the preſent) of her ancient title, to be called a Citie, (becauſe that during theſe tryumphes, ſhee puts off her formall habite of Trade and Commerce, treading euen Thrift it ſelfe vnder foote, but now becomes a Reueller and a Courtier. So that, albeit in the end of the firſt Stanza tis ſaid,

Yet for all this, is't not pittie
Troynouant is now no more a Cittie.

By a figure called *Castigatio* or the mender, heere followes prefently are proofe; wherein tytles of Sommer Arbor; The Eagles neft, a wedding Hall, &c. are throwne vpon her, the leaft of them being at this time by vertue of Poeticall Heraldrie, but efpeciallie in regard of the State that now vpholds her, thought to be names of more honour, than that of her owne. And this fhort Apologie, doth our verfe make for it felfe, in regard that fome, (to whofe fetled iudgement and authoritie the cenfure of thefe Deuifes was referred,) brought though not bitterly the life of thofe lines into queftion: But appealing with *Machætas* to *Phillip*, now thefe reafons haue awakend him: let vs followe King *Iames*, who hauing paffed vnder this our third gate, is by this time, gracioufly receauing a gratulatorie Oration from the mouth of Sir *Henry Mountague*, *Recorder* of the Citie, a fquare lowe gallorie, fet round about with pilafters, beeing for that purpofe erected fome 4. foote from the ground, and ioyned to the front of the Croffe in *Cheape*; where likewife ftood all the Aldermen, the Chamberlaine, Towne-clarke, and Counfell of the Citie.

The Recorders Speech.

High Imperiall Maieftie, it is not yet a yeere in dayes fince with acclamation of the People, Citizens, and Nobles, aufpitioufly heere at this Croffe was proclaimed your true fucceffion to the Crowne. If then it was ioyous with Hats, hands, and hearts, lift vp to heauen to crie King *Iames*, what is it now to fee King *Iames*? Come therefore O worthieft of Kings as a glorious Bridegroome through your Royall Chamber: But to come neerer, *Adest quem querimus.* Twentie and more are the Soueraignes wee haue ferued fince our conqueft, but Conquerour of hearts it is you and your Pofteritie, that we haue vowed to loue and wifh to ferue whilft *London* is a Citie. In pledge whereof my Lord Maior, the Aldermen, and Commons of this

Citie, wiſhing a golden Reigne vnto you, preſent your Greatnes with a little cup of gold.

At the end of the Oration three Cups of gold were giuen (in the name of the Lord Maior, and the whole Body of the Citie,) to his Maieſtie, the young Prince, and the Queene.

All which but aboue all (being gifts of greater value) the loyall hearts of the Citizens, beeing louingly receaued; his Grace was (at leaſt it was appointed he ſhould haue beene) met on his way neere to the Croſſe, by *Syluanus* dreſt vp in greene Iuie, a Cornet in his hand, being attended on by foure other *Syluans* in Iuie likewiſe, their bowes and quiuers hanging on their ſhoulders, and winde Inſtruments in their hands.

Vpon ſight of his Maieſtie, they make a ſtand, *Syluanus* breaking forth into this abrupt paſſion of ioy.

Syluanus.

Stay *Syluans*, and let the loudeſt voyce of Muſicke proclayme it (euen as high as Heauen) that hee is come.

Alter Apollo redit, Nouus En, iam regnat Apollo.

Which acclamation of his was borne vp into the ayre, and there mingled with the breath of their muſicall Inſtruments: whoſe ſound beeing vaniſhed to nothing, Thus goes our Speaker on.

Syluanus.

Moſt happie Prince, pardon me, that being meane in habite, and wilde in apparance, (for my richeſt liuorie is but leaues, and my ſtatelieſt dwelling but in the woodes,) thus rudely with piping *Syluanes.* I preſume to intercept your royall paſſage. Theſe are my walkes: yet ſtand I heere, not to cut off your way, but to giue it a full and a bounteous welcome, beeing a

Meſſenger ſent from the Lady *Eirene* my Miſtreſſe, to deliuer an errand to the beſt of all theſe Worthies, your royall ſelfe. Many Kingdomes hath the Lady ſought out to abide in, but from them all, hath ſhee beene moſt churliſhly baniſhed : not that her beautie did deſerue ſuch vnkindnes, but that (like the eye of Heauen) hers were too bright, and there were no Eagles breeding in thoſe neſts, that could truly beholde them.

At laſt heere ſhe ariued, *Deſtinie* ſubſcribing to this Warrant, that none but this Land ſhould be her Inheritance. In contempt of which happines, Enuie ſhootes his impoiſoned ſtings at her heart, but his Adders (being charmed) turne their daungerous heads vpon his owne boſome. Thoſe that dwell far off, pine away with vexing to ſee her proſper, becauſe all the acquaintance which they haue of her, is this, that they know there is ſuch a goodly Creature as *Eirene*, in the world, yet her face they know not : whilſt all thoſe that heere ſleepe vnder the warmth of her wings, adore her by the ſacred & Cœleſtiall name of *Peace*, for number being (as her bleſſings are) infinite.

Her daughter *Euporia* (well knowne by the name of *Plentie*, is at this preſent with her, (being indeede neuer from her ſide) vnder yonder Arbour they ſit, which after the daughters name is called, *Hortus Euporiæ* (*Plenties Bower* :) Chaſt are they both, and both maydens in memorie of a Virgine, to whom they were nurſe children : for whoſe ſake (becauſe they were bound to her for their life,) mee, haue they charged to lay at your imperiall feete, (being your hereditatie due) the tribute of their loue : And with it thus to ſay.

That they haue languiſhed many heauie moneths for your preſence, which to them would haue beene, (& proud they are that it ſhall be ſo now,) of the ſame operation and influence, that the Sunne is to the ſpring, and the ſpring to the earth : hearing therefore what trebble preferment you haue beſtowed vpon this day, wherein befides the beames of a glorious Sunne, two other cleare and gracious ftarres fhine cheerefullie on thefe her homely buildings : Into which (becaufe no dutie fhould bee wanting) fhee hath giuen leaue euen to Strangers, to bee Sharers in her happines, by fuffering them to bid you likewife welcome. By mee (once hers now your vaffaile,) fhee entreates, and with a knee finking lower than the ground on which you tread, doo I humbly execute her pleafure, that ere you paffe further, you would deigne to walke into yonder Garden ; the *Hefperides* liue not there but the Mufes, and the Mufes no longer than vnder your protection. Thus farre am I fent to conduct you thither, proftrately begging this grace, (fince I dare not, as beeing vnwoorthie, lackey by your royall fide) in that yet thefe my greene Followers and my felfe may bee ioyfull fore-runners of your expected approch, away *Syluanus.*

And being (in this their returne) come neare to the Arbor, they gaue a figne with a fhort florifh from all their Cornets, that his Maieftie was at hand: whofe princely eye whileft it was delighting it felfe with the quaint obiect before it, a fweete pleafure likewife courted his eare in the fhape of Muficke, fent from the voyces of nine Boyes (all of them Querifters of Paules) who in that place prefenting the nine Mufes fang the dittie following to their Viols and other Inftruments.

But, leaft leaping too bluntly into the midft of our Garden at firft, we deface the beautie of it, let vs fend you round about it, and furuey the Walles, Allies, and quarters of it as they lye in order.

This being the fafhion of it.

The paffages through it were two gates, arched and grated Arbor-wife, their heigth being 16. foote, their breadth 10. from the roofe, and fo on the fides, downe to the ground, Cowcumbers, Pompions, Grapes, and all other fruits growing in the land, hanging artificially in clufters : Betweene the two gates, a payre of ftayres were mounted with fome 20 affents : at the bottome of them (on two pillers) were fixed two Satiers carued out in wood; the fides of both the gates, being ftrengthened with foure great French frames ftanding vpon pedeftals, taking vp in their full height 20. foote.

The vpper part alfo caried the proportion, of an Arbor, being clofde with their round tops, the midft whereof was exalted aboue the other two, *Fortune* ftanding on the top of it. The garnifhments for the whole Bower, being Apples, Peares, Cheries, Grapes, Rofes, Lillies, and all other both fruits and flowers moft artificially molded to the life. The whole frame of this fomer banqueting houfe ftood (at the ground line) vpon 4 foote ; the *Perpendicular* ftretching it felfe to 45. Wee might (that day) haue called it, *The Muficke roome*, by reafon of the chaunge of tunes, that danced round about it ; for in one place were heard a noyfe of cornets, in a fecond, a confort, the third, (which fate in fight) a fet of Viols, to which the Mufes fang.

The principall perfons aduancde in this Bower, were, *Eirene* (*Peace*) and *Euporia* (*Plenty*) who fate together.

Eierene.

Peace: Was richly attired, her vpper garment of carnation, hanging loofe, a Robe of White vnder it, powdred with Starres, and girt to her : her haire of a bright colour, long, and hanging at her back, but interwouen with white ribbands, and Iewels ; her browes were encompaft with a wreath compounded of the Oliue, the Lawrell, & the Date tree : In one hand fhee held a *Caducæus*, (or *Mercuries* rod, the god of eloquence :) In the other, ripe eares of corne gilded : on her lap fate a Doue : All thefe being enfignes, and furnitures of *Peace*.

Euporie.

Plenty : Her daughter ſate of the left hand, in changable colours, a rich mantle of Gold trauerſing her bodie : her haire large and looſely ſpreading ouer her ſhoulders : on her head a crowne of Poppy & Muſtard ſeede ; the antique badges of *Fertilitie* & *Abundance*, In her right hand a *Cornucopia*, filde with flowers, fruits, &c.

Chruſos.

Directly vnder theſe, ſate *Chruſos*, a perſon figuring Gold, his dreſsing, a tinſell Robe of the colour of Gold.

Argurion.

And cloſe by him, *Argurion*, Siluer, all in white tinſell ; both of them crownde, and both their hands ſupporting a Globe, betweene them, in token that they commaunded ouer the world.

Pomona.

Pomona, the goddeſſe of garden fruits ; ſate at the one ſide of Gold and Siluer ; attirde in greene, a wreath of frutages circling her temples : her armes naked : her haire beautifull, and long.

Ceres.

On the other ſide ſate *Ceres*, crowned with ripened eares of Wheate, in a looſe ſtraw-coloured roabe.

In two large deſcents (a little belowe them) were placde at one end,

The nine Mufes.	*Clio.* *Euterpe.* *Thalia.* *Melpomene.* *Terpficore.* *Erato.* *Polymnia.* *Vrania.* *Calliope.*	With muficall inftrumentes in their hands, to which they fung all the day.

At the other end.

The 7 liberall Artes.	*Grammer.* *Logique.* *Rhetorique.* *Muficke.* *Arithmeticke.* *Geometry.* *Aftrology.*	Holding fhieldes in their hands, exprefsing their feuerall offices.

Vpon the verie vpper edge of a faire large Freeze, running quite along the full breadth of the Arbor, and iuft at their feete were planted rankes of artificiall Artichocks and rofes.

To defcribe what apparrell thefe Arts, and Mufes wore, were a hard labour, and when it were done, all were but idle. Few Taylors know how to cut out their garments: they haue no Wardrob at all, not a Mercer, nor Merchant, though they can all write and read verie excellently well, will fuffer them to bee great in their bookes. But (as in other countries) fo in this of ours, they goe attirde in fuch thin clothes, that the winde euerie minute is readie to blowe through them: happy was it for them, that they tooke vp their lodging in a fummer arbour, and that they had fo much muficke to comfort them, their ioies (of which they do not euerie daie taft,) being notwithftanding now infinitelie multiplied, in this, that where before they might haue cryed out till they grew horfe, & non would heare them, now they fing.

Aderitque vocatus Apollo.

Chorus in full voices anſwering it thus.

Ergo alacris Syluas, & cætera rura voluptas
Panaque paſtoreſque tenet, Driadaſque puellas,
Nec Lupus inſidias pecori, nec retia Ceruis
Vlla dolum meditantur, amat bonus otia Daphnis;
Ipſi lætitia voces ad ſidera iactant
Intonſi montes: ipſæ iam carmina Rupes,
Ipſa ſonant Arbuſta, Deus, Deus ille!

Syluanus (as you may perceiue by his office before) was but ſent of an errand; there was another of a higher calling, a Trauailer, and one that had gon ouer much grownd, appointed to ſpeake to his Maieſty, his name *Vertumnus*, the maiſter Gardner, and husband to *Pomona*: To tell you what cloathes hee had on his backe were to doo him wrong, for hee had (to ſay truth) but one ſuite; homelie it was, yet meete and fit for a Gardener: In ſteade of a hat, his browes were bound about with flowers, out of whoſe thicke heapes, here and there peeped a queene apple, a cherie, or a peare, this boon-grace hee made of purpoſe to keepe his face from heate, (becauſe he deſired to looke louelie) yet the ſunne found him out, and by caſting a continuall eye at him, whilſt the old man was dreſſing his arbours, his cheekes grew tawnie, which colour for the better grace, he himſelfe interpreted bluſhing. A white head he had, & ſunne-burnt hands: in the one he held a weeding hooke, in the other a grafting knife: and this was the tenor of his ſpeech. That he was bound to giue thanks to heauen, In that the arbour and trees which growing in that fruitfull Cynthian garden, began to droop and hang downe their greene heades, and to vncurle their criſped forlocks, as fearing and in ſome ſort, feeling the ſharpeneſſe of Autumnian malice, are now on the ſudden by the deuine influence apparelled with a freſh and more liuely verdure than euer they were before. The nine Mufes that could expect no better entertainement than fad banifhment, hauing now louely and amiable faces: Arts that were threatned to be trod vnder foot by Barbarifme, now (euen at fight of his Maieftie who is the Delian Patron both of the Mufes & Arts) being likewife aduanced to moft high preferment whilft the very rurall & Syluane troopes dancd for ioy: the Lady therfore of the place *Eirene*, (his miftris) in name of the Prætor, Confuls & Senators of the City, who carefully pruine this garden, (weeding out al hurtful & idle branches that hinder the growth of the good,) and who are indeede, *Ergatai Piftoi*, faithfull Laborers in this peice of ground, Shee doth in al their names, (& he in behalfe of his Lady) offer them felues, this Arbor, the bowers & walkes, yea her children gold & filuer, with the louing & loyall harts of all thofe the Sons of peace, ftanding about him, to be difpofde after his royal pleafure. And fo wifhing his happie Arriual, at a more glorious bower, to which he is now going, yet welcoming him to this, & praying his Maiefty not to forget this poore Arbor of his Lady, Muficke is commanded to cary all their praiers for his happie reigne, with the loud *Amen* of all his Subiects as hie as heauen.

Cant.

Shine Titan fhine.
Let thy fharpe raies be hurld
Not on this vnder world,
For now tis none of thine.

These firft 4. lines were fung by one alone, the fingle lines following, by a *Chorus* in full voices.
Chor. No, no tis none of thine.

2

But in that fpheare,
Where what thine armes infolde,

Turnes all to burnisht gold,
Spend thy guilt arrowes there,
Chor. Doe, doe, shoote onelie there.

3

Earth needes thee not:
Her childbed daies are done,
And Shee another Sunne,
Faire as thy selfe has got.
Chor. A new new Sunne is got.

4

O this is hee!
Whose new beames make our Spring,
Men glad and birdes to Sing,
Hymnes of praise, ioy, and glee.
Sing, Sing, O this is hee!

5

That in the North
First rizing: shonne (so far)
Bright as the morning Starre,
At his gaie comming forth.
Chor. See, see, he now comes forth.

6

How soone ioies varie?
Here staide hee still! O then
Happie both place and men,
But here hee list not tarrie.
Chor. O griefe! hee list not tarrie.

7

No, no, his beames,
Must equall deuide,

Their heate to Orbes beſide,
Like nouriſhing ſiluer ſtreames.
Chor. Ioies ſlide awaie like ſtreames.

8

Yet in this lies
Sweete hope: how far ſoeuer,
Hee bides, no cloudes can ſeuer,
His glorie from our eyes.
Chor. Drie, drie, your weeping eies.

9

And make heauen ring,
His welcomes ſhowted loudelie,
For Heauen it ſelfe lookes proudly,
That earth has ſuch a King.
Chor. Earth has not ſuch a King.

His Maieſtie dwelt here a reaſonable long time, giuing both good allowance to the ſong & Muſick, and liberally beſtowing his eye on the workemanſhip of the place: from whence at the length departing, his next entrance was, as it were, into the cloſet or rather the priuy chamber to this our Court royall: through the windowes of which he might behold the Cathedrall Temple of Saint Paule: vpon whoſe lower batlements an Antheme was ſung, by the Quiriſters of the Church to the muſicke of loud inſtruments: which being finiſht, a latine Oration was *Viua voce* deliuered to his grace, by one of maiſter Mulcaſters Schollers, at the dore of the free-ſchole fownded by the Mercers.

Oratio habita, & ad Regem, & coram Rege præ ſchola Paulina.

(.·.)

BReuis ero, ne ingratus ſim, Rex ſereniſſime, licet, & plané, & plenè putem Regem tam prudentem, in tam profuſa ſuorum lætitia, ita ſe hodie patientia contra taedium armauiſse, ne vllius tædij ipſum poſset tædère. Aedificium hoc magno ſumptu ſuo extructum Dominus Johannes Collettus Eccleſiae Paulinæ Decanus, ſub Henrico ſeptimo, maiestatis tuæ prudentiſſimo abauo, erudiendae pueritiæ conſecrauit, vt huius ſcholæ infantia tuo in Regnum Anglicanum iure coetanea exiſtat. Tanta magnificentia conditum parique magnificentia dotatum fideliſsimæ Mercerorum huius urbis primaria ſemper, hodie etiam Prætoriæ ſocietati tuendum testamento moriens commendauit. Quæ ſocietas, & demortui fundatoris ſpei, & noſtræ educationis ſtudio fidem ſuam ſanctiſſime exoluit. Hic nos cum multis alijs erudimur, qui communi nomine totius pueritiæ Anglicanæ, a Domino Rege, licet ſponte ſua ad omnia optima ſatis incitato, humillimè tamen contendimus, vt quemadmodum ſua ætatis ratione, in omni re adultioribus proſpicit, ita in ſummae ſpei Principis Henrici gratiam tenerioribus, parique cum ipſo ætate pueris, in ſcholarum cura velit etiam conſulere. Virgæ enim obſequium, ſceptri obedientia & parit, & præit inquit preceptor meus. Quique metu didicit iuuenis parere puerque, grandibus imperiis officioſus erit. Habent ſcholæ Anglicanae multa, in quibus Regiam maieſtatis correctionem efflagitant, ne inde in Academias implumes euolent vnde in Rempublicam implumiores etiam è prima nuditate emittuntur. Quod malum à Preceptore noſtro accepimus: qui annos iam quatuor ſupra quinquaginta publice, priuatimque erudiendæ pueritiae praefuit, & hæc ſcholarum errata, cum aliquo etiam dolore ſuo, & paſſim, & ſparſim deprehendit. Nostra hæc ſchola fundatorem Collettum hominem tam pium; tutores Merceros homines tam fidos conſequuta, quam eſſet fœlix, ſi placeret, Domino etiam Regi, quod Regibus Angliae, ad ſummam apud ſuos charitatem ſaepiſsimè profuit, huic Mercerorum principi ſocietati, fratrem ſe, & conciuem adſcribere, Quantum huic vrbi ornamentum, quantum ſocietati honeſtamentum, Quantum ſcholae noſtræ emolumentum? Quantu setiam Regi ipſi honos inde accederet, mauult, qui hoc vult alias inter alia per otium Regi ſuo apperire, quam hodie cum tædio & præter aream eidem explicare. Omnipotens Deus Ieſus Christus & cum eo, ac per eum noſter, et Pater, et Deus ſereniſsimum Regem Iacobum, honoratiſſimam Reginam Annam, nobiliſsimum Principem Henricum, relinquamque Regiæ ſtirpis ad omnia ſummam natam ſobolem diu nobis ita incolumes tueatur, vt cum huius vitæ fecundiſsimum curriculum confeceritis, beatiſsimam vitæ cælestis æternitatem conſequamini. Dixi.

Our next Arch of triumph, was erected aboue the Conduit in Fleetſtreete, into which (as into the long and beauteous gallery of the Citie) his Maieſtie being entered; a farre off (as if it had beene ſome ſwelling Promentory, or rather ſome inchanted Caſtle guarded by tenne thouſand harmeleſſe ſpirits) did his eye encounter another Towre of Pleaſure.

Preſenting it ſelfe.

Foureſcore and ten foote in height, and fiftie in breadth; the gate twentie foote in the perpendicular line, and fourteene in the ground line: The two Poſternes were anſwerable to theſe that are ſet downe before: ouer the poſternes riz vp in proportionable meaſures, two turrets, with battlementes on the tops: The middeſt of the building was laid open to the world, and great reaſon it ſhould be ſo, for the Globe of the world, was there ſeene to mooue, being fild with all the degrees, and ſtates that are in the land: and theſe were the mechanicall and dead limmes of this carued bodie. As touching thoſe that had the vſe of motion in it, and for a neede durſt haue ſpoken, but that there was no ſtuffe fit for their mouthes.

The principall and worthieſt was *Aſtræa*, (*Iuſtice*) ſitting aloſt, as being newly deſcended from heauen, gloriouſly attirde; all her garments being thickely ſtrewed with ſtarres; a crowne of ſtarres on her head: a Siluer veile couering her eyes. Hauing tolde you that her name was *Iuſtice*; I hope you will not put mee to deſcribe what properties ſhe held in her hands, ſithence euery painted cloath can informe you.

Directly vnder her, in a Cant by her ſelfe, was *Arate* (vertue) inthronde, her garments white, her head crowned, and vnder her *Fortuna*: her foote treading on the Globe, that moude beneath her: Intimating, that his Maiesties fortune, was aboue the world, but his vertues aboue his fortune.

Inuidia.

Enuy, vnhandsomely attirde all in blacke, her haire of the same colour, filletted about with snakes, stood in a darke and obscure place by her selfe, neere vnto *Vertue*, but making shew of a fearefulnesse to approach her and the light: yet still & anon, casting her eyes, sometimes to the one side beneath, where on seuerall Greeces sate the foure cardinall vertues:

Viz. { *Iustitia.* / *Fortitudo.* / *Temperantia.* / *Prudentia.* } In habiliments, fitting to their natures.

And sometimes throwing a distorted and repining countenance to the other opposite seate, on which, his Maiesties foure kfngdomes were aduanced.

Viz. { *England.* / *Scotland.* / *France.* / *Ireland.* }

All of them, in rich Robes and Mantles; crownes on their heads, and Scepters with pensild scutchions in their hands, lined with the coats of the particuler kingdomes: for very madnesse, that she beheld these glorious obiects, she stood feeding on the heads of Adders.

The foure Elements in proper shapes, (artificially and aptly expresing their qualities) vpon the approch of his Maiestie, went round in a proportionable and euen circle, touching that cantle of the Globe, (which was open) to the full view of his Maiestie, which being done, they beſtowed themſelues in ſuch comely order, and ſtood ſo, as if the Eronie had beene held vp on the tops of their fingers.

Vpon diſtinct Aſcenſions, (neatly raiſde within the hollow wombe of the Globe) were placed all the ſtates of the land, from the Nobleman to the Plough-man, among whom there was not one word to bee heard, for you muſt imagine as *Virgil* ſaith :

Ægl. 4. *Magnus ab integro ſeclorum naſcitur ordo.*
*Iam redit at * virgo redeunt Saturnia regna.* Aſtræa.

That it was now the golden world, in which there were few parts.

All the tongues that went in this place, was the tongue of *Zeale,* whoſe perſonage was put on by *W. Bourne,* one of the ſeruants to the young Prince.

And thus went his ſpeach.

THe populous Globe of this our Engliſh Ile,
Seemde to mooue backward, at the funerall pile,
Of her dead female Maieſtie. All ſtates
From Nobles downe to ſpirits of meaner Fates,
Mooude oppoſite to Nature and to Peace,
As if theſe men had bin Th' Antipodes,
But ſee, the vertue of a Regall eye,
Th' attractiue wonder of mans Maieſtie,
Our Globe is drawne in a right line agen,
And now appeare new faces, and new men.
The Elements, Earth, Water, Ayre, and Fire,
(Which euer clipt a naturall deſire,
To combat each with other, being at firſt,)
Created enemies to fight their worſt,
See at the peacefull preſence of their King,
How quietly they moude, without their ſting :
Earth not deuouring, Fire not defacing,

Water not drowning, & the Ayre not chaſing:
But proping the queint Fabrick that heere ſtands,
Without the violence of their wrathfull hands.
  Mirror of times, lo where thy *Fortune* ſits,
Aboue the world, and all our humaine wits,
But thy hye Vertue aboue that: what pen,
Or Art, or braine can reach thy vertue then?
At whoſe immortall brightnes and true light,
Enuies infectious eyes haue loſt their ſight,
Her ſnakes (not daring to ſhoot-forth their ſtings
Gainſt ſuch a glorious obiect) downe ſhe flings
Their forkes of Venome into her owne mawe,
Whilſt her ranke teeth the glittering poiſons chawe,
For tis the property of *Enuies* blood,
To dry away at euery kingdomes good,
Eſpecially when ſhee had eyes to view,
Theſe foure maine vertues figurde all in you,
Iustice in cauſes, *Fortitude* gainſt foes,
Temprance in ſpleene, and *Prudence* in all thoſe,
And then ſo rich an Empyre, whoſe fayre breſt,
Contaynes foure Kingdomes by your entrance bleſt
By *Brute* diuided, but by you alone,
All are againe vnited and made *One*,
Whoſe fruitfull glories ſhine ſo far and euen,
They touch not onely earth, but they kiſſe heauen,
From whence *Aſtræa* is deſcended hither,
Who with our laſt Queenes Spirit, fled vp thither,
Fore-knowing on the earth, ſhe could not reſt,
Till you had lockt her in your rightfull breſt.
And therefore all Eſtates, whoſe proper Arts,
Liue by the breath of Majeſtie, had harts
Burning in holy Zeales immaculate fires,
With quenchles Ardors, and vnſtaind deſires,
To ſee what they now ſee, your powerful Grace,
Reflecting joyes on every ſubjects face.
Theſe paynted flames and yellow burning Stripes,
Vpon this roab, being but as ſhowes and types,
Of that great Zeale. And therefore in the name
Of this glad Citie, whither no Prince euer came,

More lou'd, more long'd for, lowely I intreate,
You'ld be to her as gracious as y' are great:
So with reuerberate ſhoutes our Globe ſhall ring,
The Muſicks cloſe being thus: God ſaue our King.

If there be any glorie to be won by writing theſe lynes, I do freelie beſtow it (as his due) on Tho. *Middleton*, in whoſe braine they were begotten, though they were deliuered heere: *Quæ nos non fecimus ipſi, vix ea noſtra voco.*

But hauing peiced vp our wings now againe with our owne feathers: ſuffer vs a while to be pruning them, and to lay them ſmooth, whilſt this ſong, which went foorth at the ſound of Hault-boyes, and other lowde inſtruments, flyes along with the trayne.

Cant.

Where are all theſe Honors owing?
Why are ſeas of people flowing?
Tell mee, tell me Rumor,
Though it be thy Humor
More often to be lying,
Than from thy breath to haue trueth flying:
Yet alter, now that faſhion,
And without the ſtreame of paſsion,
Let thy voyce ſwim ſmooth and cleare,
When words want gilding, then they are moſt deere.

Behold where Ioue and all the States,
Of Heau'n, through Heau'ns ſeauen ſiluer gates,
All in glory riding
(Backs of Clowds beſtriding)
The milky waie do couer,
Which ſtarry Path being meaſur'd ouer,
The Deities conuent,
In Ioues high Court of Parliament.
Rumor thou doeſt looſe thy aymes,
This is not Ioue, but One, as great, King IAMES.

And now take we our flight vp to Temple-bar, (the

other ende of this our Gallery) where by this time, his Majeſtie is vpon the poynt of giuing a gratious and Princely Fare-well to the Lord Major, and the Citie. But that his eye meeting a ſeauenth beautifull obſect, is invited by that, to delay awhile his (lamented) departure.

The Building being ſet out thus.

The Front or Surface of it was proportioned in euery reſpect like a Temple, being dedicated to *Ianus*, as by this inſcription ouer the *Ianus* head may appear.

Iano Quadri fronti
Sacrum.

The height of the whole Aedifice, from the grownd line to the top, was 57. foote, the full bredth of it 18. foote : the thicknes of the Paſsage 12.

The perſonages that were in this Temple, *are theſe.*

1. The principall perſon, *Peace.*
2. By her ſtood, *Wealth.*
3. Beneath the feet of Peace, lay *Mars* (War) groueling.
4. And vpon her right hand (but with ſome little deſcent) was ſeated *Quiet*, the firſt hand-maid of *Peace.*
5. Shee had lying at her feete, *Tumult.*
6. On the other ſide was the ſeconde hand-mayd, *Libertie* at whoſe feete lay a Catte.
7. This perſon trod vpon *Seruitude.*
8. The third handmaid was *Safety.*
9. Beneath her was *Danger*,
10. The fourth attendant was, *Fœlicitie* :
11. At her feete, *Vnhappines.*

Within the Temple was an Altar, to which, vpon the approch of the King, a *Flamin* appeares, and to him, the former Genius of the Citie.

The effect of whofe fpeech was, that whereas the *Flamin* came to performe rites there, in honour of one *Anna* a goddeffe of the *Romaines*, the Genius vowes, that none fhall doe Sacrifice there, but himfelfe, the offring that he makes being, the Heart of the Citie, &c.

And thus haue wee (lowely and aloofe) followed our Soueraigne through the feauen Triumphal gates of this his Court Royall, which name, as *London* receiued at the ryfing of the *Sunne*; fo now at his going from her (euen in a moment) She loft that honour: And being (like an Actor on a Stage) ftript out of her borrowed Majeftie, fhe refignes her former fhape & title of Citie; nor is it quite loft, confidering it went along with him, to whom it is due: For fuch Vertue is begotten in Princes, that their verie prefence hath power to turne a Village to a Citie, and to make a Citie appeare great as a Kingdome. Behold how glorious a Flower, Happineffe is, but how fading. The Minutes (that lackey at the heeles of *Time*) run not fafter away then do our joyes. What tongue could haue expreft the raptures on which the foule of the Citie was carried beyond it felfe, for the fpace of manie houres? What wealth could haue allurde her to haue clofde her eies, at the comming of her King, and yet See, her Bridegrome is but ftept from her, and in a Minute (nay in fhorter time, then a thought can be borne) is fhe made a Widdow. All her confolation being now, to repeate ouer by roate thofe Honors, which lately fhe had perfectly by hart: And to tell of thofe joyes, which but euen now, fhee reallie behelde; yet thus of her abfent, beloued, do I heare her gladly and heartily fpeaking.

Infreta dum Fluvii Current: dum montibus vmbræ,
Virg. *Luftrabvnt Conuexa, Polus dum fidera pafcit,*
Semper Honos, Nomenque tuum, Laudefque manebunt.

The Pageant in the Strond.

THE Citie of *Weſtminſter* and Dutchy of *Lancaſter*, perceiuing what preparation their neighbor citie made to entertain her Soueraigne; though in greatnes they could not match her, yet in greatnes of Loue and Duetie, they gaue teſtimonie, that both were equall. And in token they were ſo, hands and hearts went together: and in the Strond, erected vp a Monument of their affection.

The Inuention was a Rayne-bowe, the Moone, Sunne, and the ſeauen Starres, called the *Pleiades*, being aduaunced betweene two *Pyramides*: *Electra* (one of thoſe ſeauen hanging in the aire, in figure of a Comet) was the ſpeaker, her words carrying this effect.

That as his Majeſtie had left the Citie of London, happy, by deliuering it frô the noyſe of tumult: ſo he would crowne this place with the like joyes; which being done, ſhee reckons vp a number of bleſsings, that will follow vpon it.

The worke of this was thought vpon, begun and made perfect in xij. daies.

As touching thoſe fiue which the Citie builded, the *Arbor* in Cheap-ſide, and the Temple of *Ianus*, at Temple-bar, were both of them begun and finiſht in ſixe weekes. The reſt were taken in hande, firſt in March laſt, after his Majeſtie was proclaymed, vpon which, at that time, they wrought till a Moneth after S. *Iames* his day following, and then gaue ouer by reaſon of the ſicknes: At this ſecond ſetting vpon thê, ſix weekes more were ſpent.

The Citie elected ſixteene Comitties, to whom the Mannaging of the whole buſines was abſolutely referred: of which number, foure were Aldermen, the other graue Commoners.

There were alſo Committies appoynted as Ouerſeers, and Serueyors of the workes.

Artificum Operariumque in hoc tam
celebri apparatu, ſumma.
ſumma.

THe Citie imployed in the Framing, building, and ſetting vp of their fiue *Arches*, theſe officers and worke-men.

A Clarke that attended on the Committies.
Two officers that gaue Summons for their meetings. &c.
A clarke of the Workes.
Two maſter-Carpenters.
Painters.
Of which number, thoſe that gaue the maine direction, and vndertooke for the whole buſines, were only theſe ſeauen.

William Friſelfield.
George Moſſe.
Iohn Knight.
Paul Iſacſon.
Samuell Goodrick.
Richard Wood.
George Heron.

Caruers. 24

Ouer whom, Stephen Harriſon Joyner was appoynted chiefe; who was the ſole Inuentor of the Architecture, and from whom all directions, for ſo much as belonged to Caruing, Joyning, Molding, and all other worke in thoſe fiue Pageants of the Citle (Paynting excepted) were ſet downe.

Ioyners. 80
Carpenters. 60
Turners. 6
Laborers to them. 6
Sawyers. 12
Laborers during all the time, and for the day of the Triumph. 70

Beſides theſe, there were other Artificers, As: Plommers, Smythes, Molders.

To the Reader.

Reader, you muſt vnderſtand, that a regard, being had that his Majeſtie ſhould not be wearied with teadious ſpeeches: A great part of thoſe which are in this Booke ſet downe, were left vnſpoken: So that thou doeſt here receiue them as they ſhould haue been deliuered, not as they were. Some errours wander up and downe in theſe ſheetes, vnder the Printers warrant; which notwithſtanding may by thy authoritie be brought in, and receiue their due Correction.

FINIS.

NOTES AND ILLUSTRATIONS.

Page 1.

The Shomakers Holiday.

On what authority is this play fometimes afcribed to Barten Holiday and to others? That Dekker was the author, even if Henflowe's testimony were wanting, is, as will be feen, abundantly proved by internal evidence.

The original edition of this comedy, as alfo that of *Old Fortunatus,* is printed in black letter.

Page 20.

wher's Cifly Bumtrinket *your maid?*

The same term is ufed by Richard Brome in the Beggars' fong, in the comedy of *The Jovial Crew.* Dekker also ufes it in *Satiromaftix* (p. 220).

Page 81.

The Comedie of Old Fortunatus.

Hazlitt fays that this play "has the idle garrulity of age, with the frefhnefs and gaiety of youth ftill upon its cheek and in its heart." The plan is founded on an old German romance, which was reprinted and tranflated a great many times during the fixteenth century. Dekker has preferved the original names and the main outline of the ftory.

Page 83.

Some cal her Pandora.

From the evils Pandora is said to have brought on mortals, and the fenfe in confequence generally attached to her name, this feems a fomewhat equivocal compliment; but Dekker alludes only to her name, which fignifies *all-accomplifhed,* and perhaps to the correſponding deſcription of her in the "Theogony" of Heſiod. Gloriana, Cynthia, Belphœbe, and Aſtrea, were undoubtedly appellations applied to Elizabeth by the Poets of her time, although there is probably no other inſtance in which ſhe is praiſed under the name of Pandora.

PAGE 87.

Patience is a vertue : would I were not vertuous, thats to ſay, not poore, but full of vice, (thats to ſay, full of chinckes) Ha, ha, ſo I am, for I am ſo full of chinckes, that a Horſe with one eye may looke through and through me.

This is probably an alluſion to a line found in Lyly's Grammar :

Effodiuntur opes, *irritamenta* malorum.

as by chinks, in the firſt inſtance, money is meant, and the holes in his dreſs in the ſecond.

PAGE 89.

My tongue ſpeakes no language but an Almond for Parrat, and cracke me this Nut.

It is ſomewhat difficult to affix any preciſe meaning to theſe phraſes, which, however, occur not unfrequently in the writings of the time. There is a ſcarce black letter work named "An Almond for a Parrot ;" and a play called "Crack me this Nut," was performed at the Roſe Theatre in 1595. This latter is alſo one of the titles of a pamphlet of Lyly's.

PAGE 93.

Fortune her ſelfe is ſaid to view thy fall.

We should probably read "ſad" here inſtead of *ſaid.*

PAGE 95.

Iſ through Golds ſacred hunger thou doſt pine.

This is the *Auri ſacra fames* of Virgil (ſee Æn. III. 57) ; the word "ſacred" being of courſe uſed in the ſenſe of accurſed.

PAGE 95.

a wiſeman poore,
Is like a ſacred booke thats neuer read,
To himſelfe he liues, and to all els ſeemes dead.
This age thinks better of a gilded foole,
Then of a threedbare Saint in wiſedomes ſchoole.

Our poet may here allude to a paſſage in the Book of Eccleſiaftes, ix. 14, sqq. "The poor man's wifdom is defpifed, and his words are not heard."

PAGE 96.

thou wilt repent
That for the love of droffe thou haft defpifed
Wifedomes divine embrace.

It is evident that many of the fentiments in this fcene were drawn by our poet from the choice made by Solomon in the beginning of his reign, of wifdom, in preference to riches, or honour, or power over his enemies, or length of life, as recorded in the First Book of Kings: and it fhould be remembered to their honour that many noble images and illuftrations were derived from the fame divine fource by the dramatic poets of that age.

PAGE 96.

Gold is the ftrength, the finnewes of the world.

"No wonder," fays Campbell, who quotes this Scene in his Specimens, "poor Dekker could rife a degree above the level of his ordinary genius in defcribing the bleffings of Fortunatus's inexhauftible purfe: he had probable felt but too keenly the force of what he expreffes in the mifanthropy of Ampedo,

"I'm not enamour'd of this painted idol," &c.

PAGE 97.

yet I feele nothing here to make mee rich,
here's no fweete Muficke with her filuer found.

"Mufic with her filver found" is a quotation from a poem by Richard Edwards, in *The Paradife of Dainty Devices*, 1576, 1597. The ftanza containing thefe words is alfo quoted in Romeo and Juliet, towards the end of the fourth act. A fimilar expreffion "Muficke with her filuer tongue" occurs again in the *Comedy of Old Fortunatus*. Dekker feems indeed to have had a fpecial fondness for this phrafe, for we read alfo in *Satiro-maftix*.

"Muficke talke lowder, that thy filver voice," &c.

PAGE 124.

Whether it were lead or lattin that hafpt downe thofe winking cafements.

The word *latten*, which occurs in act I. of *The Merry Wives of Windfor* has been differently explained by the commentators.

Theobald ſuppoſes it to have been the old orichalc; Malone that it was made of copper and calimini, and Steevens, who quotes the paſſage in the text, seems inclined to think it tin. Chaucer ſays in *The Frankeleines Tale:*

"And this was, as the bookes me remember,
The colde froſty ſeſon of December.
Phebus waxe old and hewed like *laton*,
That in his hote declination
Shone as the burned gold with ſtremes bright:
But now in Capricorne adoun he light,
When as he ſhone ful pale, I dare wel ſain."

PAGE 125.

what ſhall we learne by trauaile
ANDEL. *Faſhions.*
SHAD. *Thats a beaſtly diſeaſe.*

"Infected with the faſhions" is one of the diſorders of Petruchio's horſe, as deſcribed by Biondello in act 3. of *Taming of the Shrew.* "It is ſo called in the Weſt of England," ſays Grey, "but by the beſt writers on farriery, *farcens* or *farcy.*" Steevens, among other inſtances of its uſe by the old writers, adduces the paſſage in the text.

PAGE 125.

when my purſourſhip ends, ile reſigne, and cap you.

Cap you, from the context, muſt mean, *take from you the cap.* In the *Knight of the Burning Peſtle*, the hoſt threatens to *cap* Ralph, unleſs his reckoning be immediately paid, which is reſented by the honeſt citizen as an unpardonable indignity.

PAGE 129.

O Deformitie,
Thy fairenes is not like to Agripynes,
For (dead) her beautie will no beautie haue,
But thy face lookes moſt louely in the graue.

In the original the word in parentheſis is miſprinted *dread.* For the very obvious correction made in the text I have the high authority of Charles Lamb, who ſays of the ſcene which theſe lines cloſe:—"The humour of a frantic lover is here done to the life. Orleans is as paſſionate an inamorato as any which Shakeſpeare ever drew. He is juſt ſuch another adept in love's reaſons. He talks 'pure Biron and Romeo,' he is almoſt as poetical as they, quite as philofophical, only a little madder." *Specimens* (1808) p. 62-63.

PAGE 133.

With fiftie bard Horfes prawncing at his heeles.

"Bard," *i.e. barbed* or adorned with trappings. So in Heywood's Foure Prentices of London :

"Shall our *bar'd horfes* climb yon mountain tops," &c.

PAGE 136.

la pauyne Hifpanola.

The pavan, whieh is here fpoken of, is faid in the *Alchemift* of Ben Jonfon, to be a Spanifh dance. It is alfo mentioned in the laft fcene of *Twelfth Night.* It feems to have been a majeftic and ftately dance, and is particularly defcribed by Sir John Hawkins in a note on *Twelfth Night.*

PAGE 147.

But I in wilderneffe tottred out my youth.

"Wildnefs" is probably the correct reading.

PAGE 151.

The path that leades to Vertues court is narrow,
Thornie and vp a hill, a bitter iorney,
But being gon through, you find all heau'nly fweetes,
The entrance is all flintie, but at th' end,
To towers of pearle and chriftall you afcend.

One is irrefiftibly reminded in reading thefe fine lines of a fimilar paffage in Tennyfon's *Ode on the Death of the Duke of Wellington.*

PAGE 155.

whilft thou art commenfing thy knauerie there, ile proceede Doctor Dodipoll here.

A comedy called "The Wifdom of Dr. Dodipoll," was printed in 1600: it is to this that Dekker alludes, as alfo in *Satiro-maftix*, p. 262, "Wut fweare by Parnaffus and lye too, Doctor Doddipol?"

PAGE 159.

to marke how like tree bul-beggara dey ftand.

Bull-beggar and bull-bear were words of the fame meaning as the modern *bug-bear.* Gable Harvey in his *Four Letters and certain Sonnets*, ufes both. "He was proved a filly *bull-bear*; a very puff of wind; a thing of nothing." "Some odd wits forſooth will needs be accounted terrible *bull-beggars*, and the only kill-cows of their age." See alſo Pierce's *Supererogation*.

PAGE 160.

Puts Gallowayes hornes off.

This ſtage-direction is evidently an error. For Galloway we ſhould doubtleſs read Montroſe and Longavile.

PAGE 175.

May ſtill to fortie two, and one yeere more,

So the original; but there is very little doubt we ſhould read "add." As Elizabeth ſucceeded to the Crown only in November, 1558, and the preſent play was printed in 1600, it ſeems certain that ſhe could not have reigned more than forty-two years.

PAGE 177.

SATIRO-MASTIX.

This play is an anſwer to Ben Jonſon's *Poetaſter*, which had been brought out at the Blackfriars by the children of the Queen's chapel in the previous year. Marſton and Dekker had, it ſeems, perſiſted for ſome years in ridiculing Jonſon on the ſtage, till he found it neceſſary to draw up the Poetaſter, in which, together with the untruſſing, the whipping, and the ſtinging, he anticipated and anſwered many of the accuſations ſubſequently brought againſt him in the *Satiro-maſtix*. As Marſton and Dekker had headed the cabal againſt him, he introduced them under the reſpective names of Criſpinus and Demetrius; Marſton is very diſtinctly marked: Dekker might, perhaps, have "ſat ſtill unqueſtioned"—at leaſt with poſterity—had not the juſtice of the ſatire filled him with rage, and induced him to appropriate the character of Demetrius to himſelf in an angry recrimination. He was (apparently to his own ſatisfaction) put forward by the reſt as their defender. Jonſon muſt have been aware of this, for he makes one of the players ſay of Dekker, "his doublet's a little decayed, otherwiſe he is a very ſimple honeſt fellow, ſir, one Demetrius, a dreſſer of plays about the town here; we have hired him to abuſe Horace, and bring him in in a play."

Dekker, being both a rapid and a popular writer, the choice of a champion was not injudicious. The *Satiro-maſtix* was produced in 1602. Jonſon had played with his ſubject; but Dekker writes in downright paſſion, and foams through every page. He makes no pretenſions to invention, but takes up the characters of his predecessor, turns them the *seamy side without*, and produces a coarse and ill-wrought caricature. Tucca who, in Jonson's hands, is amusing with all his insolence and rapacity, degenerates with Dekker into a mere candidate for Tyburn. Nor is this the worst. In transferring the scene from the court of Augustus to England, Dekker has the inconceivable folly to fix on William Rufus, a rude and ignorant soldier, whom he ridiculously terms "learning's true Mæcenas, poesy's king," for the champion of literature, when his brother, Henry I., who aspired to the reputation of a scholar, would have entered into his plot with equal facility.—GIFFORD, *Memoir of Ben Jonson.*

"William Rufus, 'learning's true Mæcenas, poesy's king,' it may be presumed, was the ignorant William Shakespeare, "skilled in the hawking and hunting languages;" so that Dekker's selection appears to have been peculiarly appropriate. The wits of Elizabeth were not asleep.

In this comedy Shakespeare is King William, and Lyly is Sir Vaughan ap Rees; the remark of Tucca, "be not so tart my precious Metheglin," identifies Lyly with Amorphus, reminding us of the Metheglin and Pythagorical breeches in *Cynthia's Revels,* which, I hold, are satirical allusions to the transmigrations through Sir Hugh Evans and Captain Fluellen; whilst in the remark, "you nasty Tortois, you and your itchy poetry break out like Christmas, but once a year," we have probably the germ of Caliban."

SHAKESPEARE AND JONSON. Dramatic *versus* Wit-Combats. Auxiliary Forces: Beaumont and Fletcher, Marston, Dekker, Chapman, and Webster. Lond.: J. Russell Smith, 1864, p. 52.

PAGE 179.

Non potes in Nugas dicere plura meas,
Ipse ego quam dixi.—Qui se mirantur, in illos
Virus habe: Nos hæc nouimus esse nihil.

This is from Martial. Epig. lib. XIII. 2, *In Detractorem.*

PAGE 181.

Monstrum horrendum, informe: Ingens cui lumen ademptum. Virgil, *Aen.* III, 658.

PAGE 183.

Populus me sibilat, at mihi plaudo.

Horace, Satir. lib. I. 1. 66.

Satiro-mastix.

Page 184.

To this play the author prefixed a lift of *Errata* (which have, of courfe, been corrected in the prefent edition), with the following addrefs, *Ad Lectorem* : " In fteed of the Trumpets founding thrice, before the Play begin : it fhall not be amiffe (for him that will read) firft to beholde this fhort Comedy of Errors, and where the greateft enter, to give them in ftead of a hiffe, a gentle correction."

Page 212.

thefe true heires of Ma. Juftice Shallow.

The two plays of Shakefpeare, in which the character here alluded to, appears—*i. e.*, the Second Part of K. Henry IV. and The Merry Wives of Windfor—were brought out in 1600—1602. The allufion in the text feems to prove that the famous juftice had already become a houfehold word.

Page 214.

One word Sir Quintilian in hugger mugger.

In hugger-mugger—i. e., in private, fecretly. The phrafe occurs in *Hamlet*, Act iv. Sc. 5.

" we have done but greenly
In *hugger-mugger* t'inter him."

Page 216.

Miftris Miniuer caps.

This expreffion, which recurs frequently in the *Satiro-maftix*, is ufed by Simon Eyre as a term of reproach in *The Shoomakers Holiday* (*vide antea*, p. 72) : "Vanifh mother Mineuer-Cap, trip and goe."

Page 218.

Mother Mumblecruft.

This name, which is applied by Eyre to his wife in *The Shomakers Holiday*, is given in *Ralph Roifter Doifter* to one of the principal characters : it is alfo ufed in the *Pleafant Comedy of Patient Griffell*, 1603.

Page 221.

Th'aft a breath as fweet as the Rofe, that groews by the Beare-garden.

The promixity of the Hope, while yet a bear-garden to the

Rofe, may be gathered from the above paffage. The atmofphere at the Rofe was, it would feem, impregnated with the effluvia from the Hope.—*Collier.*

PAGE 229.

TUC. *Thou haft been at Parris Garden haft not?*

HOR. *Yes, Captaine, I ha plaide Zulziman there.*

Paris Garden was at an early date employed as a theatre for dramatic reprefentations, and it feems to have been of an hexagonal fhape. *Zulziman* was a character in fome play which has not furvived.

PAGE 229.

My name's Hamlet reuenge.

This is the fecond allufion in *Satiro-maftix* to the writings of Shakefpeare. The earlieft known edition of Hamlet bears date 1603; but it feems to have been acted fome time before it found its way into print.

PAGE 231.

Ile tagge my Codpeece point *with thy legs.*

This expreffion occurs alfo in *The Shomakers Holiday* (*fuprà*, p. 68): "My *Codpeece-point* is ready to flye in peeces euery time I thinke vpon miftris *Rofe.*"

PAGE 251.

Smiles on my cheekes arife,
To fee how fweetly a true virgin dyes.

"The beauty and force of this fcene," fays Charles Lamb," "are much diminifhed to the reader of the entire play, when he comes to find that this folemn preparation is but a fham contrivance of the father's, and the potion which Cœleftina fwallows nothing more than a fleeping draught, from the effects of which fhe is to awake in due time, to the furprife of her hufband, and the great mirth and edification of the king and his courtiers. As Hamlet fays, they do but 'poifon in jeft.' The fentiments are worthy of a real martyrdom, and an Appian facrifice in earneft." But as Terrill and his bride both believed the facrifice to be real, we cannot concur in thefe ftrictures of the gentle Elia.

PAGE 257.

Saue thee, my moft gracious King a Harts faue thee, all hats and caps are thine, and therefore I vaile: for but to thee great Sultane Soliman, &c.

Compare the final ſcenes of *The Shomakers Holiday*, where Simon Eyre talks in much the ſame way to the King. "Sim Eyre knowes how to ſpeake to a Pope, to *Sultan Solyman*, to *Tamberlaine*, and he were here." Both Eyre and Tucca aſk of their Sovereign the boon of his preſence to grace a banquet. The difference is that the *bonhonnie* of the former is genuine and natural, and that of the latter aſſumed and artificial.

PAGE 265.

Epilogus.

In the Epilogue to Dekker's *Satiro-maſtix*, Tucca addreſſes the audience generally as "*two penny tenants*," having previouſly told them, "Ill ſee you all here for your two-pence a-piece again, before I'll loſe your company," as if the price had been, for ſome reaſon, temporarily lowered to that rate. This play was performed before 1602, by the Lord Chamberlain's ſervants and by the Children of St. Pauls. In the body of it, Tucca ſpeaks degradingly of "penny-bench theatres," where "a gentleman or an honeſt citizen" might ſit "with his ſquirrel by his ſide cracking nuts;" which agrees with a paſſage in his Gull's Horn-Book, 1609, where he remarks, "your groundling and gallery commoner buys his ſport for a penny," as if the admiſſion to the yard, where people ſtood, and to the gallery, where they ſat, were the ſame.

PAGE 267.

The Magnificent Entertainment, &c.

With this is uſually found at the end: B. JON: [Ben Jonſon] *his Part of King James his Royall and Magnificent Entertainement through his Honorable Cittie of London, Thurſeday the* 15 of *March* 1603. So much as was preſented in the firſt and *laſt of their Triumphall Arch's. Printed at London by* V. S. *for Edward Blount*, 1604.

Of Dekker's portion another edition exiſts, "Edinburgh, Printed by Thomas Finlaſon and are to be ſauld at Niddries wynde heide. Anno Dom. 1604. with Licence."

PAGE 274.

Where the neat Sunne each Morne himſelfe attires,
And gildes it with his repercuſsiue *fires.*

This is a word of very uncommon occurrence. It is uſed in Fanſhawe's tranſlation of the Luſiad:

"Whofe *repercuffive* lyre fhall have the fate
To be renowned more than fortunate."

Dekker ufes the word again in his Pageant of *Troia Nova Triumphans* (vol. III., p. 243).

PAGE 282.

Gracious-ftreet.

See alfo *The Shomakers Holiday*, p. 69: "the great new hall in Gracious ftreete corner." The prefent name, Gracechurch-ftreet, is but little more correct than the corrupted appellation of Dekker's time. St. Bennet Grafs-church, at the fouth-weft corner of Fenchurch-ftreet, was fo called from its vicinity to the Grafs-market, formerly held clofe by. The cuftoms or duties of this market, in the reign of Edward III., are printed in Stow's *Survey*, ed. 1603, p. 214.

PAGE 290.

Alter Iefiades, alter Amoniades.

Jefiades, *i.e.*, Solomon, the grandfon of *Jeffe*. It is almoft needlefs to obferve how much the King admired this agnomen, or how often it was attributed to him. In the Preface to his Works, by Bifhop Montacute, we read "God hath given us a Solomon, and God above all things gave Solomon wifdom," &c. *Amoniades* probably fignifies Apollo, the fon of Jupiter (Ammon).

PAGE 293.

The Mart, where as well the Froe, as the Burger, are buying and felling.

Froe is the Dutch word for a woman. It is ufed by Beaumont and Fletcher in *Wit at Seven Weapons*, Act. V.

"Buxom as Bacchus' froes, revelling, dancing,
Telling the mufick's numbers with their feet."

PAGE 294.

Sermo ad Regem.

Gifford is at a lofs to know where Dekker got thefe Latin verfes—"perhaps," he fays, "from his own ftores; for he had a fmattering of Latin, which he is fomewhat too fond of fhowing."

Page 297.

A woman in a watchet roabe.

Watchet is a light blue-colour. The word is Saxon, and is uſed by Milton and Dryden.

Page 302.

Troynouant *is now no more a Citie.*

The name of *Troynovant* here given to London, and alſo in a Pageant by Dekker, entitled *Troia Nova Triumphans* (1612), is derived from the once popular fable of Geoffry of Monmouth, who declares that Brute, a lineal deſcendant of Æneas, "the grandſon of Jupiter, by his daughter Venus, builded this citie about the year of the world 2885," (or 1008 years before the nativity of Chriſt), and named it Trinovantum, Troy-novant, (or New Troy), in remembrance of Troy, from whence he came, calling the country Britain after his own name.

Page 314.

One of maiſter Mulcaſters Schollers.

Dr. Richard Mulcaſter, then Maſter of St. Paul's School, "a native of Carliſle, was educated at Eton, whence he was ſent to King's College, Cambridge, where he took the degree of B.A., 1553-4, but afterwards removed to Oxford, and was elected a Student of Chriſt Church; proceeded M.A. and became eminent for his ſkill in Greek. After ſpending more than five years at Oxford, he made ſo great a proficiency in ſeveral ſorts of learning, that he was unanimouſly choſen maſter of the ſchool erected in 1561 in the pariſh of St. Laurence, Pountney, by the Worſhipful Company of Merchant-taylors of that City. In 1596 he ſucceeded one Joh. Harriſon in the Chief Maſterſhip of St. Pauls School in London, and ſoon after had the rich parſonage of Stamford Rivers in Eſſex beſtowed on him by Queen Elizabeth. He died there 15th April 1611, having reſigned Paul's School three years before."—Wood's *Athenæ Oxonienſes.*

Page 317.

I hope you will not put me to deſcribe what properties ſhee held in her hands, ſithence every painted cloath can informe you.

Properties, i.e., enſigns proper to her character—a theatrical term. *Sithence* is "ſince." *Painted cloth* was cloth or canvas painted in oil with a variety of devices and verſes interſperſed.

Page 318.

Scepters with penſild ſcutchiors in their handes.

i.e. (not having *penſils*, ſmall flags, but) painted; ſo in an earlier paſſage of this pageant: "They held in their handes penſild Shieldes; vpon the firſt was drawne a Roſe," &c.

Page 318.

where, on ſeuerall greeces, ſate the foure cardinall vertues.

This word, uſed in ſeveral places by Shakeſpeare, was variouſly ſpelt, grice, greece, greeſe, grieze, grize, griſe, &c.; and ſeems to be formed from *greſſus*, or contracted from *degrees*. It ſignified a ſtep, or a flight of ſteps. See Lydgate's *Warres of Troy* (ed. 1555):—

> "She gan anone by *greeces* to aſſende
> Of a Touret in to an hye pynacle."

Page 318.

that cantle of the globe which was open to the full view of his Maieſtie.

Cantle, or *cantel*, ſignifies portion, piece, or parcel.

"Cant," which occurs anteà p. 317:—"Directly vnder her in a Cant by herſelfe" is a contraction of this, and means a niche or corner, like the Dutch *kant*, from which both words are probably derived.

Page 319.

And ſtood ſo, as if the Eronie *had* beene held vp *on the tops of their fingers.*

Qy. "ourany"? ſuggeſts Mr. Dyce (Notes to Middleton's Works, v. 209).

ADDITIONAL NOTES.

PAGE 181.

Horace *hal'd his* Poetaſters *to the Barre.*

Alluding to the trial of the Poetaſters, which takes place before Auguſtus and his poetical jury of Virgil, Ovid, Tibullus, etc., in Ben Jonſon's play.

Ib.

Horace *made himſelfe believe, that his* Burgonian wit *might deſperately challenge all commers.*

Dekker alludes here to the baſtard of Burgundy, who conſidered himſelf unmatchable, till he was overthrown in Smithfield by Woodville Earl Rivers.

ERRATA.

PAGE	LINE
329	20 *for* probable, *read* probably.
339	6 *for* bonhonnie, *read* bonhomie.

END OF FIRST VOLUME.

CPSIA information can be obtained
at www.ICGtesting.com
Printed in the USA
BVHW042247140219
540160BV00056B/1416/P

9 781162 976334